SECOND CHANCE

ROBERT A. DIVINE

Robert A. Divine was born in Brooklyn, New York, in 1929 and educated at Phillips Exeter Academy and Yale University, where he received his Ph.D. in 1954. Since then Professor Divine, who has won a teaching-excellence award, has been at the University of Texas, and he is now Chairman of its History Department. A specialist in American diplomatic history, he began research for this book while a Fellow at the Center for Advanced Study in the Behavioral Sciences at Stanford, California. His other books are American Immigration Policy, 1924-1952; American Foreign Policy: A Documentary History; The Illusion of Neutrality; and The Reluctant Belligerent. He lives in Austin, Texas, with his wife and three children.

Robert A. Divine

SECOND CHANCE

*The Triumph of Internationalism in
America During World War II*

Atheneum   New York

1967

To Barb

Acknowledgments

I AM INDEBTED to staff members of the many libraries in which I carried on the research for this book, especially the Hoover Library on War, Peace and Revolution at Stanford University; the University of Texas Library; the Manuscripts Division of the Library of Congress; the National Archives; Butler Library at Columbia University; the Harry S. Truman and Franklin D. Roosevelt presidential libraries; and Firestone Library at Princeton University. E. Taylor Parks of the Department of State's Historical Office helped me secure access to the Department's files in the National Archives. I wish to thank Chester Kielman, Archivist of the University of Texas, for calling my attention to the David Andrew Simmons Papers. Claire Christman, Anna Tower and Ted Cooper of the staff of the Center for Advanced Study in the Behavioral Sciences performed many helpful services.

Former Senator Joseph H. Ball and Clark M. Eichelberger of the Commission to Study the Organization of Peace generously shared with me their reminiscences of the internationalist movement. I also want to thank James Reston for disclosing the source for his coverage of the Dumbarton Oaks conference and Arthur Krock for permitting me to cite his correspondence with Secretary of State Hull.

This book could not have been completed without the generous financial assistance of the Penrose Fund of the American Philosophical Society, which enabled me to visit libraries in other parts of the country, and the Research Institute of the University of Texas, which freed me from teaching duties so that I could carry on research and writing. I am especially grateful to the Center for Advanced Study in the Behavioral Sciences, and its director, Ralph Tyler, for giving me the chance to begin this study under ideal conditions.

Finally, I wish to thank Thomas F. McGann for relieving me of administrative chores while I was writing this book and Colleen T. Kain for invaluable secretarial assistance. My wife, Barbara Renick Divine, shared in the fun and drudgery of this project from the beginning, and she made a major contribution with her careful editing of the entire manuscript.

Contents

SECOND CHANCE

Prologue

PRESIDENT HARRY S. TRUMAN arrived in San Francisco on the afternoon of June 25, 1945, to witness the climax of the founding conference of the United Nations. A crowd of more than a million cheered him as his motorcade moved slowly from Hamilton Field to the Fairmont Hotel. For two months, delegates from fifty nations had been drafting the Charter for a new world organization. Now their work was complete. In the final plenary session, held in the War Memorial Opera House, Lord Halifax, the presiding officer, asked the delegates to signify their approval by a standing vote. As the diplomats rose in unison, the audience of three thousand burst into sustained applause. It was, Halifax said, "one of the historic moments of history." [1]

The next day, June 26, the delegates assembled at the Veterans' Building auditorium to sign the Charter they had approved the night before. Broadway designer Jo Mielziner had helped the State Department staff prepare for the ceremony. Indigo-blue drapes covered the walls, relieved only by the multicolored backdrop formed by the fifty silk flags of the member nations. A royal-blue runner led from a narrow opening in the drapes to a huge circular table in the center of the stage. The Charter, bound in blue morocco trimmed with gold, lay on the table in front of a single blue-upholstered chair.

At the stroke of noon the Chinese delegation filed through the drapes to begin the ceremony. Delegates from the Soviet Union, Great Britain and France followed, each giving a brief speech after signing the Charter. The United States was scheduled to be the last of the fifty nations to sign, but at 3:15, after the Nicaraguan delegation, the American representatives entered the auditorium so that President Truman could watch them before he addressed the conference at the Opera House.

Secretary of State Edward R. Stettinius, Jr., was the first to sign for the United States, with Truman beaming his approval. The six other American delegates added their signatures, and then the small nations continued the process well into the evening, although most of the spectators left to hear Truman's speech.[2]

At 4:30 the President delivered the closing address of the San Francisco conference. After praising the delegates for achieving "a victory against war itself," Truman recalled an earlier effort at world order. "By this Charter, you have given reality to the ideal of that great statesman of a generation ago—Woodrow Wilson." And then he continued, "If we had had this Charter a few years ago—and above all, the will to use it—millions now dead would be alive." Truman ended his speech and the conference with a ringing appeal, "Let us not fail to grasp this supreme chance to establish a world-wide rule of reason—to create an enduring peace under the guidance of God."[3]

Thus, for the second time in the twentieth century, the United States had helped create an international organization for peace. In 1919 the Senate had refused to sanction American participation in the League of Nations; in 1945 few feared a repetition of that tragedy. After Pearl Harbor a small group of articulate internationalists had set out to convince the American people that their refusal to join the League had led to the Second World War. Only a new organization of nations, they preached, could guarantee an end to wars. By June of 1945 the internationalists had created such overwhelming public support that Senate approval of the United Nations Charter was a certainty. The American people were determined not to waste their second chance.

This book chronicles the transformation of American attitudes toward international organization during the Second World War. The focus is on the international movement, not on the policy and diplomacy of the United States government.[4] Many aspects of postwar planning are neglected, especially the significant attempts at international trade and monetary reform, in order to treat thoroughly the public preoccupation with collective security. Wars have deep roots in the economic and social conditions of nations, but Americans from 1941 to 1945 were concerned primarily with the problem of armed aggression and the techniques of preventing its recurrence. Looking to the past rather than to the future, they tried to learn from the mistakes of an earlier generation, only to find themselves stunned by the explosion of the atomic bomb and the onset of the Cold War. Yet their efforts were not completely in vain. The organization they helped create has endured despite the perils of a nuclear age, and it still embodies the hopes of mankind for permanent peace. And if they failed to banish war from the world, they succeeded in ending the tradition of American isolationism.

I

Defenders of the Faith

O N THE EVENING of January 10, 1923, over seven hundred prominent New Yorkers gathered for a banquet at the Hotel Biltmore to celebrate the third anniversary of the League of
Nations. After dinner George W. Wickersham, who had served as
Attorney General in the Taft administration, rose to announce the
formation of the League of Nations Non-Partisan Association. The sole
purpose of this new group, Wickersham declared, was to secure American entry into the League at the earliest possible moment. Wickersham
would serve as chairman of the organization and John H. Clarke, a
Democrat who had recently retired from the Supreme Court, would be
president. The audience cheered when it was announced that Mrs.
Emmons Blaine, Cyrus McCormick's daughter, had contributed $10,000
to finance this new campaign.

Shortly after ten o'clock Justice Clarke rose to deliver the principal
address of the evening. Clarke was an imposing figure, his thick white
hair, broad forehead and firm chin suggesting strength as well as wisdom. He spoke for over an hour, praising the League and bemoaning the
absence of the United States from its ranks. "If we remain out of it," he
warned, "the next war will come as the last one did, without our having
any opportunity to prevent it and with only the privilege of fighting our
way out of it." He went on to argue that the League issue had never had
a fair chance in the United States because it had become enmeshed in
partisan politics. "The purpose above all others of this organization for
which I am speaking tonight is to do what we can to lift it out of party
politics and to place it again before our country in a candid, nonpartisan
way for reconsideration upon its merits." Then Clarke invoked the
name of Woodrow Wilson, calling on his listeners to give the best that

6

was in them for the great cause. He hoped for a quick and decisive victory, "But if the contest shall be long, still we are enlisting to see it through to the end. . . . It is not too late for us to share in the moral leadership of the world," he concluded, "nor for us to prove again that statesmen and politicians are often blind when the people see the vision and the light." [1]

The men and women in the audience rose to their feet in a spontaneous tribute to Clarke's oratory and to the cause which they shared. Wave after wave of clapping swept through the hall. The League of Nations, rejected by the Senate in 1919 and by the American people in the election of 1920, had come to life again in the United States. A dedicated group of internationalists had determined to confront the nation with the fact of the League's existence and to compel a reconsideration of the American refusal to join. Though optimistic, they were, as Clarke said, "enlisting to see it through to the end." In 1923 few realized how long that would be.

I

The League of Nations Non-Partisan Association was founded to carry on the work begun by the League to Enforce Peace. In 1914, with the outbreak of the World War, a group of peace enthusiasts in New York City had come together to discuss ways in which war could be prevented in the future. Hamilton Holt, the energetic editor of the *Independent,* an influential weekly, was the moving force in these discussions which led to the formation of the League to Enforce Peace in the spring of 1915. In a convention held in Independence Hall in Philadelphia on June 17, the League was formally organized. William Howard Taft served as president, and though the group was nonpartisan, Republicans dominated its leadership. The goal of the League was to form a universal organization whose members would agree to submit all disputes to an international court. If a nation went to war without presenting its grievances to the court, the other members were bound to use their armed forces to punish the nation that had begun the hostilities.

Though the issue of American entry into the European war overshadowed the League to Enforce Peace in its first year, it gained great prestige in May 1916 when Woodrow Wilson spoke at its first National Assembly. Asserting that "what affects mankind is inevitably our affair," Wilson advocated American participation in "any feasible association of

7

nations" with a commitment to use force to preserve peace. When the United States entered the war in 1917, the League devoted much of its activity to winning the war and urged that the wartime coalition of Allies and Associated Powers become the nucleus for the postwar organization for peace. The members of the League applauded Wilson's decision to press for "a general association of nations" in the fourteen points, and when the text of the League of Nations Covenant was published in the United States during the Paris Peace Conference, spokesmen for the League to Enforce Peace praised it as a major step "toward the suppression of war and the promotion of permanent peace." [2]

In April 1919 President Wilson announced that the Allies had accepted a series of amendments to the League Covenant Wilson had offered at Paris to accommodate critics in the United States. The League to Enforce Peace responded with an endorsement of the Covenant and inaugurated a massive campaign to win public support for American acceptance of the League of Nations. But within a few months the organization was caught up in the bitter partisan controversy which enveloped the Covenant. In June, Elihu Root, former Secretary of State, offered three reservations to the League Covenant which he thought all Republicans could support. The most important dealt with Article 10, "the heart of the Covenant," which committed signatories to guarantee the territory and the independence of all member nations. Root proposed that the United States exempt itself from this guarantee which he felt the American people would not honor in time of crisis. Henry Cabot Lodge, chairman of the Senate Foreign Relations Committee, eventually put forth fourteen reservations to the Covenant, including one which severely limited American responsibility under Article 10 and provided that American armed forces could not be used under any article of the Covenant without the prior consent of Congress in each case.

During the summer and fall of 1919 the unity of the League to Enforce Peace gradually cracked. When William Howard Taft publicly accepted the reservation on Article 10, the executive committee issued a statement opposing all reservations, yet voted to retain Taft as their president. In November, when the Senate formally accepted the Lodge reservations, the League to Enforce Peace held a crucial meeting of its executive committee. Hamilton Holt offered a motion opposing all reservations to the Covenant. It was defeated, ten to five. Then the majority voted to support whatever reservations were necessary to secure

8

Senate approval. On November 18 the executive committee issued a public statement calling on the Senate to approve American entry into the League of Nations on the terms that Lodge had decreed. On that same day, however, Woodrow Wilson wrote to Senator Gilbert M. Hitchcock, the minority leader, asking him to inform the Democratic senators that he opposed acceptance of the Covenant with the Lodge reservations.[3]

On November 19 Hitchcock read Wilson's letter to the Democratic caucus, and the senators agreed to follow the wishes of their President. That afternoon they joined with "the irreconcilables," a group of extreme isolationists led by William E. Borah and Hiram W. Johnson, to vote against American entry into the League of Nations with reservations. A few minutes later the irreconcilables, who opposed the Covenant in any form, voted with the reservationists led by Lodge to defeat a motion to enter without any qualifications. The public outcry at the rejection of a treaty which eighty percent of the Senate favored in principle brought about a second vote in March 1920. This time twenty-one Democratic senators disobeyed Wilson and voted for acceptance of the Covenant with the Lodge reservations, but still the treaty fell seven votes short of the necessary two thirds. The disagreement over reservations, especially over the degree of sovereignty the United States would surrender to the new world body to prevent aggression, had fatally divided the overwhelming majority of senators who expressed a desire to see the United States become a member of the League of Nations.

The defeat of the Covenant ended the formal activities of the League to Enforce Peace. The organization continued in existence until 1922, but its members sought new channels to express their conflicting ideas on international organization. In the election of 1920, when the Democratic party nominated Governor James M. Cox of Ohio on a pro-League platform, Hamilton Holt, Irving Fisher, a Yale economist, and a number of other members of the League to Enforce Peace formed a group called "Pro-League Independents" to campaign for Cox. With financial help from Bernard M. Baruch, Fisher chartered a railway car and traveled around the nation urging GOP internationalists to vote for the Democratic ticket. Holt persuaded 121 prominent Republicans to sign a manifesto which appeared in the press on October 18 endorsing the League of Nations and repudiating the Republican candidate, Warren G. Harding.[4]

Many members of the League to Enforce Peace, however, stayed loyal to the Republican party and accepted the ambiguous statement of

9

Harding advocating an "association of nations." Worried by defections, party leaders asked Elihu Root to draft a statement that prominent pro-League Republicans could sign endorsing Warren Harding. On October 15 the statement appeared, signed by thirty-one well-known Republicans, including Charles Evans Hughes, Henry L. Stimson, George W. Wickersham and Herbert Hoover. Five of the signers, including Wickersham and Hoover, were members of the executive committee of the League to Enforce Peace. The statement declared that only Harding could bring the United States into the League of Nations, since Cox was committed to retaining Article 10, which the American people would never accept. Therefore, the thirty-one claimed the election of Harding was the best way to "advance the cause of international cooperation." [5]

The election of Harding by a huge majority did not necessarily signify a repudiation of the League of Nations. The voters were registering their dissatisfaction with the Wilson administration and the problems brought on by the war and its aftermath. But only six weeks after his inauguration the new President declared, "In the existing League of Nations, world-governing with its superpowers, this Republic will have no part." Though Harding continued to talk of forming an "association of nations," he never acted to give any substance to this nebulous phrase. For his Secretary of State, Charles Evans Hughes, Harding's stand was embarrassing. Hughes had signed the statement of the Republican thirty-one, and he was challenged by Hamilton Holt and George Wickersham to live up to his principles. Hughes considered resigning, but he finally accepted Harding's position. Most of the other Republican thirty-one kept silent, bitter at the administration's policy, but unwilling to break with their party. [6]

Most internationalists gave up the fight after the election, but a few remained loyal to their cause. Hamilton Holt, a lifelong Republican, now moved into the Democratic party, embracing it as the most useful vehicle for the League issue. In 1921 Holt founded the Woodrow Wilson Democracy and called on all friends of the League to "tread the path of the opponents of slavery, who continued fighting even though election after election went against them." The comparison with the abolitionists was apt. Convinced of the righteousness of his cause, Holt directed a steady tattoo of criticism at the Harding administration in public letters, editorials and speeches. Avoiding the complex arguments over the use of force and Article 10, he called for entry into the League so that the United States could "resume its rightful place in the moral leadership of the world." Though he won considerable attention in the press, Holt failed to convert the leaders of the Democratic party, who attributed Cox's defeat to his advocacy of the League. Cordell Hull, then a congressman from Tennessee and chairman of the Democratic National Committee, tried to soothe Holt while he avoided the demand that the Congressional elections of 1922 be waged on the League issue. Holt scored his only success with Woodrow Wilson, but the former President, living in seclusion in Washington, no longer controlled his party. The Democrats, like the Republicans, preferred to forget the League of Nations.[7]

In the early 1920's another converted Republican joined Hamilton Holt in his lonely campaign. He was Raymond B. Fosdick, a young lawyer who had come under Wilson's sway while an undergraduate at Princeton. Fosdick had left the Republican party in 1912 to work for Wilson's election, and during the war he had served as chairman of the Commission on Training Camp Activities under Secretary of War Newton D. Baker. In May 1919, just after he had returned from a trip to France, Wilson asked him to serve as Under Secretary General of the League of Nations. Fosdick went to London to take up his new duties under Sir Eric Drummond, the first Secretary General. Working with his fellow Under Secretary, Jean Monnet, Fosdick found the new job engrossing; but when the United States failed to join the League, he felt compelled to resign. As he prepared to leave England, he told his wife, "I do care deeply and, I confess, passionately about America's desertion and the chance we've missed to make this world a fit place to live in instead of a place to fight in." But Fosdick did not give up hope. On the voyage back to the United States, he wrote to Drummond that "the cause is by no means lost. Rather the fight has just begun. . . . In the United States, the issue can never be settled until it is settled right."

After Harding's election, Fosdick resumed the practice of law and, as a sideline, formed the League of Nations News Bureau. He began with one experienced newsman and a secretary, but he soon expanded the staff with the help of several wealthy Wilsonians. For three years Fosdick's news bureau distributed thousands of press releases and documents which served to remind the American people that even without their participation the League of Nations was carrying on the work for peace. Like Holt, Fosdick also engaged in extensive public speaking, and he waged a one-man war against Charles Evans Hughes when he discovered that the State Department was pigeonholing all communications from the League. "Do expediency and party loyalty," he taunted in a

11

letter to the New York *Times*, "justify a Secretary of State in playing hide-and-seek with an agency which is working for the world's peace?" Hughes quickly announced that the State Department would reply to all notes from Geneva.[8]

Though Fosdick and Holt kept the League from dropping out of the American consciousness, both men were aware that a more formal organization was essential. In the summer of 1922, after returning from attending sessions of the League in Geneva, Holt learned that John H. Clarke had resigned from the Supreme Court at the age of sixty-five, announcing that he wanted to serve his neighbors "and some public causes." Knowing that Clarke believed ardently in American membership in the League of Nations, Holt joined with Everett Colby, a New Jersey attorney and member of the Republican National Committee, to form the League of Nations Non-Partisan Committee. Holt then met with Clarke, who agreed to lead the new campaign for American entry. With Clarke's prestige, Holt was quickly able to secure the necessary financial support from a half-dozen wealthy New Yorkers. Holt then opened negotiations with George Wickersham, who had founded the American Association for International Organization earlier in the year. For a moment the merger of the two groups was threatened when Woodrow Wilson wrote to Clarke opposing cooperation with any Republicans. Holt went to see Wilson in early November, and though the former President refused to endorse the new organization, he did agree not to denounce it publicly.[9]

The great obstacle to the founding of the new organization was Article 10. Wickersham, and many other Republicans, refused to endorse American entry into the League of Nations without reservations voiding any commitment to employ force against an aggressor. Remembering the bitterness of 1919 and the partisan division on this issue, Clarke suggested a compromise formula broad enough to unite the divided internationalists. The new society would work to educate American opinion to induce the government to enter the League of Nations "on such terms as may seem wise, provided only that they be consistent with our constitution and consonant with the dignity and honor, the moral responsibility and power of our Republic." At a dinner meeting at the Union Club in New York City on December 20, Holt, Clarke, Fosdick and Wickersham agreed on this statement of purpose and arranged for the banquet at the Hotel Biltmore on January 10, 1923, to launch the League of Nations Non-Partisan Association. The internationalists had finally patched over their quarrel and were once again united in a common cause.[10]

12

I I

The new organization quickly built up momentum. By the end of January there were over two thousand members on the rolls. A paid staff, including several who had worked for the League to Enforce Peace, conducted its day-by-day activities in New York. Though Clarke made the policy decisions, Hamilton Holt was the sparkplug, devoting nearly all his time to the work of the Association. As chairman of the Finance Committee, he engaged in extensive fund-raising activities which were so successful that the organization was soon able to spend $10,000 a month promoting the League of Nations. In the summer and fall of 1923 Holt went on an extensive speaking tour, lecturing in smaller cities throughout the nation and helping set up branches of the Association in thirty-six states. The financial support that Holt had gathered began to dwindle, however, and in the latter part of 1923 John Clarke insisted on an economy program which brought the speaking tours to a halt. Though 3,100 individuals contributed to the Association in 1923, most were small subscribers who could not sustain the massive publicity campaign that Holt desired.

The most effective work was carried on through the printed page. In the fall of 1923 the Association began publication of the *League of Nations Herald,* a bi-weekly newsletter which carried stories on League activities in Geneva and on the crusade for American entry. By April 1924 the *Herald* had a circulation of thirty-five thousand and had become a vital link between headquarters in New York and the members scattered across the country. The Association had also taken over Fosdick's League of Nations News Bureau and distributed documents and press releases on the League to libraries, universities and civic groups. In addition, the New York office put out a steady stream of pamphlets praising the work being done in Geneva and exhorting Americans to become informed about opportunities for international cooperation. The League, wrote Raymond Fosdick in one of these pamphlets, is not a superstate, but "a simple instrument for bringing nations together in conference around a table." On the inside cover, bold print asked, "What is your Mental Age in regard to Foreign Affairs? Why be an International Illiterate?" Readers were told to join the League of Nations Non-Partisan Association, pay dues of only one dollar a year and do their part to get America into the League in order to prevent another World War.[11]

1. Defenders of the Faith

The Association's exhortations failed to move the politicians. In April 1923 President Harding reiterated his opposition to the League, informing the American people that his administration had "definitely and decisively put aside all thought of the United States entering the League of Nations. It doesn't propose to enter now, by the side door, the back door or the cellar door." Harding's words were extremely discouraging, but when he died that summer, internationalists hoped that his successor would be more receptive. Calvin Coolidge had been sympathetic to the League in 1919, but in his State of the Union message to Congress on December 16 he refused to break with Harding's policy. Calling the League "a foreign agency," Coolidge declared that "the United States sees no reason to limit its own freedom and independence of action by joining it."

1924 was an election year, and the leaders of the Association decided to make a supreme effort to get the political parties committed to American entry into the League. Though many of the Republican members of the organization objected, John Clarke persuaded the executive committee to try to secure planks favoring entry into the League in both the Democratic and Republican platforms. In March the *League of Nations Herald* joyously announced the end of "the silence during recent years of the friends of the League while irreconcilable politicians and mendacious correspondents and editors have deliberately misrepresented the facts. . . ." The executive committee hired seven professional organizers to help form campaign committees in each of the 435 Congressional districts in the nation to work directly on the delegates who would attend the national party conventions. A Speakers Bureau was organized, with more than a thousand men and women ready to speak before civic groups, women's clubs and church organizations.

A new spirit of optimism swept through the internationalist ranks. Mrs. James Lees Laidlaw, director of this campaign, told members of the Association that "there is no manner of doubt" that a majority of the American people were "for our entrance into the League of Nations." "The moral commitment to American membership in the League of Nations," wrote one enthusiast, "is a pent-up flood in every one of the four hundred and thirty-five Congressional Districts of the country." Raymond Fosdick was convinced that only one element stood in the way of the popular will. "Surely the cause of world peace in which we Americans have so deep a concern," he wrote, "should not be dragged at the chariot-wheels of a small political junta, in rebellion against its own leadership." [12]

The internationalists, hypnotized by their own rhetoric, failed to comprehend the political realities in 1924. A delegation led by Irving Fisher and Everett Colby appeared before the Republican Resolutions Committee to argue for a plank authorizing entry into the League "provided the Covenant . . . can be so Americanized as not to surrender to other nations our independence of judgment and action." Yet even this watered-down statement was unacceptable to the Republicans, who still viewed the League as Wilson's handiwork. The GOP adopted a platform opposing membership in the League and rejecting "any obligations under the Covenant."

The Association hoped for greater success with the Democrats. John Clarke addressed the Resolutions Committee in late June, asking for an unequivocal pledge by the Democratic party to do all in its power to secure American entry into the League of Nations. But the Democrats, torn by an urban wing championing Al Smith and a rural faction favoring William G. McAdoo, and split over a proposal to denounce the Ku Klux Klan, were in no mood to revive the divisive issue of the League. The platform neatly sidestepped the question by declaring that "there is no substitute for the League" and calling on Congress to conduct a national referendum on the issue of American entry. A small minority within the party, led by former Secretary of War Newton Baker, was appalled by this cavalier dismissal of Wilson's dream. In early 1924 Baker had written Raymond Fosdick that he was "going to stick to the ship . . . and go down, if I have to, with colors flying" in the fight to get the party committed to the League. True to his word, Baker challenged the report of the Resolutions Committee on the floor of the convention in a passionate speech, but the delegates spurned his appeal and voted to accept the plank on the League by a two-to-one majority.

The executive committee of the League of Nations Non-Partisan Association decided not to endorse either party in the presidential campaign. The Democratic nominee, John W. Davis, who was chosen as a dark horse when the Smith and McAdoo forces stalemated, personally favored American participation in the League, but he refused to make it a campaign issue. Reiterating his faith in the League, he stated that he would limit his policy, if elected, to American cooperation with Geneva. Though this slim promise of future collaboration died with the overwhelming victory of Calvin Coolidge in November, the internationalists refused to admit defeat. Writing to Newton Baker, Raymond Fosdick promised to "rise and continue to shout for the League of

15

Nations. I shall never acquiesce . . . ," he declared. "There are plenty of Presidential campaigns ahead. I have just been reading the life of William Lloyd Garrison, and it's a mighty stimulus in times like these." [13]

The evangelical determination that Fosdick voiced ensured that the League of Nations Non-Partisan Association would survive after the shock of the election, but it became a very different organization. At a meeting on December 10, 1924, the board of directors adopted a new statement of policy. American entry into the League of Nations was now to be an "ultimate aim" of the Association. For the present, the organization would devote itself to encouraging cooperation with League agencies engaged in humanitarian activities, to planning for a disarmament conference, and to securing American membership in the World Court.[14]

Frustrated by the apathy of the American people, the directors of the Association bet on the future. In January 1925 they created an experimental educational committee on a six-month trial basis. The committee studied the high-school curriculum in the New York area and prepared outlines and brochures so that teachers could educate young people "in the existence and aims of the League of Nations." Pleased with the success of this approach, the directors created a permanent Education Department in October and financed the publication of a *Manual for Teachers* to be used in history and civics classes studying the League of Nations. In a few months the first printing of ten thousand copies was exhausted, and the Association brought out a second edition under the title *Essential Facts in Regard to the League.* The anonymous authors of this pamphlet carefully refrained from advocating American entry into the League. Instead they worked more subtly, describing the activities in Geneva and stressing that the League was not a superstate, but "*a method of cooperation* open to those states which wish to use it." Admitting the liabilities as well as the advantages of the League, *Essential Facts* did not let the reader escape without a reminder that "the present League marks mankind's first groping effort towards that noble goal" of international organization and cooperation.[15]

The Education Department soon became the mainspring of the Association, with six full-time workers carrying on its activities. In 1926 the department experimented with a high-school contest on the League of Nations. Fifteen hundred students took an examination based on *Essential Facts* in an effort to win a free trip to Geneva to see the League at work. The contest was an immediate hit, and the Association repeated it every spring. Students from schools throughout the nation participated and other civic groups, including the Rotary Club and the American Association of University Women, gave regional and local prizes to stimulate interest. The Association especially encouraged high schools in rural areas and small towns to participate in order to ensure that people in remote parts of the country would be informed about the League of Nations. The contest undoubtedly achieved the Association's aim of "acquainting thousands of selected high school students, destined to be leaders in their communities and perhaps in world affairs, with the principles and facts of world cooperation."

In 1927 the Association extended its educational activity to college youth with a model League of Nations Assembly at Syracuse University. Students from eleven colleges attended the two-day conference as delegates from the various member nations and discussed the current issues being debated in Geneva. This do-it-yourself project proved to be so popular among college youth that they organized the Middle-Atlantic Model Assembly and arranged a conference each year at a different college in that region. The next year similar groups were formed in New England and the Middle West with the aid of the Association, which helped prepare the agenda, furnished reference material for the student delegates and gave advice on procedure. "It is not impossible that delegates from the United States to future League assemblies," wrote the director of the Association, "will have gained their first experience of both the difficulties and the satisfactions of international cooperation in these miniature assemblies." [16]

While the educational work flourished, the other activities of the Association languished. In July 1925 the bi-weekly *Herald* became the *League of Nation News* and switched to monthly publication. The speaking tours continued, but the Association lost its most dynamic lecturer in September when Hamilton Holt resigned to become president of Rollins College in Florida. Raymond Fosdick continued to address audiences in behalf of the League, speaking to more than sixty groups across the country in 1925. Yet even he began to doubt that the United States would join the League in the near future, though he still believed that eventually the nation would enter "with reluctant feet." In 1927 John H. Clarke grew weary of the ineffective campaign to win over public opinion and resigned as president. The board of directors made him honorary president and chose George Wickersham as his successor. Under Wickersham's leadership, the Association did not even try to secure pledges in favor of the League in the party platforms of 1928. In the contest between Al Smith and Herbert Hoover, the League of Nations was never mentioned as the voters wrestled with the issues of prohibition, Catholicism and continued prosperity.[17]

The Association once again proved its adaptability with a thorough reorganization in January 1929. Dropping the words "Non-Partisan" from its name, it acknowledged that entry into the League was no longer a live issue. Wickersham continued as president; Fosdick became chairman of a five-man executive committee which determined policy; Philip C. Nash, a political scientist, became the paid director of the organization; and Herbert Feis, a professor of economics at the University of Cincinnati, took over the editorship of the *League of Nations News*. The Association was still remarkably healthy. There were 19,341 members operating through ten state branches. In addition, the Association maintained a Midwest office in Chicago to serve the eleven states of that area and operated an information office in Washington. The budget for 1929 was $112,000, much of it spent on educational activities, and the treasury was solvent, with a balance of over $10,000 at the year's end.

The organization now stated its purpose as "furthering American cooperation with and ultimate membership in the League of Nations." Among the more immediate goals, greatest stress was placed on the educational campaign "regarding the history of the League of Nations, its purposes, methods and achievements." An editorial in the *News* made clear the new emphasis. Stating that the central interest of the Association was "the maintenance and furtherance of international peace," the editor offered to cooperate with any group, regardless of attitude toward the League, in the cause of world peace. "The League of Nations Association asks only this," he continued, "that the great experiment which is now being carried on at Geneva should be given fair consideration by the United States." Thus the action group formed to agitate for immediate American entry into the League of Nations had become an educational organization to keep the American people informed about the League and to convince the next generation that international organization was the only alternative to war.[18]

III

Though the League of Nations Association had waged a lonely campaign for entry into the League in the twenties, by the end of the decade a large number of organizations had sprung up to inform the American

18

people on world affairs. Most did not take on a stand on the League issue; instead they sought to convince the American people that the nation was inevitably involved with the rest of the world. They suggested that the United States should attempt to influence the course of international affairs by pursuing an active policy, but they carefully refrained from advocating specific measures. Yet their goal was similar to that of the League of Nations Association—ultimate American acceptance of international cooperation as the sure road to lasting peace. "The first step," wrote one of their number, "is to train an elite to think, feel and act internationally."

The most openly pro-League of these organizations was the Woodrow Wilson Foundation. In 1921, when Wilson received the Nobel Peace Prize, a group of women in New York City decided to establish a similar award in Wilson's name. A committee was quickly formed, headed by Franklin D. Roosevelt, and including Bernard M. Baruch, Henry Morgenthau, Sr., Mrs. William G. McAdoo and Hamilton Holt. In early 1922 the committee began an ambitious campaign to raise an endowment of one million dollars. Holt led the drive, which was remarkably successful, netting $800,000 in six months from over two hundred thousand contributors. Wealthy donors later pushed the fund over the million mark. Adopting the name Woodrow Wilson Foundation, the directors established an annual prize of $25,000, which was awarded for the first time in 1924 to Lord Robert Cecil, British advocate of the Leagues of Nations. In subsequent years the Foundation used its funds to honor both individuals and organizations, giving occasional grants to the League of Nations Association. In 1929 the directors gave the $25,000 prize to the League of Nations "in recognition of ten years' service in the cause of world peace." The League Council reciprocated by using the money to commission an American sculptor to design a monument to be placed in the Peace Palace at Geneva in memory of Woodrow Wilson. In this same year the Foundation joined with the League of Nations Association to establish the Woodrow Wilson Memorial Library in New York.[19]

Other groups worked in the 1920's to arouse American interest in international affairs. In 1918 a small group of liberal journalists and intellectuals, led by Charles A. Beard, Herbert Croly and Paul Kellogg, began meeting in New York to discuss ways of supporting Wilson's peace program. Calling themselves the "Committee on Nothing at All," they gradually expanded into a formal organization, adopted the name League of Free Nations Association and worked hard for the Covenant in 1919. After the Senate rejection, the group became the Foreign Policy

Association and dedicated itself to "spreading a knowledge of foreign affairs among the mass of intelligent people throughout the country." Though its founders were Wilsonians, the Foreign Policy Association cultivated an objective stance, attempting to assess issues from every possible position. Yet the Association never denied its sympathy for the League of Nations. In the 1930's it shared office space with the League of Nations Association and became a co-sponsor of the Wilson Memorial Library.

The Foreign Policy Association was far more influential than the Woodrow Wilson Foundation. By the end of the decade it had over ten thousand members and branches in seventeen cities. Each month the Association held luncheon meetings in New York and in its branch cities at which experts discussed current world problems. In 1932 fifty thousand people attended the luncheons, and millions more heard the discussions over the radio. The Association also developed a research department in the mid-twenties which sent a weekly *Foreign Policy Bulletin* to newspaper editors throughout the country. These bulletins summarized developments overseas and helped ensure coverage of foreign news in the American press. Relying on the mass media, the Foreign Policy Association succeeded in reminding the American people of the world beyond their borders.[20]

Another New York-based group, the Council on Foreign Relations, employed very different techniques in an effort to influence American business, professional and governmental leaders. The Council was founded in 1921 when a group of prominent New York businessmen who had organized during the war to host distinguished foreign visitors merged with a nucleus of intellectuals who had served together as advisers to Wilson at the Paris Peace Conference. The bankers and lawyers provided the money and the rank-and-file membership; the scholars furnished the ideas and the leadership. Limited to 650 members, 400 from New York City and 250 from the rest of the country, the Council's roster read like a Who's Who of American business and professional men. Partners from J. P. Morgan and Company mingled with Ivy League professors, international lawyers with syndicated columnists, State Department officials with clergymen. The Council never took positions on public issues, but its members shared a common belief that the United States should play an active role in world affairs.

The Council's principal activity was to bring its varied membership together for dinner meetings, study groups and conferences. They avoided formal lectures and relied instead on discussion so that experts in business, government and research might "each profit from the knowledge and experience of the other." These sessions took place in the Council's headquarters, a brownstone house in New York City, and though occasionally the studies undertaken by members led to publication, the Council deliberately conducted its activities in seclusion. The one exception was *Foreign Affairs*, a quarterly journal of international relations which first appeared in 1922 and soon became the foremost American periodical of its type. Yet the scholarly quality of its articles restricted its circulation to the academic and expert circles served by the Council. This elitist approach carefully obscured the full impact of its activities, but the Council undoubtedly converted a significant segment of the American economic and governmental leadership to internationalism.[21]

An older organization, the Carnegie Endowment for International Peace, also played an important role in promoting interest in world affairs. Founded in 1910 with a gift of ten million dollars from Andrew Carnegie, the Endowment devoted itself to promoting international cooperation. Under its first president, Elihu Root, it avoided involvement in the debate over the League of Nations, but in 1925 Nicholas Murray Butler, the president of Columbia University and an ardent supporter of the League, replaced Root and cautiously expanded the work of the Endowment. When the League of Nations Association began its educational activities, the Endowment provided financial support, first with small grants, later with an annual subsidy of $4,000. The major emphasis, however, was placed on reaching college students. The Division of Education and Intercourse greatly expanded a wartime program of forming international-relations clubs on college campuses; the number grew from 24 at the war's end to 670 by the mid-1930's. The Endowment supplied the clubs with books, periodicals and occasional lecturers; once a year student leaders met at regional conferences to hear distinguished speakers and to hold round-table discussions on international problems. The Carnegie Endowment also offered universities grants to begin formal courses on world affairs. By 1931, due in part to this stimulus, American colleges were offering 3700 semester courses in international relations.[22]

The continuing American interest in the world found expression in a variety of other ways in the years after World War I. Franklin D. Roosevelt joined with other internationalists to help found the Walter Hines Page School of International Relations at Johns Hopkins University in 1930. Similar graduate schools designed to train experts in foreign affairs and conduct research on world problems developed in the early 1930's: notably Princeton's School of Public and International Affairs and the Fletcher School of Law and Diplomacy at Tufts. In 1921 Harry Garfield, the president of Williams College, asked Bernard Baruch to finance a summer Institute of Politics at Williamstown. For the next twelve years distinguished foreign and American scholars gathered in the Berkshires to lecture to journalists, teachers and elderly ladies and gentlemen on international issues. Similar institutes were held in Colorado, Virginia, Georgia and Southern California at sporadic intervals. Though most provided little more than a glimpse at the complexities of world affairs, they did contribute to the international education of the American people. The very fact they were held indicates a hunger for knowledge that belies the view that the American people had turned their backs on the world in 1919.[23]

The cumulative effect of the activities of the League of Nations Association, the Foreign Policy Association, the Council on Foreign Relations and the other organizations was to create a body of internationalists in the United States. These men and women represented only a small minority of the American population, but they were capable of exerting great influence. Not all favored American entry into the League of Nations, but they shared a common faith in international cooperation. Discussion, arbitration and conciliation were the techniques they believed would banish war from the world. Above all else, they worshiped Woodrow Wilson, finding in his ideals their deepest convictions and vowing that one day they would make his vision of peace and brotherhood a reality.

The most striking characteristic of the internationalists was their homogeneity. Virtually all were old-stock Protestant Americans. Descendants of English and Scottish settlers, they were Anglophiles who believed that the United States had inherited England's role as arbiter of world affairs. As representatives of a social class that had taken on many characteristics of a caste, they showed little sympathy for the plight of colonial peoples. The world they wanted to save was limited to Europe and its overseas possessions; they took Latin America for granted and neglected the Orient. Bankers, lawyers, editors, professors and ministers predominated; there were few salesmen or clerks and no workmen in their ranks. The business community was represented by men who dealt in the world markets—Thomas J. Watson of IBM; John Foster Dulles of Sullivan and Cromwell, the leading international law firm in the nation; Thomas W. Lamont of J. P. Morgan and Company. Small manufacturers, real-estate brokers and insurance executives were conspicuously absent.

Above all, the internationalists lived in the Northeast, with only isolated cells scattered through the provinces in university towns and such cosmopolitan centers as San Francisco and New Orleans. Twenty-six of the twenty-seven directors of the League of Nations Association in 1929 lived within three hundred miles of New York City. The Association had branches in three of the six states of New England but only a Chicago office to serve the eleven-state Middle West. The Council on Foreign Relations and the Foreign Policy Association were equally east-coast oriented. The internationalists dutifully sent missionaries on tour through the hinterlands, but here their homoegeneity betrayed them. Mingling so much with each other and so rarely with the man on the street, the internationalists were never able to comprehend prevailing public attitudes on foreign affairs. One moment they believed that they were on the verge of converting the American people to an unswerving commitment to international cooperation. Then sudden setbacks like the election of 1924 convinced them that the people were confirmed isolationists who would never allow the United States to play its rightful role in world affairs. They failed to realize that most Americans were neither intensely isolationist nor internationalist, but confused and uncertain about the complexities of foreign policy. Mistaking this confusion for indifference, the internationalists continued to preach the Wilsonian abstractions which they alone understood. They made few converts.

IV

In September 1931 the Japanese army swept through the Chinese province of Manchuria, overrunning the area in a few months' time and creating the puppet state of Manchukuo. China appealed to the League of Nations, and after weeks of discussion the Council appointed an investigating committee. A year later the League adopted the committee's report condemning the Japanese as aggressors, but took no further action. In its first test, Article 10 had failed. In 1933 Hitler came to power in Germany, instituting a dictatorship under the Nazi party. Though relatively circumspect in his foreign policy at first, Hitler gave warning of his future plans when he abruptly withdrew from the League in October. Two years later the Italian dictator, Benito Mussolini, defied the League by invading Ethiopia. In Geneva the Council placed limited economic sanctions on Italy, but England and France, fearful of driving Mussolini and Hitler together, refused to permit embargoes on oil, the key to the Italian war effort. As a result, Mussolini completed his conquest in February 1936, and the League of Nations ceased to be a factor in international politics.

In the United States the League of Nations Association continued its varied activities despite the setbacks abroad. In 1933 students from 140 colleges participated in model League Assemblies; ten thousand high-school youths took the examination to win a trip to Geneva. The directors broke with tradition by holding the annual convention "in the land of the Chicago *Tribune*," meeting in midwestern cities in 1931 and 1933. The Association still relied on oratory to carry its message. Each year twenty-five members attended a speakers' institute at the headquarters in New York, and when they passed written and oral tests, they were certified as lecturers. Every two weeks the national office sent out *Speakers' Notes*, a bulletin giving the Association's line on recent events overseas, to the more than six hundred qualified lecturers. Yet the vitality of the Association declined. In 1932 the *League of Nations News* ceased publication, replaced by the *Chronicle*, a six-page monthly in newspaper format put out by the Chicago office. An effort to secure one million signatures on petitions asking the government to state the terms on which it would join the League reached only a third of its goal. And membership fell nearly in half to ten thousand.

The most serious problem facing the Association in these depression years was finances. The annual budget of $112,000 in 1929 dropped to $84,000 in 1932 and then to $53,000 the next year. The board of directors devoted its meetings to discussing means of raising money. In response to a desperate plea to Nicholas Murray Butler, the Carnegie Endowment raised its subsidy from $4,000 to $11,646 in 1935. The Woodrow Wilson Foundation provided an additional $5,000, and with this support the Association was able to keep five regional offices functioning. In 1934 the Association moved into new quarters on the twenty-first floor of a building at 8 West 40th Street in New York City, sharing expenses and space with the Woodrow Wilson Foundation and the Foreign Policy Association. As economic conditions improved, larger contributions from members and money from increased sale of publications enabled the Association to survive.[24]

The internationalists continued to look for significant changes in the attitude of the American people. In 1932 they were greatly encouraged by a referendum in western Massachusetts in which election officials placed a question on the ballot asking voters if they favored entry into the League of Nations. Sixty-three percent of the more than 40,000 who participated answered yes. Two years later, when this question was put to 217,000 voters in many parts of Massachusetts, sixty-two percent expressed a desire to enter the League.[25]

The election of Franklin D. Roosevelt and the return of the party of Woodrow Wilson to power in 1933 failed to cheer the internationalists. Though Roosevelt had campaigned for the League as Cox's running-mate, his ardor had cooled during the 1920's. In an article in *Foreign Affairs* in 1928, he wrote, "We should co-operate with the League as the first great agency for the maintenance of peace . . . ," but he stopped short of advocating American entry. Four years later, when he was seeking the Democratic nomination, he specifically opposed American participation in a speech to the New York State Grange. The Democratic platform in 1932 championed international "consultation and conference," but it made no mention of the League. After the election Roosevelt's appointment of Cordell Hull, who worshiped Woodrow Wilson, as Secretary of State offered some solace. From Florida, Hamilton Holt wrote to Attorney General Homer Cummings, expressing his hope that "the President will be persuaded to take his former position in favor of the League of Nations. I am sure the country will follow him if he will." [26]

Once again Holt was to be disappointed. In the mid-1930's the United States moved further into isolation as the world crisis deepened. For two years Senator Nye conducted a far-ranging Senate investigation of the munitions industry which led him to charge that bankers and "merchants of death" had deceived Wilson and brought about American entry into the World War. Responding to Nye's accusation and to Mussolini's African adventure, Congress passed a series of neutrality laws to keep the United States out of the next conflict. Under the mandatory provisions of this legislation, the President was compelled to ban the shipment of arms and the granting of loans to foreign belligerents. To the dismay of the internationalists, this meant that the United States could neither cooperate with the League in applying sanctions nor aid the victims of armed aggression. Instead of leading the nation into the League, Roosevelt was following Congress in a policy of rigid isolationism.

Meanwhile, significant changes were occurring in the leadership of the League of Nations Association. In 1933 Raymond Fosdick followed

George Wickersham as president and tried to infuse the organization with his unquenchable enthusiasm. "A new generation is growing up," he told the members, "unhampered by the political prejudices of a dozen years ago." Two years later, however, Fosdick resigned to become president of the Rockefeller Foundation. Though he continued to support the work of the Association, his departure marked the passing of the old guard.

Two remarkably able men now took over the affairs of the Association. The first was James T. Shotwell, a professor of history at Columbia University, who succeeded Fosdick as president. A Canadian by birth, Shotwell had come to the United States to study under James Harvey Robinson at Columbia. Though Shotwell started his teaching career as a specialist in medieval history, a trip to Europe in 1905 led to a lifelong interest in contemporary international affairs. During the World War he became a member of the Inquiry, a group of scholars who helped Wilson prepare for the Paris Peace Conference. From this experience, he developed the idea for an economic and social history of the World War which the Carnegie Endowment agreed to sponsor. As general editor of a series which eventually ran to over 150 volumes, Shotwell spent most of the twenties in Europe, lining up authors and overseeing the work of two hundred collaborators in sixteen countries. A restless and inquisitive man, Shotwell lobbied for revision of the League Covenant in Geneva in 1923, launched a major crusade to unify the warring factions of the peace movement in the United States and played a key role in the origin of the Pact of Paris. As president of the Association, he continued the able leadership of Clarke, Wickersham and Fosdick, and, like them, he carried on the Wilsonian spirit. "At a time when the moral forces of humanity were surrendering to bleak despair," he wrote of Wilson in his autobiography, "he summoned them again to action. . . . Never before had any single individual in secular history been able to exert an influence like this."

When Shotwell became president, the Association was administered by Clark M. Eichelberger, who had become the executive director in late 1933. Born in Freeport, Illinois, in 1896, Eichelberger was a graduate of the University of Chicago. He had first gone into social work, but after serving in the army during the World War he became a lecturer on world affairs. In 1927 he began working for the Association as director of the Chicago office. He did an outstanding job, reviving interest in the League in the hostile Middle West and editing the *Chronicle* so successfully that it replaced the *News* as the Association's voice in 1932. Eichelberger possessed a warm, outgoing personality, a charm of manner, and a deep, rich voice that made him an extremely persuasive spokesman for the internationalist cause. He and Shotwell formed a very effective partnership. Eichelberger ran the daily affairs of the Association and stimulated the members in monthly editorials and frequent speaking engagements. Shotwell concentrated on securing continued financial support from the foundations and wealthy contributors and on developing new policies for the Association to pursue.[27]

The great challenge facing the new leaders was the breakdown of the League of Nations. In 1936 the board of directors approved a policy statement which began, "The conquests of Ethiopia and Manchuria confront the world with a failure of the collective system, as applied, to maintain the principles of the Covenant of the League of Nations. . . ." The remedy was obvious—probe for the flaws in the Covenant, remove them and press forward with a reorganized League. Eichelberger was convinced that the unwillingness of the leading nations to vote for sanctions had crippled the League, and he urged a revised Covenant that would bind the members to aid victims of aggression. But in 1938, when Hitler seized Austria and then, at Munich, forced the western democracies to accede to his demands for Czech territory, the internationalists acknowledged the complete ineffectiveness of the League. However, they did not abandon the principle of collective security; the editorials in the *Chronicle* now stressed the need to work for "the collective system." "The first task confronting us is a constant reiteration of the ideals of international society," declared the board of directors in November 1938. "These principles housed in the League of Nations and its allied bodies cannot be forever lost." [28]

As they reluctantly turned away from the League, Eichelberger and Shotwell stressed the necessity of American cooperation with other nations to prevent war. When President Roosevelt gave his Quarantine Address at Chicago, suggesting that aggressors be outlawed by peace-loving nations, they were overjoyed. "This is the collective system manifesting new vitality," Eichelberger declared, while Shotwell saw the speech as "a milestone in the long march of nations" away from war. The Association played a major role in the formation of the American Union for Concerted Peace Efforts, which sought to prevent the United States from giving aid to nations which waged war in violation of treaty commitments. The Union was composed of the leaders of a large number of peace groups. Eichelberger served as chairman and directed

27

the efforts from the Association's headquarters in New York. In 1939 the Union led a drive to revise the neutrality legislation so that the United States could discriminate against aggressors. With Shotwell's support, the Association threw all its resources into this effort, celebrating a Peace and Security Week from April 26 to May 3, sponsoring a conference attended by 146 prominent educators and churchmen in Washington and airing four radio broadcasts. This effort was useless; Congress adjourned in July with the neutrality legislation intact.[29]

Throughout these bleak years the internationalists never lost faith. They ignored a public-opinion poll in 1937 which showed that only twenty-six percent of the American people felt that the United States should have joined the League of Nations in 1919. With great passion, they presented a different reading of history. "Had the United States joined the League of Nations," wrote Clark Eichelberger after Hitler seized Austria, "democracy would have triumphed, the League of Nations would have been the outstanding force for peace in the world and the Nazi soldiers, representing a more brutal militarism than that of the Kaiser, would not again be on the march to dominate Europe." After Munich he proclaimed, "If, as many people say, the World War has finally been lost, it was lost twenty years ago in the United States Senate. . . ." In March 1939, after Germany swallowed up the remainder of Czechoslovakia, Eichelberger renewed the charge. "The United States won the war and lost the peace. . . . Since aggression started in 1931 to the present occupation of Czechoslovakia, the world has had plenty of evidence of the alternatives to the policies of Woodrow Wilson. . . ."

As the shadows of war lengthened across Europe in 1939 the internationalists looked forward to the peace that would follow and a new opportunity to create a more enduring society of nations. "Let the fair-weather friends of collective peace and security drop by the way," wrote William Terry. "Those whose abiding faith and unceasing efforts will eventually make the dream of world peace a reality will not lose heart. . . ."[30]

2

War

OFFICIALS of the League of Nations assembled in Geneva on the morning of September 1, 1939, for a long-awaited ceremony. Ten years before, the League had decided to use the $25,000 prize from the Woodrow Wilson Foundation for a memorial to the American President. Sculptor Paul Manship had designed a huge bronze sphere, and now, in anticipation of the League's twentieth anniversary, the globe was lowered into position on the central terrace of the Peace Palace. Beneath it the officials placed a tablet with the inscription, "To the Memory of Woodrow Wilson, President of the United States, Founder of the League of Nations."

On the same morning, several hundred miles to the northeast, German troops crossed the border into Poland. A week before, Adolf Hitler had concluded a non-aggression pact with the Soviet Union which he believed would permit him to conquer Poland without interference. For the first time Hitler had miscalculated. Neville Chamberlain, the English Prime Minister who negotiated the Munich agreement, learning from Hitler's treachery in Czechoslovakia, promised Poland in March 1939 to come to her aid if Germany attacked. Reluctantly the French had agreed to stand with Britain. On Sunday, September 3, both nations sent ultimatums demanding that Hitler withdraw his forces from Poland. When the Nazi dictator refused, England and France declared war.

For the internationalists, World War II came as an awful fulfillment of their prophecies. "You . . . must be all but ill," wrote novelist Marjorie Kinnan Rawlings to Hamilton Holt, "knowing that American participation in a League of Nations with teeth in it, would have avoided all of this." The League of Nations Association issued a statement asserting, "The tragedy of the moment is grim justification for the ideals of the League of Nations. The Association's task will be to do its part in planning the world of tomorrow." In his editorials Eichelberger urged members to begin working immediately to prevent a third world war. "Nothing in this time of travail has weakened our faith in the possibility of enduring peace," he wrote, asking his followers to launch a new crusade "for American leadership in preparing for and building a better new world." [1]

In its first meeting after the outbreak of the war, the Association adopted a twofold policy. Reaffirming their belief in "an international community that practices cooperation and seeks justice," the members pledged to work for "a new world on the other side of the devastation which the nations are entering." But for the present they would devote themselves to securing all-out American aid to England and France in their fight against Nazi Germany. "There can be no future for what we believe in," they declared, "unless aggression is stopped and the free nations of Europe restored." With this mandate Clark Eichelberger formed a new pressure group to secure changes in the Neutrality Act to permit American aid to the European democracies. Persuading William Allen White to provide the formal leadership, Eichelberger announced the creation of the Non-Partisan Committee for Peace Through Revision of the Neutrality Act. Several hundred prominent educators, businessmen, publishers and clergymen joined in the effort, which ended successfully in November 1939 with the repeal of the arms embargo. When the Nazi blitzkrieg swept over western Europe in the spring of 1940, Eichelberger once again called on White to form the Committee to Defend America by Aiding the Allies. For the next year and a half the Committee absorbed the energies of the internationalists. Eichelberger served as its executive director, and he used the Association's offices in New York to carry on a massive propaganda campaign. With branches in over three hundred cities, the Committee to Defend America played a vital role in building public support for a policy of increased aid to Britain and eventual involvement in the war.

In the midst of this campaign Eichelberger never forgot the ultimate goal. ". . . the issue today," he told the members of the Association, "is between the organization of a world by force under the dictators and the reorganization of a democratic world on the principles of the League of Nations." In speeches to local chapters of the Association and the Committee to Defend America he stressed the importance of mobilizing public opinion to create "a democratic society of nations" at the war's end. Eichelberger returned from a trip to the West Coast in the summer of 1940 deeply impressed by the changing public attitude. "Cynicism toward the League of Nations has disappeared," he reported. "Audiences responded spontaneously when I pointed out that had . . . the United States fulfilled its responsibilities in 1919, the tragedy of a second world war might have been avoided." [2]

James T. Shotwell responded to the outbreak of war by resigning from the presidency of the League of Nations Association in order to concentrate on forming a new group devoted to planning for the postwar world. In the fall of 1939 he invited fifty leading experts in international relations to join with him in this venture. Though Eichelberger served as director, Shotwell sought a broader base than the League of Nations Association, and he finally secured the co-sponsorship of the American Association of University Women, the Church Peace Union and the National Board of the YWCA. Determined to stress seriousness of purpose, Shotwell insisted on adopting a cumbersome title, the Commission to Study the Organization of Peace.

The Commission held its first meeting on Sunday, November 5, 1939, at the Murray Hill Hotel, described by one member as an "ancient relic of Victorian luxury." Twenty-eight men and women conferred all day in a bare and cheerless room, stopping only for a brief luncheon in the hotel's dining room. The participants, among them Virginia Gildersleeve, John Foster Dulles, Owen Lattimore, Max Lerner, William Allen White and Monsignor John A. Ryan, made Shotwell president of the Commission and William Allan Neilson, the former head of Smith College, chairman of the executive committee. They formed three committees to carry out their work and agreed to continue meeting in all-day Sunday sessions once a month.[3]

Two months later Clark Eichelberger announced the existence of the Commission to the public. Its major purpose, he explained, was to enable a small group of experts to engage in an intensive examination of the problems of peace. A studies committee, headed by Clyde Eagleton, professor of international relations at New York University, would direct the preparation of reports which the Commission planned to publish. Then a second committee would stimulate public discussion by forming groups throughout the country to meet and consider the reports. In publicizing the work of the Commission, its spokesmen emphasized that it was "not a League of Nations move." Instead it hoped to "review the past without prejudice" in order to prepare for the creation of a new world organization for peace.

Soon more than one hundred members were attending the monthly meetings of the Commission and they included the nation's most distinguished authorities in international affairs. At these sessions they listened to papers prepared by Clyde Eagleton, John Foster Dulles and Shotwell and began drafting their first report. In order to capture public attention, the Commission launched a series of radio broadcasts in January 1940 over the CBS network which were carried on ninety stations around the country. Aired on Saturday evenings at 6:30, these fifteen-minute programs presented Shotwell interviewing guests who gave their views on the basic question "Which Way to Lasting Peace?" The Commission encouraged listeners to form study groups of their own and furnished them with reprints of the broadcasts and a brochure entitled *In Time of War Prepare for Peace.* "Man is still the director of his destiny," this leaflet declared. "With intelligent leadership and vision, he can build a new and better world through the *organization of peace.*" The response was so favorable that in the spring the Commission began a second series of radio broadcasts aimed at college students. Scheduled for Saturday afternoons, these programs consisted of a panel discussion by students on the theme of peace. To stimulate study groups on the campuses, the Commission offered $600 in prizes for the groups which submitted the most imaginative reports of their discussions.[4]

While the Commission sought publicity for its work, the Council on Foreign Relations approached the State Department with a proposal to study postwar issues secretly and make its deliberations available to the Department. Secretary of State Cordell Hull approved, and with financial support from the Rockefeller Foundation, the Council appointed four study committees. Norman H. Davis, head of the American Red Cross and close friend and adviser to Hull, coordinated the work of the Council's committees. Under his direction, they prepared reports on such problems as armaments, colonial territories, economic relations and aggression. As the war in Europe intensified, however, these studies focused more and more on the current problems of American foreign policy and neglected long-range issues.

The Council's study groups stimulated the State Department. In a long meeting with his principal advisers on December 27 Cordell Hull decided to form a high-level committee to "survey the basic principles which should underlie a desirable world order to be evolved after the termination of the present hostilities." In early January Hull announced the creation of this Advisory Committee on Problems of Foreign Relations, thus carefully disguising its main job of studying postwar issues. The Under Secretary of State, Sumner Welles, was chairman of the body, and all but two of its members were officers of the Department. The exceptions, Norman H. Davis and George Rublee, a New York lawyer, were both men who had intimate ties with the State Department. The Committee quickly divided into three subcommittees to conduct its studies, but the pressure of the war in Europe soon prevented the already overburdened Department officers from carrying out their plans.[5]

The Commission to Study the Organization of Peace proved more successful. Though Shotwell suspended the monthly meetings during the summer, the members met again in the fall and approved the final draft of their first report, which was made public on Armistice Day, 1940. Two days before, Clark Eichelberger had joined with Shotwell in a radio broadcast to give the public a preview of the Commission's report. "We are at last aware," he told a nationwide audience, "that the challenge to world peace has become a challenge to civilization itself." James Shotwell then summarized the Commission's findings and urged the American people to take up the quest for lasting peace. "At a time like this, when the old landmarks are disappearing, we must keep our bearings and chart our course so as not to repeat the mistakes of the past." [6]

The report did not offer any blueprints for the future, but it did provide the guidelines that Shotwell promised. The chief argument was for the creation of a new and stronger league of nations with sufficient force to prevent aggression. "Only by organization to develop and uphold the law of nations can civilization stand up against the ever-advancing machinery of modern scientific warfare," the authors contended. ". . . law can be enforced only if the power of the community, overwhelmingly greater than the power of any of its members, is brought to bear when and where lawlessness begins." But the authors never spelled out how this power was to be wielded. They disclaimed any intention of creating a world superstate with its own police force, yet they called for limitations on national sovereignty greater than those demanded in the League Covenant. The report did urge nations to submit disputes to an international court, to forego the use of armed force except in self-defense, to cooperate economically, to disarm, and to recognize and respect basic human rights. The report concluded with the cryptic statement, "The world must evolve from League to federation."

In papers attached to the report, James Shotwell and Clyde Eagleton spelled out more fully their conceptions of a future world organization.

33

With Manchuria, Ethiopia and Czechoslovakia in mind, Shotwell wrote, "It is aggressive war which the peace movement must concentrate upon, for if we can get rid of it, we can get rid of all war by making defense a cooperative police action." By narrowing down the complex causes of war to the single factor of unprovoked aggression, the internationalists believed they had found the key to lasting peace. "What we now have to do is to make the use of force the monopoly of the international government," wrote Eagleton, "and forbid its use by any State against another." Yet even he was not prepared to advocate the universal world body which would be necessary to exercise such unlimited power.

The vague tone of the Commission's first report disguised a fundamental ambivalence about the existing League of Nations. On the one hand, the internationalists realized that the League had failed because it did not possess the available military force to halt the aggression of Mussolini and Hitler. They were thus willing to scrap the experiment at Geneva and begin again with a more effective organization. But the League was still close to their hearts, and they viewed the next effort at world order as a continuation of the task Wilson had begun. Most of all, they wanted to convince the American people that their rejection of the League in 1919 had been a tragic mistake. "The Commission," stated the report, "aims to do its utmost to lead the American people to see more clearly than they did twenty years ago that, for selfish and unselfish reasons alike, all their efforts must have as their ultimate goal the creation of a better world in which to live." [7]

I

"The coming spring," wrote Clark Eichelberger in March 1941, "may be the most critical spring that mankind has seen since the dawn of history." Nothing less than the "fate of civilization for centuries to come" was at stake. Millions of Americans shared his deep concern. Though Britain had survived the German blitz from the air, she remained a lonely outpost of resistance against a Nazi Germany that now dominated the European continent. Stirred by England's gallant fight and alarmed by Germany's awesome power, the United States had abandoned its aloof neutrality. In September 1940 President Roosevelt announced that he had transferred fifty American destroyers to England in return for the rights to build eight air and naval bases on British territory in the Western Hemisphere. Later in the year, when Churchill informed Roosevelt that Britain was fast running out of money to pay for purchases of war supplies in the United States, the President submitted the lend-lease program to Congress. Comparing it to giving a neighbor some garden hose to fight a fire, Roosevelt asked Congress for permission to provide Britain with the weapons and matériel she needed free of charge. In March 1941 Congress passed the lend-lease bill by overwhelming margins and appropriated an initial seven million dollars to finance this aid.

Internationalists, after decades as an unheeded minority, now became the spokesmen for a new national consensus on foreign policy. They were less than gracious in their new role. "The time for controversy is past," declared the Committee to Defend America, adding that any who opposed aid to Britain were "subversive elements." "To agitate for a reversal of policy," Clark Eichelberger warned the isolationists, "would be tantamount to sabotage." Caught up in the passions of war, Eichelberger and his followers condemned neutrality as evil. "Each nation today is in some degree or other either the ally of Germany or the ally of Britain and America; the ally of fascism or the ally of democracy." Pursuing the logic of his position, Eichelberger advocated extending additional aid to Britain even if it meant eventual American participation in the war.[8]

The Committee to Defend America became the chief focus of the internationalist movement in 1941. When William Allen White resigned as chairman in January in protest against the group's increasing militancy, Eichelberger took over as acting chairman. The Committee had lobbied strenuously for passage of lend-lease, and during the spring began demanding that the American Navy convoy British ships across the Atlantic to ensure the delivery of vital supplies. Yet even in the midst of these current issues, Eichelberger never forgot the long-range goal. In a policy statement issued on March 17 by the Committee, he said that victory for the democracies would be meaningless unless it brought about a new world order. "Public opinion must be mobilized now," his statement concluded, "so that America will play an effective part in the organization of a lasting peace and will this time see the job through."[9]

In these hectic months the activities of the League of Nations Association tended to languish. Dr. Frank G. Boudreau succeeded Shotwell as president in January 1940, and he confined the work of the Association to the educational field. The annual high-school contest continued,

35

but in 1940, with Hitler's conquest of Europe, the Association changed the award to a trip to South America. The questions also changed; in 1941 the students were asked to discuss four ways in which national sovereignty should be limited "in order to organize durable peace." Similarly, the model assemblies altered their structure with the demise of the League of Nations. The students who gathered at Lehigh College in March 1941 came as delegates to a world peace conference. The most significant initiative taken by the Association was the founding of the Free World Association as a successor to the American Union for Concerted Peace Efforts. The new group, which was composed of representatives of American peace societies and exiles from German-occupied European countries, came into existence on June 15, 1941, at a conference in Washington. Clark Eichelberger served on the board of directors of the Free World Association, and the Carnegie Endowment helped finance its activities. Its major undertaking was the publication of *Free World*, a monthly journal which printed news from occupied Europe, discussed peace aims and advocated "an international system of collective security." [10]

The Commission to Study the Organization of Peace was very active in 1941, distributing 100,000 copies of its first report. Working through women's clubs, churches and civic organizations, the Commission cooperated with three hundred study groups across the nation and mailed material to 3,500 individuals. A leaflet, *How to Study the Organization of Peace*, gave interested readers comprehensive advice on how to set up and run discussion groups. In January the studies committee started work on a second report, which the members decided should focus on the postwar problems of relief and reconstruction. This report was not released in 1941, but in June, James Shotwell made public a new statement of policy. "The American people are now paying the price of two decades of international irresponsibility," he began. Stating that the war in Europe had finally convinced the American people that they were "part of the world community," Shotwell listed seven goals for the future, including lower tariffs, an international bill of rights, the free exchange of ideas, and American financing of postwar reconstruction. Shotwell failed to clarify the Commission's conception of the future world organization, calling simply for "a substitute for war which can adequately settle disputes, remedy injustice and maintain rights between nations." [11]

In 1941 a member of the Commission, John Foster Dulles, helped the Federal Council of Churches create a new body to join in the quest for postwar world order. Dulles came from a family which had specialized in diplomacy. His grandfather, John W. Foster, had served briefly as Secretary of State in the Harrison administration, and his uncle, Robert Lansing, had headed the State Department under Wilson during the First World War. Dulles' career as a diplomat began in 1907, when he accompanied his grandfather to the Second Hague Peace Conference in the Netherlands. Graduating from Princeton, he had become a lawyer concentrating on international finance. He served on the War Trade Board during World War I, and then attended the Paris Peace Conference as an adviser to Wilson on financial matters. In the 1920's he joined the staff of Sullivan and Cromwell, and within ten years he became the managing partner of this distinguished law firm. A devout Presbyterian, Dulles attended a Conference on Church and State held at Oxford in 1937 which moved him profoundly. He was struck by the spiritual bonds between the Christians from all over the world who participated in the meeting. "From that time on," he wrote in 1943, "I began to think and plan my work through Christian rather than through secular groups."

In December 1940 Dulles drafted a statement on "The American Churches and the International Situation" which he presented in Atlantic City to the biennial meeting of the Federal Council of Churches. The Council quickly approved his major recommendation and established a Commission to Study the Bases of a Just and Durable Peace. Dulles was chairman of the new group, and he spent the early months of 1941 recruiting more than a hundred prominent clergymen and laymen. By May, Dulles, working with a twenty-five-man Committee of Direction, had decided on a dual role for the Commission. First, the members had to engage in intensive study to inform themselves fully on world affairs. Then they must develop lines of communication so that they could share their knowledge with all Protestant churchmen and thus bring Christian influence to bear on the eventual peace settlement. Dulles was not yet sure of the policies he wished the Commission to advocate, but in a speech to a Methodist group in May he firmly renounced isolationism. "The sovereignty system is no longer consonant either with peace or with justice," he declared. "It is imperative that there be transition to a new order." A month later he was writing David Lawrence, the columnist, "I am rather appalled at what seem to me the lack of any peace aims which would serve the dual purpose of giving inspiration to our present military effort, and also serve to educate and crystallize public opinion. . . ." [12]

37

2. War

The inability of the internationalists, both secular and Christian, to formulate concrete plans for world organization led to a growing public enthusiasm for the ideas of Clarence Streit. A Missouri-born journalist, Streit covered the League of Nations for the New York *Times* throughout the 1930's. As he sat in Geneva and watched the League disintegrate, he developed a radically different concept for world order. Beginning with a sketch in a *Times* article in 1933, Streit evolved his plan, writing and rewriting until he had a book-length manuscript. Four publishers rejected his work, and he resigned from the *Times* in 1939 to publish his manuscript privately when finally Harper's agreed to bring it out under the title *Union Now*. It achieved immediate success and underwent fourteen reprintings in the next two years.

In *Union Now* Clarence Streit found in the American experience after the Revolution the perfect model for the world to follow. The states at first had joined in a loose confederation which failed to govern adequately and subsequently gave birth to a federal union. The League of Nations, Streit argued, was the world's attempt at a confederation in the twentieth century, and it must give way to a union of the democratic nations which would eventually expand into a universal organization. The test for membership in the union Streit proposed was democracy—only nations which believed in self-government and the freedom of the individual could join. He restricted the founders to fifteen nations: the United States, Great Britain, the self-governing British dominions, and the countries of Western Europe, including France, Belgium, Holland, Switzerland and Scandinavia, but excluding Germany, Italy and the Soviet Union. "The Great Republic," he wrote, "would be organized with a view to its spreading peacefully round the earth as nations grow ripe for it."

In this utopian organization the citizens would enjoy the benefits of a union defense force, a union customs-free economy, union money and a union postal and communications system. But, like the American states, the member nations would retain complete home rule and separate powers of government to handle local matters. The structure of the union would also resemble that of the United States, with a Congress having a lower house based on population and a Senate in which each nation would be equally represented. Streit wanted a president, but he thought a five-member executive board would work better. Stressing the need for prompt action, Streit suggested that the President of the United States issue a Declaration of the Dependence of Free Men, invite the other democracies to sign it, and then hold a constitutional

38

convention. Streit had no doubt that such a plan was feasible. "If we *will* Union we can achieve Union, and the time we take to do it depends only on ourselves." [13]

Thousands of readers responded so enthusiastically that Streit formed the Inter-democracy Federal Unionists in 1939. After a year under this cumbersome name, the organization was rechristened Federal Union, Inc., and began an active drive to recruit members. By early 1941 there were sixty chapters formed and organizers were planning sixty more. The specific nature of Streit's plan, its stress on democracy and its exclusively Anglo-Saxon and Nordic character appealed to many Americans who had been shaken out of their apathy toward foreign affairs by the war. Celebrities were particularly drawn to Federal Union. At a rally in New York City's Mecca Temple in late 1940, W. Somerset Maugham, Robert E. Sherwood and Raymond Massey spoke to three thousand in behalf of Streit's plan. Clare Boothe Luce, Thomas Mann and Dorothy Thompson joined Streit in addressing a dinner meeting at the Waldorf-Astoria on January 22, 1941. Mrs. Luce summed up the feelings of many of Streit's supporters. "There is no other peace plan or war aim being presented anywhere, by anyone, or any group of statesmen, but this plan and aim. Dare we refuse it?"

Old-line internationalists became alarmed at the surprising success of Federal Union. Ruhl Bartlett, a diplomatic historian, wrote in *New World*, the monthly journal of the League of Nations Association, that Streit was guilty of perverting history. Denying that the American situation in 1789 and the world crisis in 1940 were comparable, Bartlett pleaded, "Let us not try to organize the world on the basis of Mr. Streit's historical myth." Other internationalists agreed. William Terry objected to the exclusive nature of the *Union Now* plan, and pointed out that in practice it would mean "a new order imposed on the world by an Anglo-American federation." This was precisely its appeal. At a time when the American people were applauding England's gallant struggle against Hitler, they rallied to the idea of a world federation based on the leadership of the Anglo-Saxon nations.[14]

By the summer of 1941 the American people had traveled a long way from the isolationism of the 1930's. In a Gallup poll taken in May, thirty-eight percent of those questioned wanted the United States to join a league of nations after the war, while only thirty-nine percent objected. Thus, nearly half who expressed an opinion favored international organization. The lessons of the war, coupled with the ceaseless activity of internationalist pressure groups, had convinced many Americans that the United States had to play an active role in the postwar world. As yet, no one was sure what that role would be. In a long editorial in *Life* entitled "The American Century," Henry Luce expressed the new mood. Claiming that the United States had passed up "a golden opportunity . . . to assume the leadership of the world" in 1919, Luce called upon the American people to help Roosevelt succeed where Wilson had failed. It was time, he said, "to accept wholeheartedly our duty and our opportunity as the most powerful and vital nation in the world." But Luce was unable to describe the nature of the new internationalism he preached. "It will take shape," he concluded, "as all civilizations take shape, by the living of it, by work and effort, by trial and error, by enterprise and adventure and experience." [15]

II

President Roosevelt carefully refrained from taking part in the movement toward international organization. In his State of the Union address to Congress in January 1941 he limited his view of the future to "the co-operation of free countries, working together in a friendly, civilized society." The President then called for a world order based upon freedom of speech, freedom of worship, freedom from want and freedom from fear. But Roosevelt refused to go beyond the vague ideals of the four freedoms. He made no mention of international organization, suggesting instead that freedom from fear could be achieved through universal disarmament. Two months later Clark Eichelberger wrote to the President, urging him to arouse public opinion in favor of future American entry into a world organization. "The reaction against cooperation which produced the tragedy of 1919–1920," Eichelberger wrote, "must not be repeated." Roosevelt ignored this plea. "If you, personally, or those associated with you," he replied in May, "have any concrete suggestions or proposals, I would appreciate it if you would place them before the Secretary of State." [16]

The State Department seemed equally uninterested. The Advisory Committee on Problems of Foreign Relations set up in January 1940 had quietly died. Leo Pasvolsky, a Special Assistant to the Secretary of State, deplored the lack of planning for the postwar world in the Department, and in November 1940 he asked Cordell Hull to create a Division of Special Research. On February 3, 1941, the Secretary issued a secret departmental order establishing the new division.

Leo Pasvolsky now became the government's chief planner for international organization. Born in Russia, Pasvolsky arrived in the United States in 1905 and attended City College and Columbia University in New York. He worked for a brief period as a journalist, and then joined the staff of the Brookings Institution, a private research firm in Washington, as a specialist on Eastern European trade and commerce. Pasvolsky entered government service as an economic expert during the depression, and in 1936 Cordell Hull made him his personal assistant. A short, owlish man, Pasvolsky shunned publicity, preferring to work unobtrusively preparing Hull's speeches and drafting departmental memoranda. In his new job as Chief of the Division of Special Research, he quickly assembled a small staff of economists, political scientists and journalists to carry on long-range studies. In the spring of 1941 he tried unsuccessfully to revive the Advisory Committee, but Hull was too absorbed in the day-by-day problems of the European war to act. Undaunted, Pasvolsky continued his research effort, waiting for a more favorable moment to begin detailed planning for the postwar world.[17]

Vice President Henry A. Wallace broke the administration's silence on international organization in a nationally broadcast speech to the Foreign Policy Association on April 8, 1941. The tall, rumpled Iowan had expressed isolationist sympathies in the 1930's when he served as Secretary of Agriculture, but Hitler's aggressive acts had transformed him into an ardent interventionist. Chosen personally by Roosevelt as his running mate in 1940 despite conservative protests, Wallace was viewed as the embodiment of the New Deal and the likely successor to the presidency. Addressing the dinner guests of the Association at the Waldorf-Astoria, he declared, "The United States now has her second opportunity to make the world safe for democracy." He attacked the isolationists who continued to oppose American aid to Britain, blaming them for the war and its many tragedies. The United States should adopt a "Bill of Duties," he continued. "With such a bill we can help build a Pax Democratica which will bless us and the whole world for a century to come." Then he became more specific. "There must be worked out an international order sufficiently strong to prevent the rise of aggressor nations." The audience cheered long and loudly; the next day the New York *Times* praised Wallace for opening "a new chapter" in American foreign policy.[18]

Another high administration official, Under Secretary of State Sumner Welles, found Wallace's words encouraging. When Cordell Hull became seriously ill in June, Welles served as Acting Secretary, a job he filled with distinction. Welles was a model diplomat, tall and erect in bearing, elegantly dressed in hand-tailored suits which he changed at least twice a day in the Washington heat, and never without his ivory-handled walking stick. Aristocratic in appearance, he sported a neatly trimmed mustache beneath his prominent nose and imposing forehead. An intimate friend of the President, Welles came from the same patrician New York background and had also attended Groton and Harvard. In college he determined on a career in diplomacy, choosing Latin America as his special field. He entered the foreign service in 1915, and after two years in Tokyo, where he developed a lifelong hatred of the Japanese, he served in the American embassy in Buenos Aires. In 1921 he returned to Washington to head the Division of Latin American Affairs at the age of twenty-eight. Four years later, after liquidating an American intervention in the Dominican Republic begun by Wilson, he clashed with Calvin Coolidge and resigned from the Foreign Service. He lived in great luxury at Oxon Hill, the Maryland estate of his second wife, Mathilde Townsend. When Franklin Roosevelt ran for the presidency in 1932, Welles contributed heavily to the campaign and was rewarded with the post of Assistant Secretary of State. Despite a disastrous beginning in Cuba in 1933, he played a major role in developing the Good Neighbor policy and in 1937 Roosevelt promoted him to Under Secretary.

Welles was a striking contrast to Tennessean Cordell Hull, and the two men gradually became antagonists. Hull could never forgive Welles for his aloof manner and snobbish air, and he resented his subordinate's easy access to the White House. Yet Hull appreciated the efficient way in which Welles supervised the daily administration of the Department and he was grateful to him for entertaining visiting foreign dignitaries at Oxon Hill. Other members of the Department appreciated Welles' keen and pragmatic intelligence, instinctive knowledge of diplomatic tactics and enormous capacity for work. But he rarely inspired the personal loyalty that colleagues felt for Hull. They viewed him as a condescending aristocrat, and journalists agreed, branding him a "cool fish" and a "copybook diplomat." Beneath this austere exterior, however, Welles believed passionately in the ideals of Woodrow Wilson and he soon became the most eloquent prophet of a new world order.[19]

On July 22, 1941, with Hull still recuperating from his illness, Sumner Welles spoke for the government at the laying of the cornerstone for a new wing of the Norwegian Legation. He paid tribute to the people of Nazi-occupied Norway, describing the ceremony as "an act of faith in the ultimate victory of the forces of human liberty, in the triumph of civilization itself over the forces of barbarism." He called for the defeat of Hitler and lamented that the "blind selfishnesss of men here in the United States" had kept the country out of the League of Nations. Then he looked to the future. "I cannot believe that peoples of good will will not once more strive to realize the great ideal of an association of nations through which the freedom, the happiness, and the security of all peoples may be achieved."

The internationalists were overjoyed. The New York *Times* printed the text of his address and called it "the most specific declaration of peace aims that has been made by the spokesman of any Government since the war began." Recognizing his closeness to the President, the *Times* concluded, "Mr. Welles commits this country to responsibility for making peace and keeping it." Members of the LNA praised Welles for advocating "an association of nations" and the directors reprinted the speech in a pamphlet and distributed it across the country. Hull was less pleased when he returned to the State Department, but he did nothing to retract Welles' commitment of the administration to a future world organization.[20]

A month later Welles accompanied Roosevelt on a sea journey to Newfoundland to meet with Winston Churchill. At this Atlantic conference the two leaders discussed the course of the war, agreeing to extend aid to Russia, invaded by Germany in June, and to take a stiffer attitude toward Japanese aggression in Southeast Asia. Roosevelt brought up the question of the postwar world, suggesting that Britain and the United States issue a declaration of principles. Churchill was delighted, and he quickly presented a five-point statement drawn up by his staff. The first four points condemned aggression, promised self-determination in territorial changes, affirmed the right of self-government and free speech, and pledged fairer economic practices after the war. The fifth point declared that the two nations would "seek a peace which . . . by effective international organization will afford to all States and peoples the means of dwelling in security."

Sumner Welles took the British draft and made extensive revisions in it, but he retained the fifth point virtually intact. He then showed it to the President, who immediately struck out the phrase "by effective international organization," substituting a new article calling for the disarmament of the aggressors. The next day Churchill asked Roosevelt to reconsider this deletion, but the President refused. According to Welles, Roosevelt explained to Churchill that his advocacy of international organization would create "suspicions and opposition" in the United States. Moreover, the President stated that he personally did not think a new League of Nations would be effective. Instead, he preferred "an international police force composed of the United States and Britain" to keep order in the world. When Churchill warned that internationalists in the United States and Britain would be very disappointed, the President replied that "the time had come to be realistic."

Later that day both Sumner Welles and Harry Hopkins, Roosevelt's most trusted adviser, argued with the President. Welles was appalled that Roosevelt believed a new league would be futile, and he pleaded for Churchill's original fifth point. The President was unmoved, repeating his conviction that England and the United States would have to run the world alone in the immediate postwar years. When Welles and Alexander Cadogan, the British Under Secretary of State for Foreign Affairs, completed a new eight-point statement which ended with a call for disarmament of aggressors "pending the establishment of a wider and permanent system of general security," Roosevelt accepted this indirect hint at international organization. His earlier objections reflected a genuine disillusionment with the League, but he also was following his highly developed political senses. He remembered the bitter feelings stirred up by the League issue in the United States in the 1920's and the completeness of the American rejection of the Covenant. Hard pressed by isolationist criticism of his current policies, he did not want to engage in a needless debate over future international organization.[21]

The Atlantic Charter was made public on August 14, 1941. Isolationists criticized it, hinting that Roosevelt had entered into a secret alliance with Britain, but the terms of the document were so vague and benign that they found little to question. Despite the absence of any specific mention of a world body, most internationalists praised the Charter. Clark Eichelberger congratulated Roosevelt and Churchill for directing the people's attention to the postwar world. "In every schoolhouse, church, radio station, newspaper office, and home there should be full discussion of the kind of world we want when victory has been won," he wrote. A pamphlet published by the Commission to Study the Organization of Peace saw in the Charter "the general principle of collective action [which] must be the foundation of the future world order." The author believed that the reference to a "wider system of general security" in the eighth point looked forward to a world organization.

John Foster Dulles disagreed. At the first full meeting of the Commission to Study the Bases of a Just and Durable Peace, he pointed out "the striking omission" from the Atlantic Charter of "any proposal for a permanent association of nations." In October the Commission published an analysis of the Charter written by Dulles. He endorsed the principles espoused by Roosevelt and Churchill, but stated, "The Declaration seems to reflect primarily the conception of the old sovereignty system." He then called for the creation of "an international federation for peace" which would include all the nations of the world. Dulles ruled out the use of force in this organization, limiting its power and authority to the moral realm. Other Commission members wanted to go further and create a world body with the armed power to enforce its decrees. "The use of force for the preservation of law and order by a world society that is heroically and steadfastly bent upon establishing justice is not immoral," wrote Walter Van Kirk. Dulles did not disagree, but he preferred to proceed in slow stages toward such a world government.[22]

President Roosevelt remained silent, but in October 1941 Secretary of the Navy Frank Knox expressed the Commander-in-Chief's viewpoint. Speaking to the American Bar Association, Knox proposed that the British and American navies join together at the war's end "to stop new aggression . . . at its beginnings." Knox claimed such a joint effort would guarantee peace for "at least 100 years." "Sometime, somewhere, an international order may emerge which need not rely on force, but that time, unhappily, is a long way off," he warned. "In the interim, a justly conducted, peace-loving force must intervene to save the world from self-destruction."

Sumner Welles replied to Knox in a speech at Wilson's tomb in the basement of the Washington Cathedral on Armistice Day. Recalling Wilson's struggle and defeat in 1919, Welles said the realists of that day jeered at the idealism of international organization. Wilson, he reminded his audience, had predicted that if the United States rejected the League the next generation would fight a second world war. "Solely from the standpoint of the interest of the American people themselves," Welles asked, "who saw straight and who thought straight twenty years ago?" The American people, he continued, "have entered the Valley of Decision. . . . I believe that they will turn again for light and for inspiration to the ideals of that great seer, statesman, patriot, and lover of his fellow men—Woodrow Wilson—whose memory we here today revere." [23]

Less than a month later the United States entered World War II. The untiring efforts of the internationalists had convinced many Americans that they had made a great mistake in 1919, but the failure of the League stood as a powerful reminder that international cooperation without the effective use of force was worthless. Although the voices of Henry Wallace and Sumner Welles summoned the people to honor the ideals of Woodrow Wilson, many hung back, sharing their President's secret doubts that a universal organization could deal successfully with the problem of aggression. Bewildered by the contradictory calls for an American Century, Union Now, Pax Democratica and a new League of Nations, they hoped the war would somehow bring forth a formula they could embrace wholeheartedly.

3

"The Century of the Common Man"

TWO DAYS after the Japanese attack on Pearl Harbor, President Roosevelt spoke to the American people in a fireside chat. "In these last few years—and, most violently, in the last few days— we have learned a terrible lesson," he told them. "We have learned that our ocean-girt hemisphere is not immune from severe attack—that we cannot measure our safety in terms of miles on any map." He warned the people of the terrible struggle that lay ahead and the sacrifices that would be demanded of them. But he closed his somber address on a hopeful note. "We are going to win the war and we are going to win the peace that follows."

Internationalists shortened Roosevelt's appeal to "Win the War, Win the Peace," and made it their slogan. Editorials and articles in *Changing World*, the monthly journal of the League of Nations Association, hammered at this theme. "To win the peace means just that," wrote Chester Rowell, "to assure that the collective force of united nations stands ready and able to enforce the peace on an outlaw nation again seeking to break it." Clark Eichelberger called for a great crusade for "the building of a new order of international society." Another writer was even more specific: "To win the peace requires the total mobilization of American public opinion in support of a world peace organization, with full American participation." [1]

Many expressed the feeling that the nation must not repeat the mistakes of 1919. Senator Charles O. Andrews of Florida, writing to Hamilton Holt, vowed he would work in the Senate "to insure the future peace of the world and if possible thus prohibit the future

47

generations from having to face the scourge of blood, sweat and tears that you and I have had to face practically twice in one generation." His colleague, Senator Joseph H. Ball of Minnesota, told his constituents, "This time we must win all of the war to end all wars, not just that part of it fought on the battlefields." Nothing would be more tragic, he wrote, "than to win the war at the cost of tremendous sacrifices and then throw it all away by losing the peace, with the whole thing to be done over again in twenty years." President James B. Conant of Harvard was sure the American people had finally learned their lesson. When the war is over, he told the New England Society of New York in a speech on December 22, 1941, "isolationism will be as extinct as the volcanoes on the moon. . . . The flight from reality of the 1920's will not again be repeated while any of the present generation are still alive." [2]

On January 2, 1942, the government announced that the United States, Great Britain, the Soviet Union, China and twenty-two other nations at war against the Axis had signed a Declaration of the United Nations. Cordell Hull and his aides in the State Department had first suggested this statement, and when Churchill arrived in Washington in late December, he and Roosevelt immediately agreed, making numerous changes in the original draft. The President himself thought of the name "United Nations," and he burst into Churchill's room in the White House, interrupting his bath, to secure the British Prime Minister's concurrence. Hull insisted that Russia and China be permitted to serve as co-sponsors of the Declaration with the United States and Britain, and on January 1 the Soviet and Chinese ambassadors joined with Roosevelt and Churchill in signing the document. The next day the representatives of twenty-two smaller nations added their signatures.

The Declaration created a wartime alliance of United Nations who promised to wage war against the Axis powers with all their resources and not to sign a separate peace. In addition, the signatories accepted the principles of the Atlantic Charter as a "common program of purposes," and promised "to defend life, liberty, independence and religous freedom, and to preserve human rights and justice." A final clause permitted other countries who entered the war in the future to join the United Nations.[3]

Advocates of international organization hailed the Declaration as a major step toward their ultimate goal. Clark Eichelberger believed it committed the United States "to participation in international collective action," while the *New Republic* rejoiced that Roosevelt had laid the foundation for "a dynamic international union for the benefit of all." But the President interpreted the Declaration quite differently. In his State of the Union message that January he stressed the immediate goal of winning the war, describing the United Nations as a coalition to defeat Germany and Japan. He barely alluded to the postwar dreams of the internationalists. A month later, in a radio speech to the nation, the President again devoted himself exclusively to the war effort. He made no mention of international organization, and referred only to his hopes for a just peace based on the four freedoms and the Atlantic Charter.

Concerned by the President's neglect of the United Nations concept, Eichelberger wrote to Marvin McIntyre, a White House aide, in April, informing him of a plan to celebrate United Nations month in May. He asked McIntyre to see if the President would write a letter "saying that he thought it a fine idea to urge people to be aware of the United Nations dedicated to winning the war and winning the peace." Roosevelt liked Eichelberger's proposal, but in his reply, drafted by Archibald MacLeish, he carefully avoided any mention of peace or the postwar world. Focusing solely on the war, the President praised the plan "to inform our people of the United Nations' aspect of the struggle." A month later Eichelberger wrote to McIntyre again, describing his efforts to convert the American people to the cause of international organization. McIntyre showed the letter to the President, who responded, "Tell him . . . for heaven's sake not to do anything specific at this time—as things are changing every day." [4]

While President Roosevelt concentrated on the winning of the war, the State Department began a new effort at postwar planning. In September 1941 Leo Pasvolsky had proposed to Hull the creation of a new advisory committee to work on all phases of postwar foreign policy. Hull and Welles discussed the idea with the President, who gave his approval, and in October Welles drafted a letter to Roosevelt formally requesting permission to go ahead. But the crisis with Japan diverted the Department's attention, and the letter, now signed by Hull, was not sent until December 22. The Secretary proposed the establishment of the Advisory Committee on Post-War Foreign Policy, composed of both administration officials and "several prominent persons from outside the Government." The Committee, with Hull as chairman, would study and recommend solutions to the "vast and complicated problems of international relations which will confront us and the world after the final defeat of the forces of aggression." On December 28 the President returned the letter with the handwritten notation, "C.H. I heartily approve. F.D.R." [5]

49

3. "The Century of the Common Man"

The drafting of the United Nations Declaration and the diplomatic problems resulting from entry into the war prevented an immediate convening of the Committee. In early February, Cordell Hull once again became seriously ill and left Washington to recuperate in Florida. Sumner Welles, who had been in Brazil attending the Rio conference of foreign ministers, served as Acting Secretary of State. Discovering that Hull had not yet appointed the Advisory Committee, Welles sent letters on February 9, 1942, to the persons Roosevelt and Hull had approved, informing them of their new assignment. There were six members of the State Department, including Leo Pasvolsky, and four other government officials, Benjamin V. Cohen and David K. Niles of the White House staff, Milo Perkins from Henry Wallace's Board of Economic Warfare, and Paul H. Appleby of the Department of Agriculture. The five members from private life were Norman H. Davis, of the Council on Foreign Relations and the American Red Cross; Hamilton Fish Armstrong, editor of *Foreign Affairs*; Myron Taylor, former head of U.S. Steel who had served as Roosevelt's Personal Representative to the Pope; Isaiah Bowman, president of Johns Hopkins University and a geographer who had been a leading member of the Inquiry; and Anne O'Hare McCormick, columnist and foreign-affairs analyst for the New York *Times*. All were exceptionally able people, and all were dedicated internationalists.

The fifteen members of the Advisory Committee gathered in Welles' office at the State Department on the afternoon of February 12. At the outset they agreed to keep their existence secret. The war was going badly on every front, and they felt it imperative to wait for a favorable turn in the fighting before directing public attention to the problems of peace. Aware that many private groups were already conducting postwar studies, they decided to encourage such organizations to submit their ideas to the State Department. This decision led to a close relationship between the Department and the Council on Foreign Relations; by summer, several employees of the Council joined the staff of the Division of Special Research as part-time consultants. The members of the Advisory Committee felt that they should confine themselves to postwar issues and not deal with any aspect of the war effort. Before adjourning, they set up six subcommittees to meet weekly to conduct their work and report periodically to the full group. Sumner Welles appointed himself chairman of the all-important Subcommittee on Political Problems, which encompassed international organization.[6]

When Cordell Hull returned to Washington on April 20, the Com-

mittee had met twice more and was making substantial progress. On
May 2 the Secretary attended the fourth meeting, held in his office. Hull
thanked the members for their generous contributions to the vital work
of postwar planning, and then warned of the grave difficulties that lay
ahead. Recalling the fight over the League of Nations, he spoke of
"sinister influences" that would oppose a constructive peace. "We need
to make better preparation for world peace than was made at the close
of the First World War," he continued. "Even then the chances are
only about one to two that a sound peace can be carried to fruition."
After this pessimistic prediction, Hull informed the Committee that
this was their last full meeting. In the future they would carry on all
their work in subcommittees. Hull believed that such compartmental-
ization would insure secrecy on policy recommendations and permit him
and President Roosevelt to make the final decisions on the nature of the
postwar world. In addition, this procedure would severely restrict the
influence of Sumner Welles.

Hull's fear of isolationism was deep-seated. He was determined to do
everything possible to avoid the partisan controversy that had wrecked
Wilson's peace plans, and he was particularly concerned about Congress. In January he had asked Assistant Secretary of State Breckinridge
Long to keep the Senate Foreign Relations Committee secretly informed on all major developments in American foreign policy. Long, a
Missouri Democrat who had served in the State Department during
World War I and was an ardent Wilsonian, appeared before the Senate
committee periodically, although he had difficulty in keeping his
briefings off-the-record. On May 27, Hull took a far-reaching step,
inviting Senators Tom Connally and Warren Austin to become members of the Advisory Committee. Both accepted immediately and began
serving on Welles' political subcommittee. Connally, chairman of the
Senate Foreign Relations Committee, was a logical choice. A Texan
with a fiery temper, he wore a black string tie and long frock coat that
made him appear to be a caricature of a southern senator. He was
shrewd enough to use this exterior to disarm his opponents, who soon
learned that he was a tough and able fighter. Austin was a rarer phenomenon—a pre-Pearl Harbor Republican internationalist. Though he
came from Vermont, he was neither canny nor taciturn. His low rank on
the Foreign Relations Committee and his tendency to ramble made him
a questionable symbol of bi-partisanship.[7]

When the two senators joined the political subcommittee, Sumner
Welles had secured agreement that an international organization should

be formed during the war. The subcommittee had in mind a "United Nations Authority" which would include all the countries fighting the Axis but with the United States, Britain, Russia and China playing the dominant roles. On June 25 Cordell Hull invited James Shotwell to become a member of the political subcommittee. Two days later the group decided to create a special subcommittee on international organization to draw up a specific plan for study and discussion. Sumner Welles agreed to serve as chairman; the other members were Shotwell, Isaiah Bowman, Ben Cohen, Green H. Hackworth, the State Department Legal Adviser, and Leo Pasvolsky.

The new subcommittee met on Saturday mornings in Welles' office. Shotwell suggested that Clark Eichelberger be brought in as a consultant, and beginning in July he met regularly with the group. At first each member submitted a rough outline plan of a world body, and then they decided to spend the summer studying previous efforts at international organization, culminating in an article-by-article appraisal of the Covenant of the League of Nations.[8]

While this work went on in strict secrecy, members of the Division of Special Research pressed for a more open approach. In a memorandum to Pasvolsky on April 14, 1942, Charles Yost pointed out that there were thirty-six private organizations engaged in postwar studies, all eager to cooperate with the State Department. Yost suggested that their enthusiasm "be discreetly guided in channels which seem to the Department useful." Otherwise, he warned, "they will presumably go galloping off in twenty directions at once and in the end may confuse more than they educate." In April, Edgar Ansel Mowrer of the Office of Facts and Figures, the government's propaganda agency, told a State Department official that his office wanted to exploit the United Nations "idea" to build up public opinion in favor of international organization. Pasvolsky responded by forming within his division a Post-War Trends Unit to study public opinion through an analysis of speeches, books, magazine articles and newspaper editorials and a Public Relations Unit to keep in touch with the private organizations. The two new groups were limited to gathering information; neither could engage in activities designed to influence public sentiment.

The administration firmly resisted all further efforts to publicize its postwar planning. Citizens who made inquiries were simply told that the State Department was engaged in "a series of studies of long-range postwar issues." Cordell Hull, fearful of isolationist criticism, impressed all new members of the Advisory Committee with the importance of keeping its work confidential. The New York *Times* published a brief report in July that Sumner Welles and some members of Congress were making a survey of postwar problems, but otherwise the press was silent. As a result, the American people had no idea of the intensive effort their government was making to prepare for the future peace.

I

The government's silence did not inhibit private organizations. Five days after Pearl Harbor, Clyde Eagleton sent a memorandum to all members of the Commission to Study the Organization of Peace; "Our task now is not merely to study, but actually to formulate and announce as rapidly as possible the principles and procedures regarded as proper by the American people for the organization of the world after this war," he wrote. In a radio broadcast the next day, James Shotwell warned that the postwar world would not be prepared for anything "so splendid as the immediate establishment of a stronger and more universal League of Nations." Instead, he advocated an "Anglo-American directorate" to run the world during the immediate postwar years.

Shotwell was reflecting the ideas expressed in the Commission's second report, released to the public on February 14, 1942, at an all-day session in the ballroom of the Hotel Biltmore. Entitled "The Transition Period," this document dealt with the problems of relief, reconstruction and rehabilitation that would face the world at the war's end. The authors urged that the victors form a temporary coalition to undertake this enormous task as trustees for a future world organization. "When stability has been sufficiently restored," the report concluded, "a conference of all nations, defeated or otherwise, should be called for the purpose of formulating the principles and institutions of the world order in which all states will be expected to participate." There was no mention of a new league of nations, nor any reference to the possibility of the wartime United Nations becoming the basis of a permanent international organization.[10]

Though the Commission had the second report printed in the April issue of *International Conciliation* and distributed twenty-five thousand copies of specially bound reprints, it quickly repudiated the concept of a long transitional period. On February 13, 1942, Clark Eichelberger proposed that the studies committee begin work on a third report exploring ways in which the United Nations could "be expanded into the universal society of nations which the Commission has demanded as the basis of the future structure of peace." In urging this course, he warned against repeating the mistake of World War I, when the formation of the League was "nurtured in the inevitable reaction of the post-war period." The members of the Commission agreed, authorizing the studies committee to prepare the third report on the United Nations as the vehicle for a postwar security organization.

Throughout the first half of 1942 the Commission stressed the need to begin planning for peace during the war. Edward R. Murrow furnished the slogan, "We must plan or perish;" Shotwell and Eichelberger supervised the publication of a series of flyers, pamphlets and study guides which hammered away at this point. "A new world is in the making," one brochure proclaimed. "A vision big enough to plan for that new world must be developed." A pamphlet which the Commission prepared for high-school teachers began, "We must make certain that such a war as this one does not take place in another 25 years." This literature advocated transforming the wartime coalition into a world organization, but it failed to give any details. Instead, readers were told to form study groups and begin discussing "a democratic world order where law will reign, violence will be restrained and the peoples of the world will work together to solve our real problems of hunger, disease, and ignorance." The blueprints for this promised land, the pamphlets implied, would come later.[11]

Shotwell and Eichelberger, deeply involved in the administration's Advisory Committee studies, realized that they could best further the cause of international organization by concentrating on public opinion. Accordingly, Shotwell took advantage of his position as director of the Division of Economics and History of the Carnegie Endowment to ask the trustees to allocate $50,000 to establish regional centers for the study of international affairs. On May 7 the executive committee agreed to give Shotwell $25,000, with $15,000 to go to the Commission to provide all the necessary study materials. In the course of the year, International Relations Centers opened in Chicago, Minneapolis, Des Moines, Denver, San Francisco, Dallas and Chapel Hill. The centers coordinated the work of local agencies interested in foreign policy, and sponsored speeches, forums and panel discussions designed to influence public opinion. In San Francisco a political scientist, Guy Talbott, took the lead in forming the Carnegie center, cooperating with representatives of the League of Nations Association, the Commission to Study the Organization of Peace, and the Foreign Policy Association. Talbott used a

54

$5,000 grant from the Endowment to provide meeting rooms, a small library and a weekly newsletter. Quincy Wright, a distinguished professor of international law, was chairman of the Chicago center, which was jointly supported by the Carnegie Endowment and the Woodrow Wilson Foundation. Wright's group and twelve other Chicago organizations established a Woodrow Wilson auditorium where enthusiasts could gather to hear lectures on world affairs.[12]

The Commission to Study the Organization of Peace took advantage of the new centers by creating regional commissions in many of the same cities. Working through local branches of the League of Nations Association, Eichelberger and Shotwell invited experts in international relations to join with business, labor and civic leaders to form local commissions. These groups met once a month to discuss the postwar world using materials provided by the New York headquarters. The goal was to win over community leaders and train them to conduct local campaigns on behalf of international organization. By the end of the year, thirteen regional commissions were established and had distributed two million pieces of literature to some nine hundred study groups. "The Commission to Study the Organization of Peace," wrote James Shotwell to a midwestern publisher, "is flourishing beyond my fondest hopes." [13]

The League of Nations Association faced a much more difficult situation. The new wartime coalition led to insistent demands for a change in name to "The United Nations Association." Mrs. Emmons Blaine, who had been one of the prime contributors to the Association since its founding, ended her donations in 1942, announcing that she would devote herself to the cause of the United Nations. Informing Eichelberger of this defection, the head of the Association's Midwest office pleaded for abandonment of the League of Nations title. Eichelberger refused. In a letter to Marvin McIntyre at the White House, he commented, "we should not take down the flag and give the McCormicks and Pattersons a chance to gloat." But he added, "We fully understand that we must talk in the symbols of today rather than yesterday; that is why our emphasis is on the United Nations and the Atlantic Charter."

The Association's board of directors finally resolved the dilemma by retaining the old name but embracing the United Nations in a new statement of policy announced in July 1942. The directors declared, "The United Nations must not only win the war, but guide the world during the period of reconstruction and become the nucleus of a universal society of nations." They promised to continue their educational activities, to support the Commission to Study the Organization of Peace, and to cooperate with all who "have learned from the tragic experience of the last twenty years" in founding a new world order. Then, to prove their vitality, they launched their first membership drive in a decade, asking,, "Will we lose the peace again?"

The Association infused its educational program with the new United Nations emphasis. When the sixteenth annual high-school contest was held on March 27, 1942, the first question read, "Describe three features of the first League of Nations which you think should be retained in the new international order." The Middle Atlantic Model League Assembly convened at Hamilton College as a United Nations conference, with students coming as delegates from the twenty-six member countries. In 1942 the Association sponsored a study of international relations in the training of teachers, which led to a statement published early in 1943 by twenty-eight prominent educators, calling for a major revision of the public-school curriculum. Condemning isolation as "neither possible nor desirable," the statement urged that the schools "show the inevitable trend of events toward organization of the world as a community of nations."

The Association, however, still acknowledged its ties to the past. On January 10, 1942, the directors observed the twenty-second anniversary of the League of Nations in a ceremony at Wilson's tomb. Senator Carter Glass delivered the address, reminding his listeners of Wilson's dream. "I think it is particularly appropriate that we should on this occasion rededicate ourselves to the great cause for which the first world war was fought and for which our beloved President gave his life." [14]

The Woodrow Wilson Foundation, almost totally inactive in the 1930's, came to life again during the war. At their twentieth annual board meeting in 1942, the directors took note of "a nation-wide return to the broad ideals of international cooperation and organization presented to the world by Woodrow Wilson." They made a large contribution to the Commission to Study the Organization of Peace and affirmed a new feeling of confidence "in the triumph of Mr. Wilson's international philosophy." In the fall Mrs. Quincy Wright, the Foundation president, announced the establishment of a reference center on all phases of postwar planning at the Woodrow Wilson Memorial Library. She stated that World War II had provided an opportunity for the completion "of the task of world organization which the late President Wilson had the vision to initiate." [15]

Members of the Foundation were thrilled when Otto Preminger produced on Broadway *In Time to Come,* a play about Wilson's peace efforts. Written by Howard Koch and John Huston, it was extremely sympathetic to Wilson, viewing him as betrayed by Clemenceau in Paris and Henry Cabot Lodge in Washington. Using their imaginations liberally, the authors contrived a confrontation between Wilson and Lodge at the White House in which the President pleads with the senator to give his League a chance. An arrogant and unbending Lodge refuses. The final scene takes place on March 4, 1921, as Wilson leaves the White House. "What may seem a failure at this time will one day find its justification as a model for what must never be allowed to happen again," Colonel House comments. "Surely the day will come when your idea of the nations united to preserve the peace of the world will be put forward again." Brooks Atkinson, drama critic of the New York *Times,* praised the play as an "earnest, sincere, crisply-written drama about an overwhelming theme. . . . There, by the grace of God, went a chance to prevent the scourge of warfare that is now breaking the aching back of the world." Other critics were less impressed, and though the League of Nations Association bought out one evening's perform-ance, the play closed after only a brief run.

The Wilson revival, however, flourished. In 1942 the American Coun-cil of Public Affairs published a selection of Wilson's speeches edited by Saul K. Padover. In the introduction Padover eulogized the late Presi-dent, calling his defeat "the most colossal and heroic failure of modern times." Writing in *Changing World,* George M. Dutcher, a young historian, proclaimed, "Today Wilson's ideals are ours. His unfinished work is our supreme task." He and other internationalists saw in Wilson the inspiration they needed. Avoiding a careful analysis of the League's failure and ignoring the complexities of collective security, these enthu-siasts embraced the wartime United Nations coalition as the genesis of a new version of the League of Nations.[16]

II

There were many internationalists in 1942 who wanted to go much further than the Wilsonians toward world federation. In early March, 377 Protestant ministers and laymen attended a national study confer-ence in Delaware, Ohio, held under the auspices of the Federal Coun-cil's Commission to Study the Bases of a Just and Durable Peace. It was a distinguished gathering: the delegates included fifteen bishops, seven seminary and eight college presidents, and such prominent laymen as John Foster Dulles, Irving Fisher and Harvey Firestone, Jr. At the outset, the conference approved fourteen guiding principles recommended by Dulles' Commission. In vague and evangelical terms, the delegates condemned "a world of international anarchy" and affirmed the need for "a true community of nations." They rejected isolationism, advocated limitations on national sovereignty, and called for worldwide disarmament after the war. Then they broke into committees to engage in intensive study and prepare a "message" on world order to be sent to every Protestant congregation in the country.

The "message" adopted by the conference on March 5, 1942, was specific and detailed. The delegates called for the creation of a world government consisting of a parliament, an international court and appropriate executive agencies. Nations would give this world government power to regulate international trade, to settle disputes between countries and to control all military forces except those needed for domestic order. To enforce its authority, the world body would possess "adequate international police forces" and the power to levy "worldwide economic sanctions." The conference realized that such a far-reaching change in international affairs could not be affected overnight, but they insisted that Christians should begin working for such an ultimate goal, accepting more limited organizations only as transitional bodies, not as substitutes for world government. Though this "message" went far beyond the views John Foster Dulles had expressed earlier, he and his Commission were soon busy spreading it to all Protestant churches. Dulles even sent the "message" to the State Department, which asked for ten additional copies.[17]

The churches were not alone in championing world federation. A year before, the North Carolina legislature had passed a "declaration of the Federation of the World" by overwhelming margins. Introduced by Robert Lee Humber of Greenville, this resolution asked Congress to take the initiative in calling "a World Convention of Nations at the earliest feasible time, for the formulation of a Constitution for World Government." By March 1942 similar resolutions had been introduced in the legislatures of six other states. New Jersey acted favorably in May 1942, and a few months later the New York legislature passed a milder version calling for "an international organization of all nations." National political leaders took little notice of the resolutions, however, and Congress never debated a call for "A World Convention of Nations."[18]

In January 1942 Clarence Streit made a plea for "the immediate union of the democracies within the framework of the broader anti-Axis coalition" which produced a number of favorable letters to the New York *Times*. When critics charged that such a union would divide the United Nations by omitting such allies as Russia and China, Streit altered his policy. In press releases in early May, the board of directors of Federal Union announced that henceforth they would follow parallel policies to "win this war for good and all." In addition to the union of democracies, they advocated the immediate formation of an all-inclusive international organization in which Russia, China and other countries of the United Nations excluded from the union could play major roles.

In June, when Federal Union held its second annual convention in St. Louis, the members endorsed the new dual policy and then went a step further. After a heated floor fight, the delegates adopted a resolution calling for "a Federal Union of those people with whom we have compelling natural ties." Dropping the insistence on democracy, the resolution stated that "this nucleus union should be open to all peoples who are prepared to share the rights and responsibilities of the union." The delegates called on the United States, Mexico and Canada to form a committee to draw up a draft constitution for the new federal union. The Massachusetts chapter was soon able to demonstrate the popularity of the new program. In November 1942 they succeeded in getting a referendum asking the President and Congress to convene a constitutional convention for a federal union on the ballot in over a quarter of the state's electoral districts. Three out of four of the 270,000 voters in these areas favored the proposal. The vote had little practical value, but it did encourage Clarence Streit and his followers in their quest for a world union.[19]

Other internationalists championed Anglo-American cooperation. In *A Democratic Manifesto*, published in mid-1942, Emery Reves focused on nationalism as the root of world evil and urged the United States to join with England in compelling nations to surrender their sovereignty to the world community. "Anglo-American supremacy means general progress for all mankind," he wrote. Lionel Gelber, a Canadian writer, agreed. Arguing for a new and more powerful League, he placed his greatest faith in "Anglo-American friendship as the buttress of world order." A British advocate of world government, Lord Davies, tried to initiate formal Anglo-American cooperation by working through Congress. He formed a British Parliamentary Executive Committee in January 1942 in hopes that Congress would appoint a similar committee to discuss the war effort "and the establishment of a durable peace." In May, Parliament officially invited Congress to send a ten-man delegation to Britain for this purpose, but American senators refused the invitation, claiming it was too early to talk of peace. Lord Davies was undaunted. He wrote to Hamilton Holt in July urging him to push for "an English-Speaking federation as the sheet-anchor or core of the World Confederation." [20]

The utopian character of the drive for world federation led to an inevitable reaction. In April 1942 Nicholas Spykman, an eminent political geographer at Yale, published *America's Strategy in World Politics* to inform the American people of the underlying realities of international affairs. Frankly embracing power politics, Spykman repudiated both the pre-war policy of isolationism and the alternative of a future international organization. "Plans for far-reaching changes in the character of international society are an intellectual by-product of all great wars," he wrote, but they never altered "the fundamental power patterns." Spykman predicted that neither league nor federation would work, and he suggested Americans instead adopt a balance of power policy. The United States, he argued, should use its detached position in the Western Hemisphere to play off one country against another. "The new order," he concluded, "will not differ from the old. . . . It will be a world of power politics in which the interest of the United States will continue to demand the preservation of a balance of power in Europe and Asia." [21]

Spykman's geopolitics found an echo in a much more influential book, *The Problems of Lasting Peace* by Herbert Hoover and Hugh Gibson. First published in June 1942, the book was an immediate best-seller; it went through ten printings in six months and the *Reader's Digest* published a brief condensation in August. Walter Lippmann called its publication "a notable event" and John Foster Dulles praised it as "an extraordinarily able and timely contribution." Even Cordell Hull was impressed—he asked an aide to read the book and prepare a summary of its main ideas.

The former President and his co-author, a retired Republican diplomat, began with a long historical analysis of "seven dynamic forces that make for peace and war." They warned that man could never abolish these forces; at best he could learn to control them. This pessimism pervaded the book. "We cannot avoid the haunting fear," they wrote, "that the decline and fall of the League and other liberal efforts were a part of a decline and fall of civilization on the continent of Europe—a vast compound of impersonal forces driving inexorably to some dreadful fate." The League failed, they argued, not because the United States abstained, but because England and France reverted to "the old power diplomacy" that Europeans had always pursued.

In the final section of their book, Hoover and Gibson reviewed fifty principles which they felt were essential for a just and lasting peace. Though they gave no blueprint, they did contend that the secret to peace lay in separating the enforcement of peace from an international organization. They wanted to create a new world body which would focus solely on the peaceful settlement of disputes. ". . . such a Council, out of experience and successful precedent, could be expected to build up the fabric of international law and steadily guide the movement of nations toward abolition of war." The new league would rely solely on the good faith of nations and world opinion. The victors in the war, the Allied Nations, would form a separate military alliance to disarm potential aggressors, preserve order, and crush any threats to world peace. This separation, the authors believed, would permit nations to retain their full sovereignty yet provide a realistic means of using force to keep the peace. Nowhere did they spell out the relationship between the universal international organization and the military coalition of victorious powers.[22]

Herbert Hoover would have been very surprised to learn that President Roosevelt, his bitter political enemy, had arrived at a very similar assessment of the postwar world. Roosevelt continued his public silence, but he brought up the subject when the Russian Foreign Minister, Vyacheslav Molotov, visited Washington in late May 1942. After a dinner at the White House, Roosevelt told Molotov that at the Atlantic Conference he had informed Churchill that he could not "visualize another League of Nations with 100 different signatories; there were simply too many nations to satisfy. . . ." Roosevelt then said that he thought the United States, Russia, England and possibly China should police the world and enforce disarmament by inspection after the war. According to Harry Hopkins, "The President stated that the population of our nations and friends was well over a billion people and that we would be the 'policemen' and that we at least could be sure of peace for 25 years; at any rate until all of us now living are dead." When Molotov asked if this was the President's "final and considered judgment," Roosevelt answered affirmatively and asked Molotov to communicate his ideas to Stalin.

Two days later, at another White House conference, Molotov informed the President that Stalin approved Roosevelt's proposal that the Big Four police the world. "This idea," Molotov said, "had the full approval of the Soviet Government, which would support it fully." Then Roosevelt turned to the Soviet Ambassador to the United States, Maxim Litvinov, who had represented Russia at Geneva in the 1930's, and playfully asked whether he was ready to abandon the League of Nations. "Anything for the common cause," Litvinov replied.[23]

The realistic outlook of Hoover and Roosevelt completed the broad spectrum of views internationalists were developing on world organization by mid-1942. Nearly all were agreed that the United States would have to assume major responsibility for the shaping of the postwar world. But they could agree on little else. Wilsonians talked in terms of a new League of Nations; idealists dreamed of a world federation that would unite all mankind; realists looked forward to a new balance of power in which the victors policed the world. The American people, confused by these conflicting visions, longed for new prophets to guide them into the future.

III

Wendell Willkie did not look like a prophet. A big, rumpled man with unruly hair and a hoarse voice, he burst onto the political scene as a dark horse at the Republican convention in 1940. Born in Indiana, he was an authentic midwestern American, with a broad drawl, a directness of manner and a disdain for pomp and protocol that endeared him to millions. He had practiced law in Ohio and then had risen to the presidency of Commonwealth and Southern, a utility company that fought unsuccessfully to prevent the government from developing public power in the Tennessee Valley. Although a Democrat, Willkie won the admiration of Republicans for his fight against TVA, and with the backing of the Eastern wing of the party, he won the nomination in 1940. Willkie was never an isolationist, and in the campaign against Roosevelt he did not challenge the President's conduct of foreign affairs until the closing weeks, when in desperation he charged that Roosevelt was leading the nation into war. When questioned later by an isolationist senator, Willkie dismissed these remarks as "campaign oratory." He loyally supported Roosevelt's policies after the election, undertaking a mission to England in 1941 and doing everything he could to prevent his adopted party from blocking American entry into the war.

After Pearl Harbor, Willkie dedicated himself to transforming the Republican party from isolationism to internationalism. In an article in the New York *Times* in February 1942, he stated his belief that the American people "have moved far in the last twenty years toward the Wilsonian dream." Affirming that "he who wins wars must maintain the peace," he told Republicans that it would be suicidal for them to permit the Democrats to monopolize the issue of internationalism. He realized that his task would not be easy. Isolationism was deeply ingrained in the Republican party, and such respected leaders as Senators Robert A. Taft of Ohio and Arthur H. Vandenberg of Michigan viewed Willkie's internationalist crusade as a direct challenge to their command of the GOP. But Willkie was determined to reverse the Republican stand on international organization, even at the risk of personal defeat.[24]

Willkie began by submitting a resolution to the National Committee just before it met in Chicago in April 1942. In this statement Willkie asked the party "to undertake now and in the future whatever just and reasonable international responsibilities may be demanded in a modern world." Senators Taft and Wayland Brooks of Illinois countered with resolutions which avoided any mention of postwar commitments. Though Willkie did not attend the meeting in Chicago, the National Committee finally approved a statement which declared that "our nation has an obligation to assist in bringing about understanding, comity, and cooperation among the nations. . . ." The Committee balked at Willkie's plea to assume "just and reasonable international responsibilities," but it did recognize that after the war "the responsibility of the nation will not be circumscribed within the territorial limits of the United States."

"Wendell L. Willkie succeeded today in removing the brand of isolationism from the Republican party," the New York *Times* reporter James A. Hagerty wrote from Chicago. Other commentators agreed, calling the National Committee's statement a "vindication of Woodrow Wilson" and "the strongest and boldest statement of Republican foreign policy" since the election of Roosevelt. "Nothing has gratified me more in years," wrote Breckinridge Long in his diary. "Shades of Henry Cabot Lodge . . . and the army of destruction of 1920." In their enthusiasm, the internationalists failed to note the ambiguity of the party's stand. Senator Taft found the statement completely harmless and announced that he would support it. In his diary Senator Vandenberg commented that the idea that Willkie had won a great victory was

63

"sheer bunk." He termed the statement "shadow-boxing with platitudes." "I agree with this general statement," he continued. "*I* do not see how *anybody* could disagree with it." Vandenberg was right. The most die-hard isolationist did not oppose "understanding, comity, and cooperation among the nations," so long as the United States was not compelled to use force to preserve the peace. The National Committee's statement was merely the party's first attempt to accommodate itself to the changed wartime situation, not a radical reversal in policy. For Willkie, the long campaign against isolationism had just begun.[25]

IV

In the spring of 1942 another political leader, Vice President Henry Wallace, decided it was time to speak out again on the postwar world. He was now fifty-four years old, but his clear blue eyes, full dark hair barely touched with gray, and strong white teeth made him appear much younger. His long face, sad in repose, brightened when he broke into a shy, tentative half-smile. He was ill at ease as Vice President. In his office at the Capitol he removed the private bar where John Nance Garner had helped visitors "to strike a blow for liberty," and in the Senate chamber he dozed for hours at a time in a tall swivel chair while debate droned on. As chairman of the Board of Economic Warfare, he was in charge of an important agency with more than three thousand employees, but he delegated its administration to Milo Perkins, conferring with him from time to time by telephone. His restless energy sought more creative outlets. When Florence Harriman, former minister to Norway and an old friend, asked him to address the American Free World Association's annual banquet in New York City, he quickly accepted. He dictated the speech in a three-hour burst, polished a few phrases on the typed copy and then sent it to the President to read. "The object of this speech is . . . to encourage downtrodden peoples of the world by letting them know how strong the people of the United States feel," he told Roosevelt.

On the evening of May 8 Wallace delivered the address, which he entitled "The Price of Free World Victory." "This is a fight between a slave world and a free world," he began. He told the Free World Association audience that the common people throughout the world were on a march toward freedom that constituted "a long drawn-out people's revolution." In this struggle, the American role was to build a lasting peace after the war. "We failed in our job after World War I," Wallace charged. "We did not build a peace treaty on the fundamental doctrine of the people's revolution." Then he gave a homey illustration. "Half in fun and half seriously, I said the other day to Madame Litvinov, 'The object of this war is to make sure that everybody in the world has the privilege of drinking a quart of milk a day.'" In a memorable flight of rhetoric, he proceeded to attack Henry Luce. "Some have spoken of the 'American Century.' I say that the century on which we are entering—the century which will come out of this war—can be and must be the century of the common man." Wallace then concluded with a messianic call for a "people's peace": [26]

> The people's revolution is on the march, and the devil and all his angels cannot prevail against it. They cannot prevail for on the side of the people is the Lord. . . .
> Strong in the strength of the Lord, we who fight in the people's cause will not stop until that cause is won.

The next morning the New York *Times* headlined its account of the speech, "Attack on Alaska is Seen by Wallace." Other papers followed suit, commenting on the Vice President's brief reference to a possible Japanese invasion of Alaska and ignoring the main thrust of his remarks. The *Times* did not deem the address important enough to print the full text. Wallace's oratory might have gone unnoticed had not Ralph Ingersoll, editor of the left-wing newspaper *PM*, intervened. When he found that his staff planned to give the speech only perfunctory coverage, Ingersoll had the front page redone in order to print the full text. Then he accused other newspapers of deliberately suppressing the speech.

The furor Ingersoll aroused made Wallace's address famous. Liberal columnists began praising the Vice President for his vision and courage, quoting the phrases "century of the common man" and "people's peace." Raymond Clapper went so far as to label it "the Gettysburg address" of World War II. John Foster Dulles, returning from a trip to England, wrote to Wallace on July 27, "Your point of view has made a very deep impression over there." A New York publisher brought out the speech as a pamphlet selling for seventy-five cents which quickly went through four editions. The Carnegie Endowment published it in the June issue of *International Conciliation* and it proved so popular that the sale of reprints financed a Spanish edition for Latin America. "The Price of Free World Victory" eventually appeared in twenty languages. Wallace's office was so besieged with letters praising the speech and asking for copies that he could send only one to each person. The Office of Facts and Figures finally reprinted the speech as a pamphlet for free distribution to satisfy the huge demand.

Not all the comments were favorable. Bruce Barton made fun of Wallace's allusion to a quart of milk for everyone in the world, and Merwin K. Hart, in a speech to the Organization of Native Born Citizens, charged that Wallace was trying "to extend the New Deal throughout the earth." Raoul de Roussy de Sales, the American correspondent for *Paris-Soir,* was more perceptive. "What is striking about this speech," he wrote in his diary, "is its mystical character." What Wallace failed to realize, de Sales continued, was that Hitler was Wallace's "Common Man" gone mad. A few years later Dwight Macdonald cited the speech to demonstrate that Wallace was "an oratorical gasbag, a great wind of rhetoric blowing along the prevailing trade route of Stalinoid liberalism." [27]

It was a bad speech, but it filled a great void. The war was going poorly, and Americans hungered for a voice to tell them that they were engaged in a noble struggle that would lead to a better world. For all the hollowness of his oratory, Wallace perceived their need and gave them the lift they so badly wanted. By doing so, he emerged as the administration's leading spokesman on the postwar world.

Sumner Welles was disturbed by Wallace's vagueness, and he decided to offer the American people a more specific view of the future in a speech on Memorial Day. Speaking in the amphitheater at Arlington National Cemetery, Welles chastised the United States for its long retreat into isolation. "We are now reaping the bitter fruit of our own folly and of our own lack of vision," he declared. The only remedy was to abandon isolationism in the future. The men fighting on the battlefields, Welles prophesied, "will insist that the United Nations undertake the maintenance of an international police power in the years after the war. . . . I believe they will demand that the United Nations become the nucleus of a world organization of the future to determine the final terms of a just, an honest and a durable peace."

Internationalists were quick to seize on Welles' call for "an international police power" and "the nucleus of a world organization." Anne O'Hare McCormick called it "the first official blueprint of the Roosevelt peace policy"; James Shotwell thought it was "the most important utterance of the United States government on post-war problems." The New York *Times* reported that the public reaction was completely favorable, indicating that isolationism had subsided in the United States. Foreign comment was equally favorable. The Soviet press reprinted the speech, stressing Welles' call for the United Nations to become the basis of an international organization after the war. Welles was so encouraged that he repeated this plea in a speech at a United Nations rally in Baltimore on June 17.[28]

Cordell Hull was irate. He told Breckinridge Long that Welles had made these speeches without consulting him. On June 20 he summoned Welles to his office and dressed him down for publicly committing the government to policies not yet approved. Welles replied that the President had told him it would be all right to send up some "trial balloons" on the postwar world. Hull snorted at this "illusory consent weasled out of the White House" and finally secured a promise from Welles to submit all future speeches for approval. Yet even this did not satisfy the Secretary, who remained agitated, telling an aide a few days later that he could no longer trust Welles. Hull finally decided to make a speech himself to let it be known that "certain recent speeches" did not exactly conform to his ideas on the postwar world.

For over a month five high-level State Department officers labored over the text of Hull's speech. There were daily "speech conferences" in the Secretary's office where, Long said, "each paragraph, each sentence, each word" was "examined in its relation to the whole picture." By the end of June they were working on a fifth draft; the speech was not finished until mid-July. Then Hull sent a copy to the President, who told a press conference on July 21 that the forthcoming radio address was "a very able and conclusive summary of the present world situation." [29]

On the evening of July 23, 1942, Hull sat down at his desk in the State Department before a battery of microphones which would carry his words across the country and, by short-wave, across the world. The Secretary was very nervous; he asked Breckinridge Long to sit beside him and take over if his voice gave out. In plodding tones Hull read the carefully prepared text. For the millions of listeners, it must have been a disappointing experience. Hull gave a long and uninspired recital of the events leading to war, claiming that Americans were "forced to fight because we ignored the simple but fundamental fact that the price of peace . . . is the acceptance of international responsibilities." Turning to the postwar world, Hull declared, "It is plain that some international agency must be created which can—by force, if necessary—keep the peace among nations in the future. There must be international cooperative action to set up the mechanisms which can thus insure peace." Hull deliberately refrained from describing the details of such mechanisms, and he avoided any suggestion that the United Nations could form the nucleus of a postwar international organization.

Reactions to the Secretary's speech were mixed. Conservative commentators were pleased, interpreting it as a direct rebuttal to Wallace and Welles. Citing Roosevelt's advance endorsement, Arthur Krock claimed that the speech proved that the administration was pursuing a realistic rather than a utopian approach to peace. *Time* praised Hull for injecting "a little hard Tennessee muscle into the milk-and-honey promises of men like Henry Wallace." The editors of the *New Republic* took a different view, calling the speech "a flop." "It will take more than Secretary Hull to turn this war, in the minds of millions of plain people all over the world," they wrote, "into a war to maintain the status quo." Raoul de Sales felt that the speech was "completely insipid." Foreigners, and even Americans, he commented, expected more than the "familiar sermon" Hull gave them. ". . . a world dominated by the present American leaders is a fearful thought," he observed sardonically.

Despite their personal reactions, however, most commentators did point out that the Secretary of State had called for an "international agency" to keep the peace "by force, if necessary." By speaking out boldly, Sumner Welles and Henry Wallace had forced their more reluctant colleague to commit the administration to support the general concept of international organization. Yet they had not succeeded in converting Franklin Roosevelt. On August 14 the President sent a public message to Churchill celebrating the first anniversary of the Atlantic Charter in which he termed winning the war "the single and supreme objective of the United Nations." He dismissed the postwar issue with one brief sentence: "When victory comes we shall stand shoulder to shoulder in seeking to nourish the great ideals for which we fight." [30]

V

Public-opinion polls revealed that the internationalists had won over a majority of the American people. In early July 1942 George Gallup reported that "a profound change in viewpoint on international affairs" had taken place in the United States since 1940. Of those questioned, 59 percent responded affirmatively when asked if the United States should join a new league of nations after the war, and only 22 percent expressed opposition. Discarding the 19 percent who had no opinion, Gallup concluded that 73 percent of the people favored entry into a world organization, a sharp rise from 50 percent in July 1941 and 33 percent in 1937. A poll taken by the National Opinion Research Center in Denver confirmed these findings. The question "Should the United States join a union of nations if one is formed after the war?" drew favorable responses from 72 percent of a national sample. Only 15 percent opposed such a policy. Jerome S. Bruner, a Princeton psychologist, concluded from his own studies that isolationists composed only 10 to 15 percent of the American population.

A State Department survey reached a similar estimate, but warned that "thus far opinion has been elicited and expressed only in vague terms. . . . The public as yet is generally unaware of the specific implications of international organization and of the price they will have to pay for such organization." A *Fortune* poll in June 1942 revealed that when asked to select a particular policy they wanted the nation to follow after the war, only 34 percent wanted to take an active part in "a new league or association" of nations. Indeed, *Fortune* discovered that a majority of the American people preferred to postpone planning for peace until they had won the war. Bruner noted a similar disinterest in postwar problems. In a poll in January 1942 only 23 percent of those questioned had heard of the Atlantic Charter, and only one in three of this group could correctly identify one of the eight points. No symbol, Bruner concluded, had yet fired the imagination of the American people about the postwar years.

The Council on Foreign Relations, reporting on the views expressed by its twelve regional committees of American leaders, stated that "Pearl Harbor changed no one's thinking very much." A member of the Detroit committee commented that the war had "created at least an outward semblance of unity behind the Government, but it was a negative, not a positive state." Another Midwesterner put it more succinctly: "Only time can show whether isolationism was killed, or only stunned, at Pearl Harbor." All the committees agreed that the United States should accept responsibility for world order after the war, but they divided sharply on specific programs. Pre-war isolationists tended to favor "impregnable military strength and strategic position," while interventionists championed "a world association of nations and a police force to prevent aggression." But all felt it was too early to discuss detailed plans for America's role in the postwar world.[31]

George Gallup found that the most remarkable shift in viewpoint had taken place among Republican voters. In 1937 only 23 percent had favored entry into the League; now, in the summer of 1942, 70 percent wanted the United States to join a postwar world organization. Willkie's influence had obviously had an impact, but he was no longer alone in urging Republicans toward internationalism. In May, Thomas E. Dewey, one of the contenders for the Republican presidential nomination in 1940 and now candidate for governor of New York, spoke out. "Enlightened national interest requires that out of this war we help create a stabilized world," he declared in his first campaign speech. "We must learn to work together with other nations for peace." Harold Stassen, the young Republican governor of Minnesota, went much further in a speech to the National Governors' Conference on June 22. He wanted the United States to take the lead in forming "a world association of free peoples" that would have its own police force to prevent aggression.

Internationalists looked forward to an "offensive" against the isolationists in the fall Congressional elections. "One of the first major moves in this offensive," Clark Eichelberger wrote, "should be banishing from the Congress every isolationist member who is up for reelection this year. . . ." He warned his followers not to be fooled by those who pretended to have changed their views. "The burden of proof is on each of them," he continued. "Any 'former isolationist' who does not unequivocally renounce publicly his former isolationism, for the peace as well as the war, should be defeated." A writer in *Changing World* pleaded with readers to become active in the Congressional campaign. "Perhaps your best service in international politics this fall can be rendered by ringing door bells in the interest of the candidate sure to stand for the best in international politics." [32]

Wendell Willkie continued his drive to purge the Republican party of its isolationist legacy. In July he came out against Representative Stephen A. Day, a Republican from Illinois, saying that if he were a citizen of the state, he would not vote for him. In early August, Willkie called reporters into his law office in New York to read a public statement on the forthcoming election. He urged all Republican candidates to sign a three-point pledge promising not to exploit the war as a political issue. The first two points called for unity with our allies in winning the war, but the third was more controversial. " . . . when the war is over," the pledge stated, "we must set up institutions of international political and economic cooperation and adjustment among the nations of the earth" and "devise some system of joint international force."

No candidates came forward to sign Willkie's pledge, but a month later 115 Republican congressmen issued a postwar manifesto drawn up by J. William Ditter of Pennsylvania and Everett M. Dirksen of Illinois. The plank on foreign policy stated that "the United States has an obligation and responsibility to work with other nations to bring about a world understanding and cooperative spirit which will have for its supreme objective the continued maintenance of peace." And then, lest any isolationist voters become alarmed at this vague call for international cooperation, the representatives added, "In so doing we must not endanger our own independence, weaken our American way of life or our system of government." Even so, forty Republican congressmen found this statement too strong, and the New York *Times* hailed it as "a major political document" which removed the stigma of isolationism from the party.

The primaries, held in the summer and early fall of 1942, shocked the internationalists. Nearly all the prominent isolationists who had opponents triumphed. Stephen Day easily won renomination in Illinois, and Hamilton Fish, a strident isolationist who represented President Roosevelt's Hyde Park area, defeated his opponent by a two-to-one margin despite the opposition of Dewey and Willkie. The only isolationist defeats came in Cleveland, where the Democratic incumbent lost to an administration candidate, and in Minnesota, where internationalists scored a major triumph. Governor Stassen and Senator Ball beat off isolationist challengers, and Walter Judd, a political unknown, upset Congressman Oscar Youngdahl, a bitter critic of Roosevelt's foreign policy, in a Minneapolis district.[33]

President Roosevelt kept aloof from the political struggle in 1942. In a speech to students on September 3 he made an oblique reference to isolationists, condemning "little men of little faith" who "play petty politics in a world crisis." But he did not speak in behalf of Democratic candidates or call for a repudiation of isolationism as Willkie had. He continued to avoid specific mention of postwar plans, alluding to the future peace in only the most general terms. In a Columbus Day address he acknowledged that it was useless to win the war unless it stayed won. "We, therefore, fight for the restoration and perpetuation of faith and hope and peace throughout the world."

In August the President took a major step to influence public opinion. Inviting Wendell Willkie to a luncheon at the White House, the

President asked his 1940 opponent to take a round-the-world trip through Russia and China to dramatize the United Nations aspect of the war.[34]

On the morning of August 26, Willkie boarded a converted army bomber nicknamed the *Gulliver* at Mitchell Field on Long Island, accompanied by Gardner Cowles, the publisher of *Look*, and Joseph Barnes, a foreign correspondent for the New York *Herald Tribune*. In the next forty-nine days Willkie and his companions flew 31,000 miles. After a brief stop in the Middle East, they spent several days in Russia, where Willkie brushed aside American foreign-service officers and gained headlines in the United States by echoing the Soviet demand for an immediate second front in Europe. The climax of the trip came in China. Willkie got along well with Chiang Kai-shek, who helped convince him that it was time to sound the death knell for western imperialism. In a statement issued in Chungking in early October, Willkie called for "firm timetables" for the liberation of colonial peoples. Roosevelt bridled at this pointed insult to Great Britain, and when Willkie landed at Minneapolis on October 14, the President asked him to come directly to the White House to make his report.

An estimated thirty-six million Americans heard Willkie give a radio speech on the evening of October 26 describing his trip around the world. He repeated his plea for a second front in Europe and called for an offensive against Japan in Burma. Devoting most of his remarks to the Far East, he again called for an end to imperialism. "We must fight our way through not alone to the destruction of our enemies but to a new world idea," he told his radio audience. "We must win the peace." He closed with a plea for "an active, constructive" American policy in the postwar world.[35]

Willkie's speech was extremely successful. He received a flood of letters praising his ideas, and liberal journalists eulogized him. Samuel Grafton called him "the first United Nations statesman," and the *New Republic* thanked him for challenging the notion that the war was primarily "an Anglo-American affair." Raoul de Sales was astonished by the enthusiasm of the American press for Willkie's speech, noting that he was compared to Marco Polo. "People trusted him precisely because his observations are superficial and simplified," de Sales decided, "and because they provide a key to everything." Roosevelt tried to mask his own pique at Willkie. When a reporter asked him to comment on the address, he replied, "I don't know. I suppose the easiest thing to say is to paraphrase an old cigarette advertisement: there isn't a controversy in a carload of speeches." In a letter a few days later to an old friend, Roosevelt was more candid. "He had a good thought," he wrote of Willkie's speech, "but was just a bit too immature to carry it through. He could only see the little things—and he has not yet forgotten that he ran for President two years ago." [36]

Roosevelt received a jolting setback on November 3, 1942, when the American people went to the polls. The Republican party made impressive gains, picking up forty-four seats in the House and nine in the Senate. It was their best showing since the 1920's, and they came very close to winning control of Congress. On the state level, Thomas E. Dewey became the first Republican governor of New York in two decades, and victories by Earl Warren in California, John W. Bricker in Ohio, and Leverett Saltonstall in Massachusetts heralded the arrival of a new generation of leaders to revitalize the party. At the same time, all but five of 115 congressmen with isolationist voting records were re-elected, including Hamilton Fish, Stephen Day, and Claire Hoffman of Michigan. In the Senate, Senator Wayland Brooks survived an internationalist challenge, while George Norris, a staunch supporter of Roosevelt's policies, lost to Kenneth Wherry, thus ending a brilliant forty-year career at the age of eighty-one.

The election created widespread gloom. English observers feared that the United States would once again repudiate its responsibilities as a world leader at the war's end. The editors of the *New Republic* warned of a repetition of the tragedy of 1919–1920, with Dewey to become the new Harding. In the press, explanations ranged from "a revolt of the middle classes, including the farmers, against the New Deal" to "a big, silent, sinister anti-war" vote. Most commentators noted the extremely light turnout at the polls—only twenty-six million people voted, nearly a fifty percent decline from 1940. With millions of men in service and many civilians who had moved to new war jobs unable to vote, the normal Democratic majority had nearly vanished. Moreover, the people were disillusioned with the course of the war. Since Pearl Harbor, American forces in the Pacific had met with defeat after defeat, and in Europe the United States Army had not yet seen action. Frustrated by wartime controls and restrictions and craving military victories, the American people had voted against the Roosevelt administration.[37]

There was, however, no genuine isolationist resurgence. The new congressmen and senators soon proved open to internationalist persuasion. The older isolationist spokesmen like Fish and Day had survived despite their foreign-policy stands because the political tide was running

73

strongly against the administration. Most of the new Republican leaders were clearly in sympathy with Willkie. Stassen in Minnesota, Warren in California, Saltonstall in Massachusetts, even Dewey in New York—these men had not taken rigid stands against American entry into the war before Pearl Harbor, and they now wanted the United States to play an active role in the world. But for the internationalists, the elections were disappointing. They had looked forward to a complete victory and had achieved only a stalemate. Haunted by memories of World War I, they would not be satisfied until the last isolationist had been driven from public life.

4

Revolt in the Senate

WHILE THE AMERICAN PEOPLE were going to the polls on
November 3, an armada was moving across the Atlantic
Ocean toward French-held North Africa. On the morning
of November 8, American troops waded ashore at three places in Morocco and Algeria. Despite clandestine efforts to win over the French
army commanders in North Africa, the troops encountered heavy fire
from shore batteries and machine-gun emplacements. Three days later
the Vice Premier of Vichy France, Admiral Jean Darlan, who was on a
visit to Algiers, signed an armistice with General Mark Clark which
ended the French resistance. The American forces then began moving
eastward toward their true objective, the German Afrika Korps com-
manded by General Erwin Rommel. Hitler responded quickly, sending a
large army into Tunisia to protect Rommel's flank. By early 1943 the
American troops were engaged in battle with the German army as
Rommel drew back to Tunisia determined to resist this effort to sweep
his forces from Africa.

In the Pacific, Americans also took the offensive in late 1942. The
navy had won revenge for Pearl Harbor in July, when American planes
destroyed four Japanese aircraft carriers in the Battle of Midway and
turned back a Japanese thrust toward Hawaii. In August marines landed
on Guadalcanal Island in the Solomons to protect the supply line to
Australia. The landings went smoothly, but three days later a Japanese
naval force sank four cruisers and forced the American naval commander
to withdraw his remaining ships. The marines were stranded, with
only a small landing strip to keep them supplied and reinforced. During
the next two months the Japanese sent in over twenty thousand men to
recapture Guadalcanal. The beleaguered marines resisted desperately,
killing six Japanese for every man they lost, until finally the American

navy, in a series of costly night engagements, regained control of the waters around the Solomon Islands. In February the Japanese withdrew, acknowledging defeat for the first time since their invasion of Manchuria in 1931.[1]

The landings in North Africa and the victory at Guadalcanal gave the American people a great lift. In the months since Pearl Harbor, defeat and frustration had weighed heavily upon them, leading to an unspoken fear that they might lose the war. Now all was changed. The United Nations had taken the initiative, and on all fronts the American, British and Russian forces were driving the German and Japanese armies back toward their homelands. More and more, Americans looked ahead to the even more demanding job of building an enduring peace.

I

The prophets of a new world order now spoke out with assurance. In a speech to the New York *Herald Tribune* Forum on November 17, 1942, Sumner Welles urged the United Nations to start creating the "world of the Four Freedoms" by setting up agencies to deal with postwar relief and reconstruction. He advocated a world police force to achieve "freedom from fear" and concluded with a plea for "some form of organized international political cooperation to make the rules of international living and to change them as the years go by." A month later he spoke at the dedication of a chapel erected in memory of President Roosevelt's mother at St. Paul's Church in Mount Vernon, New York. Charging that American refusal to enter the League had led to World War II, Welles asked, "Do we realize that an association of the free peoples of the United Nations when the war is won is just as essential to the future security of this country?" Only American participation in a world organization, he asserted, would assure "that this catastrophe will not occur again." In a speech at Toronto in February 1943 he was more specific, calling on the United Nations to set up machinery to study postwar economic problems. "Only through our combined efforts," he told his Canadian audience, "can we make certain that the victory which we will win in battle can become in fact the victory of peace." [2]

Wendell Willkie was equally insistent on the need to plan for peace. In speeches in New York City in November he criticized the administration for its silence on postwar problems, demanding "global solutions for a global war." "We must learn to work together; we must learn to work with all our allies that we may win both the war and the peace," he told the New York *Herald Tribune* Forum. "We must work together today; tomorrow will be too late." Speaking on the radio in early January, he reminded his listeners that Wilson failed because he waited until the war was over before planning for peace. "Successful instruments of either national or international government are the result of growth," he declared. "They are not created in a day. . . . They must be created now while we fight." He concluded by proposing that Roosevelt take the lead in forming a United Nations Council to direct both the winning of the war and the planning of the peace.[3]

Willkie also continued his efforts to revamp the Republican party. After the elections National Chairman Joseph W. Martin, congressman from Massachusetts, announced his resignation and called a meeting of the National Committee in St. Louis in early December to select his successor. When Willkie learned that Senator Robert A. Taft and Colonel Robert R. McCormick, publisher of the Chicago *Tribune,* planned to nominate Werner Schroeder of Illinois, he was furious. Schroeder was an isolationist who had just managed the successful reelection campaign of Senator Wayland Brooks. Willkie sent an aide to St. Louis to coordinate the opposition of eastern Republicans to Schroeder's candidacy. When the Committee met on December 7, the Willkie group put up an unknown thirty-five-year-old Oregon businessman, Frederick E. Baker. On the first ballot Schroeder and Baker deadlocked with forty votes apiece. Baker advanced slightly on the second ballot, but failed to gain a majority. At this point Joe Martin called a recess. Conferring with the leaders of the opposing factions, Martin finally persuaded them to compromise on a third candidate, Harrison Spangler of Iowa. An hour later, when Martin reconvened the committee, Baker and Schroeder walked down the center aisle arm-in-arm to withdraw and announced their support for Spangler. The Committee then elected him unanimously.

"Not a victory, perhaps," commented Willkie in New York, "but it averted catastrophe." The press gave a similar interpretation, suggesting that Willkie's intervention had stymied the plans of midwestern isolationists to recapture control of the party. Few seemed to realize that Spangler was a pre-war isolationist who had supported Taft at the 1940 Republican convention. In a press conference on December 8, however, Spangler tried to steer a middle course, announcing that he realized that the Atlantic and Pacific were no longer moats protecting America from the outside world. But then he hastily added, "My job is to build up an army of voters in the United States, . . . and I don't think there are any votes in China or Mongolia or Russia that I can get for the Republicans." [4]

Spangler's election as National Chairman aptly symbolized the shifting crosscurrents on foreign policy that continued to flow through the Republican party. In December former President Herbert Hoover delivered a speech in Chicago, his first major address since American entry into the war. He championed a "conditional peace"—a long cooling-off period after the war before any final peace settlement was made. Warning that "we cannot fly to the realms of peace on the wings of phrases and oratory," he suggested that the United Nations should police the world while their leaders tackled the problems of peace one at a time. A few weeks later Harold E. Stassen went to the other extreme in voicing an appeal for a "United Nations of the World." Speaking to the Minneapolis branch of the Foreign Policy Association, the young Republican governor sketched out an elaborate world federation consisting of a world parliament, a seven-member executive council, an international court and a United Nations Legion to keep the peace. "On this basis," he told his audience, "the citizens of this state in the years ahead would be not only citizens of Minnesota, not only citizens of the United States of America, but also citizens of the United Nations of the World." In contrast, Willkie's call for a wartime United Nations Council seemed modest and realistic. [5]

Among the Democrats, Henry Wallace remained the most outspoken internationalist. On November 8, 1942, he addressed the Congress of American-Soviet Friendship in Madison Square Garden, flaying the isolationists in both political parties. In 1919, he declared, "isolationism came out of its cave and not only killed any possibility of our entering the League, but made it certain that we would adopt international policies which would make World War II almost inevitable." He went on to praise Russia, pointing out that the Soviets were bearing the brunt of the war against Hitler. "In order that the United Nations may effectively serve the world, it is vital that the United States and Russia be in accord as to the fundamentals of an enduring peace based on the aspirations of the common man," he concluded. "The American and Russian people can and will throw their influence on the side of building a new democracy which will be the hope of the world."

A month later the retiring president of the National Association of Manufacturers, William P. Witherow, replied to Wallace. Speaking to the War Congress of Industrialists, Witherow declared, "I am not making guns or tanks to win a 'people's revolution.' I am making armament to help our boys save America." Witherow was particularly upset by Wallace's vague schemes for postwar American aid for other countries. "I am not fighting for a quart of milk for every Hottentot, or for a TVA on the Danube," he told his fellow manufacturers. In January Roane Waring, the national commander of the American Legion, joined in the assault on Wallace. "Let's plan the future of Timbuktoo and Patagonia," he told a Congressional audience, "after we have destroyed the military might of the Germans and the Japs."

In his New York *Times* column Arthur Krock charged that Wallace was advocating a postwar give-away of American resources. Angered by this criticism, the Vice President wrote to Krock to clarify his position. "I do not now and never have had in mind," Wallace wrote, "that the United States would over a long period of time play the role of Santa Claus to the rest of the world." Krock replied on December 8 that after rereading Wallace's speeches, he was impressed with their "humanitarian quality," but he still believed that the Vice President was calling for "a post-war Utopia, paid for entirely by the United States and handed out to any that may ask for it." Krock then sent copies of this correspondence to Cordell Hull's secretary and wrote in the *Times* that administration officials were worried that Wallace's speeches had alienated millions of Americans who were ready to abandon isolationism.[6]

Undaunted, Henry Wallace agreed to speak out again when the Woodrow Wilson Foundation invited him to make a nationwide radio address on Wilson's birthday. Calling his critics "self-styled 'realists,'" Wallace compared them to the men who had opposed the League of Nations. He praised Woodrow Wilson, denying that he had failed. "Now we know that it was the world that failed," he said, "and the suffering and war of the last few years are the penalty it is paying for its failure." He proceeded to discuss the specific problems of world organization, suggesting an international police force, a world council and an international court as essential elements. He favored a regional approach which would permit "the maximum of home rule that can be maintained along with the minimum of centralized authority" in a world federation. "Now at last," he proclaimed, "the nations of the world have a second chance to erect a lasting structure of peace—a structure such as that which Woodrow Wilson sought to build but which crumbled away because the world was not yet ready."

The internationalists cheered Wallace's brave words. The *Christian Century*, which had opposed entry into the war, hailed the speech as "the most important outline of peace aims so far put forward by an administration spokesman"; the editors of the *Nation* applauded his idealism, noting that it was "based on common sense." The speech was reprinted in all the London papers, with editors recording their "warm agreement" with his ideas. The *Daily Herald* paid Wallace the nicest compliment, labeling him "a realist." Officials in the State Department were less enthusiastic. In his diary Breckinridge Long called Wallace one of the "Post War Dream Boys" who wanted to "feed the world, clothe the world, and house the world." "The effect of Wallace's speeches," Long noted, "is somewhat dimmed by the realization of the people that we have not enough of some things for ourselves—to say nothing about giving chunks of it to people overseas." Long commented that Hull agreed with him. "He thinks his Trade Agreements offer the best solution for a post-war world." [7]

While Wallace spoke grandly of a global New Deal, he did advocate one practical way to keep the peace—the creation of an international air force. He first mentioned this concept in his November 8 speech to the Congress of American-Soviet Friendship. Noting that airplanes increased the horrors of war, he also pointed out that they could help the cause of peace. "When this war comes to an end," he said, "the United Nations will have such an overwhelming superiority in air power that we shall be able speedily to enforce any mandate. . . ." In December he told a graduating class of Army Air Force cadets that an international air squadron, "consisting of adequate numbers of planes and strategically located bases," could enforce peace easily. He described this plan more fully in a radio interview with Raymond Clapper, proposing a worldwide network of international airports as bases for this peace-keeping force. On February 5, 1943, he wrote to President Roosevelt to propose a "United Nations Organization" with only two specific functions—power to outlaw international cartels and authority to establish a chain of international airports for the exclusive use of the United Nations. In a magazine article in March he told how air power could be used to halt aggression. "If economic quarantine does not suffice," he wrote, "the United Nations' peace force must at once bomb the aggressor nation mercilessly." Sumner Welles was a little dubious about Wallace's panacea. When the Vice President sent him a letter on this subject, Welles replied, "It is obvious that, in event that arrangements are worked out to maintain peace, air force must play a considerable part."

Despite the attacks of conservative critics, the jealous disdain of the

State Department, and the fuzziness of his thinking, Wallace remained the leading administration spokesman on the postwar world in early 1943. *Newsweek* noted that his speeches had lifted him "spectacularly out of Vice Presidential obscurity." He had captured the attention of the American people and, more than any other individual, had compelled them to look beyond the war to the peace that would follow.[8]

II

The turn in the tide of the war had little impact on the State Department. The committees set up in the spring of 1942 to analyze postwar problems continued their weekly meetings without publicity. When a British visitor asked Hull why the American government was so slow in discussing the issues of peace, the Secretary replied that the people were not ready. "There is bitter feeling against what is called neglect in prosecuting the war," he explained. Public opinion, he added, was opposed to "sitting down and engaging in long-winded conversations and formal conferences about postwar policies and programs."

Many disagreed with Hull. Joseph M. Jones, a former journalist who headed up the Post War Trends unit in the Division of Special Research, bombarded Pasvolsky with memos advocating a more active program to influence public opinion. On September 24 he warned that American morale was very low and that the people were dissatisfied with the administration's silence on postwar issues. Jones felt it was essential for the Department to adopt "a more open and cooperative attitude towards private and public groups in the United States groping for solutions." After the elections in November he renewed this plea, declaring that the administration's silence had contributed to the Republican victory. Jonathan Daniels, a White House aide, agreed. In a memorandum to Marvin H. McIntyre in December, he predicted that the 1944 election would turn on the issue of peace. "Indeed, as after the last war, the political decision of the people of the United States may determine the future of security in the world," he wrote. Daniels asked McIntyre to urge the President to begin cultivating public support for a "decent peace."[9]

The deal in North Africa with Admiral Darlan, who had collaborated with Nazi Germany, touched off widespread criticism of the State Department's postwar aims. The editors of the *New Republic*, warning that the Department was honeycombed with conservatives intent on

81

preserving the status quo, wanted the President to take over the task of making peace himself. In January 1943 *Life* printed an editorial reviewing *Peace and War, 1931–1941*, a collection of documents on American entry into the war. The editors condemned the State Department for failing to educate the American people on the Nazi menace in the 1930's and urged that in the future the United States abandon "words and legalistic exhortation" in favor of "action and deeds." In a letter to Hull on January 25, Henry Luce explained what he meant. "It is my belief that public discussion is the highway to a future American internationalism—and the only highway that leads to such a goal," he wrote. "Open and forthright discussion of all policies, past and present, is the only means, in my opinion, by which a genuine international policy—a policy of deeds as well as words—can in the future be sustained in the United States."

Though Hull politely thanked Luce for his views and granted him an interview, the policy remained unchanged. The Secretary did permit Kingsbury Smith to write an article in *American Mercury* describing in vague terms the postwar studies conducted by the Department. "Behind the scenes in Washington," Smith began, "a new world is being planned for you. If the plans materialize, you are going to be given a try at running the world." The article failed to live up to this exciting prospect, however, and the main conclusion was, as the Secretary had wanted, that Hull and not Henry Wallace was in charge of the administration's postwar planning.[10]

Otherwise, the work of the various subcommittees went on in silence. The one on international organization, chaired by Sumner Welles, continued to meet weekly, usually on Saturday mornings. After studying the League Covenant, the group began work on a draft charter. In early January it had reached some tentative conclusions, which Welles passed on to Roosevelt during a two-hour White House conference. The major decision was to adopt a regional approach, dividing the world into a series of councils similar to the Pan-American conferences. Each regional body would send representatives to a world Executive Council on which the United States, the Soviet Union, Britain and China would have permanent membership. According to Welles, Roosevelt was doubtful about this arrangement, fearing that the small nations would have too much authority. The President preferred to have the Big Four in full control, and he suggested to Welles that his committee focus on functional agencies to deal with such problems as food, health and relief.

4. *Revolt in the Senate*

During this period another offshoot of the Advisory Committee, the security subcommittee, was also studying the problem of keeping the peace. Under the chairmanship of Norman H. Davis, this group agreed that it was mandatory for a future world organization to have military power at its disposal. In October, Breckinridge Long submitted a draft plan for a world organization "based on the availability of force to secure peace." In early 1943 the members accepted Wallace's idea for an international air force and asked army and navy aviation experts to advise them on details. In essence, they wished to create a truly international air corps which would attack immediately if any nation committed an act of aggression. If an air strike failed to halt the aggressor, then the member nations would send in ground forces. Long believed that this plan would be acceptable to the American people provided that the United States possessed the power to veto such action.

In January, Cordell Hull replaced Welles as chairman of the political subcommittee. Disturbed by the Under Secretary's direct access to the President, Hull insisted that all plans, including those emanating from the subcommittee on international organization which Welles still headed, pass through his office. The Secretary then moved to broaden Congressional participation, inviting Senators Walter F. George of Georgia and Elbert Thomas of Utah, Representatives Sol Bloom of New York and Luther A. Johnson of Texas, all Democrats, and Republican Representative Charles A. Eaton of New Jersey to join the Advisory Committee. A few weeks later he asked Senator Wallace H. White, a Maine Republican, to become a member. All but George were members of the foreign-relations committees in Congress, and each was assigned to one of the subcommittees studying postwar problems. Still convinced that the American people were unwilling to focus on the future peace, Hull made no further changes in the Department's activities.[11]

Throughout 1942 President Roosevelt was equally circumspect. On December 9 Josephus Daniels, who had been his superior as Secretary of the Navy during World War I, asked him to issue a statement on Woodrow Wilson's birthday to "pay some tribute to his vision." The President politely declined, saying: "honestly I cannot spend the two or three days necessary to prepare a speech or radio talk." When Rabbi Charles E. Shulman of Illinois asked him to give a statement of war aims more precise than the vague ideals of the Atlantic Charter, Roosevelt remained evasive. "The processes of coalition war and the agreements which make it possible are weaving the material of future policies," he replied in a public letter, "and their patterns can be described

83

with increasing definiteness." He urged Shulman and other clergymen to discuss postwar issues with the American people, but he said that they needed no special mandate from the government—they held this commission from God.

On January 1, 1943, the President celebrated the first anniversary of the United Nations Declaration with a brief public statement. He emphasized the importance of unity to the war effort, but he also alluded to the future, affirming the need "so to organize relations among Nations that forces of barbarism can never again break loose." In a press conference later that day he was just as vague. ". . . the most important war objective," he told the reporters, "is to maintain peace so that all of us . . . will not have to go through another world cataclysm again." [12]

A week later Roosevelt delivered his annual message to Congress. Again he concentrated on the war. Although he warned against becoming "bogged down in argument over methods and details" of the future peace, he did speak out against a return to isolationism. "We . . . have learned that if we do not pull the fangs of the predatory animals of this world, they will multiply and grow in strength—and they will be at our throats again once more in a short generation." He dismissed the League of Nations as a "formula . . . based on magnificient idealism" which only proved that peace must be built on firmer foundations than "good intentions alone." He saw only one solution:

> Bound together in solemn agreement that they themselves will not commit acts of aggression or conquest against any of their neighbors, the United Nations can and must remain united for the maintenance of peace by preventing any attempt to rearm in Germany, in Japan, in Italy, or in any other nation which seeks to violate the Tenth Commandment, "Thou shall not covet."

For the first time Roosevelt revealed to the American people a glimpse of his determination to secure a peace based on power. Though he did not disclose his plan for the Big Four to police the world, his cautioning against "methods and details" and his criticism of the League of Nations stood in sharp contrast to the lofty preaching of Welles, Wallace and Willkie. "The Roosevelt doctrine," commented Ernest K. Lindley, "is that we must shatter at the source any threat to the peace of the world." On January 24, after a ten-day conference with Winston Churchill at Casablanca, the President announced that the United States and its allies would demand the unconditional surrender of the Axis nations. By ruling out the possibility of a negotiated peace,

Roosevelt clearly emerged as a realistic statesman who had repudiated Wilsonian idealism.[13]

III

Public-opinion polls showed that more and more Americans were moving toward internationalism. The National Opinion Research Center reported that the majority in favor of the United States joining "some sort of organization of nations after the war" had increased from 62 percent in November 1942 to 72 percent the following January. Equally important, the earlier reluctance to discuss the future peace had melted away. A Gallup poll in December showed that 73 percent of the population wanted the government to "take steps now, before the end of the war," to establish a new world organization.

Heartened by this public support, internationalist leaders demanded more action from the Roosevelt administration. *Free World* called for "a definite and positive plan of the kind of world for which we are fighting, a plan which outlines the new world organization." The editors favored immediate formation of a United Nations Supreme Council to conduct the war and plan the peace. Clark Eichelberger echoed this cry in *Changing World*. He called upon the statesmen "to organize the United Nations and implement the Atlantic Charter; to lay the foundation of peace while the war is being won." The *New Republic* joined in the demand for a United Nations Supreme Council, asserting that it was essential for "a democratic organization of the world." When the United Nations failed to create such a body at the Casablanca conference, the internationalists were bitterly disappointed. "We must fulfill the worldwide demand that this shall be the century of the common man," the *New Republic* proclaimed in an editorial entitled "The Moral Crisis of the War." "And we must recognize that political decisions of the leading Allied governments—and most of all our own—are now creating a tide setting powerfully in the opposite direction." [14]

Clark Eichelberger was determined to reverse this tide. On October 19, 1942, he wrote to President Roosevelt asking for an appointment to discuss "ways in which we could help now in the urgent task of preventing the rise of isolationism." "I have become more and more convinced," Eichelberger wrote, "that the next peace will be won or lost before the war is won." The President agreed to see him during the last week of

October, but Roosevelt was too busy to keep the appointment. Instead, Eichelberger conferred with Henry Wallace, who secured him another appointment with the President on November 13. At this meeting Roosevelt surprised Eichelberger by describing his plan for the Four Policemen to disarm and patrol the postwar world. The President suggested that Eichelberger change the name of the League of Nations Association to "The United Nations Association" and launch a new campaign to win public support, but he asked not to be associated publicly with this effort.

Eichelberger eagerly followed up the President's suggestion. He arranged for the League of Nations Association, the Commission to Study the Organization of Peace and the American Free World Association to form a Council of United Nations Committees. The major aim of the new group was to stimulate the formation of local units in communities across the nation to prevent "a disastrous repetition of the 1919–20 mistake." Eichelberger originally hoped to have these units functioning by January 1 to celebrate the first anniversary of the United Nations Declaration, but he soon realized that greater coordination was necessary. In mid-December he called for a meeting of national leaders in New York City on January 3 to draw up detailed plans for the United Nations movement.[15]

On December 22 Eichelberger again wrote to the President informing him of the forthcoming meeting and asking him to "outline with characteristic boldness your plans for international machinery" in his annual message to Congress. "The announcement of your program," he told the President, "will facilitate the task of mobilizing public opinion." In an accompanying note to Marvin McIntyre, Eichelberger said the January 3 meeting could be postponed until after the President's speech if that would prove helpful. Roosevelt, alarmed by Eichelberger's enthusiasm, seized on this suggestion, but when McIntyre phoned Eichelberger on December 31, it was too late to cancel the meeting. Eichelberger, however, agreed to avoid publicity and to clear any public statement with the White House.[16]

On January 3 fifty prominent Americans, including Florence Harriman; Thomas Lamont of J. P. Morgan and Co.; Thomas J. Watson of IBM; Chester Rowell, publisher of the San Francisco *Chronicle*; James Reston of the New York *Times*; Gardner Cowles of *Look*; and Malcolm Davis for the Carnegie Endowment, met at the Hotel Commodore. At the end of the day the conferees decided to form a new Citizens Council for the United Nations to coordinate the activities of the many existing groups interested in world organization. The group honored Eichelberger's promise by keeping the meeting off-the-record and deferring a public announcement of its existence. In reporting to the White House, Eichelberger stressed that the meeting focused solely "on the best means of reaching the majority of the people with the necessity of the United States' taking its place in the United Nations of the World." Another informant told the President that there was an "astounding" degree of harmony among the participants and that all agreed to support "the President . . . on the United Nations program after the war."

For the next two months Clark Eichelberger worked with those attending the January 3 meeting to perfect the plans for the Citizens Council for the United Nations. At subsequent meetings they agreed to form local United Nations Committees by working through churches, women's clubs, veterans' organizations, chambers of commerce and labor unions. The Citizens Council would supply speakers and literature; the local committees would carry on the day-to-day campaign to win public support for international organization. After an unsuccessful effort to get Bernard Baruch to serve as national chairman, Eichelberger made public the formation of the new Council in mid-March. He and Shotwell were members of the executive committee; Melvin Hildreth, a Washington attorney, was listed as chairman. In the announcement, the founders stated their goal as the transformation of the wartime coalition into "the nucleus of the final United Nations of the world." They urged all like-minded people to form local committees to begin agitating in their newspapers, on the radio and through their clubs for the United States "to take its rightful place in the organization of nations which must follow the war." [17]

While the new United Nations group was forming, more than a thousand people gathered on February 27, 1943, at the Hotel Commodore for a day-long meeting to discuss the third report of the Commission to Study the Organization of Peace. Representative J. William Fulbright of Arkansas, then an unknown freshman legislator, delivered the main address. He spoke out boldly for a "world organization to prevent war," stating that a majority in Congress favored such a course. Clark Eichelberger presented the Commission's report, which called upon the United Nations to form a "continuing conference" immediately to begin planning for the peace. "The most urgent need for the future," the report asserted, "is that the United Nations be welded together so closely that their union can withstand the effects of the postwar reaction." The "continuing conference" would be a temporary body which would lead ultimately to a universal world organization with the power to keep the peace. "Force is inescapable in human affairs," the report concluded. "It cannot merely be abandoned; it must be controlled and used." [18]

The Commission to Study the Bases of a Just and Durable Peace, the Protestant church group headed by John Foster Dulles, was also active in the United Nations movement. After a trip to England in the summer of 1942, where he had conferred with Foreign Minister Anthony Eden, Dulles approached Sumner Welles with a proposal for closer cooperation between the State Department and his Commission. Welles approved, but Pasvolsky thought it would interfere with the Department's studies, and he persuaded the Under Secretary to drop the idea. After this setback, Dulles proposed to the Commission that it avoid advocating a specific peace plan, but instead formulate and publicize "those basic moral principles which undergird a peaceful world." The Commission approved this policy, and on February 7, 1943, Dulles submitted a draft of "Six Pillars of Peace" which the members unanimously adopted. "We regard it as by all odds the most important statement on the issues of peace thus far forthcoming from American Christians," commented theologian Henry P. Van Dusen.

At noon on March 18, 1943, a group of financial, labor, educational and religious leaders attended a luncheon on the sixty-fifth floor of the RCA Building in Rockefeller Center. Dulles told this distinguished audience that the Commission was releasing the text of "Six Pillars of Peace" in order to secure an American commitment to "a future of organized international collaboration." Dulles stressed the need for a prompt decision. "If the United Nations of this war are to continue to be united, the time to cement that unity is now." He hoped the Commission's Six Pillars would compel the government to act. "If so," Dulles concluded, "we will have made a momentous advance toward victory and done that which will give us a reasonable chance for a durable peace." [19]

The Six Pillars consisted of a call for "continuing collaboration of the United Nations," and a peace based on international economic reform, social change, independence for colonial peoples, worldwide disarmament and religious and intellectual freedom for all mankind. In the pamphlet presenting these principles, Dulles explained that all these goals depended on the establishment of a new world organization. In describing this body, he firmly committed the Commission to the use of force to preserve peace. "The economic and military power of the world community," Dulles wrote, "should be subject to mobilization to support international agencies which are designed to, and do in fact, serve the general welfare."

Under a shorter name, the Commission on a Just and Durable Peace, Dulles' group distributed the "Six Pillars of Peace" throughout the nation. They sent copies to sixty thousand ministers in an effort to reach the fifteen million members of Protestant churches. On March 26 Dulles and two clergymen met with Roosevelt at the White House. Dulles handed the President a copy of the pamphlet describing it as a "simple statement" which was "designed to evoke from the American people a mandate to their Government to build a structure of peace on the bases set forth." Three days later Dulles sent Roosevelt a draft statement for possible use in a future address. The President passed it on to Samuel Rosenman, his chief speech-writer, telling him "to find a way to make public use" of the Six Pillars.[20]

By March 1943 the internationalists were poised for a great crusade to place the United States on record in favor of international organization. Seeing in the United Nations an appropriate symbol for peacetime cooperation, they had created the machinery to influence public opinion and avoid a repetition of the postwar letdown which they believed had doomed the League of Nations. Though their ideas were still hazy, they agreed on the concept of a security organization possessing sufficient military force to prevent aggression. All they needed was a specific plan to offer as a rallying cry to the American people.

IV

The Seventy-eighth Congress convened on January 6, 1943, for its first session. In the House, three Republican isolationists, Representatives Everett M. Dirksen and Jessie Sumner of Illinois and Karl Mundt of South Dakota, introduced resolutions proposing postwar planning commissions. Though the details differed, each wanted to create a body of congressmen, senators and private citizens to advise the President on the future peace. In the Senate, Alexander Wiley, a Republican from Wisconsin, resubmitted a resolution he had first offered in September 1942 calling for a similar Foreign Relations Advisory Council. Hull had opposed this resolution in the fall, writing Wiley that he preferred to consult informally with members of the Senate. In offering it again,

Wiley said his only motive was to avoid a repetition of "what happened after the last war." Breckinridge Long was doubtful, noting in his diary that the purpose of these Republican resolutions was to "embarrass the President." [21]

Long was probably right, but the same charge could not be made against three resolutions offered a few weeks later by Democrats. On January 25 Representative John Kee of West Virginia proposed that the President negotiate immediately with the other United Nations to create an international organization. Representative Fulbright introduced a resolution on February 19 calling for the House Foreign Relations Committee to conduct a study to develop "a specific plan or system by which peace may be maintained through cooperative international action." In the Senate, Guy M. Gillette of Indiana offered a proposal for the President to negotiate a treaty with the other United Nations embodying "the program of purposes and principles enunciated in the Atlantic Charter." Gillette told the Senate that such a "United Nations Post-War Peace Charter" would reassure the world about the altruistic peace aims of the United States and its allies.

The press greeted this resolution with surprising warmth. The *New Republic* called Wiley's proposal "a thoughtful idea which needs to be explored"; *Time* believed that the new Congressional interest in the postwar world marked a sharp turn away from isolationism. The New York *Times* was even more enthusiastic. Praising the Gillette proposal, the editors called for a resolution affirming "American participation in the guarantee of peace in the postwar world." Such a resolution was necessary to "assure our friends and warn our enemies that we are in the world to stay," the *Times* argued. In early March, Arthur Krock stirred up great interest when he reported that Senator Bennett Clark of Missouri, a leading pre-war isolationist, was planning to sponsor a joint resolution favoring American entry into a future international organization. "The passage of such a resolution," commented the editors of the *Nation*, "would have an electric effect on the United Nations and would assure him [Clark] a place in history." [22]

The State Department was not sure how to deal with the resolutions. When Sol Bloom, chairman of the House Foreign Affairs Committee, asked for comments on the Kee proposal, Hull replied that he found its spirit "entirely in accord with the foreign policy of this administration" and promised to work for international organization "as rapidly as events make further progress possible." At the time, the Secretary and his aides were busy preparing for the forthcoming visit of Anthony

Eden, which Churchill had suggested to Roosevelt in early February. In a memorandum on March 6, legal advisor Green Hackworth discussed the dilemma facing the Department. "We cannot, of course, afford to give the impression that we object to consideration of post-war problems by the Congress," he wrote. "The most that we can do is to endeavor to avoid embarrassments in the international field at this particular juncture." Hackworth particularly feared public hearings at which isolationists would voice criticism of Britain and Russia. Concluding that postwar issues required "the most painstaking use of the diplomatic process," he recommended telling Congress "to leave these matters to the Department for the time being."

Hull decided to rely on the discretion of Tom Connally, chairman of the Senate Foreign Relations Committee. On March 6 Connally created a special three-man subcommittee composed of Arthur H. Vandenberg, Walter F. George, and Guy Gillette as chairman. He asked them to study the Gillette and other postwar resolutions and then report back to the Foreign Relations Committee. He and Hull evidently hoped that the subcommittee would delay any further action by Congress until the Secretary had explored "questions arising out of the war" with the British Foreign Minister.[23]

The Congressional interest in peace, however, had taken deeper root than Hull realized. A small group of senators, led by Joseph H. Ball of Minnesota, was determined to prevent the issue from being brushed aside. Ball, a young, obscure senator who was a protégé of Harold Stassen, came from a rural Minnesota background. When he was seventeen, he rented fifty acres of land, borrowed a team of horses and a plow, and raised a crop of seed corn that paid for his first year at Antioch College in Ohio. After three years his money ran out and he left Antioch, working as a telephone lineman, a steam-shovel operator and a chemical researcher before settling down as a reporter in Minneapolis. He came to know Stassen as a political columnist for the St. Paul *Pioneer-Press*, and in 1940, when Stassen became governor, he appointed Ball to a vacant Senate seat. Over six feet tall and slightly stooped, Ball looked much older than his thirty-eight years. He had a rugged, deeply lined face, an iron-gray cowlick and thick dark eyebrows that gave him, as one commentator noted, "the combination of brooding melancholy and grinning humor that makes swooning lady journalists think immediately of Lincoln."

In the Senate, Ball's candor and lack of pretense antagonized the older members. He did not receive any major committee assignments, but in 1941 the leaders placed him on a new investigating committee chaired by Senator Harry Truman of Missouri. The Truman committee soon won public attention for its disclosures of corruption in war industries, and Ball formed close ties with the other members, particularly with Democrats Truman and Carl A. Hatch of New Mexico and fellow Republican Harold H. Burton of Ohio. After Pearl Harbor, Ball became convinced that the United States should take the lead in forming a new world organization, and in the spring of 1942 he spoke on this theme during an extensive tour of Minnesota. "Our civilization will never survive continual war," he told his constituents, and he was delighted to discover how many agreed with him. He campaigned primarily on foreign-policy issues in 1942, and he interpreted his surprise victory as a mandate for internationalism.[24]

When he returned to the Senate in early 1943, he began discussing the need for international organization with Burton, Hatch and Truman. They all believed the United States should act during the war to found a new world body, and they decided to sponsor a resolution to commit the Senate to such a course. Since Harry Truman had his hands full with the investigating committee, they asked Lister Hill of Alabama to join them in his place. Ball drafted a resolution which they showed to over a dozen sympathetic senators. The administration did not take an active part in the framing of the resolution, though Ball remembers Henry Wallace being "benignly present" at one of the drafting sessions. Contrary to legends that later sprang up, neither Willkie nor Stassen influenced Ball, and Truman played only a background role. Ball, Burton and Hatch took the initiative, with Hill added at the last moment to give the bi-partisan balance.

The resolution which Ball drafted was far more specific and detailed than the ones introduced earlier in the session. It began with a call for the United States to ask the United Nations to form a permanent international organization during the war. Ball and his colleagues then proposed that the new world body have the power to carry on the war, occupy territory liberated from the Axis, administer relief and economic rehabilitation, and provide machinery for the peaceful settlement of disputes. Most important, they advocated the creation of a United Nations police force to "suppress by immediate use of . . . force any future attempt at military aggression by any nation." Deliberately framed "to be out in front of public opinion," the Ball resolution boldly challenged the Senate and the administration to come to grips with the issue of international organization.[25]

92

In early March, Ball took the final draft to Sumner Welles, who was serving as Acting Secretary while Hull vacationed in Florida. Welles was enthusiastic, urging Ball to introduce the resolution in the Senate promptly. On Saturday, March 13, the four senators called a press conference in Senator Hill's office to make public their proposal, which they said would be formally presented to the Senate on March 16. They declared that their goal was to get at least two thirds of the Senate on record now in favor of a strong world organization. Ball told the reporters that they had talked with many pre-war isolationists who promised to support the resolution. When a journalist asked if they were calling for a new League of Nations, Senator Hill broke in sharply, saying, "Please don't bring that in. This has no relation to the League of Nations, nothing like it." At the end of the press conference they disclosed that they would meet with the President the next day.

At 2:30 on Sunday afternoon Ball, Hill, Burton and Hatch went to the White House along with the two senior Democrats on the Foreign Relations Committee, Tom Connally and New York's Robert F. Wagner. The President, accompanied by Welles, Harry Hopkins and James F. Byrnes, who had resigned from the Supreme Court to serve as economic mobilizer, greeted them cordially. For over an hour the four senators discussed their plan with the President. Roosevelt indicated his agreement in principle, but he advised the senators to wait, fearing that they might stir up a fierce reaction from isolationists if they pushed for Senate approval at this time. When they emerged from the White House, Senator Hill told reporters there might be a delay, but Ball was adamant. "We want to be ready with a program when the war is won," he declared. "We are trying to put into words the minimum things we think will be necessary for a permanent peace."

The next day the New York *Times* carried comments by Senator Burton K. Wheeler, a Montana Democrat and ardent isolationist. Announcing that he would wage a "long, bitter fight" against the Ball resolution, Wheeler opposed "any entangling alliances or any international police force." He then attacked the Soviet Union, saying that he was suspicious of "what Mr. Stalin wants, what he will demand and what he'll take." [26]

Despite this warning, Ball rose on the Senate floor on March 16 to introduce the measure which the press had now dubbed the B_2H_2 resolution. In a brief speech he said that he, Burton, Hatch and Hill were acting in behalf of a larger group of senators who were deeply concerned about the future peace. They advocated "a collective world

93

security system" as "the best hope of maintaining the peace and stability of the world after the war." Ball said it was vital for the Senate to act now in order to reassure our wartime partners. "The only way to find out whether our allies are prepared to join us in that collective effort is to ask them," Ball asserted. Reminding his colleagues of the Senate's rejection of the League of Nations in 1919, Ball concluded, "History must not repeat itself; that tragedy must not happen again."

In a press conference that day, reporters tried to get the President to commit himself on the B_2H_2 resolution. When one asked him if he shared the belief that "we should attempt to win the war first," he declined to comment, calling this idea "a glittering generalization." When another reporter asked if there was any plan to form a United Nations Council, he again sidestepped, saying only that the State Department was keeping in close touch with our allies. Finally, Roosevelt closed out the subject by saying that for the present he preferred to avoid "any specifics" on postwar issues. The next day the New York *Times* ran a front-page story stating that the President had been "cool" toward the Ball resolution at his press conference.

Three days later Roosevelt tried to correct this impression at another press conference. "I wasn't cool toward the resolution at all," he said. He explained that he did not feel he had a right to interfere in a matter before the Senate, but he did favor "having the world know that the United States is, as a whole, ready and willing to help in maintaining future peace." When a reporter asked if it would be correct to say that Roosevelt endorsed "the broad principle" of the Ball resolution, the President replied, "Yes. Yes." [27]

Cordell Hull felt quite differently. When he returned from Florida on March 14 to begin his conversations with Anthony Eden, he was much disturbed by the Ball resolution. In a meeting with the Gillette subcommittee two days later, he said he would have given anything to have kept it off the Senate floor. He expressed concern that isolationists would make scathing assaults on Russia and Britain that would injure the war effort. "He counseled extreme caution in doing *anything*," Arthur Vandenberg noted, even suggesting that, to prevent a full-scale debate, senators simply sign a general statement of their postwar intentions. However, when Eden queried Hull about the Ball resolution, Hull admitted that "a suitable expression of this sort by Congress would have a splendid effect abroad." The Secretary then proceeded to give the British Foreign Minister a detailed lecture on the American constitutional system, pointing out the relationship between the executive and

94

legislative branches and stressing the need to confer extensively with senators to achieve "understanding and unity on every essential phase" as "an indispensable prerequisite to any successful action by the Senate." Eden evidently understood Hull, for at a luncheon with members of Congress on March 18 he told them he felt it was too early to discuss details of the future peace.

Between his meetings with Eden, Hull conferred daily with Senate leaders to head off debate on the Ball measure. On March 19 he told Senator Gillette that it would be necessary to draft a new resolution which would pass the Senate "overwhelmingly." Three days later Hull called Gillette, Connally, George and Vandenberg into his office to read them a new resolution drafted by the State Department. The two-paragraph text simply called for the "relentless" prosecution of the war against the Axis and declared that the Senate "advocates participation by the United States in the creation and maintenance of an international organization to insure permanent peace." That same day Hull told Anthony Eden that "with proper and careful management" he believed the Senate would pass some resolution "which will express approval . . . of an international permanent peace ogranization." [28]

In Congress the B_2H_2 resolution was referred to the Senate Foreign Relations Committee. On March 24 Chairman Tom Connally issued a public statement denying that the administration favored its passage. Privately, he told reporters that if his committee sent the measure to the Senate floor, "There'd be the damnedest gut-pulling you ever saw, and that's just what the President doesn't want, or any of us want now." The next day Connally announced that he had appointed an eight-man subcommittee which he himself would chair to study the proposal. The other members were George, Vandenberg and Gillette, whose three-man group was now disbanded, and Elbert D. Thomas, Democrat of Utah; Alben W. Barkley, the Democratic majority leader from Kentucky; Wallace H. White, Republican of Maine; and Robert M. La Follette, Jr., a Wisconsin Progressive and an outspoken isolationist. Connally promised that this group would work "promptly, and thoroughly and earnestly," but in private he said the subcommittee would sit on the Ball resolution until public opinion rallied strongly, and then it would report out "a very broad-guage, generalized resolution."

The President approved of Connally's strategy. When James Byrnes told him what Connally planned to substitute for the B_2H_2 resolution, the President said that Hull had some ideas which he thought would "fit in well." The next day Roosevelt sent Byrnes a resolution he had

95

drafted, telling him to pass it on to Connally when "the thing comes down to the matter of language." The President's draft was vaguer than the Ball resolution, but it did call for a world organization to settle disputes peacefully and proposed "the maintenance under the United Nations, of sufficient forces to suppress any future attempt at military aggression by any nation." [29]

Hull now abandoned the two-paragraph State Department proposal and issued a public statement announcing that the administration favored "the broad principles of resolutions introduced in Congress," but would leave to the Senate the task of "working out a resolution which will be generally acceptable." He was encouraged when Vandenberg wrote to him on March 24 to support his view that the Ball resolution was too specific. Thanking the Michigan Republican for his "cordial and interesting letter," Hull said he thought that "very full and elaborate conference among each and all Senators desirous of working out a common plan or formula with respect to this matter will probably be the single available course calculated to succeed." [30]

Many others, however, were unhappy over the obvious reluctance of the administration to deal openly with the B_2H_2 proposal. Henry Wallace called it "a very constructive suggestion," and Wendell Willkie sent the four senators a telegram endorsing their idea. "Let me know if there is anything I can do to help," he offered. Twenty-six of the fifty-five new Republican members of the House issued a statement on March 21 praising the resolution. "The only sure way to keep the United States out of future wars," they declared, "is not to have future wars." Even Breckinridge Long, one of Hull's most loyal aides, viewed the Ball resolution as "one of the most important developments of our time in American politics." He especially liked the bi-partisan nature of the measure, believing that it heralded the possibility of a "*national* foreign policy" that transcended the narrow partisanship of the past.

By the end of March it was clear that the Ball resolution had aroused the entire nation and provided the internationalist movement with the focus it had lacked. The administration had succeeded in preventing a floor debate in the Senate, but Hull, Roosevelt and Connally could not dampen the enthusiasm engendered by the four senators. The New York *Times*, which had editorialized that the resolution was "less likely to solve problems than to raise them" likened it to a "time-bomb" which no one wanted to go off but which absorbed everyone's attention. the *New Republic* preferred to speak of "a tiger that burns bright in the forest of the night." The tiger was national hostility and power politics, which only the unity advocated in the B_2H_2 resolution could overcome. The editors of the *Nation* made the most perceptive comment, noting that now "the peace of the world is no longer the almost exclusive concern of Vice-President Wallace and Wendell Willkie." The great crusade to assure the United States a second chance at world leadership was under way.[31]

5

One World

INTERNATIONALIST LEADERS immediately recognized the importance of the Ball resolution. On April 3, 1943, Clark Eichelberger wrote to the local United Nations Committees to inform them that the Citizens Council for the United Nations had purchased thirty thousand copies of Ball's speech introducing the measure in the Senate. He asked them to distribute these reprints in their communities, stating that passage of the resolution was necessary to assure our allies that this time the Senate would not block American entry into a new world organization. In *Changing World* he wrote a long analysis of the resolution and urged his readers to work for its passage. The editors of *Free World* also stressed the Senate measure, seeing it as a sign that the American people were "determined to establish a United Nations organization which will end once and for all the threat of another world conflict."

The Ball resolution had its greatest impact, however, in the formation of new internationalist groups which sprang up to work for its adoption. In a report to the directors of the League of Nations Association on March 27, Eichelberger recommended that all the scattered efforts in behalf of international organization be merged into a new United Nations Association. The directors approved and authorized Eichelberger to make the necessary arrangements. When he found that an organization devoted to lobbying for a specific measure would not have the tax-exempt status enjoyed by the League of Nations Association, Eichelberger decided to make the Citizens Council for the United Nations the vehicle for the proposed coordination. For the next three months Eichelberger perfected the details of the merger. Finally, on July 16, the charter members of the United Nations Association met in New York to elect their officers and begin a drive for the "entrance of the United States into a permanent organization for collective security."

On July 30, 1943, the new group made itself public. The leaders were all familar internationalists—Shotwell, Eichelberger, William Allen White, Chester Rowell, Thomas J. Watson and Melvin Hildreth, who served as president. Their program included planks favoring the establishment of democratic regimes in liberated countries, efforts to better the living standards of all people, and a world organization with "police power to prevent or suppress aggression." But for the present they focused on the B_2H_2 resolution, calling for a mammoth letter-writing campaign to force the Senate to act on this measure. The United Nations Association followed the same structural pattern as the Citizens Council, serving as a coordinating body to establish and work with local committees. The leaders made no attempt to enroll individual members, and for financing they relied on the generous support of a few wealthy donors, notably Marshall Field, Thomas Lamont and Hugh Moore, the president of the Dixie Cup Company and an ardent internationalist.[1]

With encouragement from Eichelberger and Shotwell, many of the local branches of the League of Nations Association transformed themselves into United Nations Committees. The Massachusetts chapter made this change in May, holding a benefit performance of the film *United We Stand* in Boston. This movie, produced by Twentieth Century-Fox and narrated by Lowell Thomas, traced the theme of international cooperation from the signing of the Treaty of Versailles down to the United Nations Declaration. "Ushers in costumes of the United Nations, stirring music by foreign-born groups, a downtown theatre turned over to the Association for the occasion," wrote an enthusiastic correspondent in *Changing World*, "combined to make this a social, educational and financial success." In Texas a new organization, known as the Texas Committee on Postwar Organization, was formed to carry on the work of the United Nations Association. This group favored the Ball resolution and waged a campaign to win over Senator Connally. The most active committee in the Midwest was the Minnesota United Nations Committee, which had more than a thousand members by midsummer. In August they manned a booth at the Minnesota State Fair and distributed thousands of pieces of literature, including texts of the B_2H_2 resolution. The St. Louis Committee, formed by the local branch of the League of Nations Association, concentrated on finding a candidate to oppose isolationist Senator Bennett Clark.

By the end of the summer the United Nations Association was well established, with committees active in all parts of the country. In New York, Mrs. James Lees Laidlaw, a veteran of the League battles in the 1920's, headed up a Congressional committee which hoped to create a bi-partisan local group in every Congressional district in the country to press for the Ball resolution. Soliciting members for these groups, she wrote, "We need minute men and women like you." The Association published a brochure, *Unite for Victory*, which strongly supported the B_2H_2 measure. In *Changing World*, Melvin Hildreth stated that the goal was "to make certain of victory in war and in the maintenance of that victory in peace." Warning against renewed isolationist onslaughts from the "sneering Senators" and "neurotic newspapers," he concluded:

> Democracy is not dead; but it can live only in an organized world. America is the last best hope of earth in building such a world. The time has come when America must keep her momentous rendezvous with destiny.[2]

In April 1943 Edgar Ansel Mowrer, foreign correspondent for the Chicago *Daily News*, and W. W. Waymack, editor of the Des Moines *Register* and *Tribune*, organized the Non-Partisan Council to Win the Peace. Mowrer had been active in Freedom House, a New York organization which pressed for both social reform at home and international cooperation abroad. He had presented the idea of forming the Non-Partisan Council to a group of liberal internationalists at a meeting at the Cosmopolitan Club in New York on March 11, 1943, stating that the aim "is to build up an irresistible public demand that the U.S.A. negotiate and enter into a system of collective security." When Ball introduced his resolution the next week, Mowrer and Waymack decided to make its passage their primary goal. In order to win midwestern support, Mowrer announced the formation of the Non-Partisan Council at a luncheon at the Palmer House in Chicago on April 16. Unlike the United Nations Association, the Council made no effort to establish local branches, but instead concentrated on coordinating the activities of national organizations interested in promoting the Ball resolution. The membership consisted of representatives of these groups, including the League of Nations Association, the United Nations Association, Freedom House, the Church Peace Union, and the Carnegie Endowment, which financed many of the Council's activities.

Though the Non-Partisan Council held its weekly meetings in New York City, in May the members voted to set up a Washington office to direct the lobbying activity in behalf of the B_2H_2 resolution. In June they began work on a pamphlet entitled *Your Congress Can Win the Next War Now.* The Council distributed more than a hundred thousand copies of this booklet, with the Carnegie Endowment alone ordering fifteen thousand. It was an impassioned plea for adoption of the Ball resolution which began with a series of questions—"Do you want another bloody, ruinous war in 25 years? Did the U.S. Senate in 1919 unwittingly vote for Pearl Harbor?" The anxious reader was told that only by passage of the B_2H_2 resolution could the United States prove its good intentions to its wartime allies. The Council also joined with Freedom House in running a full-page advertisement in the New York *Times* entitled "Stop World War III." Blaming "the long depression, Hitler in Germany, the League failure, the war, Pearl Harbor, our hundreds of expended billions, our dying and our dead" on American rejection of the League in 1919, the advertisement called for a world organization backed up by "an international police force." The Council distributed fifteen-thousand reprints of this page to groups across the country to display on their bulletin boards.[3]

A third new internationalist pressure group, the Women's Action Committee for Victory and Lasting Peace, also developed in March 1943. It was a successor to the National Committee on the Cause and Cure of War, a peace society headed by Carrie Chapman Catt that was a casualty of the war. Dr. Esther Caukin Brunauer, the director of the American Association of University Women, organized this new group, which included representatives of the General Federation of Women's Clubs, the YWCA, the League of Women Voters and a dozen other national organizations. At its first meeting in New York on March 21, the members agreed to "carry on a campaign for every congressional measure essential to the full participation of our country in all international efforts to secure . . . a just and lasting peace." They hoped to form committees of women in each Congressional district to write to their senators and congressmen "each time the Committee sends out a call for action." In April the Women's Action Committee endorsed the Ball resolution and asked members to press for Senate adoption. Like the Non-Partisan Council, the committee favored an international police force and distributed a pamphlet arguing for the creation of such a body to keep the peace.[4]

While these action groups worked for passage of the Ball resolution, the Commission to Study the Organization of Peace continued its educational activities. On June 5, aided by a grant from the Carnegie Endowment, the Commission began a thirteen-week series of radio broadcasts over the NBC network entitled "For This We Fight." On the first program Senators Elbert Thomas and Warren Austin discussed a future international organization, calling on the Big Four to take the lead during the war by forming a United Nations Council. Sumner Welles, Supreme Court Justice Owen Roberts, Nelson A. Rockefeller, Thomas W. Lamont, John Foster Dulles and many other well-known Americans appeared on subsequent broadcasts to advocate entry into a postwar collective-security organization. These programs had a far-reaching impact; according to the Hooper ratings, over four million Americans, nearly one-quarter of the available audience, tuned in each Saturday evening. United Nations Committees often sponsored the programs locally, and when a station failed to carry the broadcast, they swiftly applied pressure to remedy the oversight.

Convinced that isolationism was strongest among rural dwellers, the Commission launched an ambitious effort to reach American farmers in the summer of 1943. With the cooperation of farm organizations and churches, the New York office arranged for study groups to meet during the second week in August to discuss a pamphlet prepared by the Commission. Titled *Winning the War on the Spiritual Front*, this handbook argued that "this is our last chance to unite with the other nations to prevent the coming of a third world war." In an effort to reach their rural readers, the authors said that war was as obsolete as using a hand sickle to harvest grain and that nations needed to come together for the same reason that pigs huddled together on a cold night! "Neighboring is a two-way proposition," the pamphlet concluded. "This is just as true with nations as it is with individuals." It is impossible to tell how successful this appeal was, but at least the Commission had made an effort to reach beyond the urban audience to which it normally spoke.

The Commission did not take a public stand on the Ball resolution. The reason was undoubtedly fear of losing its tax-exempt status as an educational group, for its leaders clearly favored the ideas in the Senate proposal. In April, Clark Eichelberger wrote to the Studies Committee suggesting that the fourth report deal with the problem of security. "The public is overwhelmingly in favor of an international police force," he averred, "but the idea has not really been broken down to an examination of international air force, United Nations control of strategic bases, etc. etc." The members concurred and devoted themselves to a detailed study of the mechanics of using force to keep the peace.[5]

The reaction of the internationalists to the Ball resolution, while it led to some effective activity, revealed a crucial weakness in the movement. For months internationalist leaders had prepared for a major campaign to arouse the American people. When an obscure group of senators finally provided them with a specific program, they responded by creating three new organizations to secure public support. The overlapping activities of the United Nations Association, the Non-Partisan Council and the Women's Action Committee probably bewildered as many Americans as they enlightened. The frantic claims that this was the last chance to stop World War III rang hollow, while the plans to put pressure on congressmen and senators were far too elaborate for a non-election year. In their eagerness to crush isolationism, they risked overselling the Ball resolution.

The sole restraint on the internationalists in 1943 was financial. The war had diverted the giving of many wealthy individuals who had sustained the movement in the 1920's and the 1930's. The Carnegie Endowment had come to the rescue, providing an increasingly larger share of the operating funds of the Commission to Study the Organization of Peace ($24,000 in 1943) and subsidizing such new groups as the Non-Partisan Council. Malcolm Davis became the officer in charge of supervising these Endowment grants, but an intense sympathy with the internationalist cause hampered his judgment. He supported each new group with great zest, failing to restrain the naive optimism of its founders. Thus the Endowment, which could have served as the coordinator of the internationalist movement by rationalizing activities, forbidding duplication and stating priorities, instead encouraged the multiplication of groups and functions. The result was an incoherent movement, split into too many competing units, which failed to take full advantage of the favorable wartime climate and the impetus provided by Senator Ball and his associates.[6]

I

"I am dedicating my life to arousing the American people so that the Senate cannot prevent the United States from taking its place in world leadership," Wendell Willkie declared in a speech on March 26, 1943. In the four months since the election Willkie had been busy writing an account of his trip around the world. Gardner Cowles and Joseph Barnes, who had accompanied him, prepared outlines and drafts. Each morning Willkie went to the apartment of Irita Van Doren, the New

York *Herald Tribune's* book-review editor and a good friend, and together they worked on the final draft. Cowles, Barnes and Mrs. Van Doren helped give it a professional touch, but the blunt prose bore Willkie's unmistakable imprint. When he was finished, he took the manuscript to Simon and Schuster and agreed on a title: *One War, One Peace, One World.* On April 8 it appeared under the shorter and more dramatic name *One World.*[7]

Two thirds of the book was an anecdotal account of Willkie's journey to the Middle East, Russia and China, punctuated with brief philosophical comments. On the second page Willkie stated his thesis: "There are no distant points in the world any longer." He then went on to say that his trip had taught him that the destiny of the United States was intimately connected with the fate of the peoples of Europe, Asia and Africa. He described his ten-day visit to Russia, noting the heroic efforts of the Soviets in the war against Germany and discounting the possibility of future antagonism. He admitted that Stalin was an enigma, but he believed that "it is possible for Russia and America, perhaps the two most powerful countries in the world, to work together for the economic welfare and the peace of the world." He was even more optimistic about China. Praising Madame Chiang Kai-shek and the Generalissimo, he asserted that a new China was emerging that would make western domination impossible in the future.

In the last third of *One World,* Willkie drew on his experiences to deliver a sermon on internationalism. His main impression, he wrote, was "that there exists in the world today a gigantic reservoir of good will toward us, the American people." In order to preserve this reservoir, which was filled with "the clear, invigorating water of freedom," the American people would have to assume their rightful responsibilities in the world. Rejecting both isolationism and imperialism as disastrous policies, Willkie said the United States must work for the creation of a new world of freedom for every race and nation. He called for peace "planned on a world basis," and he urged that the United States begin immediately by establishing a United Nations Council with representatives from all the member nations. Beyond that, he refused to be specific, saying simply that "successful instruments of either national or international government are the result of growth." The important thing was to begin the cooperative venture. "Continents and oceans are plainly only parts of a whole, seen, as I have seen them, from the air," he wrote. "And it is inescapable that there can be no peace for any part of the world unless the foundations of peace are made secure throughout all parts of the world." [8]

Reviewers were kind to *One World*. Reinhold Niebuhr found Willkie's internationalism "wise" and was impressed by his "remarkable grasp of the essential realities." Malcolm Cowley thought Willkie had come a long way in his thinking and that now he was "exactly 128 years ahead of the State Department," which Cowley saw still planning in terms of the Congress of Vienna. Other commentators praised *One World* as "an exceedingly interesting report," "one of the hardest blows ever struck against . . . isolationism," and "an eagle's view" of the world. A few found Willkie's ideas naive, but the only strong criticism came from a Catholic newspaper in Massachusetts which condemned it as "pro-Russian."

The American people proved even more receptive; *One World* enjoyed the most phenomenal sale of any book published in the United States. Simon and Schuster had prepared a first printing of 40,000 copies in a one-dollar paperback edition and 13,000 more in cloth selling for two dollars. These were sold in two days, and the publishers soon had two printing plants working twenty-four hours a day from four sets of plates. At the end of the first week 197,130 copies had been sold; within three weeks *One World* had passed the half-million mark, and sales continued at 25,000 a day. Simon and Schuster, which had budgeted $15,000 for promotion, quadrupled this figure, placing advertisements in fifty newspapers across the nation. By the first week in May, Willkie's book headed the non-fiction list in every city surveyed by the New York *Times.*

Much of the appeal of *One World* lay in Willkie's report on China and Russia. Most Americans knew little about these distant allies, and they were eager to learn about them first-hand from Willkie, who had talked with their leaders and gone where reporters were normally forbidden. Equally important, Simon and Schuster marketed the book brilliantly, distributing the paperback edition through magazine outlets at the same time that bookstores sold the hard-cover copies. The Union News Company stocked it in 75,000 outlets, mostly newsstands and cigar stores, and set up eye-catching displays of the book in its choicer locations. By saturating the market, Simon and Schuster enabled Willkie's message to reach millions of Americans.[9]

". . . we hope devoutly that Mr. Willkie speaks for the entire Republican party," wrote a reviewer in *Changing World*. Most political observers were sure that he did not, but two midwestern Republicans, Deneen Watson and Dennison B. Hull, decided to capitalize on the success of *One World*. Without consulting Willkie, Watson, a young lawyer who had been an aide to Illinois Governor Dwight Green, announced the formation of the Republican Postwar Policy Association. On May 3 seventy-five Republican leaders attended a luncheon at the La Salle Hotel in Chicago to launch the new organization, which would be financed by Hull, a wealthy architect active in the internationalist movement. Watson told his fellow Republicans that unless the party repudiated isolationism, they would lose again in 1944. "The way to beat Mr. Roosevelt in his Fourth Term grab is to take the foreign issue away from him," Watson declared. The group then adopted two resolutions, one calling for the immediate formation of a United Nations Council and another backing the Ball resolution.

The Postwar Policy Association, dubbed "Betrayal, Inc." by the Chicago *Tribune*, undertook a campaign to ensure the adoption of an internationalist plank at the 1944 Republican national convention. Watson hired Leo Casey, a New York public-relations man who had worked for Willkie in 1940, to help him in the East. For the next few months Watson and Casey spoke to hundreds of state and county leaders who would be delegates, warning them that a failure to embrace internationalism would be politically disastrous. They held a second meeting in New York in July, at which Watson spoke to three hundred eastern Republicans, who responded by passing a resolution calling on the party to support "an organization of nations to assume full responsibility in maintaining world peace." [10]

Watson's activities, especially his direct approach to the party stalwarts, alarmed National Chairman Harrison Spangler. Though Willkie had kept aloof from the Postwar Policy Association, Spangler viewed it as a veiled drive to secure his nomination in 1944. On May 31 Spangler retaliated by creating the Republican Postwar Advisory Council to draw up a statement of policy on the postwar world. The Council was composed of forty-nine party leaders, including governors, congressmen, senators and national committeemen, but Willkie's name was conspicuously absent. When asked about this omission, Spangler blandly replied that Willkie held no official position within the party structure, but that his views would always be welcome. Pre-war isolationists predominated, with Arthur Vandenberg, senior Republican on the Senate Foreign Relations Committee, the likely leader. In a press comment on June 1, Vandenberg agreed to serve on the Council, commenting, "We shall vigorously cooperate with the forces of international progress, but we shall remain irrevocably the independent and sovereign United States of America." A few days later Willkie issued a statement, saying he found it "regrettable" that men like Senators Ball and Burton had been left off the Council. "I, of course," he added, "intend to fight for those things in which I believe, irrespective of the action of any pre-convention committee."

The creation of the Postwar Advisory Council, despite its isolationist cast, marked a significant victory for Republican internationalists. Ball's resolution in the Senate, Willkie's broad appeal in *One World*, Watson's maneuvering among the party professionals—these tactics had forced Spangler to acknowledge the importance of the postwar issue. He dared not risk splitting the party, and thus he sought, as *Time* noted, "to build bridges across the deep chasms that divide its leaders on U.S. foreign policy." [11]

I I

In Congress the Connally subcommittee resented the intense publicity stirred up by the B_2H_2 resolution. At their first meeting, on March 31, the senators decided not to hold any public hearings. Wallace White suggested that they simply table the measure without further discussion, but Vandenberg objected, warning that then the administration would accuse them of choking off discussion of the future peace. The subcommittee finally agreed to ask Secretary Hull for his viewpoint.

At the next meeting, on April 7, Hull reinforced the subcommittee's reluctance to act on the Ball resolution. He reiterated his fear that a Senate debate on postwar issues would lead to attacks on Britain's policy in India and Russia's territorial ambitions in eastern Europe. "Hull repeatedly said that anything of this sort could be seriously damaging to our war unity," Vandenberg reported. In response to a question from Senator Gillette, the Secretary acknowledged that "a mild, general statement of postwar cooperation" would be helpful to reassure our allies of America's postwar intentions, but he felt the risks in the Senate were still too great.

A week later the sponsors of the B_2H_2 resolution—"the four horse-men," as Vandenberg dubbed them—came before the subcommittee in a conciliatory mood. Ball said they did not insist on the language of their measure or all the points covered by it—they would accept any reasonable compromise proposal that did not totally emasculate their resolution. The vital point, the four senators argued, was that the Senate go on record in favor of American entry into a postwar security organization. They admitted that such an action would not be legally binding on a future Congress; it would be a "moral commitment," but this would be enough to allay the fears of our allies that once again the United States would retreat into peacetime isolation.

Their plea failed to move the members of the subcommittee. The group met several times again in the spring, but it refused to take any specific action, preferring to let the whole issue drift. In May the members met with Winston Churchill when he came to Washington to confer with the President, and they were delighted to find that he believed discussion of postwar issues premature. In his diary Vandenberg recorded that Churchill had taken him aside during a reception at the British embassy to warn against "opening Pandora's box." This concern for the war effort was the decisive factor in the subcommittee's decision to continue sitting on the Ball resolution. "I do not want to wind up fighting this war all alone," Arthur Vandenberg commented. "If we must quarrel with our Allies, I'd rather do it *after victory*. . . ." [12]

Throughout the spring, senators were deluged with letters urging them to act on the Ball resolution. In March the wives of Senators Ball and Hatch set up a mail-answering service to cope with the enthusiastic response to their husbands' proposal. As the internationalist organizations rallied behind the B_2H_2 measure, the volume of correspondence steadily increased, running twenty-to-one in its favor. J. A. Migel, the vice president of the American Silk Spinning Company, wrote to Senator Theodore F. Green of Rhode Island, urging him to support "the first step toward International Law and Federation." Migel hastened to add, "As a practical business man, I am not prompted in this thought by any false idealism." Irving Fisher wrote to Green to urge "collective policing" of the world, while a Missouri history professor told Senator Truman that he hoped "the spirit of Woodrow Wilson will at last come to full fruition." Senator Connally received a stream of letters urging him to release the Ball resolution from his subcommittee. In his replies he avoided a direct answer, simply saying that personally he favored an international organization and vowing, "We ought never to have another war like the present one." [13]

Women's groups were the most active in pressing for the B_2H_2 resolution. The American Association of University Women and the National League of Women Voters sent letters to Connally which they released to the press. The president of the Quota Club, an organization of women executives, sent Connally a telegram urging the Senate to voice "its determination to cooperate with other United Nations in a system of collective security." In their annual meeting of June 1943 the directors of the General Federation of Women's Clubs adopted a resolution calling for "international machinery for the establishment of a just peace and prevention of dire aggression." Mrs. Esther Caukin Brunauer, director of the AAUW and organizer of the Women's Action Committee, was responsible for promoting much of this activity. In July she climaxed it by sending each member of the Connally subcommittee a lengthy memorandum on the Ball resolution, which argued strongly for an international police force. "The establishment of a United Nations military force to suppress any attempt at military aggression," she wrote, "is the one measure that would really carry the world beyond the point where it was from 1931 to 1939." [14]

Senators Ball, Burton, Hatch and Hill actively campaigned to ensure public support. They spoke on the radio, addressed mass rallies and made public appearances throughout the Northeast. The Free World Association planned a debate in which Senators Ball and Hatch would defend their resolution against Senator Gerald P. Nye and another isolationist, but this event was canceled when no one could be found to join with Nye. The wives of the four senators traveled with their husbands, speaking to groups of ladies and posing for newspaper pictures. Joseph Ball proved to be the most effective speaker of the foursome, and he soon had more engagements than he could fill. In his addresses he hammered away at the need for prompt action, calling his measure the "Win-the-Peace-Now" resolution. "In view of Senate action on the Versailles treaty twenty-three years ago," he told a New York audience in April, "our allies can scarcely be blamed for questioning whether the United States will collaborate as effectively in maintaining peace as it is now in winning the war."

The most controversial feature of the B_2H_2 resolution was the fifth point, which called for an international police force to prevent aggression. Senator Robert Taft, a leading pre-war Republican isolationist, saw it as a threat to American security. "It must be just as easy for such a force to bomb New York," he declared, "as it will be to bomb Berlin as a punishment for what is found to be aggression." Appearing on one of the "For This We Fight" radio broadcasts sponsored by the Commission to Study the Organization of Peace, Taft stated, "My own view is that an international superstate with an international police force is fantastic." In a commencement address at Grove City College in Pennsylvania, he reiterated his objections to any surrender of sovereignty by the United States, saying that he favored a world organization "along the same general lines suggested in the League of Nations." Senator Hiram Johnson, the extreme isolationist from California, was blunter. He termed an international police force "preposterous and absurd." [15]

These attacks led the Associated Press to conduct a poll of the Senate which was released on April 19. All ninety-six senators were asked whether they favored "committing the Senate and the country now to a post-war course of preserving the peace through an international police force?" To the dismay of internationalists, only twenty-four replied yes. Thirty-two senators gave negative responses, and forty more refused to commit themselves. "This would seem to end all Senate chance for the Ball resolution," commented Vandenberg in his diary, "because even its authors agree that it would be fatal to have a sharply divided Senate." Though the *New Republic* felt "it is nonsense to say that the battle for world cooperation to keep the peace has already been lost," Edgar A. Mowrer believed that the poll indicated that the chances for Senate passage of the B_2H_2 resolution were "well nigh hopeless." [16]

A Gallup poll published on May 2 revealed that the American people disagreed sharply with the Senate. When asked if the United States should participate in "an international police force after the war is over to try to keep peace throughout the world," 74 percent said yes. Only 14 percent expressed opposition, with 12 percent having no opinion. A breakdown by political affiliations showed that nearly as many Republicans as Democrats favored the idea. The hopes of internationalists soared with these figures, but professional pollsters were dubious. Jerome Bruner thought that few Americans really understood what an international police force involved. ". . . we are for it in the same way as we are for vaccination," he wrote. "Force stops aggression. Vaccination stops smallpox. Never mind the niceties." Another expert, Ross Stagner, doubted that many of the 74 percent who favored an international police force would accept "the reduction in national power" inherent in such a proposal. The *New Yorker* was equally skeptical. "Asking a man whether he wants an international police force is like asking him whether he wants the Rockettes," the editors commented. Considering that in 1939 another Gallup poll had showed 46 percent of the people favoring an international police force at a time when isolationism was still dominant, the internationalists had little basis for their optimism. [17]

The procrastination of the Connally subcommittee and the controversy over an international police force disturbed Representative J. William Fulbright of Arkansas. Only thirty-eight years old, Fulbright had moved from the presidency of the University of Arkansas into Congress, winning his election on a "no more war" platform. In his maiden speech in the House he declared that "our representatives should begin negotiations at once with our allies to formulate a specific and concrete system for collective security of the nations of the world." The resolution he introduced in February calling for a study of ways to preserve peace had gone unnoticed. On April 5 he tried again, submitting a new resolution that proposed "the creation of appropriate international machinery with power adequate to prevent future aggression and to maintain lasting peace." Much vaguer than the Ball resolution, and only hinting at the idea of a police force, this measure attracted little attention at first. In an effort to win administration support, Fulbright sent a copy to Sumner Welles. "I believe that we can secure favorable action on this Resolution in the House and that such action would be of assistance to the sponsors of the Ball Resolution in the Senate," Fulbright told Welles. The Under Secretary conferred with Hull, and then wrote back a guarded letter that offered little encouragement.

In early June, when it had become apparent that the Senate did not plan to act on the B_2H_2 resolution, members of the House saw a rare opportunity to take the initiative on foreign policy. Aware of the public desire for Congress to declare itself on the postwar issue, the House Foreign Affairs Committee met on June 12 to consider the Fulbright resolution. Keeping their deliberations secret, the members proceeded to redraft the measure, dropping out the reference to preventing future aggression in order to avoid any suggestion of an international police force. On June 15 Fulbright quietly introduced the new version of his proposal, which simply asked Congress to go on record "as favoring the creation of appropriate international machinery with power adequate to establish and maintain a just and lasting peace among the nations of the world, and as favoring participation by the United States therein." Later that day the committee voted to report favorably on the new Fulbright resolution, with such strong pre-war isolationists as John M. Vorys of Ohio and Hamilton Fish of New York concurring.[18]

On June 16 Vorys, the senior Republican member of the Foreign Affairs Committee, rose on the House floor to urge consideration of the Fulbright resolution. Pointing out that it was neither a blueprint for peace nor a binding commitment on Congress, he described it as "merely a statement of congressional preference in postwar policies." But such a statement was significant, he continued, for it would inform the world that "we prefer post-war participation—not post-war isolation." Though Jessie Sumner, die-hard isolationist from Illinois, charged that "it might mean giving away rights of this Government under the Constitution," other members of Congress praised the committee's action. Hamilton Fish told his colleagues that he voted for the Fulbright resolution in committee because he felt it was time to begin discussing the future peace, and then he astonished everyone by declaring, "If this is the people's war, it must be a people's peace." Henry Wallace had apparently made a convert.

The new resolution received extremely favorable treatment in the press. *Time* called it "a crystal-clear statement of American intentions to help make a good peace," while the editors of the *Nation* labeled it "a notable step toward prevention of World War III." The New York *Times* liked the simple wording of the resolution: "It says what needs to be said at this time." Senator Connally raised the only discordant note, calling it "mild and cryptic." He said the Senate Foreign Relations Committee would give careful consideration to any expression of opinion by the House, but his subcommittee planned to report out a resolution "of our own making." [19]

Representative Fulbright once again appealed to the administration for help. In a letter to the President on June 26 he stressed the political risks for the Democrats in "cautiously holding back in the effort to evolve a positive foreign policy for the post-war era." He pointed out that the Republicans were taking the lead in this area, thus threatening "to nullify foreign policy as an issue in the next campaign." "I have always thought," Fulbright told Roosevelt, "that your own success has been largely due to your courage in boldly taking the lead in the development of progressive solutions for our troubles." Impressed by this plea, the President asked Hull to consider pushing the Fulbright resolution. "It seems to me pretty good," Roosevelt wrote, "and if we can get it through the House it might work in the Senate also."

On June 28 Hull replied, informing the President that several days earlier he had spoken with Speaker Sam Rayburn about the Fulbright resolution. Rayburn had told Hull that Representative James Wadsworth, a Republican internationalist from New York, had asked him to hold off on the measure until fall. Wadsworth thought that after exposure to the sentiment in their home districts over the summer, the fifty Republicans who now opposed the resolution could be reduced to less than a dozen. "The Speaker said that he then called a meeting of Fulbright, Wadsworth and the Floor leaders, or at least John McCormack, and after talking the matter over, it was agreed that the resolution would be taken up when the House reconvenes in September," Hull reported. The Secretary endorsed this procedure to Roosevelt, but added that the Senate was "very jealous of its prerogatives on foreign policy."

The President asked Sumner Welles to prepare a reply to Fulbright, which went out under Roosevelt's signature on June 30. He told the Arkansas representative that the adoption of his resolution "would be in the highest degree desirable." "I am, of course," he continued, "in favor of having your resolution acted upon as soon as there is reasonable assurance that no prejudicial amendments would be adopted and that the largest possible measure of support can be obtained for its passage." He did not indicate when he thought that would be.[20]

On July 2, a week before Congress adjourned for the summer, Senator Arthur Vandenberg introduced a postwar resolution with fellow Republican Wallace White after he failed to find a Democrat who would join him. Their measure was even more general than the Fulbright resolution, calling simply for the winning of the war and "the participation of the United States in post-war cooperation between sovereign nations." In order not to alienate any supporters, Vandenberg and White added a final clause stating that this must be done "with faithful recognition of American responsibilities and American interests." In his diary Vandenberg noted that this resolution was framed to bar "all 'World Staters' " and assure "the continuance of the American Flag over the Capitol."

Senators Ball, Burton and Hill also spoke out on July 2, and only illness prevented Senator Hatch from joining them. All three demanded that the Connally subcommittee end its procrastination and report out their resolution when Congress reconvened in the fall. "If there is to be hope of peace there must be a collective world security system," declared Lister Hill. "The peace can be lost because of too little, too late," Ball warned, adding that his group would wait only until mid-October for the Senate Foreign Relations Committee to act—after that they would take their case to the floor of the Senate. Vandenberg disparaged this demand by saying, "we do not threaten easily," but Ball had shrewdly played on the administration's fear of an open debate. By serving notice that they would not tolerate further committee delay in the fall, the B_2H_2 senators hoped to force Roosevelt and Hull to permit Congress to declare its postwar intentions.[21]

III

The hostility of administration officials to the Ball resolution stemmed in large measure from their own indecision. Anthony Eden's visit to Washington in March compelled the State Department to focus on postwar plans, but at first officials could not reach any firm agreement. On March 21 Winston Churchill added to the confusion in a radio address to the British people in which he outlined his ideas of world order. He called for an international organization in very general terms, but his only specific suggestion was the immediate creation of a Council of Europe and a Council of Asia to handle the postwar problems of those continents. The American press displayed great interest in Churchill's proposal and wondered what role he envisioned for the United States.

On March 26 Sumner Welles submitted a "Draft Constitution" prepared by his subcommittee on international organization. This plan called for a three-branch world body which combined elements of Roosevelt's Four Policemen with Churchill's regional approach: at the top, an executive committee representing the United States, Russia, Britain and China to deal exclusively with all threats to world peace, but acting only in unanimity; an eleven-member council composed of the Big Four and seven regional representatives—two from Europe, two from Latin America, one from the Far East, one from the Middle East and one from the British dominions, to decide when there was a threat to the peace or an act of aggression; and, finally, a general conference in which all member nations would be represented. There was no provision for an international police force in the Draft Constitution; instead, each nation was to keep armed contingents available for use by the world body.

President Roosevelt evidently liked this plan, for when he met with Eden on March 27, he cited its major features in describing the kind of world organization he preferred. He told the British Foreign Minister that the regional councils Churchill had suggested were out of the question. He and Welles firmly stated their conviction that "all the United Nations should be members of one body for the purposes of recommending policy; that this body should be world-wide in scope." Roosevelt then reiterated his belief that the Big Four should make "the real decisions," since they "would be the powers for many years to come that would have to police the world." Eden indicated that he had been surprised by Churchill's regional approach and that he shared Roosevelt's belief in organizing on a "global basis." Hull sat quietly through this exchange of views, letting the President and Welles outline the American position.[22]

In early April, a few days after Eden's return to England, the *Saturday Evening Post* published an article by Forrest Davis entitled "Roosevelt's

World Blueprint." Davis had held a confidential interview with the President in December 1942, and his article, which Roosevelt had read and approved in advance, was the fullest account the public had yet received of the President's postwar plans. Davis made clear that Roosevelt was preoccupied with security against future aggression, and that he did not share Wallace's concern over "welfare politics" or a "continuing revolution" in the world. "At this time," Davis wrote, "Mr. Roosevelt primarily is concerned not with aspirations toward a better world . . . but with the cold, realistic techniques, or instruments, needed to make those aspirations work. This means that he is concentrating on power." Describing the President as closer to Theodore Roosevelt than Woodrow Wilson in his outlook, Davis said he envisioned the United Nations developing into "a society of free states, less ambitious and constraining than the League of Nations, but organic and capable of growth." Davis made no mention of Roosevelt's Four Policemen, stating only that the President opposed an international air corps or any form of a world police force. Roosevelt favored a world association on the Pan-American model, Davis concluded, with a reliance on common interest and consultation rather than binding commitments.[23]

Cordell Hull was delighted with the Davis article, which he interpreted as a rebuff to Henry Wallace and Summer Welles. One of his loyal aides, James C. Dunn, prepared an analysis of the article for Hull, concluding, "I find that the President's line follows the general ideas you have expressed." In a conversation with Breckinridge Long on April 21, the Secretary voiced his continuing resentment of Wallace and Welles, who he felt were responsible for "stirring up the Senate." Three days later he met with Isaiah Bowman, Norman Davis, Myron Taylor and Leo Pasvolsky, a committee that soon became known as the Informal Agenda Group, to consider how to proceed with plans for international organization. Bowman and Taylor both advised the Secretary to begin drawing up blueprints; "a draft," they argued, "is indispensable as a basis for understanding the problems involved."

For the next few weeks Hull mulled over this advice. He agreed on the need to begin writing a specific plan, but he wanted to bypass Welles' subcommittee and its Draft Constitution. Hull disliked the regional features of this plan, but even more he resented the fact that Welles was its author. He finally hit on an ingenious solution. On July 12 he sent letters to the several subcommittees, suspending their operations while the Department reviewed their work and decided on basic policies to pursue in the future. The suspension proved permanent, and from this time on, the Informal Agenda Group, composed of men Hull trusted, became the agency that drafted the charter for a new international organization. Thus, after a year and a half of skirmishing, Hull had finally broken Sumner Welles' domination of the Department's postwar planning.[24]

During this period the President experimented with a functional approach to the problems of peace. On February 23 he informed reporters that the administration was considering calling a United Nations conference in the spring to discuss "post-war food." This revelation caught the State Department by surprise. Hull, vacationing in Florida, was skeptical, fearing "political hazards" which might "injuriously affect our entire postwar program," but he permitted Welles to issue a public announcement that the conference would be held in the United States, probably in April. The press praised this move; *Newsweek* called it "the first test of the United Nations' resolve to win the peace." At a press conference on March 19 the President clarified the purpose of the meeting, pointing out that it would not deal with relief in the immediate postwar period. Instead, the delegates would consider the long-range issues of nutrition, means of improving agricultural techniques, and the distribution of the world's food supply. Two weeks later Roosevelt told reporters that the food conference was only the first in a series of United Nations meetings that were being planned to cover such topics as relief and postwar monetary problems.[25]

On March 30 the United States invited thirty-eight governments to send representatives to the food conference, which would be held in Hot Springs, Virginia. The delegates would be technical experts, not diplomats, and, to the dismay of the press, reporters would not be permitted to cover the deliberations. Editors across the country denounced Roosevelt for condoning "secret diplomacy," and in Congress several Republicans introduced resolutions demanding an investigation of the press ban, but Roosevelt held firm. When the conference opened on May 18 at the Homestead Hotel, reporters were limited to brief handouts from the State Department and occasional briefings by the American delegation. In retaliation, journalists lampooned the meeting, commenting on the sumptuous meals served the delegates and on the two-hundred military policemen guarding the delegates "against the menace of 50-odd newsmen." Despite these bad notices, the conference proceeded smoothly, concluding in early June with the creation of an Interim Commission on Food and Agriculture pending the establishment of a permanent United Nations agency.

President Roosevelt received the delegates at the White House after the conference adjourned. Speaking to them in the East Room, Roosevelt called this first United Nations gathering "epoch-making." "You have demonstrated beyond question," he told the delegates, "that free peoples all over the world can agree upon a common course of action and upon common machinery of action." When he finished speaking, the audience moved out to the White House garden, where Henry Wallace and Cordell Hull joined the President in the receiving line. While the Marine Corps band played, the delegates from all over the world shook hands with the American leaders. There was a slight pause in the line when the representative of Ethiopia, a country the League of Nations had so conspicuously failed to protect, stopped to give the President a picture of Emperor Haile Selassie.[26]

The successful outcome of the Food and Agriculture Conference encouraged Roosevelt to tackle the problem of postwar relief in the same way. On June 11 the State Department released the text of a draft agreement that had been formulated by the Big Four. After other governments studied the plan, a conference would be held to create a United Nations Relief and Rehabilitation Administration. Plans for UNRRA dated back to June 1942, when American and British representatives began discussing how they could aid the populations of areas liberated from German occupation and resettle displaced persons. In the fall of 1942 President Roosevelt approved the plans that emerged from these conversations and appointed Herbert H. Lehman, the former governor of New York, to be Director of a new Office of Foreign Relief and Rehabilitation Operations in the State Department. Lehman supervised American relief activities in North Africa and, together with Assistant Secretary of State Dean Acheson, began planning the American role in UNRRA.

On June 9, 1943, President Roosevelt informed the Republican and Democratic leaders of Congress that he planned to secure American participation in UNRRA by an executive agreement. The Congressional leadership raised no objections, but when Senator Vandenberg learned of this arrangement, he wrote to Hull protesting that the administration was bypassing the Senate on a vital postwar matter. On July 6, 1943, Vandenberg introduced a resolution in Congress calling for an investigation of the UNRRA draft agreement to determine whether it was a treaty requiring Senate approval. "I think this is the initial preview of methods by which post-war plans are to be made," Vandenberg declared, "and we may as well find out precisely what the pattern is to be."

In a letter to Charles L. McNary of Oregon, the Senate minority leader, Vandenberg repeated this charge, expressing a fear that Roosevelt and Hull planned to use executive agreements for all postwar commitments.[27]

The next morning, in an unprecedented display of speed, the Senate Foreign Relations Committee unanimously approved Vandenberg's resolution. Connally was furious at the administration for placing him in such an awkward situation. He appointed himself chairman of a five-man subcommittee and arranged for Hull and Dean Acheson to testify before it that afternoon at 2:30. At this meeting Connally led the attack, chastising Hull for setting "a dangerous precedent" by ignoring the Senate in the establishment of a major United Nations agency. Connally became so abusive that Hull walked out of the room, and Vandenberg and Acheson served as peacemakers, finally getting Hull to permit the Senate subcommittee to suggest changes in the UNRRA draft. The next day Vandenberg told the Senate that he had no objections to the idea of postwar relief, but he wanted assurance that "Congress is to be a constitutional partner in the plans and the decisions which shall liquidate the war."

The Senate subcommittee met again with Dean Acheson on July 14 and offered some changes in the UNRRA agreement. More important, the members asked the administration to submit the proposal to Congress as a joint resolution after it was signed so that it could be acted on by both Houses. On August 10 Hull informed Roosevelt of this request and asked his approval, warning that the UNRRA proposal was "imperiled." The President agreed, and on August 16, with Congress adjourned for the summer, Senators Theodore Green and Vandenberg met with Acheson and Francis B. Sayre of the State Department in Green's office. Acheson informed the senators that the Department had made the changes they had requested and that, once UNRRA was accepted by the other nations, the President would ask Congress to approve American entry by a joint resolution. The next day, when this arrangement was made public, Arthur Vandenberg declared, "I am hopeful that this mutual effort may be sufficiently successful to set a pattern for other post-war problems." [28]

For Roosevelt and Hull it was a sobering, but valuable, experience. They had overlooked the extreme sensitivity of the Senate, and this oversight had jeopardized an important international agreement. It must have reminded them of Wilson's tactless handling of the Senate in 1919 and served as a warning for the future. Roosevelt reacted by returning to his earlier emphasis on the war effort. In a fireside chat on July 28 in which he announced Mussolini's fall from power in Italy, the President declared: [29]

The United Nations are substantially agreed on the general objectives for the postwar world. They are also agreed that this is not the time to engage in an international discussion of *all* the terms of peace and *all* the details of the future. Let us win the war first. We must not relax our pressure on the enemy by taking time out to define every boundary and settle every political controversy in every part of the world. The all-important thing now is to get on with the war—and to win it.

I V

The United Nations Food and Agriculture Conference and the announcement of UNRRA failed to satisfy the American people. Stimulated by the B_2H_2 resolution and Willkie's *One World*, they wanted to know what else the government planned to do. Sensing this avid curiosity, publishers and magazine editors produced an outpouring of books and articles dealing with the postwar world. As a result, in the spring and summer of 1943, Americans had a chance to read and discuss every possible approach to the future peace.

The three prophets continued their call for a new world order. In a Detroit speech he had cleared with both Hull and Roosevelt, Henry Wallace called for a peace that would be "more than just a breathing space between the death of an old tyranny and the birth of a new one." Renewing the demand for a "people's peace," he promised that "the day of victory for humanity will come just as this night of terror and desolation will pass." President Roosevelt was delighted with the speech, telling Wallace, "You drew blood from the Cave Dwellers!" Sumner Welles, chastened by Hull, was more circumspect. In a speech in North Carolina on May 31 he advocated an eventual international police force, but warned that it was still too early for the government to outline its specific plans for peace. In June the Columbia University Press published a collection of Welles' earlier, bolder speeches under the title *The World of the Four Freedoms*.[30]

Though Wendell Willkie did not make any speeches in the spring, *One World* carried his message across the nation. By June it had sold over one million copies, becoming only the third non-fiction book to do so, and achieving this distinction in record time. Willkie's mail tripled, and he was forced to hire two additional secretaries to handle it. He sold the movie rights to Twentieth Century-Fox for $100,000, and then donated this sum, along with all royalties, to the American Red Cross and other war charities. Pocket Books eventually sold over half a million copies of a twenty-five-cent edition, and the armed forces distributed fifty thousand more to servicemen overseas. Magazines published digests of the book, a condensed version ran in 107 daily newspapers, and foreign-language editions appeared throughout the world. "Count two readers for every copy," commented Edward Weeks, "and then guess how many million will have read Mr. Willkie before the year is out."

In July, Simon and Schuster joined with three other publishers to bring out *Prefaces to Peace,* an anthology containing *One World,* Hoover and Gibson's *The Problems of Lasting Peace,* and selected speeches by Summer Welles and Henry Wallace. In the introduction Henry Seidel Canby cited these authors as the men who had given "the best thinking to the postwar world." The Book-of-the-Month Club distributed over 300,000 copies as a bonus to its members, and it enjoyed a brisk sale in the bookstores. Many readers evidently agreed with the reviewer Henry Steele Commager, who noted, "The conviction is growing that if we do not succeed in writing a just and lasting peace, civilization itself will collapse." [31]

Advocates of a world federation believed passionately that this was the case. In an address to the American Society of International Law on May 1, 1943, Supreme Court Justice Owen J. Roberts called for a world order based on "supra-national law." He sketched out a design for a world parliament and an international court, but he avoided details, stressing instead the need "to arouse and enliven public sentiment in this country in support of an integration of our own and other nations in a world organization." Roberts was attracted by Clarence Streit's ideas, and he sent Secretary of State Hull copies of the Union Now plan. "I see no answer to the questions now arising," he wrote, "but federation of the democracies." Later in May, Harold Stassen, who had resigned as governor of Minnesota to become a lieutenant commander in the Navy, published articles in the *Saturday Evening Post* and the New York *Times Magazine* reiterating his plan for a world confederation. Like Roberts, he wanted a world parliament and a code of international justice, but he placed a greater emphasis on the use of force. He proposed "a United Nations Legion consisting of units of air, naval and mechanized land forces" to carry out the mandates of the world government.[32]

Ely Culbertson, the bridge expert, put forth by far the most detailed plan for world federation. Culbertson had been born in Romania, the son of an American mining engineer and a Russian mother. His father developed extensive oil holdings in southern Russia, and though young Ely had once been imprisoned by the Czarist regime for revolutionary activities, the Soviets expropriated his family's property after the Bolshevik Revolution. Suddenly penniless, Culbertson earned his living by playing cards and then developed a system of bidding which made him the world's leading authority on contract bridge. Convinced that playing cards formed "a world of pure power politics" which offered clues to international behavior, he set out in 1939 to design "a postwar world system which would be as orderly, logical and responsive as a deck of cards properly manipulated." By 1942 he had completed the outline of his scheme, which he sent to more than five hundred experts in international relations. After making some minor adjustments, he made his World Federation Plan public in 1943, first as an article in *Reader's Digest*, then as a pamphlet, finally as a book, *Total Peace*.

Culbertson set out to resolve the two dilemmas which he felt doomed all other approaches to peace. The first was how to create a world government strong enough to maintain order without infringing on the freedom and sovereignty of nations. He found the solution in regionalism, dividing the world into eleven "natural" regions with the strongest country in each area serving as the "initiating-state." He likened the world federation to the sun, with the eleven regional units revolving around it as planets, held in their orbits "by psycho-social and economic forces" which he failed to define. The central body would consist of a World Supreme Court, a two-chamber legislature, the World Trustees and the World Senate, and a World President serving a six-year term. The most unusual feature of this government, Culbertson explained, was that it "*does not govern,* in the usual sense of the word." The sole power it possessed was the "Prohibition of War." He called the World Government a "Peace Trust" to which the member nations surrendered the right to wage war in return for something of much greater value—absolute security from aggression. "For the first time in history," he told his readers, "our nation can do what no other nation has done before—*declare lasting peace on the rest of the world.*"

To solve the second dilemma, the creation of an international police force powerful enough to stop aggression yet safe enough not to become an instrument of tyranny, Culbertson put forward his most ingenious idea, the Quota Force. He proposed a world army made up of twelve units. Eleven would be national contingents composed of the troops of the dominant nation in each region, but the twelfth would be a truly international force—an integrated legion made up of soldiers from the small nations operating out of strategic bases around the world. Culbertson assigned a quota to each of the eleven dominant nations, with the United States receiving 20 percent, Britain and Russia 15 percent, and others lower figures, for a total of 78 percent of the military force in the world. The international force would consist of 22 percent, and thus be larger than any single national army, yet not large enough to dominate the world on its own. The result, Culbertson reasoned, would be that each nation would possess enough military strength to defend itself but not enough for aggression. The Quota Force would place war into "a strait jacket tighter than any yet devised." [33]

Though Culbertson claimed he was trying to bridge the gap between the idealists who clamored for international organization and the realists who wished to rely on military alliances, he won little support from either group. But he did attract attention. Most internationalists dismissed him as an imperialist who used the rhetoric of world federation to advocate a plan for big-power domination of the postwar world. Albert Guerard thought that Culbertson was "deficient in the true international spirit," while Louis Fischer charged that his plan "creates a paradise for the major powers." Warning that "mathematics is not the soul of politics," Fischer concluded that "Culbertson is dealing the old cards. He almost makes you think—if you don't watch closely—that the cards are new. But they are old, and the deal is old."

A few internationalists disagreed. L. S. Rowe, the director general of the Pan American Union, sent a copy of the World Federation scheme to Leo Pasvolsky, endorsing it as a "very interesting plan" and arranging an appointment for Culbertson. Hamilton Holt enthusiastically called the Quota Force "striking, original, realistic and imaginative." Herbert M. Merrill, a *Nation* reader from Schenectady, New York, rebutted Fischer's criticism in a letter to the editors. Praising Culbertson for his revolutionary proposal, Merrill wrote in June 1943: [34]

> As for the "nature of military weapons," I might add that atomic power is almost certain to be used in any third world war which we are stupid enough to permit. There would be enough energy in a single uranium-235 bomb to erase a city like London or New York completely from the map. . . . If we're not ready to go "whole hog or none" now, *Homo sapiens* may never have another chance.

In the spring and summer of 1943 many commentators were much franker than Culbertson in advocating big-power domination of the postwar world. In *Newsweek*, Raymond Moley praised Churchill's proposal for Councils of Europe and Asia as "blunt, down-to-earth realism." In a speech in June, Moley declared that "the peace of the world will depend upon the collective will of the big four of the United Nations." In *Life*, Henry Luce published a long article by John K. Jessup advocating "a Sino-Russo-Anglo-American agreement to keep the peace of the world," and sent reprints to John Foster Dulles, Hamilton Holt and other internationalists. The most candid call for postwar alliances came from Henry J. Taylor, a businessman who had become a reporter on world affairs. After a trip to the fighting fronts in 1943, Taylor wrote a book entitled *Men in Motion*, in which he denied that American failure to enter the League had led to World War II. "Europe let herself down," he wrote, warning against American involvement in "some grand new world order." Instead, Taylor proposed a limited alliance with England and France to establish a stable balance of power after the war.[35]

In a four-part series in *Collier's* in June, Herbert Hoover and Hugh Gibson spelled out in greater detail their cautious plans for the postwar world. Obviously upset by Willkie's idealism, they began by asserting, "To many people, global planning is a field where imagination can engage in unrestrained play. It is indeed a playground where they may blow gigantic bubbles by dipping their pipes in suds of human kindness." Calling themselves realists, they denied that "a world-wide political and social revolution" was in progress. They renewed their suggestion that the major powers, acting as "Trustees of Peace," avoid an immediate postwar settlement and instead dominate the world during a long transitional period devoted to relief and reconstruction. "Then," they wrote, "when the world is stable and on the road to prosperity, the next step, the creation of a world organization, can take place." [36]

Another Republican, Clarence Buddington Kelland, proposed a far more elaborate plan in a speech to the National Republican Club in August. Kelland, a well-known writer of popular fiction and pre-war isolationist, was Republican National Committeeman from Arizona and a member of Spangler's Postwar Advisory Council. In his address he outlined "five zones of safety" as the basis of postwar American security. The first two were alliances with Britain, Russia and China to occupy the defeated Axis nations and to provide for joint military action to preserve peace. As insurance against the breakup of the Big Four, however, Kelland wanted the United States to sign an ironclad defensive alliance with Britain as a third zone of safety. His fourth zone consisted of a pact with the Latin American nations to resist any attack on the Western Hemisphere. Finally, in case all these arrangements failed, the United States should maintain overwhelming military strength as an absolute guarantee of its security. Calling for a five-ocean navy, Kelland declared, "We must so ring our land with defenses that no nation, no coalition of nations, shall be able to penetrate our fortification to reach our shores."

In presenting this scheme, which the editors of the *Nation* dubbed "a post-war variety of 'America First,'" Kelland made clear his intense nationalism. He savagely attacked Henry Wallace as "the gentleman who would cure all earthly ills with the fairy's gift of a quart of milk a day," and he insisted that the peace structure be built with "the granite of reality" and "the steel of fact" rather than with "the cobwebs of mawkish, impractical, imponderable idealism." Above all, Kelland stressed the importance of retaining national sovereignty. "We will collaborate but we will not amalgamate," he proclaimed. "We will become part of no Utopian Super-state, no partner in Union Now, no tail wagging at the end of any dog."

The five zones of safety symbolized a resurgence of traditional isolationism. Though Kelland used the rhetoric of internationalism, he asked the American people to place their ultimate reliance on a go-it-alone policy backed by armed might. In an August 16 speech in San Francisco, Roane Waring, national commander of the American Legion, also came out against "placing the destiny of this America of ours in the hands of any international organization of any kind under any circumstances." Declaring that he was a "nationalist" and not an isolationist, Waring particularly opposed an international police force. The editors of *Collier's*, objecting to the "inferiority-complex sales talk" of Wallace and Willkie, urged Americans to stand proudly on their own. They favored postwar alliances but they were prepared "to go it alone" if necessary, relying on America's enormous power. "The Eagle, in short, has excellent claws, actual and potential," the editors concluded. "He can best serve himself and the rest of the world by henceforth—generously but also hardheadedly—acting his age, size and power." [37]

By far the most sophisticated and influential formulation of the realistic viewpoint came from Walter Lippmann. As an editor of the *New Republic* he had crusaded for American entry into World War I and he had helped Wilson prepare his peace program. Though he became disillusioned with the Treaty of Versailles and opposed the League of Nations, throughout the inter-war years he advocated an active American role in world affairs in his daily newspaper column, and no one ever accused *him* of isolationism. Lippmann supported Willkie in 1940, and though they remained personal friends, he strongly disapproved of the idealistic internationalism Willkie championed, terming it "a dangerous doctrine." When *One World* appeared, Lippmann had nearly completed a book which he hoped would serve as an effective antidote. "I felt it wasn't possible to make one world," Lippmann recalled in the 1950's, "and the attempt to do it would produce a struggle rather than one world, and that the right line was to recognize the pluralism of the world and hope for an accommodation among many systems." [38]

In *U.S. Foreign Policy: Shield of the Republic*, which appeared in July, Lippmann presented the thesis that a nation must limit its commitments to its resources, must "maintain its objectives and its power in equilibrium." Toward the end of the nineteenth century the United States had made a series of enormous commitments far beyond its power to keep. As a result, Lippmann argued, "we have been compelled to fight two great unexpected wars for which we were unprepared." He saw the internationalists as continuing this disastrous national habit as they urged the nation to undertake the impossible task of policing the entire world to achieve permanent peace. Warning that "the statesman . . . can no more ignore the order of power than an engineer can ignore the mechanics of physical force," he proposed a cool and sober reappraisal of America's position in the world as a basis for postwar planning.

In the remainder of the book Lippmann offered his formula for a realistic peace—a "nuclear alliance" of the three great powers, the United States, Britain and the Soviet Union. Dismissing China and France as weaker states, he contended that England and Russia were the only nations strong enough to threaten American security in the postwar world. Since we enjoyed close ties with the British, the only real danger would be a falling-out with the Soviets. Predicting that an Anglo-American alignment against Russia "would set the stage inexorably for a third World War in Europe and in Asia as well," Lippmann felt it was essential to bring the Soviet Union into a three-power pact. "Combined action by America, Britain, and Russia is the irreducible minimum guarantee of the security of each of them," Lippmann contended, "and the only condition under which it is possible even to begin to establish any wider order of security." He concluded by urging the United States to make this "nuclear alliance" its primary postwar goal, suggesting that "a wider association of nations" might someday emerge from this vital core. [39]

U.S. Foreign Policy had the greatest circulation of Lippmann's many books. It went through seven printings in the first three months of publication, and by the end of the summer sales climbed near the half-million mark, including 300,000 copies distributed by the Book-of-the-Month Club, which made it the July selection. By August it was second only to *One World* on the New York *Times* best-seller list, and in September it climbed to the top for a brief time. *Reader's Digest* printed a condensation in the July issue, stating, "No more important book has been written for Americans in a generation." In August the editors of the *Ladies' Home Journal* ran a seven-page summary in cartoon form with brief captions below each picture. The final panel showed "civilization," portrayed as a young woman with babe in arms, going forward into "a world of order, security and well-being which today is only a dream." [40]

Lippmann also received broad critical acclaim for his book. Arthur Krock praised its "attractive and lucid" prose, while John Chamberlain called it "brilliant," hailing Lippmann for having "tossed overboard the last vestige of well-meaning but essentially futile Wilsonianism." He hoped that every American senator would read it. In a long review in *Atlantic Monthly*, Hans Kohn, a professor of history at Smith College and an authority on nationalism, congratulated Lippmann for putting history "to its best use." "We had to rebuild in this war the alliance of the last war; had we maintained it after 1918, World War II might never have come," Kohn wrote. Only the internationalists dissented, objecting to Lippmann's refusal to champion a new world organization. They pointed to his callous disregard for the small nations. "If after victory we are to have a brave new world of plenty," commented George Fort Milton, "the need for participation of all the people in their own national destinies and directions would seem too clear for argument." The secretary of the Southern California branch of the League of Nations Association was indignant at Lippmann's book: "It is really the old alliance and balance of power theory that has failed over and over again down the centuries." Breckinridge Long sent Cordell Hull a thirty-page memo challenging Lippmann's thesis and arguing for a general association of all the nations. To support his position, he asked Charles Warren, an eminent legal scholar, for his evaluation of *U.S. Foreign Policy*. To Long's intense disappointment, Warren replied that he had read it twice and thought it "excellent."

Lippmann had helped clarify the debate on the postwar world. Americans who wanted to abandon isolationism yet were not attracted by the Wilsonian slogans now had a respectable program to embrace. His cool logic made the far-fetched schemes of Harold Stassen, Ely Culbertson and Clarence Buddington Kelland suspect, and, in this regard, he did the internationalists an important service. Though Lippmann talked prviately with the President from time to time, there is no evidence that he was aware of how close his nuclear alliance was to Roosevelt's Four Policemen. With uncanny foresight and matchless skill at stating the simple in an apparently profound way, Lippman had offered the American people an attractive alternative to the prevailing idea of a new League of Nations.[41]

V

The people of America and the world face the greatest decision in the history of western civilization. Unless we meet it courageously and realistically, blazing new trails if necessary, our children and their liberties will both perish in World War Three.

Joseph Ball wrote these lines in a letter to his constituents on July 15, 1943, from Reno, Nevada. He and Representative Albert A. Gore of Tennessee were one of eight bi-partisan Congressional teams touring the country to stimulate interest in the B_2H_2 and Fulbright resolutions. Ball and Fulbright had developed the idea when they were besieged with requests from communities across the nation to speak on the postwar world. The United Nations Association agreed to sponsor the tour with help from Esther Brunauer of the Women's Action Committee and financial aid from the Carnegie Endowment. United Nations committees in each city made all the local arrangements, and the Endowment paid the travel expenses. The speakers went around the country by train, often in day coaches, and received neither fees nor political advantage, since they usually spoke outside their own states.[42]

Senator Ball and Representative Gore formed the first team to go out, arriving in Los Angeles on July 5. For the next ten days they traveled through California, Oregon, Washington, Nevada and Colorado, speaking at luncheon and dinner meetings of civic groups, talking informally with factory workers, and making formal addresses at mass rallies in Los Angeles, San Francisco, Reno, Seattle and Denver. The press covered their activities fully, and many of their speeches were broadcast over the radio. Most of the meetings Ball and Gore addressed passed resolutions endorsing the B_2H_2 and Fulbright resolutions. Guy Talbott, the director of the San Francisco International Center, was amazed at how many influential people were converted to the internationalist cause in the course of the tour.

The United Nations Association concentrated on sending teams into the Middle West; by the end of the summer every state in this region had been visited at least once, and some several times. Senator Truman and Congressman Judd of Minnesota conducted the most strenuous journey, traveling through the Great Plains states in late July and early August. They spoke to twenty-seven meetings in nineteen cities, and an estimated audience of ten thousand heard them in person, with many more listening to their addresses on the radio. "Hundreds of business people were turned away because of lack of facilities to accommodate them," reported the director of the tour. Harry Truman was impressed by the responsiveness of the people to the internationalist message. "In my tour of Iowa, Nebraska, Kansas, and part of Missouri," he wrote on August 23, "I have found that the people are awake to the situation and are no longer the strong isolationists they were in the past." [43]

Other teams traveled through New England and the Mid-Atlantic states, but the United Nations Association sent only one pair into the South, which was considered firmly internationalist in sentiment. In August, Clark Eichelberger appealed to Nicholas Murray Butler, the president of the Carnegie Endowment, for funds to send out ten more Congressional teams, but Butler refused, saying the trustees did not like to support "current political discussion." Nevertheless, the Endowment did provide enough money to finance two additional teams, one in New England and one in the Middle West. Senator Ball participated in the final swing through Illinois and Missouri, as well as taking part in a ten-day midsummer tour of the Dakotas and Minnesota.

For Ball and his fellow speakers it was a long, arduous summer of campaigning. Most of the trains they took lacked air-conditioning, and they frequently sat for hours in stifling heat on sidings while troop trains and freight cars loaded with war supplies roared past. But their presence in hundreds of cities and towns stimulated a grass-roots interest in international organization that no other technique could have achieved. John S. Dickey, a special consultant to Hull, prepared a long memo to the Secretary of State in September commenting on the effectiveness of the Congressional tours. He noted that the "middle-class and university-educated people who supported 'collective security' organizations before the war" spearheaded the local arrangements committees, but he pointed out that they succeeded in winning over entire commu-

128

nities which previously had been apathetic to international organization. For the first time, the internationalists seemed to have reached the great mass of the American people.[44]

The Non-Partisan Council, noting this success, decided to climax the whole movement with a series of mass rallies in behalf of the B_2H_2 resolution in September, just before Congress was scheduled to reconvene. They hoped to secure Henry Wallace, Sumner Welles, Justice Owen Roberts, Representative Fulbright and Senator Truman as the featured speakers in New York, Boston, Chicago, Denver and San Francisco. Henry Wallace immediately agreed to speak, preferring Chicago, where he had never made a major address, but the Council ran into difficulty with its other plans, failing to attract either the speakers or the local groups needed to sponsor the meetings. Aside from Chicago, the only rally held was in New York, where Dorothy Thompson and Senators Elbert Thomas and Harold Burton delivered addresses in behalf of the Ball resolution.

The Chicago meeting, billed as a "win-the-peace rally," attracted a crowd of twenty thousand who came to hear Sidney Hillman, Senator Ball and Vice President Wallace. In his address, which he had cleared with both Roosevelt and Hull, Wallace urged Midwesterners to abandon isolationism and take up the crusade for the "Common Man the world over." "There is no time to be lost," he declared. "Now is the time to strike while the war irons are hot." Though he devoted most of his remarks to postwar economic arrangements, he concluded with a specific endorsement of international organization and the B_2H_2 measure. "Senate Resolution 114," he proclaimed, "is a step toward a people's peace. A people's peace is the gateway on the path to the century of the Common Man." The huge audience roared its approval.[45]

VI

During the summer of 1943, Harrison Spangler tried to guide the Republican party toward a consensus on postwar foreign policy. In July he announced that the Postwar Advisory Council would meet in early September on Mackinac Island, a resort in Lake Michigan. In an effort at harmony, he met for an hour and a half on July 27 with Deneen Watson, urging him to disband the Republican Postwar Policy Association and support whatever stand the party adopted at Mackinac. Watson refused, and in August he held a meeting in San Francisco attended by more than a hundred West Coast Republican leaders. In a radio address on September 3, Watson asked the party to issue "a forthright statement on foreign policy" at Mackinac sanctioning, among other things, an international police force. Senator Robert Taft added to Spangler's difficulties by denouncing the Fulbright resolution in a speech to the American Bar Association. "It is broad enough to cover an international world state, a league of sovereign nations, [or] a British-Russian-American alliance, as proposed by Walter Lippmann," he charged.

Arthur Vandenberg shared Spangler's concern. In a letter to Thomas W. Lamont on August 4 he wrote, "I am hunting for the middle ground between those extremists at one end of the line who would cheerfully give America away and those extremists at the other end of the line who would attempt a total isolation which has come to be an impossibility." Two weeks later he drew up a draft statement for consideration at the Mackinac meeting. Following closely the resolution he and Senator White had introduced in Congress on July 2, it advocated American participation "in postwar cooperation between sovereign nations to prevent by all necessary means aggressions that might hereafter threaten the peace." Vandenberg carefully made no mention of international organization as such, and he stressed the retention of sovereignty and the protection of American vital interests. Spangler then showed the draft to other party leaders, including Senator Warren Austin, Taft and Governor Dewey of New York, and by the end of August he had secured their approval.[46]

Though the formal meeting of the Postwar Advisory Council was not scheduled to open until Monday, September 6, delegates began arriving at the Grand Hotel on Mackinac Island on the preceding Friday. More than a hundred reporters, twice the number of participants, crowded the verandas of the rambling wooden building, searching for stories on what *Newsweek* termed "the most important Republican deliberative assembly since the national convention of 1940." As the politicians drifted in, the newsmen surrounded them, seeking their views on the postwar world. On Sunday, Governor Dewey delighted the press by declaring that he favored a permanent Anglo-American alliance. "We have had a *de facto* military alliance with Great Britain practically ever since the War of 1812," he said, and he felt it "would be in our interest" to continue it after the war. In reply to a question, he also indicated that he would not object to including China and Russia in a broader security pact. The next day newspapers across the country featured Dewey's

statement on their front pages; one brief press conference had transformed the New York governor into a leading Republican internationalist.

When the conference opened on Monday morning, Spangler announced the formation of a committee headed by Vandenberg to present a foreign-policy resolution. But before the full Council adjourned
for the day, a group of internationalist governors, led by Raymond
Baldwin of Connecticut and Earl Warren of California, announced that
they could not accept the mild Vandenberg draft and demanded a
stronger statement. The governors appeared before Vandenberg's committee, where they received encouragement from Senator Austin and
Representative Charles Eaton of New Jersey. When Austin threatened
to write a minority report, Vandenberg finally capitulated, and a six-
man subcommittee, which included Austin, Eaton and two governors,
prepared a new and much longer statement on postwar foreign policy.

On the morning of September 8 the full Postwar Advisory Council
unanimously adopted the new draft, which the press termed the Mackinac declaration. The key sentence stated that the Republican party
favored "responsible participation by the United States in post-war
cooperative organization among sovereign nations to prevent military
aggression and to attain permanent peace with organized justice in a
free world." Austin and the governors had insisted on including the
word "organization," but Vandenberg had succeeded in retaining the
phrase "sovereign nations" from his original statement. Other parts of
the declaration modified this very general commitment. One sentence
stated that each international obligation had to be considered with
"careful regard for its effect upon the vital interests of the nation."
Another reflected Vandenberg's continuing fear that the administration
would try to circumvent the Senate by using executive agreements,
demanding that "constitutionalism" be observed in all postwar arrangements.[47]

The Mackinac declaration was a major triumph for the Republican
party. Willkie praised the action as "a very distinct move in the right
direction," and Deneen Watson, viewing it as a repudiation of isolationism, dissolved his Postwar Policy Association in October. Yet the reservations that Vandenberg had included ensured isolationist support.
Claire Hoffman, an outspoken Michigan congressman, commented, "As
an American Firster, I am satisfied with it." Vandenberg was immensely
pleased, feeling that he had found the "middle ground" he had been
hunting. He and Spangler had succeeded in binding the party to a

moderate internationalism which forestalled a party split and yet prevented the Democrats from exploiting the foreign-policy issue in the 1944 elections. In fact, for the first time in decades, the Republican party was out in front on foreign policy, committed publicly to an internationalist course while the Democrats remained silent. Thomas Dewey, who hoped to be the Republican candidate in 1944, expressed his gratitude in a letter to Vandenberg at the conclusion of the Makinac conference. "The Party should be grateful to you indeed," he wrote, "for a major contribution to its welfare as well as that of the country." [48]

Reporters were less enthusiastic. The New York *Times* correspondent remarked that a great discussion ensued among the newsmen about the precise meaning of the declaration. The consensus was that "it apparently required nothing specific and precluded nothing specific for the future." The editors of the *Nation* were also puzzled. "A momentous step was taken by the Republican party's Post-War Advisory Council at Mackinac Island last week," they wrote, "and we wish we knew what it was." Internationalists were disappointed in the statement. *Free World* felt it was hedged about with "mental reservations around which surviving isolationist tendencies might some day cluster." Edgar Ansel Mowrer dismissed the Mackinac declaration as "a fine example of pussyfooting."

Administration leaders disagreed on the significance of the Republican move. Henry Wallace belittled the declaration as a vague statement "in the Republican tradition of 1920." President Roosevelt ducked a direct comment in a press conference, but he revealed his feelings about its ambiguity by remarking, "Well, I always have my Thesaurus handy on my desk." Cordell Hull, however, was delighted with the outcome of the Mackinac meeting. He had been in touch with Will Hays, the movie czar and member of the Republican National Committee, and had asked him to urge other Republican leaders to join with the administration in removing the issue of international organization from partisan controversy. He interpreted the declaration as signifying Republican willingness to follow such a course.

The Mackinac declaration was the most important step yet taken toward American involvement in a future international organization. Though couched in vague and ambiguous language, like all political documents, the declaration was a striking contrast to the round robin of 1919 when thirty-nine Republican senators had signed a statement announcing in advance their opposition to the Covenant of the League of Nations. By affirming the principle of international organization while the war was in progress, the Republicans had reassured the American people and the world that they would not again adopt an obstructionist course. "The issue," wrote Anne O'Hare McCormick at the close of the Mackinac conference, "is no longer whether this nation will cooperate in maintaining peace; it is how, to what extent and in what ways we will cooperate." [49]

VII

Every index of public sentiment indicated that Mrs. McCormick was right. In the fall of 1943, major interest groups representing millions of Americans declared for international organization. The American Legion, meeting in Omaha, repudiated the views of its outgoing national commander, Roane Waring, and adopted a resolution advocating American entry into "an association of free and sovereign nations, implemented with whatever force may be necessary to maintain world peace and prevent a recurrence of war." The convention booed speeches by isolationists Hamilton Fish and Bennett Clark and proceeded to elect Warren Atherton, a strong internationalist, as its new leader. The Veterans of Foreign Wars, meeting in late September, also adopted a statement favoring "an association of sovereign powers" to keep the peace, though they weakened this resolution by adding a clause opposing "any dilution of our national sovereignty." [50]

Labor and management agreed on the need for international organization. In February 1943 the AFL, the CIO and the railroad brotherhoods had formed a postwar committee to voice labor's support for a policy of world cooperation. In a speech to the Economic Club in New York, William Green, president of the AFL, reminded his business audience that his union had supported the League in the 1920's. "The peace-loving peoples of the world," he declared, "must create agencies to establish international law and to enforce it against those who would foment war among nations." Late in 1943 the National Association of Manufacturers accepted the recommendations of its postwar committee which called for a general international organization with power to restrain aggressors.

The most dramatic appeal came on October 6, when 144 prominent Protestant, Catholic and Jewish leaders issued a seven-point "Declaration of World Peace." This ecumenical statement had taken four months to prepare and was the product of very delicate and sensitive negotiations by theologians who were in violent disagreement on many religious issues. Though phrased in general terms, the Declaration called for "international institutions to maintain the peace" and advocated "the use when necessary of adequate sanctions to enforce the law." *Christian Century* interpreted it as a "firm repudiation" of pre-war isolationism and a sign of a "new united front of American churches" in behalf of international organization.[51]

Public-opinion polls showed the American people solidly in agreement. In a canvass taken in September 1943 the National Opinion Research Center found that 81 percent of those questioned thought it was "a good idea" for the United States to join a "union of nations" after the war. Only 11 percent objected, with 8 percent expressing no opinion. This was a sharp rise from the 70 percent who had responded affirmatively to a similar question in June. Professional analysis noted that there was little regional variation with the Middle West only slightly less favorably inclined than the rest of the nation. Ross Stagner pointed out that those who completed college were far more internationally minded than individuals who had not gone beyond grade school. Correlating education with internationalism, he concluded that "more complete information about the world we live in . . . should lead to broadening of the individual's consciousness and awareness of a need for new solutions rather than a rigid adherence to old formulations." [52]

The regional committees of the Council on Foreign Relations, composed of businessmen, lawyers, educators, clergymen, doctors and bankers, agreed that the United States should commit itself during the war to an active role in an international system of collective security. There was no agreement on the form this would take, with different groups favoring a new league of nations, a Big Four alliance, and a world confederation with its own police force. Most felt it was still too early to choose a specific plan. The members of the St. Paul-Minneapolis committee expressed a widely held view in stating their feeling "that America has a responsibility for world organization which it cannot discharge alone, but only in concert with the international community."

Nearly all the committees believed that continued Anglo-American cooperation should be the foundation of postwar policy. They were less sure of the Soviet Union, revealing doubts of Russian intentions that many Americans shared. After Dewey's call for a permanent Anglo-American alliance in September, George Gallup found that the great majority of Americans approved, but only 39 percent wanted a similar arrangement with the Soviet Union. The Russians were aware of this distrust. On May 8, 1943, Soviet Ambassador Maxim Litvinov told Cordell Hull that he was concerned about "the state of mind in this country regarding isolation and also to a feeling on the part of many citizens directed against Russia." The dissolution of the Comintern in late May 1943 reassured many who had feared postwar Communist expansion, but latent hostility toward Russia and suspicion of Stalin remained as a major obstacle to complete acceptance of internationalism.[53]

There was some disagreement on the intensity of internationalist sentiment. Henry C. Link conducted extensive surveys in depth, asking the people he interviewed to give detailed reasons for the views they expressed. He concluded that the American people were genuinely internationalist in their beliefs and that they were prepared to sacrifice a substantial degree of national sovereignty to a world agency to keep the peace. A Gallup poll taken in October 1943, however, showed that when asked to name the greatest problem facing the nation in the future, 58 percent said "jobs" and only 13 percent replied "lasting peace." Jerome Bruner received similar results when he asked a cross-section whether they were more concerned with postwar domestic or international problems. More than half said they were most concerned with the future of the economy; only 16 percent expressed primary interest in foreign affairs.[54]

Despite these findings, the trend of public opinion in the fall of 1943 was running overwhelmingly in favor of international organization. *One World*, the B_2H_2 resolution, the Congressional speaking tours and the ceaseless efforts of Clark Eichelberger and his committees had aroused the people and lifted their eyes to the world that lay beyond the war. Americans had accepted the idealism of Wilson's heirs and were insisting that the United States not turn its back on the world again.

6

Commitment

IN THE SUMMER OF 1943 there was a growing awareness in the State Department that the administration was lagging far behind public opinion in the quest for enduring peace. The subcommittees of the Advisory Committee had adjourned indefinitely on July 12 at Hull's request, and the Draft Constitution for a world organization drawn up by Welles' group had been cast aside. Worried by this apparent inactivity, Myron Taylor, a member of Hull's Informal Political Agenda Group, prepared a memorandum for the Secretary on July 8. "Our failure to enter the League leaves a reasonable doubt as to our sincerity now," Taylor wrote. "To promote the world organization, therefore, some positive steps must be taken now to assure the world of our adherence." He then recommended that the United States negotiate an agreement with Britain, Russia and China pledging the creation of a postwar international organization. With Hull's approval, the staff of Pasvolsky's Division of Special Research began drafting a tentative four-power declaration.

In early August, Hull decided that he would present the proposed agreement to the British at the Quebec conference, scheduled to take place later in the month. Hull was impressed by a long memo from Pasvolsky pointing out that the greatest uncertainty was the Russian attitude toward international organization. "The sooner and the more fully we test out Moscow's intentions," Pasvolsky argued, "the clearer will be our own tasks, as well as the possibilities open to us." On August 10, Hull, accompanied by Welles, Pasvolsky, Norman Davis and Isaiah Bowman, showed the draft four-power agreement to the President. Roosevelt suggested a few minor changes and then gave Hull permission to submit it to the British at Quebec.

The "Tentative Draft of a Joint Four-Power Declaration" was a relatively brief eight-point statement in which the signatories promised to

136

continue "their united action, pledged for the prosecution of the war, . . . for the organization and maintenance of peace and security." They agreed to act together on the surrender of enemy states, the occupation of liberated territory, and all related problems. The most important commitment came in the fourth article, which called for establishing "at the earliest practicable date a general international organization, based on the principle of the sovereign equality of all nations." Until this new body came into being, however, the four governments would "act jointly in behalf of the community of nations," and only employ force for legitimate purposes. Nothing was said about a possible international police force, nor did the draft even suggest a design for the future world organization. At this point, all Hull wanted was to lay the foundations for peace with a declaration of Big Four unity.

At Quebec, Anthony Eden quickly accepted the draft, and he and Hull agreed to transmit it to Moscow for Russian consideration at a future meeting of foreign ministers. There was no public disclosure of this step, and the final communiqué of the conference stated only that the conversations had focused on military plans for the coming year. In a speech at Ottawa to the Canadian Parliament on August 25, however, Roosevelt revealed that there was "much talk of the postwar world" at Quebec. The President refused to disclose the nature of the discussion, simply comparing the United Nations to a "sheriff's posse to break up the gang in order that gangsterism may be eliminated in the community of Nations." "Surely by unanimous action in driving out the outlaws and keeping them under heel forever," he concluded, "we can attain a freedom from fear of violence." [1]

The evening before Roosevelt spoke, American papers carried the far more sensational news that Sumner Welles had submitted his resignation to the President. At a press conference upon his return from Quebec, Hull tacitly confirmed the report by refusing to deny its validity, though no official word was released for several more weeks. Columnists, intrigued by the administration's silence, speculated on a wide range of possible reasons for the showdown between Hull and Welles, with most feeling that it reflected a major policy disagreement on the administration's postwar plans. Though the evidence on Welles' resignation is still very meager, the fundamental cause appears to have been personal. Cordell Hull, convinced that the Under Secretary was working behind his back to usurp his control of American foreign policy, compelled the President to drop Welles.

6. *Commitment*

A highly critical analysis of the State Department by John Crider in the New York *Times* on August 4 touched off the episode. Crider, writing while the *Times's* Washington Bureau Chief, Arthur Krock, was out of the city, reported that the State Department was crippled by "conflicting personalities, lack of a cohesive policy, and a resulting impairment of efficiency." Crider charged that Hull was very slipshod in his administration of the Department and that foreign diplomats received a different view of American policy from each Department officer they conferred with. Hinting that the President was deeply concerned, Crider suggested that a major shake-up was in order to remedy "the sluggishness of an old-line department in meeting the rapidly changing situation now confronting it." The next day Hull issued a denial, and on August 6 Krock returned to Washington and wrote a column in defense of Hull. Acknowledging the validity of the conditions Crider described, Krock blamed Welles, charging that the Under Secretary undercut Hull continually by going behind his back to the President, by encouraging foreign diplomats to confer with him rather than with the Secretary, and by turning the Department staff against Hull. "In the opinion of this correspondent," Krock concluded, "the State Department will function smoothly and effectively when the President permits the Secretary to be the real, undisputed head of a loyal staff."

Hull repeated this advice to Roosevelt and then bluntly asked the President to choose between him and Welles. At this time Hull may well have informed Roosevelt that Welles was the target of a whispering campaign in Washington accusing him, as Hull put it to Long, of "a highly immoral bit of conduct." Hull had first heard gossip about Welles' "indiscretion" from William Bullitt in the summer of 1942. Welles had denied the accusation, and Hull and Long tended to believe him. But the rumor persisted. Long advised Welles to resign, telling him several Republican senators had heard the story and that "it was obvious that true or untrue the Republicans would use it to hurt the administration." Welles had become a serious political liability, although even without this delicate issue Roosevelt was very likely to favor Hull in the showdown the Secretary had forced. Hull had the confidence of the Senate, especially of the southern bloc which dominated the leadership and whose cooperation was essential to Roosevelt. The dismissal of Hull and his replacement by Welles would have been a political disaster that Roosevelt, despite his fondness for Welles, dared not risk.[2]

In mid-August, on the eve of the Quebec conference, Roosevelt and Hull agreed on a plan to ease Welles out of the State Department. The President would ask him to resign in order to fly to Moscow and to

Chungking to secure Russian and Chinese consent to the four-power declaration. When he returned, he could retire gracefully to private life, and thus be spared public humiliation. Welles submitted the necessary letter of resignation, but then he balked. On August 22, while Roosevelt and Hull were in Quebec, he suddenly left Washington for his summer home in Bar Harbor, leaving an amazed Assistant Secretary in charge of the State Department. When reporters learned of his abrupt departure, the stories on his resignation began to appear. President Roosevelt, however, refused to act, hoping to persuade him to accept the mission abroad. On September 4 Roosevelt wrote to Stalin about the projected meeting of foreign ministers, saying, "I do not want Mr. Hull to undertake such a long journey, so I would, therefore, send Mr. Welles, the Under Secretary of State." [3]

Remaining in seclusion in Maine, Welles became the hero of the affair. The liberal press, which earlier had viewed him as an aloof aristocrat, now hailed him as "the Department's leading advocate of friendly relations with Russia and its most far-sighted internationalist." Editors praised his role in the framing of the Good Neighbor policy, extolled his friendly attitude toward the Soviet Union and pointed out how eloquently he had pleaded the cause of international organization. Less partisan journals regretted his departure from the government in more restrained language, noting his competence as a diplomat and the fact that he was "a man you could do business with." *Time* lamented the passing of "a known and respected advocate of U.S. cooperation in international affairs. The U.S. still awaits a clarification of its foreign policy," the editors declared, "and the forced resignation of Sumner Welles made an already murky issue even more obscure."

Many observers believed that the administration was embarking on a new anti-Russian policy. The *Nation* condemned the resignation as "the product of political blackmail by Hull and the Southern bloc" and a sign of "the President's steady drift toward the right." Drew Pearson went further in a Sunday-evening radio broadcast, charging that Welles was fired because he opposed the State Department policy of making Russia bear the brunt of the war against Germany. The next morning Hull angrily denied this accusation, telling newsmen that Pearson's remarks were "monstrous and diabolical falsehoods." In his weekly press conference on August 31, Roosevelt dodged questions on Welles' resignation, but he did reply to Pearson's charges, stating that he had done serious harm to the wartime coalition. In a rare display of temper, the President called Drew Pearson "a chronic liar." [4]

Hull, described by Breckinridge Long as "supersensitive" to this "avalanche" of criticism, decided to deliver a radio address to the nation to restore public confidence in the State Department. For two weeks Long, Pasvolsky and three other high officials spent several hours a day on the speech. On September 9 Hull took it to Roosevelt, asking him to note carefully "the remarks which over-rule the Wallace theories of 'a bottle of milk a day' for every child in the world." The President approved the speech, telling an elated Hull that he did not share Wallace's view of the postwar world. Long and Hull spent an entire day polishing the final draft, and then on September 13 the Secretary delivered the address over all three radio networks from his office desk. Long was again standing by in case Hull's voice failed, but the aging Secretary made it through to the end, though Long noted that his delivery "was at best poor."

Hull's address, his first report to the American people on postwar plans in over a year, was disappointing. With characteristic vagueness, he set forth six moral principles which would undergird the peace. In one brief passage he advocated "a system of organized international cooperation for the maintenance of peace . . . based upon the willingness of the cooperating nations to use force, if necessary, to keep the peace." Though he stressed "readiness to use force" in another passage, he never defined the nature of the "organized international cooperation" he favored, nor did he even hint at the possibility of an international police force. Indeed, his speech was well within the ambiguous guidelines laid out by the Republicans in the Mackinac declaration. He did reveal that the Department had been conducting postwar studies for the past two years, and that members of Congress as well as prominent private citizens were taking part. But he failed to give any encouragement to those clamoring for the blueprints of peace, asking instead for his critics "to consider these all important post-war problems and to contribute to their solution in wholly non-partisan spirit." [5]

Two weeks later the White House formally announced Welles' resignation and the appointment of Edward R. Stettinius as Under Secretary. Neither Welles' letter nor Roosevelt's reply was made public, a startling departure from the usual practice; the announcement simply cited the poor health of Mrs. Welles as the reason for the resignation. The press received Stettinius' appointment favorably. A former executive of U.S. Steel who had been in charge of the lend-lease program, Stettinius was viewed as an able, genial, but not very forceful executive who would cure the administrative ills in the Department without threatening Hull's mastery of policy. But nearly everyone regretted the dropping of Welles, and the clumsy way in which the administration had handled it. "We are sorry," commented the editors of the *New Republic*, "that his wife's illness should be brought forward as an excuse, when everyone knows that Mr. Hull forced him out." [6]

For Hull, it was a costly victory. In removing his chief rival, he had antagonized the American people, who were already disturbed by his platitudinous speeches and excessively cautious approach to postwar planning. Fired up by the internationalist crusade which Welles had done so much to launch, Americans wanted bold, dramatic steps to assure them of a lasting peace. Unless Hull took them soon, he risked losing control over the direction of postwar foreign policy.

I

When Congress reconvened in mid-September, the senators and representatives displayed a strong interest in foreign policy. The quickening pace of the European war, which led to the surrender of Italy on September 8, focused attention on the problems of peace. A *Newsweek* survey showed that while there was little agreement on specific plans, a majority favored some form of international organization backed by force. And all were aware of a Gallup poll taken during the summer which reported that seventy-eight percent of the American people wanted their congressman to vote for the Fulbright resolution.

The House Foreign Affairs Committee, meeting in executive session on September 16, voted to seek immediate passage of the resolution. To forestall a lengthy debate and avoid isolationist amendments, they agreed to ask for a suspension of rules, a procedure which limited debate to forty minutes and forbade amendments, but which required a two-thirds vote. Representative John McCormack of Massachusetts, the majority leader, announced to the House on Friday morning, September 17, that he would make a motion to suspend the rules and pass the Fulbright resolution on the following Monday. Daniel Reed, a New York Republican, immediately protested, demanding an opportunity to offer amendments "to defend the sovereign rights of a sovereign people." "The Fulbright resolution," he charged, "is purely a wild and reckless plunge in the dark. . . ." [7]

Other Republicans joined with Reed in warning that passage of the measure without qualification might permit the administration to enter a world organization without further Congressional approval. Needing Republican votes to guarantee two-thirds approval, Chairman Sol

141

6. Commitment

Bloom called the Foreign Affairs Committee together on Monday morning at ten and offered to amend the Fulbright resolution by adding the words "through its constitutional processes" to guard against any administration attempt in the future to bypass Congress. The committee quickly accepted this change and agreed to lengthen the debate to four hours.

Early that afternoon, before a crowded House chamber, John McCormack made his motion to consider the Fulbright resolution. After a brief debate, the members agreed to suspend the rules and engage in a four-hour debate on the proposition:

> That the Congress hereby expresses itself as favoring the creation of appropriate international machinery, with power adequate to establish and to maintain a joint and lasting peace, among nations of the world, and as favoring participation by the United States therein through its constitutional processes.

Representatives Bloom and John Vorys of Ohio, the ranking Republican on the Foreign Affairs Committee, made the opening speeches in support of the resolution, stressing its bi-partisan nature. As other speakers followed them to the rostrum, the members gradually left the floor, forcing Speaker Sam Rayburn to make frequent quorum calls to ensure an audience. After two hours the House adjourned for the day, with the debate to conclude the next afternoon.[8]

Throughout the two days of debate, the proponents of the Fulbright resolution emphasized how important it was for the United States to proclaim its intention of joining a new world organization. "The people of the world are looking to us, to the great and mighty United States," declared Estes Kefauver of Tennessee. "Let us not fail them." Fulbright felt that his measure would permit our allies to "rely with assurance upon the commitments of our Executive"; "its defeat," added Albert Gore of Tennessee, "would be a great victory for the enemy." Republicans and Democrats alike referred to the Senate's repudiation of the League in 1919 and the importance of redeeming that "tragic mistake." They appealed to their colleagues to learn from "the lessons of history" so that "the children of today's heroes do not have it all to do over again in 20 years." Though many saw the resolution as the beginning of a bright new world, Representative Fulbright had more modest hopes. "It is simply the first small step in the process of building a policy which I hope may have better results than that which we have followed in the past."[9]

A small band of isolationists, nearly all midwestern Republicans, delivered a furious attack on the resolution. Seizing on the vagueness of the measure, they described it as a blank check which the internationalists would use to create a world superstate and thus destroy American sovereignty and independence. "Is this resolution offered at this time," asked Claire Hoffman of Michigan, "as the opening wedge for a United States of the World, for Union Now, for a Federated United Nations?" His colleagues responded affirmatively, warning that its sponsors intended to have the United States "play the role of Santa Claus for the rest of the world," "substitute a mongrel flag for the Stars and Stripes," and "make the President of the United States the first International President of the world." Representative Stephen Day pointed out that Fulbright was a former Rhodes scholar and concluded that his resolution was part of a conspiracy "to consummate the surrender of our American independence and the return of the United States into the British empire." Other speakers ridiculed the idea that the United States could save the world and urged the nation to recognize its own limitations and once again reject the Wilsonian dream.[10]

Another group of isolationists, however, accepted the Fulbright resolution, finding in its vague language the protection their colleagues desired. "I am voting for the resolution with the idea that it means only our efforts to get a realistic peace and maintain it," declared an Ohio Republican. "I shall never be for any commitment that gives away one iota of our national sovereignity." Karl Mundt of South Dakota could not see why there was any dispute over the resolution. "Within its boundaries," he proclaimed, "is haven enough for the most ultra-isolationist in the country as well as the most 'super-duper' internationalist in the world." Hamilton Fish announced his support more succinctly. "Nobody wants to vote against the Ten Commandments," he said. "Nobody wants to vote for sin." Others delivered passionate pleas for preserving American sovereignity and for keeping "America American" and then calmly concluded by stating their intention of voting for the Fulbright measure. Representative Melvin Maas, a Minnesota Republican, fervently declared his belief in world cooperation, but added, "I demand that the rest of the world cooperate with us for a change. I have no confidence in leagues of nations, by whatever name they may be called." It was Everett Dirksen, who had been an isolationist before the war, who straddled the issue most eloquently: [11]

I favor collaboration, organized justice, the curbing and prevention of military aggression, the disarmament of the Axis powers, a clarification of peace aims now before it is too late, a strong United States Army and Navy, the use of constitutional processes, and the preservation of our national interests.

As the debate neared an end on September 21, Representative Charles Eaton, a New Jersey Republican who had helped draft the Mackinac declaration, brought the listless House to life by chiding his colleagues for their ambiguous speeches and frequent absence from the floor. "What are we fussing about here when we haven't enough interest to fill these seats?" he complained. "If we haven't enough interest, we should get out and give room for some decent people who have a sense of responsibility about these issues." As Eaton spoke, the chamber began to fill. Declaring that the Fulbright resolution was in "full accord" with the Mackinac declaration, he pleaded for its passage to encourage "the public opinion of the world." As he returned to his seat, the members rose in tribute.

After a final speech by Bloom, the House passed the Fulbright resolution by an overwhelming margin, 360 to 29. Led by Fish and Mundt, scores of pre-Pearl Harbor isolationists joined with the majority. All but three of the opponents were Republicans, and 24 of the 29 were from the Middle West. In the New York *Times,* Turner Catledge called the vote "a display of unity unsurpassed in Congress since the declaration of war on the Axis." The next day Cordell Hull told reporters that the House had expressed "the determination of the people of the United States to collaborate effectively with other nations after the war to keep the peace." He was particularly pleased with the "non-partisan spirit" of the debate. Other observers were more critical, noting that the strong isolationist support and the nationalist tenor of the speeches made the Fulbright resolution a dubious indication of future internationalism in Congress. Senator Carl Hatch thought "it is susceptible of practically every interpretation under the sun," and both he and Ball announced that they would press for Senate passage of their more specific resolution.[12]

Tom Connally was furious at the House for daring to infringe on the Senate's monopoly over foreign policy. "God damn it," he exclaimed privately, "everybody's running around here like a fellow with a tick on his navel, howling about postwar resolutions." When the Fulbright resolution was formally sent to the Senate on September 25, he issued a more decorous statement, saying that his subcommittee would give it careful consideration. Connally added that he did not think it was wise to risk "intemperate and trouble-making debate on the floor of the

Senate." Off-the-record, Connally complained that he had been unable to get "anything definite" out of Cordell Hull on the administration's views. Frank McNaughton, the *Time* correspondent to whom Connally confided these remarks, thought that senatorial jealousy was the real obstacle. "It is irritating to Senators," McNaughton wrote to his editor, "to have a freshman Congressman, J. W. Fulbright of a rube state like Arkansas, grab the ball and run for a touchdown, when they haven't been able to cross the goal line in 20 years."

Connally's procrastination drew heavy criticism from editors who pointed out that his subcommittee had been studying the B_2H_2 resolution for twenty-five weeks without any result. Internationalists flooded the Senate with letters urging passage of either the Fulbright or the B_2H_2 resolution. This tactic proved quite effective; an Associated Press poll in early October showed that 42 of 53 Senators who expressed an opinion favored adoption of a postwar resolution.[13]

At this point President Roosevelt intervened. The easy passage of the Fulbright resolution in the House convinced him that the nation was now ready to make a firm postwar commitment. After Welles' refusal, the President had decided to send Hull to the foreign ministers' meeting in Moscow in October, and he felt it would be very helpful to have the Senate on record before the conference considered the proposed four-power declaration. In a meeting with the Congressional leadership on September 29, Roosevelt told Senator Alben Barkley, the majority leader, that the "time was opportune" to report out a postwar resolution. The President added that he wanted a very general measure which would rally support from all viewpoints. Barkley passed the word on to Senator Connally, who immediately called in reporters to announce that his subcommittee would prepare an entirely new resolution and submit it to the Senate within the next few weeks.[14]

Senator Connally completed the draft and presented it to the subcommittee on October 13. It was a three-part resolution which called for cooperation with the other United Nations in waging the war and securing peace. In the key clause, Connally recommended that "the United States, acting through its constitutional processes, join with free and sovereign nations in the establishment and maintenance of international authority with power to prevent aggression and to preserve the peace of the world." Though a little stronger than the brief Fulbright resolution, it was far weaker than the B_2H_2 proposal, lacking any mention of an international police force and asking vaguely for "international authority" rather than a specific organization. Vandenberg was delighted with the phrases "constitutional processes" and "sovereign nations"

145

which echoed the Mackinac declaration, and with his vigorous support the subcommittee unanimously approved the statement and released it to the press.

With Hull already on his way to Moscow, Stettinius called a meeting of the assistant secretaries to consider the Connally resolution. ". . . it was decided no action should be taken at this time," Stettinius reported to Hull. The Under Secretary did ask Breckinridge Long to follow the debate in the Senate closely, but otherwise the administration tried to remain aloof, fearful that any other policy would lead to isolationist charges of White House interference. What Roosevelt and Hull wanted above all else was an apparently free expression of the Senate's will.

On October 14 Senator Connally formally introduced his resolution, concentrating his plea for support on the B_2H_2 senators. "It is the best thing they can possibly get," he declared, warning that any attempt to renew the Ball resolution would endanger the cause of peace. The next day Ball, Hatch, Hill, Burton and seven other senators met to discuss strategy. They issued a brief statement announcing they would fight for a stronger resolution, and then they asked Senator Claude Pepper of Florida, a member of the Senate Foreign Relations Committee and a flamboyant internationalist, to sponsor a series of amendments to the Connally resolution. Pepper agreed, and the group met daily to perfect the wording of their proposals.[15]

The full Senate Foreign Relations Committee convened on October 19 to consider the Connally resolution. After listening to protests from the B_2H_2 senators at a closed hearing, the committee adjourned for two days. When it met again, Senator Pepper put forward the amendments, which substituted the phrase "an international organization" for "international authority" and added the words "including military force." The committee members voted 16 to 5 to reject these additions and then reported out the Connally resolution intact, with only Hiram Johnson and Robert La Follette dissenting. Speaking to reporters afterwards, Connally said that he did not expect debate in the Senate to last more than four or five days. "The resolution," he declared, "comes more nearly to expressing the crystallized opinion of the Senate and the country than any resolution which has reached the Committee on Foreign Relations."

Few agreed with Connally. When Senator Guy Gillette came out of the committee room, he announced, "The child is born." When a reporter asked, "Boy or girl?" Gillette replied, "Neuter." *Time* said that, by comparison, the mild Mackinac declaration now seemed "monumentally grand." "After stalling as long as public opinion would stand," the editors of the *New Republic* wrote, "the Connally subcommittee has now brought out a practically meaningless compromise proposal." Yet the resolution did promise to place the Senate on record in favor of American participation in a postwar world body. If internationalists persisted in their efforts to strengthen the resolution, they risked dividing the Senate majority which favored a postwar resolution, thus playing directly into the hands of the small isolationist faction. Moreover, with Hull engaged in negotiation with the British and Russian foreign ministers, prompt action was essential. A lengthy and inconclusive Senate debate would undercut his efforts to convince America's allies that the United States was firmly and irrevocably committed to an active postwar policy.[16]

Despite these hazards, the B_2H_2 group decided to wage a floor fight to amend the Connally resolution. They had the full support of the internationalist movement in this decision. Both the United Nations Association and the Non-Partisan Council to Win the Peace urged an all-out effort to pass a strong Senate resolution. They asked civic, religious and labor organizations to petition the Senate for a bolder stand, and soon the telegrams began pouring into the Senate Office Building. Father John A. Ryan, director of the National Catholic Welfare Council, rebuffed when he asked to appear before the Senate committee, wired Connally that his resolution would be far better if "the question-begging, irrelevant and confusing word 'sovereignty' were omitted." John Foster Dulles agreed, and asked Connally to sponsor "a clear and comprehensive resolution." Local chapters of women's groups bombarded senators with pleas for a "more forthright" stand for peace. "It is possible to win the war and lose the peace," telegraphed Philip Murray, the CIO leader. "It is possible for us to repeat the mistakes which led to World War II." In a statement adopted at its annual meeting, the American Free World Association declared, "The Connally resolution at best is only a declaration of good intentions, an I.O.U. written in disappearing ink." Tom Connally received hundreds of letters from people all over the country. The most forthright came from a Pueblo, Colorado man who told him, "Western people want effective international action with teeth. No pussy footing." [17]

I I

On Monday morning, October 25, Connally opened what the New York *Times* called "the most important Senate debate on international affairs since the rejection of the Versailles treaty and the League of Nations covenant nearly twenty-four years ago." Yellow light filtering through the glass ceiling, now reinforced by steel girders in case of enemy air raids, gave the green-carpeted chamber an eerie appearance. Though tourists, reporters and diplomats filled the galleries, less than half the senators were present. Some lounged in their red armchairs reading the morning paper, others wandered out to the cloakrooms while the oratory went on. Among them were four senators who had voted against the Covenant in 1919, including Hiram Johnson of California, one of the irreconcilable leaders.

Tom Connally, whose white mane and black-ribboned pince-nez gave him, as one reporter put it, the air "of a ham actor playing Senator," led the fight for his resolution. The B$_2$H$_2$ group, however, quickly took the initiative by proposing the adoption of the Pepper amendments. Dubbed the "willful fourteen," these senators included Harry Truman, Claude Pepper and Warren Austin. Day after day they questioned Connally, engaging in endless semantic duels over such words as "international authority" and "sovereign nations." Connally, whose patience was easily exhausted, bore this harassment with surprising grace, asking his critics to join with him in passing the resolution to bolster Hull in Moscow. Arthur Vandenberg backed him strongly, warning against "crystal-gazing details" and "resoluting in the dark." [18]

Joseph Ball gave the opening speech for the internationalists, pleading somberly for the Senate to declare its willingness to endow an international organization with the force to keep the peace. It was Claude Pepper, however, who sparked the debate by a dramatic appeal to the past. "I can seem to see in this debate today," he said, "the shadows of those figures who contested with Woodrow Wilson about the League of Nations. . . . The world wants to know whether we, in this body, have changed our sentiment." He attacked the vague language of the Connally resolution, comparing it to "an old Mother Hubbard" which "covers everything and touches nothing." At the climax of his speech, which went on for two days, he charged that to adopt the proposed measure would be "to begin the war against World War No. 3 by appeasement."

Other members of the B$_2$H$_2$ group followed Pepper to the rostrum while Connally sought vainly to bring his measure to a vote. Isolationists, delighted to see supporters of international cooperation at each other's throats, remained silent during the first few days of debate. Finally, on Friday afternoon, Democrat Burton Wheeler of Montana, a persistent critic of Roosevelt's foreign policy, rose to challenge the concept of international organization. Echoing the "blank check" accusations made against the Fulbright resolution, he declared that "we are asked to commit ourselves to something which later will be used against us and plague us." He vehemently denied the familiar charge that American rejection of the League had caused World War II, claiming that the British and French were responsible for sabotaging peace. Then, as Hull had always feared, he turned to accuse the Soviets of planning to swallow up the Baltic states and all of Poland. "The chances are," he predicted, "that when the war is over Russia will dominate Europe, and Communism will probably sweep the greater part of Europe." He was followed by Senator Harlan Bushfield of South Dakota, who claimed that the Connally resolution was "bound to lead to a world state." "The president of this new superstate," he concluded, "would eventually be the dictator of the world." [19]

The Senate adjourned for the weekend of October 29, no nearer to a decision on the Connally resolution than at the beginning of the week. Stettinius, assured by Leslie Biffle, the secretary of the Senate, that the debate would last only a day or two, became very anxious. On Tuesday he had wired Hull that the "resolution will pass without amendment in three or four days with less than ten votes in opposition." The next day Connally called the Under Secretary to request the President to "send word to speed the resolution along in the Senate." Stettinius conferred with James Byrnes, who advised against any interference by either the White House or the State Department. At the end of the week Stettinius reported to Hull the lack of progress, noting, "Connally is tired and harried." When reporters queried Roosevelt about the resolution at his Friday press conference, he tried to help out by saying he favored "some fairly general language." He dodged a direct endorsement of the Connally resolution, but he did give a brief lecture on the dangers of specific wording. In a letter to Irving Brant that same day he repeated this view, saying, "Remember the water is going over the dam very fast these days and what language is used today may be wholly out of date in a week or two." [20]

Cordell Hull was very disappointed at the controversy over the Connally resolution. He had left Washington on October 7, flying for the first time in his life on the beginning of an eleven-day combined air and sea journey to Moscow. The Russians had earlier raised objections to the draft four-power declaration he had submitted, arguing that China should not be included. When the conference with Eden and Molotov opened on October 19, Hull was determined to hold out for Chinese participation. In the third session, on October 21, the foreign ministers turned to the draft agreement. Eden and Molotov suggested revisions in the fourth article on international organization, changing the basis of membership from "all nations" to "all peace-loving states." Hull agreed and the three men approved the text, but Molotov still refused to accept China as a signatory since Russia was not at war with Japan. Later in the week, however, he finally gave way, and on October 30 the three foreign ministers, joined by the Chinese ambassador to Moscow, signed the four-power declaration. It was a proud moment for Cordell Hull, who recorded in his *Memoirs:*

> I was truly thrilled as I saw the signatures affixed. Now there was no longer any doubt that an international organization to keep the peace, by force if necessary, would be set up after the war. As I signed, I could not but recall my long personal battles on behalf of the old League of Nations. Now it was probable that the United States would be a member of a new security organization. . . .

On Monday morning, November 1, the government released the text of the Moscow declaration to the press. The four nations promised to seek peace together and to act jointly in arranging for the surrender and disarmament of the common enemy. In the fourth article they recognized the necessity of creating "at the earliest practical date a general international organization, based on the principle of the sovereign equality of all peace-loving states . . . for the maintenance of international peace and security." In addition, the Big Four promised to consult with each other and with other members of the United Nations "with a view of joint action on behalf of the community of nations" pending the establishment of the new world body.[21]

When the Senate convened on Monday afternoon, Connally received permission to interrupt the debate to read the text of the Moscow declaration. When he finished, he asserted that it fitted in well with his resolution and asked the B_2H_2 group to join in passing it as a tribute to Cordell Hull. Senator Ball then rose and read a press release signed by all fourteen senators sponsoring the Pepper amendments. Calling the Moscow declaration "a great beacon of hope to a war-weary world," Ball's statement pointed out that it called specifically for a general international organization. "We hope," the statement concluded, "that the Senate now will be at least as clear and forthright in its expression as the agreement signed at Moscow." Senators Hatch and Pepper then suggested that the Connally resolution be sent back to the Senate

Foreign Relations Committee to be recast in line with the Moscow declaration. Connally objected vehemently, asking instead that the Senate proceed to an immediate vote on his resolution. Later in the day Stettinius, acting on Long's suggestion, asked James Byrnes to try to persuade Connally to strengthen his measure. Again Connally refused. "He was emotional about it," Byrnes told Long, "temperamental like a prima donna."

The next day, Scott Lucas, the assistant majority leader, who had been supporting Connally, now suggested that the entire text of the Moscow declaration be included in the resolution. Senator Carter Glass, confined by illness to his Virginia home, issued a public statement urging that the Senate incorporate just the fourth article. Glass, a loyal Wilsonian who had served in the Senate since World War I, stressed the importance of this action. "It is my firm conviction," he wrote, "that if we had entered the League of Nations and the World Court, the horrendous nightmare through which we are now passing might have been averted." Breckinridge Long, deeply impressed by this plea, requested and received Roosevelt's permission to approach other senators with Glass' compromise plan. Long spoke with several of the B_2H_2 senators, who indicated their willingness to go along, and then he went to see Tom Connally, telling him "it was a matter of international political consequence" for the Senate to reaffirm the Moscow declaration. Connally finally agreed to call the Foreign Relations Committee into session the next day to consider such an amendment.[22]

On the morning of November 3 the fourteen senators supporting the Pepper amendments met in Lister Hill's office. After Elbert Thomas reported that Clark Eichelberger had called him to suggest that they "add point four of the Moscow Declaration to the Resolution," they agreed to go along. At three that afternoon the Senate Foreign Relations Committee accepted the fourth article of the Moscow declaration as an amendment to the Connally resolution. The members also approved a second addition, offered by Senator Raymond E. Willis of Indiana, which ensured that any treaty implementing the resolution would come before the Senate for approval by a two-thirds vote. They hoped that this amendment would placate isolationists, who were already suggesting that the administration planned to circumvent the Senate by using an executive agreement to join an international organization.

In the late afternoon Connally returned to the Senate floor to report his committee's amendments. With Vandenberg's vigorous backing, he received unanimous Senate approval to alter the resolution accordingly. Senator Hill immediately rose to declare, "I shall wholeheartedly support the resolution as now modified by the distinguished chairman of the committee." When the other B_2H_2 senators expressed their intention of voting for the amended resolution, Connally announced that the Senate would meet at eleven the next morning, an hour earlier than usual, in an effort to conclude the long debate.[23]

The isolationists, dismayed by the new unity in the internationalist camp, waged an intense last-minute attack on the resolution. "It contemplates the submergence of our American sovereignity into some as yet undiscovered form of supergovernment," declared North Carolina's bombastic Robert Reynolds, adding that he feared "a godless, soulless international Frankenstein." Objecting to "the loss of an iota of sovereignity to America," Senator Gerald Nye accused the administration of planning "some super-super-government that shall dictate our own destiny." Burton Wheeler delivered the most bitter speech, condemning "these cheap small-minded internationalists who are trying to solve all the problems of the world and saying, 'To hell with the United States.'"

Other pre-war isolationists, like their colleagues in the House, expressed their intention of voting for the Connally resolution, but insisted on a very narrow interpretation. Announcing that he still believed in "the policy of America first," Robert Taft accepted the resolution as an honest effort to substitute law and order for international anarchy which endangered the United States. Several Republican senators cited the omission of any reference to an international police force as the main reason for their acquiescence. Henry Cabot Lodge, Jr., expressed the feelings of many when he declared, "I favor international cooperation to maintain peace between nations, but I naturally do not favor having such cooperation perverted into a device to siphon off the power, prestige, and resources of the United States."

Administration supporters, notably those from the South, responded with an emotional outpouring of praise for Woodrow Wilson. ". . . had we but followed the brilliant statesmanship of Woodrow Wilson, who in my judgment is one of the great world figures of the ages," proclaimed James C. Eastland of Mississippi, "we would not be in this war, and this world would live in peace." Senator Andrews of Florida reminded his colleagues that they had "failed to keep the faith with our men who fought to make the world safe for democracy" in the last war, and warned that "our sons may soon sleep with their fathers who fell in Flanders field." Joseph Guffey of Pennsylvania phrased the same argument more simply, saying that "the same issues present themselves to the American people today as were presented in 1919." [24]

After two final days of debate, Connally succeeded in stopping the flow of oratory. He skillfully defeated a series of crippling amendments, and then late on Friday evening, November 5, the Senate accepted his resolution. The vote was 85 to 5. Three western Republicans—Hiram Johnson, William Langer of North Dakota and Henrik Shipstead of Minnesota—joined with Democrats Reynolds and Wheeler in casting the negative votes. Johnson, too infirm to play an active role in the debate, remained an irreconcilable, but the three other senators who had voted against the League in 1919 supported the Connally resolution. Even more surprising was the list of confirmed isolationists who reversed themselves—Gerald Nye, Bennett Clark, Wayland Brooks, to name but a few. Their defection was undoubtedly an attempt to accommodate themselves to the new internationalist mood of the electorate, but it also emphasized the inadequacy of the Connally resolution. Even with the fourth article of the Moscow declaration included, it was an ambiguous statement which evaded the crucial issue of the use of force to preserve peace. [25]

The New York *Times*, however, proclaimed, "The Senate yesterday undid a twenty-four-year-old mistake," and other editors agreed, hailing the Connally resolution as a "great triumph" which opened "the portals on a new world." The Russians joined in the chorus of praise, with *Pravda* calling it "undoubtedly an important milestone" in American foreign policy. Roosevelt was very pleased, telling Stettinius that he thought everything had gone "smoothly." He wrote a brief note congratulating Tom Connally, saying, "It is grand." Then he chided him, "But why, oh why did you let Nye vote for it?"

The B$_2$H$_2$ senators were pleased with the outcome of their long struggle. Joseph Ball, reminiscing years later, said his colleagues were glad to get the Senate on record in favor of international organization, even though they were still disappointed in the vagueness of the final text. "We were kind of walking on eggs in that debate," he recalled. Ball regretted the omission of any reference to an international police force, but Edwin James, an ardent internationalist who wrote for the New York *Times*, felt this was the key to its success. "None of us will live to see a world police force organized and directed by an international organization," he wrote. By affirming a more moderate form of collective security, James believed that the Senate was "going back a quarter of a century" to "pick up where Wilson left off." Breckinridge Long agreed. "Now we are back on the main track," he noted in his diary on November 7, "after being sidetracked and nearly wrecked in 1920." [26]

III

The Moscow declaration and the successful outcome of the foreign ministers' conference far outshadowed the Connally resolution. Cordell Hull was now the national hero, lauded by liberals and conservatives alike for his masterful diplomacy. Walter Lippmann wired Roosevelt that the Secretary had scored "a tremendous success," and in a speech in Boston on November 18 he declared that Hull had ushered in "the next period of history" by cementing the nuclear alliance with Britain, Russia and China. Raymond Moley was even more ecstatic, writing in his column that the Secretary of State had "saved rivers of blood and months of war." "Mr. Hull has achieved a foreign policy upon which all American parties and factions can agree," Moley concluded. Even Freda Kirchwey, publisher of the *Nation* and a frequent critic of the Secretary, grudgingly praised Hull for achieving a rapprochement with Russia. Another *Nation* writer gave Roosevelt the credit, claiming it was a stroke of genius to use "a conservative Southern Democrat to bring about an entente between capitalist America and Communist Russia."

A few voices dissented. In a weekly newspaper column he began writing in November, Sumner Welles criticized the four-power dictatorship inherent in the Moscow declaration and urged the creation of a universal world body immediately. Addressing the New York *Herald Tribune* Forum, Wendell Willkie urged that the Moscow agreements be broadened to include all the United Nations, while Henry Wallace, speaking to the same group, made a cryptic comment about the danger of turning "Peace II into World War III." Both the National Catholic Welfare Board and the Protestant journal *Christian Century* expressed fear that Hull had signed secret agreements at Moscow that compromised the ideals of the Atlantic Charter, though neither was able to back up this charge.[27]

Nothing could dim the luster of Hull's triumph. With his usual eloquence, Churchill praised Hull for undertaking the 26,000-mile journey in the cause of peace, calling him "the gallant old eagle." When his C-54 touched down at Washington's National Airport, President Roosevelt was on hand with Mrs. Hull and Stettinius to greet him. Congress responded with an unprecedented invitation, asking Hull to give a report on the Moscow conference to a joint session. Scott Lucas, who originated this idea, believed it would serve "as a tribute to Hull for his achievement at Moscow and as a demonstration to the world of national unity in the United States." The Secretary quickly accepted, and Long, Pasvolsky and several others "dragged through five drafts," completing the final text only an hour before Hull was due to speak at the Capitol.

At midday on November 18 Hull walked erectly to the podium of the House chamber. The congressmen and senators rose to give him a long ovation. Then he delivered a twenty-five-minute speech with much greater eloquence than his radio efforts. He reviewed the events at Moscow, praising Eden and Molotov as men of good will, and affirmed that continued cooperation between the Big Four "will be the foundation stone upon which the future international organization will be constructed." Taking note of Welles' and Willkie's criticisms, he promised to broaden the cooperation to include all the United Nations so that "there will no longer be need for spheres of influence, for alliances, for balance of power." Then he thanked Congress for "its vision and statesmanship" in passing postwar resolutions in a non-partisan spirit. "By the procedure of cooperation with other nations likewise intent upon security," he promised, "we can and will remain masters of our own fate." [28]

For Cordell Hull, it was the climax of a long career. Often ridiculed for his pious platitudes and regularly bypassed by the President, he now had his moment of personal glory. In the space of three months he had vanquished his chief rival within the State Department, secured agreement in principle with the Soviet Union on a postwar international organization and ensured that the Senate would not again sabotage the peace. Most important, he had captured control of the internationalist crusade and had redirected it into traditional Wilsonian channels.

7

How Brave Will the
New World Be?

IPLOMATS FROM forty-four countries entered the East Room of
the White House on the afternoon of November 9, 1943, to
sign an agreement establishing the United Nations Relief and
Rehabilitation Administration. President Roosevelt gave a brief speech
hailing this action as "one more strong link joining the United Nations." He stressed the need to cooperate in political and humanitarian
as well as military issues, seeing in UNRRA the kind of practical,
day-by-day activity which would lead to a better world. "The forces of
the United Nations are marching forward," he concluded, "and the
peoples of the United Nations march with them."

The creation of UNRRA, however, symbolized domination by the
Big Four much more than it did United Nations unity. The initial plan,
drawn up by the United States and Britain with Russian and Chinese
approval, had been shown to the other members of the coalition over
the summer. Though the small nations suggested a number of changes,
most of the alterations included in the final draft were ones suggested by
the Senate Foreign Relations Committee, which gave the document its
approval on September 22. Cordell Hull made the revised agreement
public the next day, announcing that the administration would join the
new organization by executive action but would seek formal Congressional consent through a joint resolution at a later date. The UNRRA
agreement called for a Council, with one representative from each
participating country, to set general policy, but the real power was given
to a Central Committee consisting of the American, Russian, British
and Chinese delegates. They would meet regularly to advise Director-

156

General Herbert Lehman, and would report their actions to the Council, which would convene only at infrequent intervals.

On November 10, the day after the White House signing ceremony, the Council held its first meeting in Atlantic City, with Herbert Lehman presiding. The delegates spent much of their time discussing the problem of finances, finally agreeing that each nation should contribute one percent of its national income to UNRRA. Under this formula, designed to raise over $2 billion, the United States would provide $1.35 billion, nearly two thirds of the total. On November 15, the day the conference adjourned, Roosevelt sent a message to Congress seeking approval for American participation in UNRRA and the necessary appropriation; both Houses eventually approved the request by overwhelming margins. In World War I the United States had acted alone to relieve the problems of starvation and misery in postwar Europe, but America now committed itself to a cooperative policy. "The UNRRA represents an attempt to take from the United States the trappings of Santa Claus," commented Blair Bolles, "and to permit the nations which will receive relief to keep the self-respect that disappears with charity." [1]

Later in November 1943 President Roosevelt journeyed nearly halfway around the world to meet with Churchill and Stalin at Teheran. This major wartime conference, the first face-to-face encounter between Roosevelt and Stalin, lasted only four days, but in that short time the three leaders discussed military and political problems ranging from the forthcoming invasion of Europe to the nature of the peace. Roosevelt went out of his way to assure Stalin that he and Churchill did not see eye to eye on all issues, playing up American opposition to British colonialism and suggesting that the United States was as likely to side with Russia as with Britain on postwar issues. The President was impressed by Stalin's toughness, which frequently bordered on discourtesy, but he came away from the meeting convinced that Russia, in the words of Robert E. Sherwood, "would prove tractable and co-operative in maintaining the peace of the postwar world." It has been fashionable ever since for historians to say that Roosevelt tried to woo Stalin with his genial charm and failed, but Walter Lippmann felt that the President was far too cynical for such a naive strategy. "He distrusted everybody," Lippmann said of Roosevelt in the 1950's. "What he thought he could do was outwit Stalin, which is quite a different thing." [2]

On the second day of the conference Stalin came to Roosevelt's quarters for a private conversation. Attended only by interpreters, the two men exchanged ideas freely and with remarkable frankness. The President used this opportunity to inform Stalin of his views on international organization. Drawing heavily on the plan Welles had drawn up in the spring, he described a three-part structure consisting of an Assembly of all the United Nations devoted to discussion of general problems but powerless to act; an Executive Committee composed of the Big Four and six regional representatives to deal with social and economic issues; and the Four Policemen, who would have sole authority to enforce the peace and prevent aggression. Stalin reacted somewhat coolly, indicating that he preferred Churchill's suggestion of regional councils for Europe and Asia. He displayed greatest interest in the Four Policemen concept, asking Roosevelt if the United States would be prepared to send troops overseas to preserve the peace. The President immediately retreated, saying that he contemplated the use only of American naval and air power outside the Western Hemisphere. The American people, he added, would be averse to committing troops to fight in Europe and Asia after the war. Minor disputes, Roosevelt explained, could be choked off with economic sanctions; in case of aggression by a large nation, the Four Policemen would issue an ultimatum, and if it were disregarded, they would bombard and, if necessary, invade the offending country. Britain and Russia would supply the troops, while the United States would furnish air and sea support. Neither Roosevelt nor Stalin commented on how they would proceed if one of the Four Policemen committed an act of aggression.

On December 1, the last day of the conference, the two leaders met again in private. Roosevelt returned to the question of postwar international organization, asking that Stalin keep their previous conversation confidential. The President said that it was too early to discuss these ideas with Churchill, and that the Four Policemen concept in particular needed further study. Stalin agreed, commenting that Roosevelt had converted him from Churchill's regional approach and that now he was convinced of the need for a worldwide international organization to preserve the peace. Roosevelt did not hold any similar private conferences with Churchill, nor did he raise the issue of international organization at any of the plenary sessions. Churchill, however, was well aware of Roosevelt's ideas from their previous meetings—the President was dissembling when he told Stalin it was too early to raise this issue with the British Prime Minister. It is doubtful, though, that Roosevelt succeeded in fooling Stalin.[3]

At the close of the conference the three statesmen drew up a declaration which was released to the world on December 6, 1943. Phrased in very general terms, the statement emphasized the unity of the Big Three in the conduct of the war and the quest for peace. Unlike the Moscow declaration, it included no reference to international organization. The three men simply pledged "to make a peace which will command the good will of the overwhelming mass of the peoples of the world and banish the scourge and terror of war for many generations." Aware that many were calling for a United Nations Council so that the small nations could participate in postwar planning, the declaration promised cooperation with "all nations, large and small" who were waging the fight against "tyranny and slavery, oppression and intolerance." "We will welcome them," Churchill, Stalin and Roosevelt declared, "as they may choose to come, into a world family of Democratic Nations." Liberal editors in the United States accepted this pledge with great enthusiasm. "To the dismay of our enemies abroad and at home, the United Nations are now a solid front," commented the *New Republic.* "This may save a million deaths on the battlefield, and a decade of waste and confusion in the peace."

On Christmas Eve the President gave the American people a personal report on the Teheran conference. Speaking over the radio from his study at Hyde Park, he lauded Churchill as a "great citizen of the world" and was even more lavish in his praise of Stalin. Describing his intense dedication to the war effort, the President prophesied that "we are going to get along very well with him and the Russian people—very well indeed." Throughout the speech Roosevelt sounded the theme of unity, reminding his audience that as long as the Big Four, representing three fourths of the world's population, stuck together, the peace was secure. He promised that they would protect the rights of small nations and not abuse their enormous power. "The doctrine that the strong shall dominate the weak is the doctrine of our enemies—and we reject it," the President declared.

But, above all else, he emphasized that the willingness to use force was the key to lasting peace. Attacking the isolationists as "cheerful idiots," he savagely ridiculed those who had championed "ill-fated experiments of former years" such as the neutrality legislation. "For too many years," he asserted, "we lived on pious hopes that aggressor and warlike nations would learn and understand and carry out the doctrine of purely voluntary peace." He promised the American people not to repeat this disastrous policy but to rely instead on overwhelming military power to halt aggression before it could menace the world. "I believe, and I think

159

I can say," he proclaimed, "that the other three great nations who are fighting so magnificently to gain peace are in complete agreement that we must be prepared to keep the peace by force." [4]

Though the President did not reveal his concept of the Four Policemen, his speech foreshadowed a peace based on big-power domination. He made no mention of a world organization and indicated that the Big Four, not an international police force, would provide the military power to prevent aggression in the future. His remarks ran directly counter to the internationalist assumption that the new world organization would be a universal body in which each nation had an equal voice. Most internationalists, still rejoicing over the Moscow declaration and the Connally resolution, failed to perceive that the real struggle still lay ahead.

I

Five thousand Protestants gathered at the Cathedral of St. John the Divine in New York on October 28, 1943, to launch the Christian Mission on World Order, a major effort by American churches to rally their members to the cause of international organization. Illness prevented the featured speaker, Sumner Welles, from attending, but he sent a message proposing the immediate formation of United Nations machinery for the postwar world. John Foster Dulles told the assembled churchmen that the nation faced a critical period in its history and urged them "to revive in our people a sense of destiny in the performance of the great work of creation." The principal address was given by Senator Joseph Ball, who advocated the building of a new world order based on justice. Praising the churches for taking the initiative, he called the campaign "the greatest crusade since Jesus sent his twelve disciples out to preach the brotherhood of man."

Following this kick-off meeting, ninety ministers and laymen, operating in teams of four or five, traveled to 102 cities around the nation to preach the principles contained in the Six Pillars of Peace program. They concentrated on local churches, speaking to special meetings of Protestant leaders and setting up study groups to grapple with the issues of peace. Spending a day in each city, these teams also addressed luncheon clubs, university convocations, women's groups and high-school assemblies in an effort to stimulate public opinion. They distributed a new guidebook prepared by Dulles' commission and arranged for local ministerial associations and councils of churches to establish Pillars of Peace Committees in each community they visited.[5]

Though the crusade only lasted for three weeks, it had a far-reaching impact. In January 1944 the Methodist Church began an ambitious drive led by Bishop G. Bromley Oxnam, a member of the Commission on a Just and Durable Peace and the presiding officer of the Methodist Council of Bishops. In early 1943 he and his fellow bishops had visited Washington to discuss postwar planning with Cordell Hull and President Roosevelt, coming away with the belief that the church should play an active role in supporting an internationalist policy. Oxnam then organized a "Crusade for a New World Order" with the goal of persuading eight million Methodists to write letters to Congress and to the administration in behalf of a lasting peace. Howard Chandler Christy, a popular artist, designed a poster with a picture of Christ over the caption "The Coming Peace and The Prince of Peace." Bishop Oxnam sent copies to every Methodist church in the country and distributed thousands of postcards displaying the Christy picture for Methodists to send to servicemen overseas promising a determined stand for a Christian peace.

The Bishop's crusade began on the evening of January 10, 1944, with mass meetings in cities across the nation attended by audiences ranging from six hundred to over a thousand. Bishop Oxnam addressed the principal gathering in Brooklyn, New York, asking all Methodist ministers to arrange for groups of two or three laymen to call on each church family and suggest that they write to the President and to their congressman and senators. Throughout January and February, ministers responded to this call, preaching sermons, holding study classes and organizing the canvass of their congregations. Laymen were told to stick to simple propositions in their letters, asking for a repudiation of isolationism and a commitment to international collaboration. With great optimism, the bishops hoped to fulfill the slogan of their campaign, "The Peace May Be Won with a Three-Cent Stamp." [6]

The Methodist crusade achieved spectacular results. Washington received one of the largest outpourings of mail in history. Unlike previous pressure-group efforts, there were very few form letters. Instead, members of Congress received penciled postcards and handwritten letters from men and women who had never before expressed their views. Most of the comments were very general, simply identifying isolationism as un-Christian and pleading for a policy of international cooperation. Some asked, "Please, may we have Christ at the peace table?" while others urged a "Christian peace" based on the principle of collaboration. There was little specific mention of international organization, the majority requesting only a policy of cooperation with other nations after the war. A few wanted to use force to preserve peace, and one Missouri man told Senator Truman that he favored an international police force "with power to restrain gangster nations forever." But most agreed with Frances Robertson of Eldon, Missouri, who wrote to Truman in a cramped hand, "As one of your fellow Christians, I beseech you to line up your influence with those who would plan an international cooperation which is unselfish and casts aside hatred and revenge, opening the way to brotherhood of all mankind."

When the deluge of mail was at its height in March, the Northern Baptist Convention announced plans for a World Order Crusade culminating on Sunday, May 7. On that day Baptist ministers would preach sermons on peace and ask members of their congregations to write letters to the Senate and the State Department. This campaign had a much sharper focus, with writers urged to advocate "world organization in which every nation is invited to participate." Under this stimulus, the flow of letters to Washington continued throughout the spring. Not to be outdone, the Congregational Church began a "personal commitment" drive in behalf of international cooperation. On Sunday, May 21, Congregational ministers presented their members with a World Order Compact and asked everyone to sign it. Modeled after the Mayflower Compact, this document asked people to pledge "to work for a just and cooperative world order" and to help establish "an international organization for the better ordering of the interdependent life of nations." [7]

The initial reaction of Protestant leaders to the Moscow declaration had been favorable. On November 16 John Foster Dulles issued a public statement by the Commission on a Just and Durable Peace hailing it as "a notable step toward realizing international order as envisaged by our Six Pillars of Peace." But in January the Commission adopted a new statement of policy expressing concern over the potential big-power domination of the postwar world. In particular, the Commission warned against an overemphasis on security and a reliance on force to preserve the status quo. In a speech in early February, Dulles reinforced this plea, asserting the need to provide for peaceful change as an alternative to armed aggression. "To identify peace with the perpetuation of any given status quo is wholly unrealistic," he affirmed. To impress their views on the President, a delegation of churchmen, including Dulles, Oxnam and Bishop St. George Tucker, called on Roosevelt at the

White House on February 15, 1944. They handed him the January statement by the Commission and urged him to work for a world organization which would be "curative and creative, not merely regressive."

Though Roosevelt listened sympathetically, Dulles became anxious at the continued failure of the administration to implement the Moscow declaration and the Connally resolution. To keep up the pressure, he framed a petition which 1,251 Protestant ministers and laymen signed calling for the immediate creation of a United Nations Council as the nucleus of a new world body. Released to the press on April 24, 1944, this appeal expressed the growing frustration of the religious leaders who were dedicated to international organization. Taking their cue from the apparent commitment of the administration in the fall of 1943, they were eager to move forward on the wave of enthusiasm they had generated among their fellow Christians.[8]

II

The internationalists found themselves in a peculiar position in late 1943 and early 1944. They rejoiced in the passage of the Connally resolution and the Moscow declaration, but they discovered that these victories had left them without an immediate program. For some, the administration's decision was a death blow. Clarence Streit's Federal Union held its annual convention at Peoria, Illinois, in mid-November, attracting a small group of maiden ladies, ministers, high-school students and university professors. The session was listless, and though the convention endorsed the four-power declaration and the Connally resolution, it was apparent that the new unity with the Soviet Union made Streit's plan for a merger of democracies as the nucleus of world organization impractical. Federal Union continued, but its membership declined and it never regained the élan it had exhibited during the first year of the war. Ely Culbertson, hoping to found a movement with his books, was also a victim of the administration's commitment to moderate international cooperation. His quota-force plan and elaborate regional scheme were quickly forgotten as the American people focused on more limited ideas of world organization.

The Non-Partisan Council to Win the Peace, formed specifically to press for passage of the B_2H_2 resolution, was more successful. After the passage of the Connally resolution, which Edgar Mowrer interpreted as a great victory, the Council agreed to keep working in support of "the fighting fourteen senators," and the members succeeded in arranging for the publication of magazine articles by Senators Lister Hill and Elbert Thomas in early 1944. At its February meeting, the Council decided to devote itself to a campaign for the creation of "a United Nations Council *now* to deal with manifold political problems facing the world." The Women's Action Committee for Victory and Lasting Peace followed the same course. In the spring of 1944 it mounted a major drive to win public support for such a council as the first step toward implementing the Moscow declaration. The twenty-three state chapters promised to bring pressure to bear on congressmen and senators through their affiliated women's clubs, and on May 18 they celebrated a United Nations Council Day. This campaign added to the already heavy Congressional mailbags. A typical letter from a Missouri constituent to Senator Truman asked him to help push for a UN Council, writing, "I am eager to do all that I can to prevent a second catastrophe." [9]

The Commission to Study the Organization of Peace continued its activities with little change, releasing its fourth report at an all-day conference at the Hotel Commodore in New York on November 20, 1943. In presenting the document, which had been written prior to the Moscow declaration, James Shotwell and Clark Eichelberger stressed the importance of creating a world organization before the end of the war. The report focused almost exclusively on the problem of security, defining war as "a crime against civilization" and calling its prevention the primary task of international organization. The authors rejected the idea of an integrated world police force, preferring to rely on the ironclad promises of member states to use their military power cooperatively to crush aggression. They did suggest the creation of a small international air force operating out of strategically located bases which could strike immediately at nations threatening the peace.

At the end of the report, the Commission presented eleven fundamentals of peace which comprised the first specific program it had offered to the American people. Pointing out to Cordell Hull that these fundamentals were "political theory" and not a "blue-print," Shotwell said they had been formulated as an antidote to "the growing confusion because of the existence of such plans as those of Ely Culbertson and Clarence Streit." The eleven fundamentals followed the recommendations in the fourth report closely, with the emphasis on a security organization to prevent aggression. "Aggressive war is a crime against mankind," the second point read. "All nations must be bound by the obligation not to resort to other than peaceful means for the settlement of disputes." Other points called for an international air force, the progressive reduction of armaments, a world court, and a political organization consisting of a general assembly, an executive council, and a secretariat. No attempt was made to spell out the powers and nature of these proposed organs, but the implication was that they would follow the League of Nations model. The one great change from the Covenant would be a firm reliance on the "organization of power" to keep the peace.[10]

In the first few months of 1944 the Commission embarked on a major effort to acquaint the American people with its program. The executive committee sought to raise $200,000 for this purpose, telling prospective donors that "the peace may be won or lost in the minds of the people before the war is over." Concentrating on simple, popular material, the Commission prepared a flyer listing the eleven fundamentals, which was sold for five dollars per thousand to members and cooperating groups. A more elaborate pamphlet, with very imaginative drawings by artist Harry Sternberg illustrating the eleven points, sold for a quarter. The Commission also published a ten-cent discussion guide, *The Peace We Want*, which was designed as a handbook for community activities. It told how to work through local radio stations, newspapers, civic groups and political clubs to influence public opinion. "There should also be available a group of V speakers," the pamphlet stated, "men and women ready to be called upon for five-minute talks at club meetings, at factories—in fact, to meet with all groups in the community." In March the Commission called on high schools throughout the nation to make world organization the theme for their June commencement exercises. "What could be more fitting than that the young people who will either live in a world of peace or live to fight the third world war," asked *Changing World*, "should consider the urgent need for such a world organization, how it best may be brought about and what its powers should be?"

The Commission printed a booklet in June 1944 which demonstrated how effective it and other internationalist groups had been in molding public attitudes. Entitled *The United States and Postwar International Cooperation*, this publication listed the many national organizations which had gone on record in favor of American participation in a new world body. According to the Commission, virtually every major veterans' group, women's club, labor union and business association had passed resolutions endorsing the Moscow declaration and affirming international organization. The most striking feature was a referendum conducted by the Chamber of Commerce of the United States which showed that 1,829 members favored American entry into a world body possessing the power to use force in the maintenance of peace, with only 71 dissenting.[11]

The United Nations Association nearly swallowed the League of Nations Association in 1944. Only a tax ruling, which defined the LNA as an educational association and the UNA as an action group, prevented Clark Eichelberger from disbanding the older organization. In February 1944 the LNA's board of directors voted to inform all members that they were automatically members of the UNA as well and to transfer the publication of *Changing World* to the newer group. Several charter members of the LNA regretted the change, and Eichelberger tried to reassure them in a form letter in March. "The efforts of two decades now bid fair to come to fruition," he told them, adding that there was no conflict between the old League of Nations and the developing United Nations. Hamilton Holt agreed. Writing from Florida, he told Eichelberger, "We who have fought for the League all these years have got to work with any group that can best carry on the principles for which the League stood, whether it be the League or an organ of the United Nations."

In April, *Changing World* passed into the hands of the UNA. Many of its state branches transferred to the United Nations Association, but the League of Nations Association continued its traditional program, holding high-school prize contests and sponsoring model United Nations conferences for college students. On June 15 the directors adopted a resolution urging the League of Nations and the United Nations to "unite in creating the strongest and most effective world organization possible." Eichelberger, deeply aware of the emotional attachment of his followers to the League, was relieved at the ease with which the transition had taken place.[12]

In the spring of 1944 financial necessity required even greater efforts at uniting the fractured internationalist movement. In March the head of the Carnegie Endowment, Nicholas Murray Butler, met with internationalist leaders at the Low Memorial Library at Columbia University and urged them to merge their activities in order to avoid wasteful duplication. In April, Hugh Moore, president of the Dixie Cup Company and a heavy contributor to Eichelberger's organizations, held a series of luncheons to discuss ways of uniting action groups which were not tax exempt. The chief spokesman for a merger was Ulric Bell, a former reporter for the Louisville *Journal-Courier* who had served as director of Fight for Freedom, one of the most active pre-war interventionist groups. He had gone to Hollywood to help produce government propaganda films during the war, and in March 1944 he returned to New York with the backing of West Coast internationalists "to round up all the scattered efforts now being made and develop a national movement for unity and sanity," as he told Grace Tully, the President's secretary.

Bell succeeded in convincing the other internationalists that a merger was essential to raise the money they needed to carry on an effective publicity program. In June he and Eichelberger announced the formation of Americans United for World Organization as a consolidation of the United Nations Association, the American Free World Association, Citizens for Victory and several smaller groups. The Commission to Study the Organization of Peace, which enjoyed tax-exempt status, remained independent. Eichelberger, who agreed to serve as chairman of the policy committee of Americans United, believed that the new organization would be able to develop a "united front" with business, labor and women's groups. "The pattern of world organization will be determined in the next 6 months," he wrote, "so this is the home stretch." Ulric Bell, whose salary was paid by the Hollywood Free World Committee, was the director of Americans United, which he saw as a response to "the fervent demands of groups throughout the country for a movement with teeth in it, which will seek to mobilize public opinion in favor of world organization." The only goal, he vowed, was "that of getting a world organization NOW."

Florence Harriman, a former minister to Norway who had been president of Free World, wrote enthusiastically to President Roosevelt on June 10 about the formation of Americans United. The President expressed his pleasure at this development, but he was skeptical of its potential effectiveness, saying, "it is highly important to get down to the grass roots. In 1920 I spoke all over the United States in behalf of the League of Nations, but my audiences were nearly all democratic or highbrow. They were all with me 100% but I do not think I made a single vote." He urged Mrs. Harriman to concentrate on those whose minds were not yet made up or who opposed international organization. "Now, as then," he concluded, "the intellectuals are nearly all with us." [13]

III

"Today, in 1944, we are living through experiences that parallel 1918," wrote Charlotte B. Mahon, director of the Woodrow Wilson Foundation. "Never before has one generation had the privilege of looking back and profiting by its own tragic mistakes. We are that generation." Under Mrs. Mahon's guidance, the Foundation did everything possible to compel Americans to learn from the experience of World War I in preparing for the coming peace. With a doubled staff, the Foundation greatly expanded the postwar-studies collection of the Wilson Memorial Library and increased its subsidies to the Commission to Study the Organization of Peace and other internationalist groups. It began its own publication program, distributing a pamphlet entitled *Our Second Chance* which contained statements by government leaders in 1918 and more recent ones by Roosevelt, Welles and Hull on opposite pages headed "Then" and "Now." Above all, the Foundation extolled the memory of Woodrow Wilson in order to "stimulate and sustain the American people in their effort to achieve Wilson's vision of a world without war." Mrs. Mahon devoted the greatest effort to a brief biography by David Loth designed to inform high-school students of the noble sacrifices made by Wilson to spare the world the agony of future wars.

To the delight of the Foundation's directors, a great Wilson revival developed in the course of 1944 as writers exploited the upsurge of public interest in the rejection of the League of Nations. Nearly all the authors were sympathetic to Wilson, treating him as a man whose tragedy was to live before his time. J. Eugene Harley, a political scientist at the University of Southern California, described the former President's ideals as forming "a veritable Rock of Gibraltar" and "a strong rallying point for all who think of the days of peace and reconstruction ahead." Gerald Johnson collaborated with the editors of *Look* to produce a pictorial biography of Wilson with the subtitle "The Unforgettable Figure Who Has Returned to Haunt Us." The last third of the book dealt with the quest for peace, and the theme of the photographs and text was the people's failure to understand the prophetic wisdom of their leader. Under a picture of Wilson speaking to a Los Angeles audience on his western tour in 1919, Johnson wrote, "The prevention of a second war depended on his convincing people and convincing them in time." Near the end there was a photograph of Wilson's tomb with the commentary, "The word 'Wilson' now has a new definition. It means peace." [14]

Several writers concentrated exclusively on Wilson's search for peace. In a very carefully researched study, Thomas A. Bailey analyzed the President's role in the Paris Peace Conference, concluding that Wilson had made a series of unwise concessions that flawed the Treaty of Versailles. But other authors lacked Bailey's scholarly objectivity and produced very one-sided accounts of the making of peace in 1919. In *Victory Without Peace*, Roger Burlingame and Alden Stevens included fictional conversations between the statesmen of the era to demonstrate how these lesser men betrayed the noble ideals of the American President. One sympathetic reviewer, admitting that the authors had oversimplified history with their portraits of "St. Wilson, virgin and martyr" and "the evil one, Senator Lodge, with his baleful leer," nonetheless thought that their account was "essentially true" and a "good preparation" for the peace that lay ahead. Karl Schriftgiesser, in a biography of Henry Cabot Lodge, described him as a man filled with a venomous hatred of Wilson, and treated the defeat of the Covenant as a conspiracy hatched at Theodore Roosevelt's sickbed and carried out against the national interest for partisan and personal motives. The book was well received by reviewers, who called it "hard-hitting" and "as timely as the morning's news," and it quickly went through four printings.

Ruhl Bartlett dealt with the repudiation of the League in a more scholarly fashion in *The League to Enforce Peace*, but his own regret at the outcome colored his narrative. In his last chapter he concluded that the defeat of the League of Nations was "the beginning of the moral collapse of America" and "the first of many milestones along the road to Pearl Harbor." Hamilton Holt, who had read the book in manuscript, told the publishers that "it will be an all-time source book as the inevitable movement towards world federation grows." In a letter to Bartlett, Holt praised his account, adding, "I regard Lodge and his friends guilty of the greatest political crime by men in high office during the history of the United States." The University of North Carolina Press advertised Bartlett's book under the caption "Will It Happen Again?" and claimed that "it shows with what sinister ease progressive leadership and the will of the people can be thwarted by a small but diabolically clever minority." [15]

Hollywood provided by far the most influential contribution to the revival. Darryl Zanuck originally set out to do a brief documentary on Wilson for the Office of War Information, but as he explored the subject, he became convinced that it merited a full-scale feature film. Encouraged by Wendell Willkie, then serving as chairman of the board of Twentieth Century-Fox, Zanuck employed Lamar Trotti to write the script. Trotti spent over two years at this task, doing extensive research himself and getting additional help from the Woodrow Wilson Foundation and Ray Stannard Baker, Wilson's close friend and biographer. Zanuck then budgeted over three million dollars for the picture, an amount surpassed only by *Gone with the Wind* at the time, and planned to spend another million in promoting it as "The Most Important Event in 50 Years of Motion Picture Entertainment." Zanuck, who also intended to produce a movie from Willkie's *One World*, knew he was taking a great gamble. "Unless these two pictures are successful from every standpoint," he told a reporter, "I'll never make another film without Betty Grable."

When *Wilson* opened in New York on August 1, 1944, the Woodrow Wilson Foundation joined with Willkie in giving a buffet supper attended by Mrs. Wilson, Mrs. William Gibbs McAdoo, the former President's daughter, Josephus Daniels, his Secretary of the Navy, and James Cox, the unsuccessful Democratic presidential candidate in 1920. The movie lived up to their expectations, chronicling Wilson's life from the time he decided to leave Princeton to enter politics down through the defeat of the League in 1919. It was a lavish Technicolor production complete with eighty-seven songs of the period, many sung by groups of Princeton undergraduates, a sentimental portrayal of the death of Wilson's first wife and his courtship of Edith Galt, and a vivid re-creation of the 1912 Democratic convention in Baltimore. It was entertainment on the grand scale, but historians could barely recognize Lamar Trotti's Wilson, played effectively by Alexander Knox. His stern personality softened and blurred, the screen Wilson became the conventional Hollywood hero, moving steadily up the ladder of political success until he is betrayed by a vindictive Henry Cabot Lodge, played as a stylized villain by Sir Cedric Hardwicke, whose lines had been approved in advance by Lodge's grandson. Colonel House appeared only as a minor character, and the movie barely hinted at the complex issues involved in the Treaty of Versailles and the League of Nations.

In the first five weeks, more than a million people saw the film in New York alone, and there were long lines outside the theaters showing it in fifty cities across the country. Some reviewers complained that it presented too sentimental and nostalgic a portrait of Wilson, and they lamented the heavy emphasis on trivial details and the failure to probe deeply into the dilemmas the President faced. Others accepted these flaws as a concession to popular taste and praised Zanuck for dealing with a significant theme. James Agee called it "a very sincere and even a brave picture," while *Newsweek* labeled it "a stirring pageant" and praised Zanuck and Trotti for their "surprising integrity and good taste." Nearly all agreed that it was a highly effective "hymn to internationalism." "On Hollywood's relatively modest scale," commented *Time*, "Producer Zanuck has performed a Wilsonian act. . . . Since, unlike

Woodrow Wilson, he is an experienced entertainer, his colorful, worshipful sermon on internationalism may serve to bring millions of Americans a few steps forward on the sawdust trail." Interviewers in the lobby of the Roxy Theatre in New York reported that the message reached the audiences, who came away voicing "a warm enthusiasm for a league of nations ideal." [16]

For the internationalists, viewing the film was a profoundly moving experience. Arthur Sweetser, president of the Woodrow Wilson Foundation and a longtime advocate of the League of Nations, felt that every American should see it. He wrote, "It is difficult to see how anyone viewing these tragic scenes of Mr. Wilson's fighting to keep out of war, of his eventual entry and superb consecration, of his struggles in Paris and then at home, of his heroic tour of the country in behalf of the League, of his tragic collapse and the final catastrophic defeat of his proposal, can leave the theatre without a choke in his voice and a vow that it shall not happen again." Hamilton Holt wrote that "nothing has heartened me so much since the defeat of the League. It looks as tho the truth was prevailing." In his diary, Breckinridge Long confided that seeing *Wilson* was "one of the most remarkable emotional experiences a man could have." He cried at several points in the movie, but it encouraged him greatly. "I have kept the faith," he wrote, "and this time the conviction of a lifetime will witness my participation in positive achievement in securing the principle so long advocated." [17]

The emergence of Wilson as the symbol of peace led to specific proposals based on his experience. In early 1944, Kenneth Colegrove, a political scientist at Northwestern University, advocated abolition of the two-thirds rule for the ratification of treaties in a book entitled *The American Senate and World Peace*. Reminding his readers that in 1919 a minority of senators had frustrated the will of the majority, Colegrove warned that a group of Republican isolationists were planning the same tactics "to torpedo the peace settlement at the end of the war." He urged a constitutional amendment to permit treaties to be ratified by a simple majority of both Houses. Edward Corwin, a noted authority on the Constitution, agreed with Colegrove, and in the Senate Claude Pepper and Guy Gillette sponsored such an amendment. Max Lerner endorsed this move in *PM*, writing, "Our job is to use the Constitution for the national welfare, and not to be ridden by one provision to our destruction." Most senators, however, resented any effort to tamper with their control over foreign policy, and the proposed amendment died in committee.[18]

Other scholars believed that Wilson's example pointed to a stronger

League of Nations as the sure road to lasting peace. Dexter Perkins, a noted diplomatic historian, wrote in *America and Two Wars* that the fundamental weakness of the Treaty of Versailles "lay in the absence of an effective organized force for the preservation of peace." Blaming the American people for this omission, Perkins admonished, "They must be more ready, much more ready at the end of the present war." Denna Fleming, a Vanderbilt political scientist, arrived at the same assessment, writing that "the League of the future must be a powerful federation, in which large powers are given to the federation—powers great enough to enforce the peace over at least the bulk of the earth's surface." Fleming advocated the creation of a small international police force and the surrender of sovereignty to the new world body. "This is the last chance," he warned, "that we are ever likely to have to help organize a decent, livable world." Both Perkins and Fleming saw continued American friendship with the Soviet Union as the cornerstone of peace, and warned against "the agitation of mischief-makers" who favored "playing power politics against Russia through the length and breadth of Europe." Fleming concluded with a plea for a return to Wilson's ideals. "More and more," he wrote, "it is becoming apparent that Woodrow Wilson was the first statesman of full world stature produced by any people."

In the first half of 1944 two academic internationalists wrote books giving more detailed plans for the creation of a world organization based on Wilsonian principles. The first was Philip Nash, president of the University of Toledo and a former executive director of the League of Nations Association. In *An Adventure in World Order*, Nash rejected both the idea of a big-power alliance and utopian schemes for a world state, and advocated instead an Assembly representing all nations which in turn would elect an eight-member executive board on which the Big Four would have permanent seats. Like other Wilsonians, Nash emphasized collective security as the key to peace, proposing a small international police force and a pledge by member nations to use economic sanctions and military contingents to restrain potential aggressors. Nash wanted each nation to act voluntarily, and no one would be compelled to furnish troops for collective action. ". . . let us put our faith in economic sanctions backed by a small police force," he wrote. "Behind this will be the combined military might of all the nations which see that aggression anywhere is a threat to them. If, when the crisis comes, men are again so blind as to miss these implications, then the white mountains of the Four Freedoms will still be unscaled."

In *The Great Decision*, James T. Shotwell wrote "All roads lead back to the political organization of the League of Nations as the starting point for that of the United Nations." Shotwell was convinced that prevention of aggressive war was the heart of the problem. Defining an aggressor as a nation which refused to use pacific means to settle disputes, he proposed a world assembly and an international court for the peaceful adjustment of quarrels between nations. If a country refused to use this machinery, the nations of the world would adopt economic sanctions and, if these failed, would supply military units to crush the aggressor. Shotwell also favored a small standing international air force which "reduces international policing to a minimum, and yet offers a safeguard against the dangers of international anarchy." "The only real solution for the problem of security is to erect a quarantine against aggression by cooperative agreement between peace-loving nations," he wrote, "to create the machinery for the prevention of war and to make it work." [19]

Despite the popular enthusiasm for Woodrow Wilson, critics were harsh on the ideas expressed by his followers. Norman Thomas bitingly dismissed collective security as "Peace through the Police," noting that men like Shotwell and Nash neglected the basic economic and social ills that drove nations to acts of aggression. Raymond Leslie Buell criticized Shotwell as an orthodox internationalist who failed to understand power relationships. "In a sense," he wrote, "this is a re-statement of the case for the League of Nations with the addition of an international air force." In *Christian Century*, Paul Hutchinson, a pre-war isolationist, charged that Shotwell had dodged the basic issue. "If you are going to have an organization to police the world's peace," he wrote, "it must know how it is going to 'police the policemen'!"

These attacks were hard to refute. In going back to the League for their model, the internationalists were caught up in the dilemma that had doomed Wilson—how to create a world body with the power to halt aggression without surrendering the essence of national sovereignty. Wilson had put his faith in the moral obligation in Article 10, believing that nations would honor their pledge in time of crisis. His followers now sought to escape by creating a token international police force to act on behalf of the world community. Such an agency could handle aggression by small nations, but it would be unable to deal with hostile action by the major powers. Collective-security enthusiasts responded by affirming their trust in the devotion of the Big Four to the cause of peace. But the editors of the *New Republic* expressed a widely held doubt about this "internationalist spirit" kindled by the Wilson revival. "How long will it survive," they asked, "when the icy winds of international realism begin to blow?" [20]

I V

Charles Beard, the distinguished historian and confirmed isolationist, viewed Wilsonian internationalism sardonically. In *The Republic*, which took the form of conversations between Beard and his imaginary Connecticut neighbors, the Smyths, he devoted a chapter to ridiculing the postwar ideas that circulated in 1944. At his suggestion, the Smyths invited advocates of a new world order to a cocktail party. One was a professor who believed that all the world's troubles since 1919 stemmed from the failure of the U.S. to join the League. Beard noted that the professor, with continuous grants from peace foundations, had waged the battle for the League with never-ending optimism, traveling across the nation to speak to "every kind of organization that would lend him ears." "Whenever I had seen him," Beard added, "he had told me the peace movement was making rapid progress." The other guests included a champion of Streit's concept of Federal Union, a believer in world economic union who wants to abolish war by giving everyone "equal access to raw materials," and a Protestant clergyman who announces that peace will come when God's law of love reigns over the world.

One by one, Beard proceeds to demolish the hopes of each of the world planners. He points out the ineffectiveness of the League in the 1930's when it possessed the force to stop Hitler, predicts that a world federation would lead to mammoth civil wars rather than eternal peace, and reminds the minister that the world has rejected the law of love for the past two thousand years. When the advocate of economic union protests that Beard fails to understand that they are dealing with a moral question, he replies, "Are all you world-planners who stand for the brotherhood of man prepared to sweep away all our immigration laws and let your brothers and sisters from every part of the world migrate freely to the United States and settle here?" After a lengthy silence, the Smyths ask Beard to state his own view of the postwar world. Beard demurs, saying that he is "oppressed" by the very idea of attempting to lay down the fundamentals of a new world order. Finally, he affirms the continued cooperation of the United Nations coalition and suggests that the members sign a treaty promising not to resort to violence for ten years after the war, which could then be renewed every decade. "This program, I believe, would be more likely to realize aspirations for the good of our country and humanity, which we all cherish, than grandiose plans for settling everything and everybody all at once and for all time and for trying to hold millions of people down by police and propaganda." [21]

Other scholars shared Beard's pessimistic reaction to the vogue of postwar planning. In *How New Will the Better World Be?* Carl Becker warned against trying to escape the harsh realities of the world through wishful thinking. As an historian, he asserted the primacy of the nation-state as the source of political power in the modern world. "It is futile to base any plans for a new and better world in the immediate future on the assumption that the sentiment of nationalism will be replaced by the love of mankind," he wrote. The Axis nations, he pointed out, were the ones seeking to establish a radically different world; the United Nations were fighting for the status quo, the preservation of a system of sovereign independent states free to determine their own form of government. He reminded his readers that power was the essence of all international relations, calling World War II "a manifestation of power politics on the grandest scale ever seen," and stating that the American goal was "to redress the balance of power against Germany and Japan." He doubted that a new world body would work any better than the League of Nations, and the most he hoped for after the war was a stable equilibrium between the large and small nations in the international community.[22]

Reinhold Niebuhr reinforced this realistic view of the future in a series of lectures at Stanford University given in January 1944 and subsequently published as *The Children of Light and the Children of Darkness.* Labeling the internationalists as children of light who held an optimistic view of human nature and potential, Niebuhr offered them little encouragement. True world order, he argued, could come only as the outgrowth of a genuine world community, not through leagues, federations, police forces or other structural devices. Given the force of existing national sovereignty, such a world community could come only after decades, and perhaps centuries, of continued international anarchy. But, unlike Becker and Beard, he also warned against reliance on the power politics advocated by the children of darkness. "A balance of power," he commented, "is in fact a kind of managed anarchy. But it is a system in which anarchy invariably overcomes the management in the end." He suggested that the children of light borrow some of the wisdom of the children of darkness, "and yet be careful not to borrow too much." Then, taking refuge in a theologian's paradox, he urged men to use their God-given freedom to create the world community, knowing that their human limitations would make the task impossible. "The world community," he concluded, "standing thus as the final possibility and impossibility of human life, will be in actuality the perpetual problem as well as the constant fulfillment of human hopes." [23]

Mortimer J. Adler, professor of the philosophy of law at the University of Chicago and author of the best-selling *How to Read a Book*, was only a little more encouraging in his popular *How to Think About War and Peace*. Noting that the postwar planners were divided into optimistic idealists and pessimistic realists, Adler proceeded to argue that both were correct. In the short run, the strength of existing nationalism prevented effective international organization, but the long-range trend favored the emergence of a unified world government. Beginning with the premise that sovereignty was the sole cause of war, Adler claimed that the world was doomed to perpetual war until all power was vested in a world government. He proposed to reach this goal by gradual stages, moving from a balance of power to a league of independent states, and then to a world federation which would prepare the way for the ultimate world government in which nationalism would disappear altogether. The current internationalism, he warned, was only a beginning; the whole process might take five hundred years, though it could be shortened to half that time by sustained effort. "Perpetual peace will never be made unless the work is begun and carried on by generations of men who will not live to see it accomplished," he concluded. [24]

These scholars all provided a much-needed antidote to the heady idealism of the Wilsonian internationalists. Their emphasis on nationalism and their reminder that the world of the future would be based on the traditions and institutions of the past helped clarify the public debate. Skeptical and pessimistic in their advice, they nonetheless revealed a latent sympathy with the internationalists, sharing their dreams but doubtful of their techniques. They were reluctant realists who pointed out the facts of international life without endorsing them.

A second group responded to the liberal internationalists by affirming the alternative of power politics. George Fielding Eliot, a well-known military commentator, wrote *Hour of Triumph* in 1944 as a plea for Big Four control of the postwar world. Vitally concerned with the problem of keeping the peace, Eliot rejected the idea of an international police force as impractical and relied instead on the military strength of

176

America, Britain, Russia and China, whom he termed "the senior wardens of the new peace." Though he confessed that he hoped a world federation would emerge someday, he doubted it would come in his lifetime. He urged the Big Four to form a United Nations Council during the war to ensure their continued collaboration when the fighting was over. He minimized the risk of a quarrel between the ruling nations "because there exists an equilibrium of distributed power among the principal states, and because the interests of those states are far more engaged in maintaining the peace than in disturbing it." [25]

Professor Nicholas J. Spykman of Yale, the leading advocate of the balance of power, died in 1943, but his research assistant revised some lectures given just before his death and published them under the title *The Geography of the Peace*. Dismissing the internationalists as dreamers, Spykman proclaimed, "Force is manifestly an indispensable instrument both for national survival and for the creation of a better world." Asserting that geography formed the basis for all postwar planning, he defined the American national interest as the preservation of a stable balance of power in Europe and Asia. He believed that Russian and British security also rested on such an equilibrium. "These three states can, therefore, provide the foundation for an effective security system," he wrote. "Since neither of the three can afford to stand alone and isolated against the rest of the world, their co-operation will serve their own best interests." [26]

One of Spykman's associates in the Yale Institute of International Studies, William T. R. Fox, elaborated on this approach to peace in *The Super-Powers*. In the first few pages Fox stated bluntly that the international community was composed of squirrels and elephants, and that only the elephants counted in postwar planning. "A blueprint for peace which posits the disappearance of all the great powers must be labeled: 'No solution,' " he added. Fox defined the essence of peace in the ability of the big powers to reconcile their conflicting interests and collaborate with each other. A community of interest already existed between the United States and Britain, he wrote, and thus he saw relations with the Soviet Union as the key to peace. "Soviet co-operation in the task of maintaining peace is neither to be assumed nor to be rejected in advance," he advised. "It is to be achieved." He asked his fellow countrymen to stop focusing on a world organization and concentrate instead on developing among the super-powers "a disposition to consult and to agree." Dismissing China as a squirrel, Fox called for a "Soviet-Anglo-American coalition" as the basis of the new world order.

Even this structure would not guarantee peace, he admitted, but "it does offer real promise that the next twenty years will be a transition to something other than a third world war." [27]

V

The controversy over the nature of the postwar world reached its peak in the summer of 1944 with the publication of Sumner Welles' *The Time for Decision* and Walter Lippmann's *U.S. War Aims*. To the surprise of the book trade, Welles' book was an immediate hit, displacing Bob Hope's *I Never Left Home* at the top of the New York *Times* best-seller list in mid-August and remaining there for the rest of the year. The Book-of-the-Month Club made *The Time for Decision* its August selection, and eventually nearly half a million copies were sold. Harper and Brothers promoted it by asserting "Only a handful of men in the world have had access to the facts on which this book is based," and many readers undoubtedly bought it because they believed Welles possessed authoritative knowledge of the administration's postwar plans. Lippmann's book attracted a much smaller audience, although it went through four printings and enjoyed a brief stay on the best-seller list. *Reader's Digest* printed a condensation of *U.S. War Aims* in September, and only the opposition of Henry Luce, who thought it too anti-Russian, kept *Life* from running a summary.

The two authors, close personal friends, wrote from very different motives. In his preface, Lippmann said that in 1943 William Allen White had urged him to add a chapter to his *U.S. Foreign Policy* to illustrate how the wartime four-power alliance could become the basis of a lasting peace. Lippmann thought it was too early then to discuss specific postwar arrangements, but by 1944 he had changed his mind. "The time has come and the way is clear to define our war aims," he wrote in the opening sentence of the book. Several years later Lippmann said that the book was "an open attempt to get away from the One World doctrine," adding that his views shocked and dismayed most of his friends. In contrast, Welles wrote out of a sincere conviction that it was time to proclaim again the ideals of Woodrow Wilson which had thrilled his generation "to the depths of our emotional and intellectual being." "It is because of my abiding confidence that the realization of most of these ideals was well within human capacity," Welles affirmed, "that I have dared to write this book." [28]

In *The Time for Decision* Welles put forth a moderate and restrained version of liberal internationalism. He viewed American relations with the Soviet Union as the greatest unknown, and he advocated an all-out effort to "persuade the Russian people and their government that their permanent and truest interest lies in co-operating with us in the creation and maintenance of a democratic and effective world organization." He wanted to establish a provisional executive council of the United Nations immediately on which the small as well as the large nations would be represented. Led by the Big Four, but responsible to all the United Nations, this body would guide the transition from the war to the formation of a world organization for enduring peace. He rejected Lippmann's call for a nuclear alliance, warning that history proved coalitions were temporary expedients that dissolved when the common danger that created them disappeared. "No international organization can conceivably survive," he predicted, "unless it is supported by the opinion of free men and women throughout the world."

Welles then outlined a structure that closely resembled the Draft Constitution he had helped prepare in the State Department. The central body would be a United Nations Executive Council composed of the Big Four and seven other members selected from the various regions of the world. Welles proposed the formation of regional organizations to handle all local problems; only when a disturbance proved beyond the scope of the regional body would the Executive Council take jurisdiction. The big powers would possess a veto power on the use of force, and if they voted sanctions, they would be expected to provide the bulk of the troops. As this system developed, Welles suggested adding a World Congress and a World Court in the future to provide for the peaceful settlement of disputes. He believed this system incorporated the experience of the Pan-American movement and provided an effective balance between the need for universal organization and the desire to maintain regional autonomy. But whether the United Nations adopted this proposal or some other, he was most concerned with securing full-scale American participation in the shaping of the postwar world. Welles ended his book by declaring: [29]

The people of the United States are once more afforded the chance to offer their co-operation and their leadership to other nations. They are granted another opportunity to help to make a world in which they, and all peoples, can safely live. The decision they now make will determine their destiny.

7. How Brave Will the New World Be?

Walter Lippmann believed that the issue of American involvement in international affairs had already been settled by events. "Instead of debating the need of any positive policy," he wrote in U.S. War Aims, "we have now to deliberate upon what kind of positive policy we need." Arguing that the peace was already taking shape, he urged Americans to realize that the nation's basic national interest was to maintain a stable balance of power in Europe and Asia. "Fundamentally," he wrote, "the security of the United States demands that we prevent the establishment of a conquering empire in any part of the great oceanic basin of the Atlantic and the Pacific." Ignoring the Pacific, he recommended that the United States join with Britain, France and Canada to form an Atlantic Community which would "pursue a common foreign policy" with the non-Atlantic world. At the same time, he forecast the emergence of two other major regional groupings, the Russian and the Chinese "orbits." "Whether there is to be a third World War in the twentieth century depends upon whether the Russians come to rest within their orbit, the Atlantic states in theirs, and whether they then concert their policies towards Germany and Japan."

Lippmann was optimistic, believing that the wartime alliance had already created the basis of this new world order. "If we preserve it and enhance it, we shall inaugurate a long peace," he predicted. "If we ignore it and wreck it, we must prepare for another series of great wars." In this system, he saw no role for the smaller nations, suggesting simply that they find their security "within the protective power of the great state" in each area of the world. Lippmann saw only one obstacle—a totalitarian Soviet Union which might reject collaboration with the West and attempt to expand its orbit by aggression. He favored a bold policy toward Russia, with the United States approaching the Soviets frankly with an offer to cooperate. "If they refuse," he wrote, "we can still do our very best to get on with them, persisting through the ordinary channels of diplomacy in the effort to prevent a third World War."

In the final section of his book Lippmann delivered a blistering attack on Wilsonian collective security. He did not object to forming a world organization to deal with social, technical and economic problems so long as it had nothing to do with the vital issue of war and peace. He defined the principles of Woodrow Wilson, which he himself had helped formulate during World War I, as a series of moral prohibitions which "forbid national states to do the things which they have always done to defend their interests and to preserve their integrity." He accused Wilson of drawing up a moral code which was beyond human capacity to observe and which the United States itself had never been able to honor. Fearful that the nation was preparing to repeat Wilson's errors, he hammered away at what he termed the "supreme spiritual error" in the Wilsonian principles. "It is the error of forgetting that we are men and of thinking that we are gods. We are not gods. . . . We are mere mortals with limited power and little universal wisdom." He concluded with a plea for his regional approach as a substitute for a universal international organization: [30]

> We have to reverse the Wilsonian pattern of collective security. We cannot build a universal society from the top downwards. We must build up to it from the existing national states and historic communities. That, I think, is what we must learn from the great experiment at Geneva and from its failure. We have, I am convinced, to learn it thoroughly. For we cannot afford to fail again.

"Mr. Welles challenges us to make a tremendous effort," commented the directors of Freedom House. "Mr. Lippmann seems to say that we cannot make it." Nearly all reviewers of the two books agreed, praising Welles for his urgent call for action. "The unexpected quality in this volume is fervor; it exudes heat as well as light," remarked Anne O'Hare McCormick. In a year-end poll of critics, *The Time for Decision* was ranked as one of the ten outstanding books of the year, while *U.S. War Aims* was not mentioned. Reviewers criticized Lippmann for carving the world into three spheres and failing to provide a unifying world organization. But most of all they reacted to his assault on Wilsonianism. "There was nothing wrong with the Wilsonian conception of collective justice and collective security," wrote Max Lerner, arguing that Lippmann had created a straw man to demolish. In *Free World*, Beryl Harold Levy claimed that the followers of Wilson were as conversant with power politics as "any vaunted super-realist." Levy then accused Lippmann of a lack of realism in his failure "to note the role of science and industry in reducing the world to a sixty-hour air suburb, highly interdependent, with no region immune from future robot attack except through collaborative maintenance of world-wide order."

The administration followed the controversy between Lippmann and Welles very closely. Breckinridge Long prepared mimeographed summaries of the books and distributed them throughout the State Department. In June, Hull asked his subordinates to conduct a full-scale reevaluation of the Department's postwar plans in light of Lippmann's proposals. After a thorough study, Hull's advisers rejected the concept of regional alliances and endorsed the idea of a universal international organization. Long was so disturbed by Welles' book that he sent a lengthy analysis of it to the President, urging him to release a public denial that it reflected administration policy. Calling Welles' statements "inaccurate" and "misleading," Long advised, "From every standpoint it seems necessary that an attempt be made to counteract the harmful effects of this book." Roosevelt evidently disagreed, for the White House maintained a discreet silence.[31]

Public interest in the two books became so great that in mid-August *Newsweek* asked Welles and Lippmann to restate their views in articles, with each author also given space to rebut the other's ideas. The resulting symposium revealed a surprising amount of agreement. Both men stressed the importance of dealing with world problems on a regional level as far as possible, and both felt that the major burden of policing the postwar world would have to be assumed by the Big Four. The core of their disagreement lay in the degree of power and responsibility they would vest in a world body. Welles insisted on an international organization made up of all nations and possessing the power to enforce peace. Aggression anywhere in the world threatened all mankind, he contended, and thus all nations must share in the job of maintaining order. Lippmann replied that no nation could safely promise to act against some unknown country in the future. "I conclude from this fact," he argued, "that generalized and hypothetical commitments to use force in the future are valueless, and in so far as they create a deceptive sense of security, they are dangerous." Instead, the most that nations could pledge was to consult together when the peace of the world was endangered.[32]

VI

By mid-1944 the American people were committed to the creation of an international organization. Public-opinion polls showed the heavy majority in favor of this policy holding steady at about 70 percent of the population. A *Fortune* poll indicated that only 8 percent preferred Lippmann's alliance strategy. The isolationists were reduced to a tiny fraction, ranging from 10 to 15 percent in most polls, with the remainder of the population undecided. Yet, at the same time, the majority in favor of collective security was skeptical of its effectiveness. Barely half the people asked whether they thought a union of nations could prevent war replied affirmatively, and 59 percent expected the United States to take part in another war within fifty years. Told to pick the statement which came closest to their beliefs about future war, the largest number selected the most pessimistic answer, "No matter what is done to prevent them there will always be wars." [33]

After months of controversy the American people had formed some definite ideas about the postwar world. They accepted the internationalists' contention that the United States had made a tragic error in repudiating the League of Nations, and many believed that this mistake had led to the present war. A pervasive feeling of guilt drove people toward the irresistible conclusion that this time they must redeem themselves by taking the lead in forming a new international organization. In this sense, the Wilson revival was an enormous success. But, at the same time, the American people rejected the idealistic overtones associated with Wilson's crusade for peace. They were not out to reform the world, and they paid little attention to evangelical calls. They did not want to bring democracy to all mankind, to carry out an international New Deal, or to remake the world in the American image. Rather, they wanted to make the world safe for the United States.

This new internationalism was thus much more closely related to pre-war isolationism than its advocates realized. Pearl Harbor had taught the American people that they could not safely retreat from the world, but they still yearned for a magic formula which would permit them to live in peace without constant involvement abroad. "What the majority want from the new international policy," commented one of George Gallup's associates, "is to make sure that *there are no more world wars.*" This stress on security revealed the continuing strength of nationalism. After a first rash of enthusiasm for an international police force, Americans began to turn away from this proposal as they realized it required a surrender of sovereignty to a world body. The realism preached by Spykman and Lippmann convinced them that an international organization had to rely primarily on the might of its strongest members. The doctrine of the full equality of all nations had little appeal for the American people. They favored an organization that was universal in scope but which rested on the military power of the United States, the Soviet Union, Great Britain and China. Unconsciously, they were moving toward the concept of the Four Policemen that Roosevelt had advocated from the outset.[34]

8

"Your Move, Mister President"

Two weeks after Cordell Hull returned from the Moscow conference, Leo Pasvolsky sent him a memorandum. Describing the Moscow declaration as a major achievement, Pasvolsky wrote, "The next step will be to secure agreement on the character, scope and operation of a permanent organization." Hull agreed, and on December 9 he called together his Informal Political Agenda Group, which had been directing postwar planning since the suspension of the Advisory Committee in June. In addition to Hull and Pasvolsky, this group consisted of Under Secretary Stettinius, three other State Department officers, Ben Cohen of the White House staff, and three men from private life, Norman H. Davis, Myron Taylor and Isaiah Bowman. Meeting nearly every day in mid-December, these men tackled the fundamental questions of the structure, functions and powers of a future international organization.

On December 21 Cordell Hull went to the White House to lunch with President Roosevelt, who had just come back from Teheran. They discussed postwar plans, and for the first time the President asked Hull to submit specific recommendations for an international organization. Hull's Agenda Group prepared an outline based on the studies the Department had conducted over the past two years. Hull spent Christmas going over their draft, and then on December 29 he forwarded the outline to the President. It was a brief document and did little more than sketch out the structure of an organization consisting of a general assembly limited in scope to the discussion of disputes, and an executive council possessing the power to use force to preserve peace. The Big Four were assigned permanent seats on the council, which might range in size from seven to eleven members. The outline listed a series of alternative ways in which the council could function, but the preferred

184

wording gave the permanent members an absolute veto. The final section listed seven "principal obligations" of member states, including a promise to settle disputes peacefully, to recognize the decisions of the executive council as binding, and to refrain from using force except when called upon by the executive council to keep the peace.

In a covering letter Hull informed Roosevelt that the Department also favored an international court and economic and social agencies as part of the world organization, but he laid the primary stress on security. The plan, he said, was based on two central assumptions. The first was "that the four major powers will pledge themselves and will consider themselves morally bound not to go to war against each other" and to cooperate in every way to preserve peace. The other premise was that the four nations "will maintain adequate forces and will be willing to use such forces as circumstances require to prevent or suppress all cases of aggression." Although the President did not give his formal assent to the outline until early February, he must have been pleased with the plan. Its principal features—the primacy of the Big Four, the retention of sovereignty, and the limitations on the authority of the general assembly—were all in line with Roosevelt's Four Policemen approach to international organization.[1]

The President, however, was not yet ready to disclose his views to the American people. In a public statement on January 1, 1944, commemorating the second anniversary of the United Nations Declaration, Roosevelt confined himself to generalities, pledging continued cooperation to win the war and establish "an international organization of all peace-loving nations to maintain peace and security in generations to come." A few days later Clark Eichelberger sent him a one-page outline of a plan for a world organization with an air force, and expressed the hope that the President would soon "find it opportune to make public" his ideas on the postwar world. Roosevelt replied in his usual breezy fashion, calling the outline "interesting" but adding that he thought it best "at this moment" not to say anything about a United Nations air force. "Such a thing might come later on—especially if everybody spoke basic English," he commented. He also punctured Eichelberger's hope by suggesting that the world organization would not need a central headquarters. Roosevelt thought the United Nations could rotate between the continents, since all they needed was "a storage warehouse for records—most of them obsolete."

In his annual message to Congress on January 11 the President made no specific mention of international organization. He did promise that "we shall not repeat the excesses of the wild twenties when this Nation went for a joy-ride on a roller coaster which ended in a tragic crash," but beyond that he simply restated the four freedoms, with greatest emphasis on freedom from fear. "The one supreme objective for the future," he declared, "and for all the United Nations, can be summed up in one word: Security." [2]

Internationalists were puzzled by Roosevelt's refusal to state his views on the postwar world, failing to realize that his political instincts controlled his actions in an election year. Though the President refused to announce his candidacy for reelection until the middle of the year, throughout 1944 he strove to avoid entangling the issue of international organization with his bid for a fourth term. Despite the Mackinac declaration, the Republicans had not taken a firm stand on the nature of the world body, and he realized that any specific administration plan would draw their fire. Remembering Wilson's difficulties, he preferred to remain aloof, masking his very definite convictions on the postwar world in vague statements while his political opponents searched for a position that would attract the widest possible public support.

I

Profound disagreement on foreign policy within the Republican party threatened to undo the unity achieved at Mackinac. Wendell Willkie continued to speak out against the isolationists within the party, denouncing nationalism and proclaiming that "the best hope for the future lies in international organization." In the Midwest, supporters of Colonel McCormick formed the Republican Nationalist Revival Committee, which called the Moscow declaration "the unconditional surrender of the United States to Europe." Nearly 1,500 of the faithful attended a meeting in Chicago to hear Senator Gerald Nye charge that Willkie was selling out the party by courting Republican support for Roosevelt's foreign policy. A poll of 3,500 precinct, county and state Republican leaders revealed that most held more moderate views, favoring an international organization but opposing disarmament after the war and the surrender of island outposts. Senator Alexander Wiley of Wisconsin reflected the prevailing nationalism in a speech advocating that the United States retain the Pacific islands taken at such great cost from Japan. "Surely, if Americans are to play a major part in the building of a post-war world of order and law and decency," he told the

Senate, "they have a right to take whatever prudent measures they may believe necessary in their own behalf."

In the early months of 1944 the most forthright Republican spokesman on foreign affairs was Senator Robert Taft of Ohio, who had stepped out of the race for the presidential nomination in favor of Governor John Bricker. With characteristic bluntness, Taft declared, "We are not fighting for democracy except for our own." He recanted his previous isolationism, but he also denounced regional alliances and a world federation. "I do believe," he told a Boston meeting of the Foreign Policy Association, "that a league of sovereign nations, agreeing upon a rule of law and order throughout the world, has today a real chance of success." He was willing to have the United States join such an organization and pledge to use force against aggression, provided that American troops were not sent out of the Western Hemisphere. In another speech he suggested that the simplest course would be to rejuvenate the existing League of Nations.[3]

The front-runners for the Republican nomination, Governors John Bricker and Thomas E. Dewey, were much more circumspect about postwar plans in their public statements. Bricker delivered a set speech throughout the country during the winter and spring condemning a "central world authority" but backing American entry into "a cooperative organization among sovereign nations after the war." Governor Dewey, never revealing his own views, preferred to attack the administration, charging in a Lincoln's Birthday address that a Roosevelt peace would lead to "a repetition of the same catastrophe which happened in 1919." Democrats in the Senate bridled at this charge. Claude Pepper, claiming that Dewey was another Harding, asserted that the Republicans "bear upon their soul the penalty of a war which has consumed another guiltless generation of men," while Scott Lucas pleaded, "Let the people remember what they did in 1920 and beware!" These partisan exchanges sounded ominously familiar to Claude Bowers, the American ambassador to Chile. He thought Dewey was "an old-fashioned reactionary candidate" whom Roosevelt could defeat easily, "but one never knows," he wrote to Breckinridge Long. "We all remember what they did to Wilson."[4]

In February 1944 Gallup polls revealed that Wendell Willkie was falling behind Dewey in the race for the Republican nomination. Though Willkie had won great respect for his internationalist crusade, he had alienated party leaders and neglected to build up an effective political organization. Believing that the party's rank and file still supported him, he decided to enter the primaries in order to overtake Dewey. The first contest took place in New Hampshire, and although Willkie captured six of the eleven delegates to Dewey's two, he was disappointed by his failure to sweep the state. In desperation he announced that he would campaign personally in the Wisconsin primary in an effort to prove his popularity in the Middle West. The risks were formidable—Wisconsin, with a heavy German population, had been the center of pre-war isolationism, and most observers felt it still was Chicago *Tribune* country. He was the only candidate campaigning actively, but there was a slate of delegates pledged to Dewey, and at the last moment backers of General Douglas MacArthur and Harold Stassen, who was serving as an aide to Admiral Halsey in the Pacific, entered the race.

Willkie opened his campaign in Richland Center on March 18, and for the next thirteen days he crossed Wisconsin, delivering forty speeches. He touched on all the major issues, attacking both the Roosevelt administration and his Republican rivals. Again and again he turned to the theme of foreign policy. At Green Bay he warned that if the party did not repudiate isolationism, Roosevelt would be elected to another four-year term; in Racine he criticized Dewey's 1943 proposal for an alliance with Britain, declaring, "If we work with just one nation, then we automatically divide the world into two groups and get ready for the next war." By the time he completed his last speech on March 30, his voice, hoarse at best, was rasping and he was near exhaustion. But instead of resting, he moved on to Nebraska to campaign in the primary there, telling reporters he expected to win a clear majority of the delegates in Wisconsin.

On April 4 the Republican voters of Wisconsin went to the polls. Dewey's delegates won fifteen of the twenty-four races; Stassen and MacArthur men won the rest. Not only did Willkie fail to win a single delegate, but he ran last in every district. Willkie was in Omaha when he received the results. After a long speech denouncing the Roosevelt administration, he told his three thousand listeners that he had an announcement to make. Reading from a prepared text, he interpreted his defeat as a sign of renewed midwestern isolationism and then withdrew from the race. As the audience rose to give him a standing ovation, he voiced his hope that the party would choose a candidate who shared his principles, promising, "I shall continue to work for these principles and policies for which I have fought during the last five years." [5]

Political commentators agreed that the Wisconsin primary ensured Dewey's nomination, but they differed on what else it signified. Liberal internationalists and partisan Democrats insisted that it proved that the isolationists still had a stranglehold on the Republican party. More conservative writers were quick to point out that Dewey and Stassen were viewed as internationalists, and that only MacArthur drew isolationist support. *Time*, which backed Dewey strongly, contended that all the Wisconsin voters rejected was "starry-eyed internationalism" and "a foreign policy of generalities." Rejoicing in Willkie's defeat, the editors continued, "Wisconsin, it seemed, had voted out of the way a massive road-block on the way to realistic internationalism." More objective analysts believed that over the years Willkie had made too many enemies on domestic as well as foreign issues. Equally important, he had managed his campaign badly, operating out of a New York headquarters and neglecting local leaders. Donald Bruce Johnson, the most careful student of Willkie's political career, has concluded, "Willkie was defeated because of his own activities, because of the long-held hostility of Republican leaders toward the 1940 candidate, and because of the uncertainty of the masses of Republican voters about his attitudes on GOP domestic policy." [6]

Dewey reacted to Willkie's withdrawal from the race by announcing his support of international organization. In a speech to the American Newspaper Publishers Association on April 27 which John Foster Dulles, an old friend, helped him to prepare, Dewey warned that the nation must not "repeat the tragic error of twenty-five years ago." In the key passage he affirmed the need "to organize in cooperation with other nations a structure of peace backed by adequate force to prevent future wars." He favored continued cooperation with Britain, Russia and China, but felt it had to be carried on through a world organization.

"He discussed some issues of the peace and went near the water—only a few faltering steps, to be sure, but closer than he has ever been before," commented the *New Republic*. The editors of the *Nation* were more caustic, asking Dewey, "Where were you when the battle was thickest, when the lines were being drawn?" They took comfort in the belief that internationalism must be popular to win the support of such an opportunistic politician, but they feared that Dewey could not control the isolationists within the pary. *Time* had no doubts about Dewey's position, hailing his speech as a statement of the "realistic internationalism" they championed. The New York *Times* and the *Herald Tribune*, the nation's leading internationalist newspapers, praised the speech and accepted Dewey as a genuine convert. Willkie remained silent, but he had every reason to take heart. Though he had met with personal defeat, his long campaign to reshape his party's stand on foreign policy now promised to remove the issue of international organization from the presidential election of 1944.[7]

I I

The State Department's public image troubled Edward Stettinius, the new Under Secretary. His experience as an executive of United States Steel and as director of the lend-lease program had taught him the importance of public relations. This genial, outgoing man, his youthful grin contrasting with his prematurely white hair, wanted to convince the American people that the State Department was an alert, efficient organization capable of planning a good peace. In December, when NBC offered the Department air time on four Saturday evenings in January to describe its activities, Stettinius quickly accepted. He appointed public-relations specialists to prepare scripts for the programs, which would consist of panel discussions by Department officers, and issued a strict warning against "ad libbing either in the form of answers to questions or otherwise."

The first "The Department of State Speaks" program dealt with postwar planning. Richard Harkness served as moderator, interviewing Stettinius, Pasvolsky and James Dunn, Political Adviser to the Secretary who had attended the Moscow conference. Pasvolsky gave a brief history of Department planning, stressing the importance of creating an international organization to prevent aggression. When Harkness asked him if collective security had been proven a failure with the League, Pasvolsky replied, "But this time, as Secretary Hull has long maintained, there must be the *clear* certainty for all concerned that breaches of the peace will not be tolerated, that they will be suppressed—by force, if necessary." Dunn described the Moscow meeting as "a dramatic and monumental milestone" in American foreign policy and emphasized the importance of Big Four unity. Following the script, Harkness asked him if this meant that these four nations would run the postwar world. "Absolutely not, Mr. Harkness!" Dunn replied, adding that Roosevelt and Hull favored "a general system of international cooperation in which all nations, large and small, would play their part."[8]

On January 15 Stettinius announced a major reorganization of the

Department designed to streamline its operations. The order established twelve major offices to handle day-by-day affairs and to free the top echelon from administrative duties. Two new committees, one on policy and another on postwar plans, were created to ensure coordination and long-range planning. Pasvolsky served as executive director of the Committee on Postwar Programs. His old Division of Special Research became the Office of Special Political Affairs under James Dunn; and within it Stettinius created a Division of International Security and Organization headed by Harley Notter, who had worked with Pasvolsky since 1941.

In his most significant innovation, Stettinius established an Office of Public Information to influence public attitudes. Though there had been close contact between private organizations and the Department in the early war years, Hull had gradually choked it off after he took command of postwar planning from Welles. The reorganization order specifically charged the new office with the task of maintaining contact with all groups interested in American foreign policy and supplying them with as much information as possible. At the same time, Stettinius also proposed a new Advisory Council on Postwar Foreign Policy to be formed under the direction of Norman Davis, Myron Taylor and Isaiah Bowman. Designed as a nonpartisan body of citizens representing private organizations who would meet twice a month with Hull to review the Department's postwar plans, this ambitious scheme never materialized. When Stettinius sent a list of possible members to the White House, Roosevelt, fearful of offending any major national-interest group, returned it with so many additions that the Department quietly dropped the idea.

Despite these structural changes, the Informal Political Agenda Group continued to work on the first complete draft of an international organization. Hull left Washington for an extended vacation in Florida in February, and under Pasvolsky, who was a perfectionist, the drafting went very slowly. Roosevelt became impatient, and in a conference with Stettinius on February 23 he suggested forming the United Nations organization right away and holding the first meeting in June. When Hull returned in March, he was very upset by this idea, which would mean bypassing Congress. Instead, he proposed a more circumspect course. In the spring he would send the American draft to Britain, China and Russia for consideration. If they had no major objections, he would then convene a conference, restricted to the Big Four, to draw up a detailed charter which would then go to the Senate for approval. The final step would be a meeting of all the United Nations to launch the new world organization. The President, aware of the enormous respect the Senate had for Hull, accepted this strategy.

On March 15 the Agenda Group completed its draft and submitted it to the Policy Committee for study. After a month of discussion Hull approved a revised version on April 24. It followed the December 29 outline closely, proposing a world organization dominated by an eight-member council. The Big Four would be permanent members, possessing a veto on all major issues, while the general assembly would elect the other four on a rotating basis. Instead of an international police force, the member nations would agree to furnish troops to put down aggression at the call of the council. In a separate agreement, the nations would stipulate the exact quantity and nature of the military forces they would keep on hand for collective police action. The assembly could discuss threats to the peace and make recommendations, but only the council could invoke force. In addition, the draft provided for an international court, agencies for social and economic problems, and a tentative trusteeship system for colonial areas.

Hull, to the dismay of his aides, decided to ask three distinguished lawyers to examine the proposal and rule on its constitutionality. He feared a repetition of the charge made against the League Covenant that any commitment to use force to keep the peace would violate the constitutional right of Congress to declare war. "The Three Wise Men," as Long dubbed them, were Charles Evans Hughes, John W. Davis, the unsuccessful Democratic presidential candidate in 1924, and Nathan Miller, former Republican governor of New York. Myron Taylor served as intermediary in this operation, which was conducted with cloak-and-dagger secrecy. To Hull's great relief, all three approved the draft and guaranteed its constitutionality.[10]

III

Throughout the winter months the administration's apparent neglect of postwar issues did not improve its public image. Walter Lippmann, Arthur Krock, William L. Shirer, Dorothy Thompson and other columnists kept asking Hull and Roosevelt to announce their policies on such critical issues as the fate of Germany and the future of Poland. The tide of battle had definitely turned, with the Soviet army rapidly expelling German forces from Russia and sweeping toward the Balkans and

Poland, while American and British troops were massing in England for the long-expected cross-Channel invasion. People wanted to know how the United States planned to restore a stable Europe in which Germany was removed as a menace to peace without opening the way to Soviet domination of the entire continent. The administration's silence led many to conclude that Roosevelt had made secret deals with Stalin and Churchill at Teheran which he dared not reveal to the public.

Senator Joseph Ball challenged Roosevelt to disclose his postwar views in a *Saturday Evening Post* article in February, entitled "Your Move, Mister President." Ball lamented the absence of any congressman or senator from the Moscow and Teheran conferences, and he warned the President that if he did not take Congress into his confidence, the Senate might well reject his postwar treaties. He suggested that Roosevelt include members of Congress in future international meetings, saying that their participation would be "the best insurance against his peace plans going awry that any President could buy." Two months later Ball wrote an article for *Collier's* charging that the administration was reverting to power politics and plotting to divide postwar Europe into spheres of influence with Britain and Russia. Warning that such a course would lose the peace, he asked for the immediate formation of a United Nations Council to deal with all postwar issues. "The 'earliest practicable date' (in the words of the Moscow Declaration)," he wrote, "for the establishment of a general international organization is now—the sooner the better."

Liberal and conservative commentators joined in the wave of criticism. Freda Kirchwey wrote in the *Nation* that Roosevelt and Hull were "tiptoeing toward the brink of a new world order," and expressed her fear of a return to the status quo and thus "a new cycle of economic disintegration, dictatorship and war." "Only a New Deal for the world, more far-reaching and consistent than our own faltering New Deal, can prevent the coming of World War III," she concluded. I. F. Stone shared her pessimism, seeing American policy as one of drift "toward all that represents the old order in Europe, Asia, and Latin America." Arthur Krock believed that the administration's inactivity would have the opposite result, permitting an aggressive Soviet Union to spread Communism throughout Europe. *Time* also feared Russian expansion, attributing Roosevelt's silence to his decision to run for a fourth term. In mid-March a group of twenty-four freshmen Republican congressmen won widespread attention when they wrote an open letter to Hull asking for a clear statement of American postwar policy. Complaining that the public had received no information on foreign policy since the Moscow conference, these Republicans commented, "Not even the United Nations Council contemplated in the Moscow Declaration appears to be functioning." [11]

When Cordell Hull returned from his Florida vacation in mid-March, he had the Department release a seventeen-point memorandum to satisfy the "growing interest" in American foreign policy. This statement, consisting of excerpts from speeches by Hull and Roosevelt over the past two years, failed utterly to satisfy the critics. Most observers dismissed it as a rehash of vague generalities, which it was, and the Chicago *Sun*, a Democratic paper, aptly described it as "Mr. Hull's 17-point mumble." Only the *Reader's Digest* came to Hull's defense. In a specially commissioned lead article in the May issue, Kingsbury Smith wrote that the Secretary was "the victim of an emotional group of publicists who believe Uncle Sam should reform the world." Praising Hull as "the wise old American eagle," Smith claimed that he had "steered a course in American foreign policy to which posterity is likely to pay tribute."

The uproar failed to deflect Hull from his determination to move slowly toward international organization. With a draft nearing completion, he was ready to begin consulting with Congressional leaders, and he would not seek wider public approval until he was sure the Senate would accept his plan. Accordingly, on March 22 he appeared before the Senate Foreign Relations Committee in a closed session and suggested that Chairman Connally appoint a small group to consult with him on the Department's plans. The next day Hull met with the twenty-four Republican congressmen, and though he informed them of this decision and told them he also planned to consult with a similar House committee, he asked them to keep this confidential. His answers to their questions were so evasive that when a reporter asked how the meeting had gone, a disgruntled Republican replied, "No hits, no runs, no errors." [12]

Realizing that he had to do something to quiet the public clamor, Hull announced that he would deliver a major policy address in April. For the next two weeks Pasvolsky, Long, Dunn and four other State Department officers worked over successive drafts of the speech, trying to include specific statements on postwar issues, only to have Hull strike them out.

Hull delivered the address over the CBS radio network on the evening of April 9 from his State Department office, with Long standing by as usual in case his voice failed. The Secretary began by emphasizing the importance of continued cooperation by the Big Four. "This is the solid framework upon which all future policy and international organization must be built," he declared. He announced that the Department was well along in developing specific plans for a new world body, but he refused to discuss details, which he said might only cause premature controversy. He did state that the projected organization must bind the member nations not to use force against each other and "provide for the maintenance of adequate forces to preserve peace" and "for calling this force into action." Then Hull revealed that he had asked Connally to appoint a bi-partisan committee to begin consulting with him on the plans for a world organization, and outlined the procedure he would follow. "After these . . . discussions, we shall be in a position to go forward again with other nations and, upon learning their views, be able to submit to the democratic processes of discussion a more concrete proposal." He closed with a plea for patience. "Once before in our lifetime we fell into disunity and became ineffective in world affairs by reason of it. Should this happen again it will be a tragedy to you and to your children and to the world for generations."

It was by far Hull's most effective wartime speech. Though a few commentators grumbled at his continued refusal to be specific, nearly all praised his plans for Congressional consultation. The New York *Times* labeled this "a revolutionary change in American diplomatic practice," one which the editors felt was a great step forward. Arthur Krock wrote, "It undermines a rock on which the foreign policy of previous administrations, notably Woodrow Wilson's, was wrecked, and with it the hope of the world." The editors of *Christian Century* and the *New Republic* agreed that Hull had made a "substantial advance" in "the democratization of policy-making" and they praised the idea of bi-partisan Congressional consultation as a sign that the administration had learned from Wilson's experience.[13]

On April 22, 1944, Tom Connally announced the names of the eight senators who would confer with Hull. He named himself chairman of the Committee of Eight, as the press called the new group, and chose three other Democrats, three Republicans and one Progressive, Robert La Follette, Jr., of Wisconsin. Seven of these men had served on the subcommittee which reported out the Connally resolution; Connally dropped Elbert Thomas of Utah in favor of Warren Austin in order to achieve the bi-partisan balance. Three of the Democrats—Connally, Walter F. George and Alben Barkley—were party regulars who could be counted on to back the administration, but the fourth, Guy Gillette of

Iowa, was a maverick. He had incurred Roosevelt's wrath in the 1930's by opposing New Deal measures and had survived the President's unsuccessful purge in the 1938 primaries. He had voted with the isolationists on many occasions before the war, and no one was certain where he stood on the issue of international organization. There was no uncertainty about La Follette's views—he was a confirmed isolationist who told his Wisconsin constituents, "Our greatest contribution to world peace will be determined by what America does for Americans." The two New England Republicans, Austin and Wallace White of Maine, were lifelong internationalists firmly committed to collective security.

The key figure, and the greatest enigma, on the Committee of Eight was Senator Arthur H. Vandenberg of Michigan. The ranking Republican on the Foreign Relations Committee and the third most senior member of his party in the Senate, Vandenberg possessed the authority to speak for his Republican colleagues that Austin and White lacked. Vandenberg was the son of a Michigan harness-maker who had gone bankrupt in the panic of 1893. Forced to earn his own living as a boy, Vandenberg had left college to become a newspaper editor in Grand Rapids. His own experience gave him a fondness for the Horatio Alger theme, and he wrote boys' stories in this vein for eastern magazines and produced three biographies of his hero, Alexander Hamilton, of whom he once wrote, "He stood at my shoulder like a big brother in my youth." In his newspaper he advocated American entry into World War I as early as 1916, but after the war he opposed the League and supported Harding in 1920, coining the slogan, "With Harding at the Helm, We Can Sleep Nights." Appointed to the Senate to fill a vacancy in 1928, he was one of only six Republican senators to survive the Democratic landslide in 1934. Always opportunistic, he supported some New Deal measures, but he became a leading isolationist in the late 1930's and opposed American entry into the war until Pearl Harbor. Then his views began to shift again, and during the debate over the Connally resolution he took a mildly internationalist position.

A big, heavy-set man with wispy white hair surrounding a large bald spot, he peered out like a foxy grandpa from behind his rimless glasses. He was a kindly and gentle man who tried always to win the good opinion of his opponents. He was not a member of the Senate's inner circle, preferring to operate as a lone wolf, but he came to be respected as the most influential Republican spokesman on foreign policy. His great failing was his love of words. "In fact," comments Richard Rovere, "he loved them almost to death." His editorials, his speeches, even his diary entries are filled with mixed metaphors, redundancies and purple prose punctuated with exclamation points, capitals and italics, which he used without the slightest sense of embarrassment. He was nevertheless an extremely clever politician who had an unfailing ability to discern the trend of public policy and move with it. If Hull could win his support for the administration's plans for international organization, the bipartisan policy would be a success.[14]

The Committee of Eight came to Hull's office on April 25 for their first meeting, with only La Follette absent. The Secretary greeted the senators cordially, and assured them that the discussion would be informal and involve no obligation on their part. He stressed the importance of postwar cooperation with the Soviet Union and the need to keep the entire issue of international organization out of domestic politics. Then the Secretary gave each senator a copy of the April 24 draft plan for an international organization, asking them to examine it and express their views at the next meeting. That evening Hull sent a telegram to President Roosevelt, who was vacationing in South Carolina, summarizing the meeting and describing the intense interest displayed by the senators as a hopeful sign.

Both Connally and Vandenberg were amazed and delighted by the conservative nature of the State Department draft. The absence of an international police force and the grant of veto power pleased Connally, who believed that "the United States should not be forced into a future war merely because the other council powers agreed to it." Vandenberg wrote in his diary, "The striking thing about it is that it is so conservative from a nationalist standpoint." He approved of the major role assigned to the council to keep the peace, and the domination by the Big Four. "This is anything but a wild-eyed internationalist dream of a world State," he wrote. "On the contrary, it is a frame-work (without passing on details) to which I can and do heartily subscribe."[15]

With the Committee of Eight due to meet again on May 2, Hull held long meetings with his advisers to discuss possible objections. He and Breckinridge Long, veterans of the fight over the League, anticipated questions on who would have the authority to commit American troops in any collective-security action to preserve the peace. The State Department draft was deliberately vague on this point, but Hull and Long felt it was essential for the President to possess this power without having to consult Congress on each occasion. At Hull's direction, Long wrote to John W. Davis, asking if he believed the President had the authority under the Constitution to use force "without the formality of a declaration of war?" Davis felt that the President did, but thought it would be best to ask Congress to delegate this power to the President when it approved formal American entry into the world organization. On the evening before the meeting, Long was very nervous. "While the curtain has not gone up—now it is time for this play to begin—the actors have had their parts assigned and are learning their pieces," he wrote in his diary, "and the great drama will soon begin to be enacted." He felt that the senators would agree to the peaceful settlement of disputes, "but will they agree to use force in the only practical way—at the direction of the President? . . . will the Senate ratify a treaty which commits the U.S. to use force without a declaration of war?"

The next day the senators did not even mention the feared issue; instead, they expressed genuine enthusiasm for the State Department's plan. Vandenberg, backed by La Follette, had only one serious objection—the question of timing. The new organization would act primarily as an agency to enforce the peace settlement made at the end of the war. Fearful of supporting an unjust peace, Vandenberg said he could not endorse any world organization until he knew the nature of the settlement. Hull countered by arguing that formation of a world organization would help ensure a good peace, but Vandenberg held to his objection. Under prodding from Hull, he agreed that the Secretary should go ahead and perfect the plans, but insisted they should not go into effect until after the peace settlement. "Otherwise we would be signing the most colossal 'blank check' in history," Vandenberg told Hull in a letter the next day.

"The Senators came this morning and practically gave the green light," commented Long on May 12. In this third meeting, Vandenberg and La Follette renewed their objection to entering a world organization before the peace was made, but they agreed that Hull should take the next step by submitting the American plan to Britain, Russia and China. Senator Gillette raised the only other major question when he asked Hull if the veto power would not permit the Big Four to dominate the world body. The other senators backed Hull strongly when he explained that the veto was necessary to ensure British and Russian participation. "We should not forget," Hull added, "that this veto power is chiefly for the benefit of the United States in the light of the world situation and of our own public opinion." At the end of the meeting, Hull suggested that the eight senators meet without him to draft a public statement endorsing the State Department's plan and recommending consultation on it with our allies. Long and Hull were delighted with the progress they had made, and Vandenberg seemed equally pleased. In his diary he wrote of Hull, "He is also manifestly eager to avoid Wilson's mistake of attempting commitments destined for ultimate congressional rejection. All in all, and again reserving details, I think his preliminary scheme is excellent." [16]

While Hull waited for the letter of endorsement from the Committee of Eight, a two-part article by Forrest Davis appeared in the *Saturday Evening Post*. Based on interviews Davis had with Roosevelt in March and approved in advance by the White House, the article was entitled "What Really Happened at Teheran." In the first installment in the issue of May 13, Davis stated that, contrary to popular belief, Roosevelt did have a "grand design" for the postwar world. "It was at Teheran that the President most clearly exhibited his tough-minded determination to enroll the Soviet Union as a sincere and willing collaborator in postwar settlements," Davis wrote. "That determination, I am able to say, is at the center of his 'great design.'" He went on to write that Roosevelt, believing Russian cooperation essential for effective world organization, had played the role of conciliator at Teheran in an effort to develop a climate of trust and allay Russian suspicions of Britain and the United States. "Mr. Roosevelt," Davis wrote, "gambling for stakes as enormous as any statesman ever played for, has been betting that the Soviet Union needs peace and is willing to pay for it by collaborating with the west."

A week later Davis concluded the article with the first public description of Roosevelt's concept of the Four Policemen. He reported that the President opposed a "heavily-organized, bureaucratic world organization" with its own police force and instead favored a simple security agency dominated by the Big Four. "He is after workable minimums, not impossible maximums," Davis wrote. He described a loose structure on the Pan-American model, capped by an executive committee of the major powers which would act as the policeman for the world in any emergency. The essence of this arrangement would be the continued unity of the wartime allies. "The period of peace for which he hopes, an era like the nineteenth century's fruitful Pax Britannica," Davis concluded, "presupposes that the powers able to make war are convinced their self-interest demands peace." [17]

Conservative critics, led by the editors of the *Saturday Evening Post*, were appalled at Roosevelt's conciliatory policy toward the Soviet Union, calling it appeasement and likening it to the policies applied to

Hitler in the 1930's. Demaree Bess had been preparing for the *Post* a piece critical of Roosevelt's foreign policy. When he read the Davis article in galleys, he immediately recast his article into a critical analysis of Roosevelt's postwar plans, and though the *Post* refused to print it in the same issue with the second Davis installment, it did appear a week later. Bess warned that the "grand design" placed the United States in the role of balance wheel between Britain and Russia, a policy which meant a huge standing army and navy after the war and enormous American commitments throughout the world. He described Roosevelt as a gambler who, like Wilson in 1919, "has placed his hopes for world security upon a single central idea." Bess believed that Roosevelt also was destined to fail because Russia was completely unreliable. Writing in the *Christian Century*, Oswald Garrison Villard reached the same conclusion. He accused Roosevelt of appeasing Stalin at Teheran, and then commented, "We thought that Woodrow Wilson blundered because of his utter ignorance of European affairs. But he had his feet on the ground compared to Mr. Roosevelt, and he was certainly much less naive."

Internationalists were even more upset by Davis' revelations of the President's idea of the Four Policemen. In a widely noted speech in New York on May 18, Sumner Welles asserted, "History does not record any example of a military alliance between great nations which has endured. . . . At best they have given rise only to a temporary and precarious balance of power." Warning against the trend to imperialism, Welles called for the creation of a wartime United Nations Council as the beginning of a world organization which recognizes "the full sovereignty of every independent nation of the world, no matter how small it may be." The New York *Times* praised his speech as "eloquent and moving," and such liberal journals as the *Nation* and the *New Republic* backed his stand for a democratic world body. The *Saturday Evening Post*, though still more alarmed over the appeasement of Russia, also endorsed Welles' views: [18]

> The present reliance on three-power decisions—with China included now and then for courtesy—may win the war, but it can never produce a peace which does not rest on the sinking sands of imperialism and personal politics on the international level. That way lies only a "war of continents" to multiply the horrors of the war of nations which now taxes our strength.

The Davis article and the resulting furor upset Hull's plan for the Committee of Eight to endorse the State Department draft.

Vandenberg believed that the disclosures confirmed his hunch that Roosevelt had made secret commitments with Stalin and Churchill, and he was more insistent than ever that acceptance of a world organization should await the peace settlement. He also did not want to commit the Republican party and its presidential candidate in 1944 to any specific program. Other members of the committee shared Vandenberg's doubts about Roosevelt's postwar plans. "We all believe in Hull," Vandenberg wrote in his diary. "But none of us is *sure* that Hull *knows* the whole story.

On May 17 the Committee of Eight approved a letter to Hull that bristled with reservations. The members approved his intention of submitting the plan for international organization to Britain, Russia and China, but they reserved their "final judgment until it may be put in final form and terms of peace are known." When Hull read this letter, he was furious. He wanted a statement from the senators which he could send to the other nations as proof that the Senate was firmly committed to the administration's policy. Suffering from a cold, he asked Long to negotiate with Connally and secure a stronger letter.

On May 18 Long and Connally met to discuss the impasse. "He and I sat there," Long recorded in his diary, "and drafted and redrafted and exercised all the ingenuity each of us had to weave our way around the idea of commitment and yet giving substantial support to the Committee's document." After six attempts they finally succeeded. Long telephoned the text to Hull, who accepted it with only two minor changes. The new wording stated that the committee was "inclined to the opinion that the document should be acceptable to the American people and considers that the proposal embodied in it is, in its present status, sufficient to justify your purpose to enter into preliminary conversations."

Connally called his committee together the next day, Friday, May 19. Nearly everyone objected to this phrasing, claiming that they had no right to speak for the American people. Vandenberg and La Follette also protested the absence of any reference to the nature of the future peace. In mid-afternoon Connally telephoned Long to ask if the letter would be published. Long said yes—the whole idea was to inform other governments of prior Senate approval in principle. Connally called back several hours later to tell Long that the committee had been unable to agree to the letter and that they would meet again on Monday.

"They are shying away like a horse from a snake," commented Long after Connally informed him that the May 22 meeting had proved equally unproductive. He went to Hull's hotel, where the Secretary was still in bed with a cold, to tell him the bad news. Hull blamed Connally, who he felt disliked him personally, and Long agreed, indicating that the chairman had become very evasive on the telephone. "I have a feeling that he would probably prefer not to be committed to anything himself," Long noted. The next day there was no further word from Connally until 5:30, when he called and asked for an appointment with Hull. On May 25 they conferred for two hours, with Hull stressing the importance of a written endorsement of the State Department plan. Finally, Connally agreed to try once more.

At the meeting the next day the senators divided six to two, with Vandenberg and La Follette refusing to sign the kind of letter Hull requested. Vandenberg, citing the Davis and Bess articles, reiterated his fear that Roosevelt had already made serious concessions to Britain and Russia and said he could not publicly endorse the administration's plan until he knew more about the peace settlement. He wanted Hull to go ahead with the plans for a world organization, however, and he suggested that the committee authorize Connally to inform Hull of this orally. Reluctantly, the majority accepted Vandenberg's proposal.

Hull called a conference of his senior advisers on May 27 to discuss the alternatives. They rejected the idea of asking the majority on the committee to sign a letter to Hull since this would reveal the split and open up the partisan debate the Secretary hoped to avoid. Long then suggested that Hull meet with the committee again, and if they persisted in their refusal to give him a written statement, the Secretary should simply announce their oral approval of the draft plan. After a long conference with the President that evening, Hull agreed to this procedure.[19]

On the morning of May 29 all the members of the committee except Alben Barkley, whose wife was ill, filed into Hull's office. According to Vandenberg, the senators took the initiative, questioning Hull about what had taken place at the Teheran conference. Vandenberg told the Secretary that he wanted him to go ahead and secure agreement with our allies on a world organization, but wait until after the peace treaties before implementing it. Realizing that the committee would not write the kind of letter he wanted, Hull showed them a statement which he planned to release to the press after the meeting, and the senators raised no objection.

That afternoon Hull called in the reporters. Describing his conversations with the senators as "frank and fruitful," he announced that he was "definitely encouraged" and was ready to proceed with "informal discussions" with Great Britain, Russia and China on plans for a world organization. He said he planned to hold further conferences with the eight senators and a similar group from the House and concluded, "the door of non-partisanship will continue to be wide open here at the Department of State, especially when any phase of the planning for a post-war security organization is under consideration."

Though the New York *Times* reporter thought Hull was "in an obviously optimistic mood," the Secretary was disappointed. He had hoped to remove any doubts our allies might have about the Senate's willingness to enter an international organization, as well as to commit the Republicans irrevocably to the administration's draft plan. Vandenberg had thwarted this strategy, but the outcome was still very auspicious for the internationalists. Of the eight senators, only La Follette had indicated opposition to the idea of a world organization, and all were willing to back Hull informally. Upon reflection, Breckinridge Long felt that he and Hull had been rather naive in expecting senators to commit themselves in writing on such a momentous issue.[20]

IV

Franklin Roosevelt was not surprised that the senators refused to endorse the State Department plan. He had told Hull in March that the Republicans would make international organization a campaign issue in the 1944 election, and the Congressional consultations only confirmed his pessimism. In early June he told Florence Harriman, "It should be clear that the Republican leaders, not knowing how to cooperate with the Democrats, know even less how to cooperate with other nations."

Though he was pleased with the Davis article, he refrained from making any direct revelations of his postwar plans. In May, Jonathan Daniels passed on a letter from Clark Eichelberger which so impressed the President that he called a conference with Hull about it. The letter, written in early April following Willkie's Wisconsin defeat, urged Daniels to prevail upon Roosevelt to "make the boldest possible speech outlining in detail his plan for a world organization." Reporting on a trip he had just made around the nation, Eichelberger said that the overwhelming majority of Americans favored international organization, but that if the administration failed to put forward some specific blueprints soon, this sentiment would "disintegrate."[21]

8. *"Your Move, Mister President"*

Roosevelt decided not to make a speech, but in his press conference on May 26 he announced that the United States had issued invitations to the other United Nations to attend a conference on international monetary and financial matters at Bretton Woods, New Hampshire, in July. Then, for the first time during the war, he volunteered information to the reporters on postwar planning. He cited the Hot Springs Food and Agriculture Conference and UNRRA, as well as the forthcoming Bretton Woods meeting, as proof that "we have got a good deal further ahead in the discussion of things" than during the First World War. When these remarks encouraged a reporter to ask why the administration had not released any details of its plans for intenational organization, the President became more cautious. He admitted discussing postwar issues with Churchill at Casablanca and with Stalin at Teheran, declaring, "I am trying to eliminate a third World War." But he said it was too early to discuss specifics since the plan was only in its first draft. "Well," he commented jocularly, "I wouldn't give out a first draft any more than I would give out a first draft of one of my speeches. It would horrify you."

On Memorial Day, later that week, Roosevelt drove out to Arlington National Cemetery to honor those who had fallen in past wars, and when he returned to the White House he called an impromptu press conference. It was very hot, and the President met the newsmen in his shirt sleeves. Earlier that day Hull had released the formal announcement that the United States had submitted a detailed plan for world organization to Britain, Russia and China for their consideration. A reporter commented on this, asking Roosevelt how he felt about the League of Nations. The President replied that he had supported the League in 1919, but that times had changed and the principles of the Covenant needed to be adapted to modern conditions. He said he was working toward the same end—"the prevention, if we can humanly help it, of another world war"—but he did not believe, as Wilson had, that it was possible to end "all wars for all time." His goal, he continued, was to cooperate with other countries

in setting up some machinery of talking things over with other Nations, without taking away the independence of the United States in any shape, manner or form, or destroying—what's the other word?—the integrity of the United States in any shape, manner or form; with the objective of working so closely together that if some nation in the world started to run amuck, or some combination of nations started to run amuck, and seeks to grab territory or invade its neighbors, there would be a unanimity of opinion that the time to stop them was before they got started; that is, all the other Nations who weren't in with them.

Roosevelt went on to praise the senators who had been consulting with Hull for their "spirit of nonpartisanship" and said that the administration was striving to develop its plans with 135 million Americans in mind as well as a great many nations, large and small.

Reporters then tried unsuccessfully to pin the President down on details of the American plan. When asked if it was radically different from the League Covenant, the President replied that he and Hull were working on "a 1944 pattern rather than a 1919 pattern." Another reporter persisted, asking Roosevelt if the plan fell within the scope of the Mackinac declaration. The President ruled that question out of bounds as too political, but he ended the discussion by saying that the State Department had drawn its ideas from many sources, including suggestions from what Teddy Roosevelt "would have called the 'lunatic fringe.' " [22]

"Franklin Roosevelt was not going to yield any U.S. sovereignty to any international organization," reported *Time* in commenting on this press conference. Internationalists were disappointed in the President's stress on sovereignty and feared that he had accepted Walter Lippmann's alliance theory. Liberal editors urged him to work for a democratic world organization that would protect the interest and preserve the self-respect of the small nations. Some of the criticisms were savage. "I think it is noteworthy that whereas President Wilson consulted the people and ignored the Senate," commented T.R.B. in the *New Republic*, "President Roosevelt consults the Senate and ignores the people." The administration plan, the *Nation* charged, "bears a striking similarity in principle to the 'new order' which the Axis has been striving to impose in Europe and Asia." [23]

Cordell Hull tried to reassure the internationalists in a press conference on June 1. "As far as this government is concerned," he stated, "whenever I have said anything on this subject, it has always emphasized the all-inclusive nature of the world situation and our disposition and purpose to see that all nations, especially the small nations, are kept on a position of equality with all others. . . ." The Secretary still worried, however, about charges of neglecting the small nations, and he feared that the Republicans would exploit this issue for partisan advantage. The long-awaited Normandy landings on June 6, and the anxious days that followed until the beachhead was secure, diverted his attention, but on June 15 he decided to release another public statement. "The people want details. They want to know what the general idea is," he told his aides, asking them to prepare a draft. Working with unprecedented speed, they completed the statement in an hour and a half, and then Hull took it to the President for his approval. Hull had the White House issue the statement under Roosevelt's name in order to answer the critics who charged that there was a rift between the two men on postwar policy. In his diary Breckinridge Long commented, "So this was conceived to tie the President in to the whole works and commit him to Hull's program. . . ."

Only a handful of reporters were lounging in the White House lobby on the afternoon of June 15 when Steve Early, Roosevelt's press secretary, handed out mimeographed sheets saying, "I think this is a pretty good story." The text described the essential features of the State Department draft plan for international organization, but it was noticeably vague on details, simply listing a council, "a fully representative" assembly and a world court as the organs. Hull emphasized its universality, stating that "the maintenance of peace and security must be the joint task of all peace-loving nations." The statement slid over the fact that the Big Four would dominate the council and have an exclusive veto power, and it failed to describe how the peace-keeping machinery would work. Instead, the administration declared: [24]

> We are not thinking of a superstate with its own police forces and other paraphernalia of coercive power. We are seeking effective agreement and arrangements through which the nations would maintain, according to their capacities, adequate forces to meet the needs of preventing war and of making impossible deliberate preparation for war and to have such forces available for joint action when necessary.

This outline of the administration's postwar blueprint, announced so casually, shocked advocates of world federation. Ely Culbertson wrote an angry letter to Roosevelt denouncing his plan as an attempt "to resurrect the bullet-ridden League of Nations." Objecting to a "triumvirate of world dictators," Culbertson said the American people wanted "a true system of collective defense against aggressors, supported by an effective international police force." A St. Louis member of Federal Union wrote to express his "disappointment" at the President's plan.

"Law must replace international anarchy," he asserted. "Only an international government can originate and enforce such law."

More moderate internationalists regretted that the plan did not remedy the fatal defect of the League Covenant—the lack of an automatic provision for the use of force in a crisis. The editors of the *Nation* lamented the administration's failure to learn the lesson of "the tragic 1930's, when short-range national interests prevented any of the powers from accepting the responsibility of checking aggression." Senator Joseph Ball thought the plan was weak, advocating the inclusion of "binding commitments by the nations within this proposed new organization to use force to suppress aggression." Clark Eichelberger masked his disappointment in a letter to the President, praising the statement but suggesting that Roosevelt include "some symbol of international police power." In a *Changing World* editorial, however, he told his followers that it was essential to have "a clear indication in advance that the forces of the nations and the world community will be used against aggression. If this cannot be stated clearly and unequivocally in the document which the United Nations will be negotiating, the cause is lost and the third world war is in prospect." [25]

The conservative nature of the organization Roosevelt proposed left little room for isolationist criticism, though some continued to worry about the fate of small nations. The most pungent analysis came from William Hard, a senior editor of *Reader's Digest* who described himself as a "nationalist." Attacking the administration for choosing the "Great Power" road to peace, he wrote, "Thus is born the Quadruple Alliance of the 20th century. It is but a copy of the Quadruple Alliance of the 19th." Like the internationalists, he bemoaned the fate of the lesser nations, saying it was not "American" to subject the majority of the human race to the domination of the great powers. But his solution was radically different; he wanted to go back to the traditional policy of Washington and Jefferson, the policy of "equal friendship" with "all powers." He suggested that the United States take the lead in forming a world union modeled after the Pan-American conferences to discuss all international questions without any binding commitments or provisions for the use of force. "The whole history of the world," he warned, "for the past 130 years teaches us that, when the power of the great powers is made the *primary* thing and when it is exalted into being the one central pillar of peace, it crashes in blood."

While isolationists and internationalists debated the role of force in keeping the peace, *Time* summed up the prevailing editorial opinion by saying, "Most Americans found the program unexceptionable—what there was of it." Praising Roosevelt for securing a beachhead for peace right after the Normandy invasion, the New York *Times* felt that the administration's plan "represents the consensus of American thought on a method to maintain peace." The editors of the *New Republic* called the plan a compromise which represented a realistic assessment of what the Big Four were likely to accept. "To avoid advance automatic commitments to the use of force is probably only good sense," they observed, "since history proves beyond any doubt that no country will go to war against the wishes of its people." They were pleased that Roosevelt had avoided Wilson's grand aspirations and hoped that his cautious approach would prove more successful.[26]

Whatever the ultimate outcome, there could be no doubt that Roosevelt and Hull had succeeded in winning a stunning tactical victory. With the Republican convention due to open in two weeks, they had occupied the safe middle ground by advocating an international organization which avoided the surrender of national sovereignty, yet held out the promise of an enduring peace. For the Republicans, the outlook was bleak. No longer could they point to Roosevelt's silence and charge that he was making secret deals, nor could they picture him as an advocate of wild-eyed internationalism. All they could do was to accept the nonpartisan role that Hull had prepared for them and ratify the administration's plans for peace.

V

Cordell Hull had left nothing to chance. On June 3 he met with a group from the House Foreign Affairs Committee which included three prominent Republicans and gave them a copy of the Department's draft plan for an international organization. Later in the month, at Senator Ball's request, Hull met with the four B_2H_2 senators and gave them a briefing on the administration's plan. Meanwhile, he authorized Myron Taylor to ascertain the views of Governor Dewey, the likely Republican candidate. Taylor, working through several prominent Republican leaders, passed the draft plan on to Dewey through intermediates, and on June 8 he reported to Hull, "I am following the matter closely but do not want to make a wrong move at this time which might injure the project." Hull finally decided it would be inappropriate to ask Dewey to endorse the plan publicly before the convention, and Taylor broke off the negotiation.

8. *"Your Move, Mister President"*

Breckinridge Long was also deeply concerned about Republican support. On June 6 he prevailed on James B. Reynolds, a member of the GOP National Committee, to give him a list of members of the Resolutions Committee which would write the party's platform. Long submitted it to Hull and asked the Secretary for permission to work with Warren Austin to secure an endorsement of the administration's plan in the Republican platform. When Hull consented, Long met with Austin and authorized him to disclose the general nature of the Department's plan to other Republicans. Long told Austin that it was important for his party to go beyond the Mackinac declaration, and then he wrote in his diary, "So now we will wait and see whether a rose grows in the garden—or a pumpkin. If it should be a rose it will be my first success in a *Republican* convention." [27]

As the time for the convention approached, Wendell Willkie used his influence to ensure an internationalist platform. Back in May he had written to twenty newspaper editors that he would wait out the presidential campaign in an effort to force the party toward his viewpoint. "Naturally," he wrote, "as a Republican, I would prefer to work within the Republican party, but I will be damned if I am going to sit by while the peace of the world is wrecked again as it was in the 1920's." When six leading Republican newspapers asked him to write a series of articles stating his ideas on the major issues in the campaign, he eagerly accepted. The first six dealt with domestic problems, but the seventh, which appeared on June 17, denounced Roosevelt's diplomacy and called upon the GOP to "frame and pursue a foreign policy that will recapture America's lost leadership." Willkie urged the party to adopt a plank advocating the immediate creation of a United Nations Council. Above all, he asked his fellow Republicans to abandon the narrow nationalism of the past. Sovereignty should not be hoarded, he declared, but instead should be used "in cooperation with other powers to create an effective international organization for the good of all."

The editors of the *New Republic* thought that Willkie's suggestions had "about as much chance of being adopted as the Sermon on the Mount has of being endorsed by the Gestapo," and they were right. In a pointed rebuke, Harrison Spangler did not invite Willkie to address the convention even though he had been the party's candidate in 1940, nor was he consulted about the platform. Instead, Arthur Vandenberg drew up a statement reaffirming the Mackinac declaration and secured the assent of Dewey and Bricker, the leading candidates, in May and early June. "So the job was just about done before we ever got to Chicago," commented Vandenberg later. [28]

8. *"Your Move, Mister President"*

On June 21, five days before the opening of the convention, the Resolutions Committee met in Chicago to prepare the platform. Representatives of internationalist groups, led by Clark Eichelberger, urged the committee to advocate an effective world organization, but the members paid little attention, with one challenging Eichelberger as a "fourth-term Democrat." Austin succeeded in getting Vandenberg to insert the words "peace forces" in his draft, but he was unable to secure any commitment to the administration's plan. Ball, who was working desperately for the nomination of Stassen as a dark horse, asked the committee to adopt a strong internationalist statement, and several governors threatened a floor fight over the foreign-policy plank. On June 24, however, the committee accepted the Vandenberg draft and incorporated it into the platform. The text, which was leaked to the press by unhappy internationalists, called for "responsible participation by the United States in postwar cooperative organization among sovereign nations to prevent military aggression and to attain permanent peace with organized justice in a free world." Like the Mackinac declaration, this pledge was hedged about with reservations in regard to American sovereignty and constitutional procedures. On the crucial issue of enforcement, the committee used Austin's ambiguous phrase "peace forces," and then added, "We believe, however, that peace and security do not depend upon the sanction of force alone, but should prevail by virtue of reciprocal interests and spiritual values recognized in these security agreements." [29]

A few hours after the convention opened on June 26, Willkie called reporters to his law offices in New York. Reading from a prepared statement, he compared the platform to the one adopted by the Republican party in 1920, denouncing its ambiguity and emphasis on sovereignty. "We should speak in words forthright, clear and strong," he asserted, and appealed to the delegates to revise the platform to include a call for a United Nations Council and a commitment to use force to maintain peace. Though Governor Walter Edge of New Jersey joined Willkie by denouncing the "rubber words" in the platform, party leaders easily suppressed a movement for a floor fight. On June 27 the convention adopted the platform with Vandenberg's wording intact, and the next day nominated Dewey on the first ballot. In his acceptance speech the nominee did not clarify the ambiguous stand of the party, stating only that he agreed that "America will participate with other sovereign nations in a co-operative effort to prevent future wars."

Breckinridge Long termed the platform "a disappointment," and feared that the administration still faced a political fight over international organization. Cordell Hull did not like it either, but he was even more upset by Dewey's acceptance speech, taking personal offense at the Republican candidate's charges that the Roosevelt administration was "old," "tired" and "quarrelsome." He wanted to issue a rebuttal that Long warned would destroy the nonpartisan policy until the President finally convinced him it would be better to remain silent. More objective commentators found little difference between the Republican platform and Roosevelt's June 15 statement on international organization. "The action proposed," commented the New York *Times*, "is about what the American people expect and will approve." Many did point out, however, that Dewey faced the problem of convincing voters that he could control the isolationists within his party. The memory of 1920 still haunted the American people, and it was up to Dewey to prove that he was not another Warren Harding.[30]

Attention now shifted to the Democrats, who were scheduled to convene in Chicago in mid-July. Though virtually everyone was sure Roosevelt planned to run for a fourth term, the President remained coy, refusing to disclose his intentions. On July 11, only a week before the convention, he read reporters a letter from National Chairman Robert Hannegan informing him that a majority of the delegates favored his renomination and asking him to declare his candidacy. Roosevelt then read his reply, in which he said he preferred to return to private life, but with the war still in progress, he would bow to the will of the people and run again.

Speculation then shifted to the vice-presidency. Roosevelt had virtually forced Henry Wallace on the party in 1940, and throughout the spring Democratic leaders had indicated their desire for a new candidate. Wallace was the embodiment of the New Deal, and politicians feared that he would alienate millions of voters who were concerned about Roosevelt's health and realized that he might not survive another term in office. Though the opposition to Wallace stemmed much more from domestic than from foreign issues, Roosevelt feared that his presence on the ticket would not only jeopardize the chances of a Democratic victory but also threaten the bi-partisan movement for international organization. Yet Roosevelt always hated to hurt a loyal associate, and he was still fond of Wallace. After months of procrastination he chose a characteristic solution, writing a public letter stating that if he were a delegate at Chicago he would cast his vote for Wallace. "At the same time," Roosevelt continued, "I do not wish to appear in any way as dictating to the convention. Obviously the convention must do the deciding." Democratic leaders immediately interpreted this as a rejection of Wallace, and a wide-open scramble for the vice-presidency began.[31]

There was less interest in the platform, although several Democrats voiced their hope that the party would take a stronger stand on international organization than the Republicans. Senator Harry Truman, one of the candidates for the vice-presidency, charged that the GOP platform was "ambiguous" and called on his party to adopt a specific pledge "that the United States will take part in world affairs this time and maintain the peace by using the Army and Navy, if necessary." Sam Rosenman, the President's chief speech-writer, drew up a draft which Roosevelt whittled down to five hundred words and then sent over to the State Department on the eve of the convention. Cordell Hull approved the plank on foreign policy, and he and Hannegan asked Tom Connally to go to Chicago to "handle the H_2's of the B_2H_2 group." Hatch and Hill had joined with Ball and Burton in a statement urging both parties to declare for a world organization "having real authority and power," and Hull wanted to block any effort to change the administration's wording.[32]

When the convention opened on July 19, internationalists led by Florence Harriman, Claude Pepper and Carl Hatch went before the platform committee to argue for a plank advocating an international air force as an integral part of the world organization. "All we ask of this resolutions committee," pleaded Mrs. Harriman, "is an endorsement of the good old American principle of collective security." Working behind the scenes, Connally was able to defeat this move, and the next day the committee reported out the administration's platform with only slight verbal changes. The internationalists persisted, offering their air-force proposal as an amendment on the floor of the convention, but the delegates rejected it by an overwhelming vote. The wording they approved followed the Moscow declaration, calling for an international organization "based on the principle of sovereign equality of all peace-loving states . . . for the prevention of aggression and the maintenance of international peace and security." On the vital issue of enforcement, the Democrats were slightly more explicit than the Republicans, suggesting that the organization "be endowed with power to employ armed forces when necessary to prevent aggression and preserve peace."[33]

Throughout the convention the Democrats paid homage to Woodrow Wilson. In his keynote address Governor Robert Kerr of Oklahoma skillfully identified Dewey with the Republican attack on the League of Nations and Roosevelt with "the kind of peace worked for, fought for and died for by the immortal Woodrow Wilson." Then he reached his climax. "The forces of isolationism crucified the great-hearted Woodrow Wilson. The same forces now strive with equal fury and frenzy to inflict the same fate on Roosevelt. But where they succeeded then, they will fail now." Josephus Daniels introduced a resolution of tribute to Wilson which ended, "We highly resolve to complete the tragically unfilled task," and the convention adopted it with great applause. Breckinridge Long confided in his diary that the repeated references to Wilson brought tears to his eyes. "A quarter of a century ago I made a hard fight for the League of Nations," he wrote. ". . . now I see my party espouse the cause I fought for and believed in and see the opposing party generally espouse the idea. . . . Perhaps I will soon feel compensated for myself, confident of peace for my grandchildren."

When it came time to choose the candidates, the delegates renominated Roosevelt by acclamation and then settled down to a floor fight over the vice-presidency. Behind the scenes Robert Hannegan produced a letter from the President endorsing Harry Truman, and though the Wallace supporters fought on, the convention nominated the Missouri senator on the second ballot. Truman was a forthright advocate of international organization who had helped initiate the B_2H_2 resolution, but the internationalists were saddened by the rejection of Henry Wallace, who had spoken out for their cause when everyone else was silent. A few were bitter. Ulric Bell, commenting on the repudiation of Willkie and Wallace, wrote, "Small comfort came to anxious Americans and a watching, wartorn world from those two little Munichs conducted at Chicago by the Democratic and Republican parties." [34]

The internationalist movement, so long the exclusive concern of a dedicated minority, had moved out into the mainstream of American politics. The sacrifices which accompanied this process were painful. Sumner Welles, Wendell Willkie and Henry Wallace had risked their careers by calling boldly for a new world order. Though they had lost their positions of leadership, they had succeeded in arousing the American people and converting them to the cause of international organization. A few die-hards regretted the compromises made to secure this consensus, but the overwhelming majority of the internationalists rejoiced in the victory they had won.

9

The Bi-Partisan Victory

THE INTERNATIONALISTS waited impatiently during the summer of 1944 for the administration to act. The Commission to Study the Organization of Peace had asked a group of experts, led by Professor Manley O. Hudson of the Harvard Law School, to draw up a draft charter for a general international organization. Hudson's group completed its task in May, and the Commission began circulating copies confidentially to its members and to government officials. When Hudson was unable to secure a personal interview with the President to present the plan to him, he sent a copy to Ben Cohen, who saw that it reached the President's desk. This draft, which was finally made public on July 31, was quite similar to the State Department plan, calling for an assembly of all nations and a council with the power to halt aggression. Though the Commission frankly stated that the draft charter was based on the experience of the League of Nations, Hamilton Holt was disappointed at the substitution of the word "charter" for "covenant" and accused James Shotwell of "soft pedalling" the League of Nations "for purely political reasons."

In midsummer the Commission published a pamphlet by Clark Eichelberger entitled *The Time Has Come for Action,* summarizing the principal features of its draft charter. Eichelberger argued for a moderate approach to international organization, pointing out that world-government enthusiasts ignored the fact that "we are living in a period when the nation-state is the basic unit of the world community." The only obligations involved in world organization, he continued, were abstention from the use of force, and agreement to settle disputes peacefully and to cooperate with other nations to prevent aggression. He stressed the importance of prompt action, warning that, after the war, "reaction, fatigue and a lessening of moral enthusiasm" might divide the

214

nations now fighting side by side and "wreck their dreams" of avoiding a third world war.[1]

Edgar Ansel Mowrer felt that the Commission's proposals were too modest. In letters to the members of the Non-Partisan Council to Win the Peace, he asserted that some surrender of sovereignty to a world body was imperative. "There must be armed forces available for use by the world organization to prevent aggression and maintain peace," he declared. Admitting that a full-scale international police force was too utopian, he suggested a small corps of troops drawn from the member nations to act as a trigger for collective security. When aggression took place, the international corps would go into action, thereby automatically committing the big powers to back them up with their armed forces.

Americans United for World Organization, the new coordinating body for all the action groups, did not advocate any specific plan in the summer of 1944. Instead, it concentrated on making arrangements for the coming Congressional elections, hoping to mobilize its supporters to defeat isolationist candidates. After Sumner Welles declined to serve as chairman, President Ernest Hopkins of Dartmouth took the office, but Ulric Bell continued to direct the day-by-day activities. Bell announced plans to work through existing committees wherever possible and to form new groups "in many unorganized communities where the isolationists, the nationalists, the cynics, and the subversives have met little or no resistance." He wrote President Roosevelt that his organization had "corraled most of the all-out people throughout the country" who stood for "a world organization with real teeth in it." [2]

The internationalists, poised for the final drive toward their goal, were delighted when Cordell Hull announced on July 17 that "informal conversations and exchanges of views on the general subject of an international security organization" would soon get under way in Washington. The conference, to be held at Dumbarton Oaks, would take place in two stages. Russia, who was not at war with Japan, would meet with the United States and Britain, and then would leave while the Chinese talked with the American and English delegations. When the Big Four had reached agreement, the other members of the United Nations would be consulted.

The State Department spent the next month preparing for the Dumbarton Oaks conference, scheduled to open on August 14 but postponed to August 21 at the request of the Soviet Union. Since the conference was designed as a meeting of experts to perfect plans for international organization, Hull decided not to include any members of Congress in the American delegation, though he promised Connally and Vandenberg that he would keep them fully informed of all developments. He asked Stettinius to head the American delegation, which was composed of nearly all the members of the Political Agenda group, six military advisers appointed by the War and Navy Departments, and Henry P. Fletcher, a former Under Secretary of State and general counsel for the Republican National Committee, who was added to continue the bi-partisan policy. By mid-August this group was meeting regularly to discuss the American plan in the light of proposals submitted by the British and Russians. The British suggested only slight modifications, but the Russians sent a draft plan on August 12 which limited the world organization to security functions, suggesting that economic, social and cultural issues be handled by other agencies. This proposal, which leaked to the press on August 15, called for an absolute veto for the Big Four and, to the delight of internationalists, an international air force to keep the peace. The American delegates quickly decided to oppose the air-force idea as impractical, but they split over the veto issue. Some favored the British view that a major power should not be able to vote in a dispute in which it was involved, but others believed that the great powers must have the right to veto the use of force in all cases. This dispute was crucial, for its outcome would decide the degree to which the big powers would dominate the world organization.[3]

I

"I have been deeply disturbed by some of the recent reports concerning the forthcoming conference," announced Thomas Dewey on August 16. "These indicate that it is planned to subject the nations of the world, great and small, permanently to the coercive power of the four nations holding this conference." In the statement, drafted with the help of Arthur Krock and John Foster Dulles, Dewey went on to warn against a four-power alliance, which he termed "immoral" and "the rankest form of imperialism." He concluded with a plea for a more democratic form of world order. "As Americans we believe with all our hearts in the equality and rights of small nations and minorities. In the kind of permanent world organization we seek, all nations, great and small, must be assured of their full rights." Dewey's blast at power politics won him headlines and editorial praise across the nation; few editors seemed aware that less than a year earlier the New York governor had advocated an alliance with Britain as the basis of America's postwar foreign policy.

The next morning Hull called a news conference at the State Department. For over an hour the Secretary, burning with indignation, lectured the fifty-five journalists lined up before him in rows of chairs like children in school. ". . . the human race at this hour, this day, this week, this year is confronted by the gravest crisis in its experience," he told them. Calling Dewey's charges "utterly and completely unfounded," Hull said the United States would protect the interests of small countries at Dumbarton Oaks and repeated his July promise that a conference of all the United Nations would make the final decisions on world organization. The Secretary then invited the Republican nominee to come to Washington and confer with him about the proposed international organization "in a nonpartisan spirit."

Dewey mulled over this proposal for a day and then sent Hull a telegram designating John Foster Dulles as his personal representative. Hull immediately accepted this arrangement, and his aides in the State Department were delighted that the Secretary had succeeded in heading off a potentially dangerous partisan assault on the eve of the Dumbarton Oaks conference. ". . . it may turn out," commented Long in his diary, "to be the most beneficent situation that could have been developed." [4]

Dewey's move thrust Dulles into public prominence for the first time. *Life* quickly published a very flattering profile in which John Chamberlain hinted that Dulles was likely to be Dewey's choice for Secretary of State. The two men had been close friends since the late 1930's, and Dulles had helped Dewey in his successful race for the New York governorship in 1942. Although Dulles had won a reputation as a forthright internationalist through his work as chairman of the Commission on a Just and Durable Peace, liberal publicists reminded their readers that as the managing partner in Sullivan and Cromwell, the leading international law firm in the nation, he was "a very conservative cartel lawyer."

Dulles tried to clarify his views on the postwar world in a press conference at the governor's mansion in Albany on August 19. Echoing ideas expressed by Herbert Hoover and Hugh Gibson in 1942, Dulles suggested that the United States, Russia, Britain and China police the defeated Axis nations. "That is a specific task which for a considerable time, at least, will be a task of the principal Allied victors and not a task of a world organization," he declared. In this way, the Big Four would not need to dominate the world body and it could be set up along more democratic lines. Then, in response to reporters' questions, Dulles said he did not plan to ask to attend the Dumbarton Oaks conference, but instead he wanted to establish a channel of communication so that Dewey could be kept informed of the progress made toward international organization during the presidential campaign.

Dewey and Dulles continued to confer in Albany in preparation for the forthcoming discussions with Hull. On August 20 Dewey told reporters that he had invited Willkie to join them, and though Willkie had declined, he had agreed to meet Dulles in New York City the next day. Dulles found the meeting "somewhat strained," and Willkie was disappointed to find that Dulles did not share his enthusiasm for an international police force. After their talk they issued a noncommittal press release saying they had "a full exchange of views" and that they both advocated a "responsible" role for the United States in world affairs. Dulles then continued on to Washington, where he was careful to seek out and listen to the diverse views of Republican Senators Taft, Vandenberg, Austin and Hiram Johnson.[5]

Dulles came to Hull's office in the State Department on the morning of August 23 for their first meeting. The two men met alone, despite the plea of Gerald L. K. Smith, the presidential candidate of the America First Party, that Colonel Robert McCormick be allowed to represent him at "this vital and history making conference." Hull began by handing Dulles the Department's draft plan and a four-page memorandum outlining the important part small nations would play in the proposed world body. The two men agreed on the need to remove the issue of international organization from politics, but for two and a half hours disagreed on everything else. Dulles resisted Hull's efforts to exempt all aspects of foreign policy from the political campaign, wanting to preserve Dewey's freedom to attack the administration on vulnerable points. "The Secretary seemed to me very stubborn," Dulles commented. "Perhaps I seemed that way to him."

When they met again the next day, Dulles began by telling Hull that he found the draft plan excellent and that he no longer was concerned over the fate of the small nations. Hull then handed him a statement his aides had prepared which said the two men had agreed on the fundamentals of international organization and that "Mr. Dulles gave assurance that the Governor on his part considers this a nonpartisan subject which must be kept entirely out of politics." Dulles immediately objected to the word "nonpartisan," insisting instead that they use "bipartisan" to suggest that the Republicans were actively participating in the formation of international organization. For nearly two hours they fought over these words. Hull stuck to his original phrasing, saying that he wanted to take the issue out of politics, not put it in. They finally decided to revise the statement in order to include both words. Hull phoned the text to the President, who approved, and he and Dulles signed the statement. Hull then asked Dulles to add the phrase "as representative of Governor Dewey" after his name, but Dulles declined; when Hull insisted, Dulles said he would consult with Dewey that evening and return for a third and final meeting the next morning.

Dulles reported the following day that Dewey had given him permission to sign the statement as his representative with some additional qualifying phrases. After a brief discussion Hull approved the change in wording and the two men called in the reporters. They stated that they had conducted a free exchange of views on international organization and were in agreement "on numerous aspects of this subject." "The Secretary," the statement continued, "maintained the position that the American people consider the subject of future peace as a nonpartisan subject which must be kept entirely out of politics. Mr. Dulles, on behalf of Governor Dewey, stated that the Governor shared this view on the understanding, however, that it did not preclude full public nonpartisan discussion of the means of attaining a lasting peace." Replying to questions, the two men stressed that their agreement covered only international organization, not other aspects of foreign policy, and they expressed an intention of conferring again during the campaign.

"We have done something unique in American politics," Dulles said afterward. He was right. Never before had the two foreign-policy spokesmen of presidential candidates met to remove a major issue from the political arena. For Hull, it was a vital step in a carefully conceived campaign to avoid a partisan split on international organization, and one that filled him with relief. When Dewey wrote to express his pleasure at the outcome of the conference, Hull replied, "I am convinced that with unity, and only with unity, we can successfully carry forward this project which means so much to the people of this generation and to the people of generations to come." Breckinridge Long was even more optimistic. "If Dewey lives up to it all—including 'non-partisan' discussion—the fight is practically over as far as Senate approval is concerned," he wrote. "This is our last chance—and this agreement may so bind the political opposition it cannot defeat us or this issue." [6]

II

The Dumbarton Oaks conference opened on the morning of August 21 at the beautiful Georgetown mansion that Robert Woods Bliss, a career diplomat and former ambassador to Argentina, had donated to Harvard University in 1940 for Byzantine studies. Surrounded by sixteen acres of grounds which included formal gardens, old pebble walks and arched bridges over ponds filled with lilies, the pink brick building contained priceless tapestries, bronzes and paintings. The thirty-nine delegates assembled in the Renaissance music room, where the Byzantine *objets d'art* and the ornate high ceilings formed a striking backdrop to the traditional U-shaped conference table covered with the inevitable blotter pads. Cordell Hull delivered the opening address, stressing the importance of force to preserve peace. "That force," he declared, "must be available promptly, in adequate measure, and with certainty." Sir Alexander Cadogan, Permanent Under Secretary for Foreign Affairs, spoke for the British delegation, and then Andrei Gromyko, the new Soviet ambassador to the United States, concluded the opening ceremony. Only thirty-five, Gromyko was a surprising choice to head the Soviet delegation, and many American observers, expecting Molotov or Vishinsky to attend, took his appointment as a sign of Russian indifference to world organization. The Chinese delegation, waiting in the wings for the Russians to depart, did not attend the first session.

The next day, to the intense annoyance of the American press, the delegates went into executive session. Military police kept reporters from entering the grounds at Dumbarton Oaks, and State Department press officers supplied very few releases on the conference activities. On August 23 journalists were on hand at the White House when President Roosevelt held an informal reception for the delegates. Dressed in seersucker suits and tropical woolens rather than in the traditional morning coats, the diplomats listened politely while Roosevelt spoke to them extemporaneously. Referring to Al Smith's advice about how to settle problems, the President suggested that the delegates take off their coats, sit down and put their feet on the table. Impressed by Roosevelt's breezy approach, Stettinius decided to take the delegates to New York the next weekend so that they could get to know each other better while sightseeing. He arranged for them to fly secretly to Manhattan, where they stayed at the Waldorf-Astoria and went out on Saturday night to the Radio City Music Hall and then on to Billy Rose's Diamond Horseshoe night club. Reporters caught up with the party on Sunday, and Stettinius quickly rounded up the delegates and flew them back to Washington.[7]

These few glimpses of the diplomats failed to satisfy the curiosity of the press, particularly when James Reston began printing authoritative accounts of the details of the conference in the New York *Times*. Reston carefully cultivated the Chinese delegates, who resented their exclusion from the first phase of the conference so intensely that they gave him the complete text of the documents being discussed at Dumbarton Oaks. During the first week Reston published a detailed outline of the American plan along with the British and Russian comments on it. Most observers believed the English were leaking the information to Reston; Lord Halifax, the British ambassador, cut off all personal contact with Reston in an effort to lessen this suspicion. Despite repeated efforts to trace this leak, the State Department never uncovered Reston's link with the Chinese, and he continued to report in depth on the progress of the conference, eventually winning a Pulitzer Prize for his series. Other journalists complained bitterly, and in Congress Senator Styles Bridges, a New Hampshire Republican and moderate internationalist, assailed the administration for its refusal to inform the people of what was going on at Dumbarton Oaks. When the State Department Correspondents Association registered a formal protest, Stettinius replied with a statement pointing out that it was traditional for diplomats to confer in private so that they could speak frankly. He promised that the final agreements reached at the conference would be made public when it was over.

The uproar became so great that Stettinius, Cadogan and Gromyko finally held a press conference on August 29. They told reporters that they had reached "general agreement" on the outline of a world organization to keep the peace, but they refused to give more than a brief description of an assembly, a council and a world court. "To go beyond this and describe the discussions in detail," commented Stettinius, "would be not only discourteous but improper." Disgruntled reporters replied that they still did not have as much information as Reston had printed, and for the balance of the conference, relations with the press remained strained. Stettinius' insistence on maintaining secrecy when Reston had effectively breached it was a serious mistake; the first international conference on world organization, which should have served to educate the American people on the issues involved, instead bred suspicions about what the State Department planned for the postwar world.[8]

Cordell Hull was careful to keep the eight senators he had conferred with during the spring informed about the Dumbarton Oaks conference. On August 23 he sent them each a copy of the revised plan which the American delegation was discussing with the British and the Russians, and two days later he met with the Committee of Eight to answer their questions about it. The conversation focused on the use of force, and Vandenberg hit hard on the point Hull and Long were most sensitive about: who would make the decision to use American troops in a collective security action? Backed by La Follette, Vandenberg insisted that the American delegate could not commit armed forces without the consent of Congress on each occasion, on the grounds that such action was equivalent to a declaration of war. Hull maintained that the President should have discretionary power to act without a formal vote from both Houses, although he would undoubtedly consult with Congressional leaders before authorizing the American delegate to vote for the use of force. Vandenberg admitted it might be all right for the President to decide to use troops in the Western Hemisphere. "But I said," Vandenberg wrote in his diary, "that I wanted it emphatically plain—so that I would not subsequently be accused of bad faith or of an attempt to 'wreck the League'—that I would never consent that our delegate on the new 'League' Council should have the power to vote us into a *major* military operation (tantamount to declaring war) without a vote of Congress as required by the Constitution."

Vandenberg renewed his objections in a long letter to Hull on August 29, insisting that Congress must pass on each decision by the American delegate to use force in preserving peace. Hull was very upset, and he finally asked Green Hackworth, the Department's Legal Adviser, to prepare an opinion on this point. Two days later Hackworth submitted a memorandum arguing that, once Congress approved American participation in a world organization with power to use force, the President would be free to commit troops as he saw fit. Hull sent this opinion to the eight senators. Meanwhile, the issue became public on August 29 when a reporter at the President's weekly press conference asked Roosevelt what role Congress would play in future decisions to use troops to halt aggression. The President replied that it was too early to go into details, but he added, "we are at one—almost—in this country, in wanting to end future wars by stepping on their necks before they grow up."

Neither Hackworth's memorandum nor Roosevelt's casual remark ended the speculation. On August 30 Walter George told Breckinridge Long that earlier that day Vandenberg and La Follette had cornered Wallace White and asked him to join them in fighting for a Congressional veto on the use of force. White, acting minority leader of the Senate and a long-time internationalist, was deeply troubled, and he had gone to George for advice. Long repeated Hull's contention that in any major crisis the President would consult with Congressional leaders, pointing out that any extensive military effort would compel the President to go to Congress for appropriations. George promised to keep White from wavering, but Long remained troubled. "This all presages a nasty partisan Republican attack—during the Dumbarton meeting—against the movement to secure peace and prevent war," he commented in his diary.[9]

Senator Harlan Bushfield, a Republican isolationist from South Dakota, confirmed Long's fears in a Senate speech on September 5. Citing Reston's reports in the New York *Times*, Bushfield declared that the American plan proposed to give the President power to declare war without the consent of Congress. Accusing Roosevelt of wanting to become "a true dictator" and "the absolute despot of the American people," Bushfield challenged the President to clarify his position in the forthcoming election campaign. Connally quickly rebutted Bushfield's charges, terming them politically inspired and asking the senators to reserve judgment on the American plan until it was published at the conclusion of the Dumbarton Oaks conference. Vandenberg came to Connally's support, telling Bushfield that the Senate could debate and decide the issue he had raised when it considered the question of American entry into the proposed world organization. He repeated his earlier suggestion that the presidential power to use force be limited to the Western Hemisphere, adding that other nations might take the primary responsibility for maintaining peace in their regions of the world. Then he warned against an excessive reliance on the use of military power to keep the peace, saying his hopes rested on the "creation of instrumentalities which will make the rules of reason omnipotent upon this earth rather than the rules of force." [10]

Hull was grateful for the backing Vandenberg gave the administration in answering Bushfield, and he now made a new effort to avert a partisan rift. On September 11 he asked Republican Hugh Wilson, a former ambassador to Germany, to convey to Dulles and Dewey his concern over the GOP senators' insistence on a Congressional veto over the use of force. "I said that this movement might endanger the whole peace program if it were not nipped in the bud," Hull later wrote, "and that it was up to the Republican leaders to do something about it before it was too late." When Dulles telephoned the Secretary the next day, Hull told him he feared that further public discussion during the Dumbarton Oaks conference might convince the British and the Russians that the administration would not be able to secure Senate approval for its own plan.

Later that day Hull met again with the eight senators and proposed a compromise. Under the American plan, each nation would agree to provide the council of the world organization with a quota of troops for use in an emergency. Hull suggested that the special agreement to provide armed forces be considered separately by the Senate. In this way, the Senate could approve American entry into the proposed international organization on its own merits, and then later decide whether Congress had to approve the use of force on each occasion. On the advice of Dewey, Vandenberg and his Republican colleagues accepted this solution. Hull was enormously relieved, believing that this compromise would remove a dangerous controversy from the coming campaign and thus ensure the success "of nearly twelve years' striving to lift foreign policies out of partisan politics." [11]

Senator Ball thought the issue was too significant to be dismissed so easily. In a speech to the Senate on September 19 he denied that the use of troops to halt aggression was equivalent to a declaration of war. "The world security organization would not be making war, but preserving the peace," he declared. "Its whole purpose is to eliminate war from the world, not make it." The delay caused by seeking the approval of Congress in a crisis could undermine the whole concept of collective security. Pleading with his colleagues to face the issue squarely and not insist on a Congressional veto, he proclaimed:

> If we make that kind of a crippling reservation so will every other nation reserve the right to decide what it will do in each particular case, and we will have no more certainty of international law enforcement than we had in the twenties and thirties.

Ball went on to say that he disagreed with many features of the plan being developed at Dumbarton Oaks, but he would bury his doubts as long as the organization possessed the power to outlaw aggressive war. But without this authority, the venture was doomed from the outset. "This time," he concluded, "let us keep faith with those who are fighting to make this second chance for a lasting peace possible." [12]

III

The conference at Dumbarton Oaks had proceeded smoothly until August 28, when Andrei Gromyko startled the British and American delegates by requesting separate memberships and votes in the General Assembly for the sixteen republics that composed the Soviet Union. No one was sure of the Russian motive, but Stalin evidently felt that he needed the votes to balance the British dominions and the Latin American nations, which he thought would always be controlled by the United States. Roosevelt, disturbed by this proposal, and aware of the impact it could have on public opinion, asked Gromyko to keep his request secret. On August 31 the President sent a cable to Stalin urging him to reconsider this demand. A week later Stalin replied, suggesting that they defer this issue for consideration at a future Big Three meeting, a course Roosevelt quickly approved.

A much more serious impasse developed in September over Soviet insistence on absolute veto power in the Security Council. The British had submitted a memorandum proposing that the great powers abstain from voting in disputes in which they were involved. The American delegates were still divided on this issue, but the majority believed that a great power should have the right to veto any decision to use economic or military sanctions. On the morning of September 8 Stettinius brought Gromyko to the White House to discuss the veto issue with Roosevelt. The President received the Soviet ambassador in his bedroom, and for thirty-five minutes he explained that it went against the American tradition of fair play to have a party to a dispute sit in judgment. He even made a folksy comparison to a husband and wife taking their differences to court—they had a right to express their views in the courtroom, but they could not expect to serve on the jury. Gromyko was unmoved, simply saying that he would repeat Roosevelt's position to his superiors in Moscow.

The next day Roosevelt sent a cable to Stalin asking him to intervene to end this deadlock. The President included his husband-and-wife analogy, and told Stalin, "We and the British both feel strongly that in the decisions of the Council, parties to a dispute should not vote if one of the members is a permanent member of the Council; I know public opinion in the United States would never understand or support a plan of international organization which violated this principle." A week later Stalin replied in an injured tone, saying that he thought the three leaders had agreed at Teheran that all decisions in the new world organization would require the unanimous approval of the great powers. He referred to the "ridiculous prejudices" some nations had against the Soviet Union, and said his countrymen felt they had to have the veto for their own protection.[13]

By mid-September the Russian stand on the veto was the sole remaining issue before the Dumbarton Oaks conference. Experts drew up a compromise voting formula reserving the veto for decisions on enforcement measures only, but both Roosevelt and Churchill objected. The split in the American delegation became acrimonious as the stalemate continued. Breckinridge Long led the faction that wanted to accept the Russian position. Pointing out that the Committee of Eight favored an ironclad veto, he argued that, far from being a concession to the Soviet Union, the veto was essential to secure Senate approval. Ben Cohen disagreed, contending that American public opinion would be outraged at any arrangement whereby a nation judged its own case. Hull finally called the entire delegation into his office, brought up the movie *Wilson* to remind the members of the dangers of division, and then suggested they try again to find a suitable compromise.

As the conference dragged on, a journalist asked Roosevelt why the meeting was progressing so slowly. "We are trying to work out a world that will be probably free from wars," the President responded, "and you just don't call a conference in the morning and solve that largest of human problems by four o'clock in the afternoon." He said that the delegates had agreed on ninety percent of the issues confronting them, adding, "Well, that is what we used to call in the old days a darn good batting average." The public unrest, however, disturbed Roosevelt, and he finally told Hull it would be best to wind up the Russian phase of the conference with the voting issue unresolved. He said he would take it up with Churchill and Stalin personally at their next meeting. On September 27 Stettinius called in the press and, repeating Roosevelt's phrase about ninety-percent agreement, announced that the meetings with the Russians would end the next day. On September 28 the Soviet delegation left Washington and the British and American diplomats began conferring with the Chinese, who had been waiting since mid-August.

226

The second phase went quickly as China accepted the agreements reached with the Russians with very few changes.[14]

The Dumbarton Oaks conference closed on October 7, when the Chinese formally approved a joint statement entitled "Proposals for the Establishment of a General International Organization." Hull sent copies of this document to all members of the Senate, and to Governor Dewey and John Foster Dulles; on October 9 he released it to the public, stressing the nonpartisan approach the administration had been following and calling on the American people to discuss the Dumbarton Oaks proposals in the same spirit. In an accompanying statement President Roosevelt expressed his pleasure that "so much could have been accomplished on so difficult a subject in so short a time." Calling the proposed international organization the "major objective" of the war, he observed that "the task of planning the great design of security and peace has been well begun."

The Dumbarton Oaks proposals contained few surprises for those who had been following James Reston's reports in the New York *Times*. They called for the establishment of a "United Nations Organization" composed of an assembly of all the member nations; an eleven-seat Security Council with five permanent members, including France; an Economic and Social Council; and an international court of justice. The proposals spelled out the security arrangements for the first time. The member nations were asked to provide, through special agreements with the Security Council, standby forces to be used to prevent aggression. A Military Staff Committee, operating under the authority of the Security Council and composed of officers from the nations with permanent seats, would direct and administer these forces when an emergency developed. It was hoped that this provision would enable the new world organization to avoid the pitfalls of the League of Nations and act quickly and decisively to prevent aggression in the future.[15]

The most striking feature was the absence of any provisions for voting on the Security Council. Roosevelt's glib reference to ninety-percent agreement could not disguise this fundamental omission which threw the entire proposal into doubt. Who decided when aggression had taken place and who voted to use sanctions were critical questions whose answers would determine the fate of the new experiment in collective security. Equally significant, the administration was also postponing the vital issue of control over the use of American troops assigned to the world organization. A Congressional veto had been the heart of Lodge's crucial reservation on Article 10 of the League Covenant in 1919 and

Hull's decision to separate this issue from the question of American entry into the proposed organization simply added to the uncertainty about America's commitment. Thus the proposals made at Dumbarton Oaks created a very misleading impression of agreement among the Big Four and between the administration and Congress. The basic issues on which the League had foundered had yet to be faced.

IV

Most Americans, forewarned by Reston's articles, accepted the Dumbarton Oaks proposals with restrained approval. The day they were released, Governor Dewey announced that he was "very happy over the result" of the conference, and on October 13 Dulles sent a letter to Hull voicing his appreciation for the proposals despite "many imperfections and inadequacies." "The main thing is to get started . . . ," Dulles continued. "For this the world owes you much." The most enthusiastic comment came from those who saw in the proposed United Nations organization a continuation of the League. Calling the agreements reached at Dumbarton Oaks "one of the greatest steps forward ever made in the history of mankind," Hamilton Holt believed that they coincided "almost 95 percent with the covenant we worked so hard to maintain in the League of Nations at the close of the last world war." The New York *Times* also noted the similarity. "The return to the idea of a League of Nations, to be called The United Nations," it editorialized, "is proof that the idea cannot die." [16]

Many observers, assuming the eventual adoption of some form of the veto for Security Council voting, recognized that the proposed world organization would be dominated by the big powers. The editors of *Time* wondered, "How can the new world order stop an aggression by one of its own Big Five?" but Walter Lippmann hailed the greater role and responsibility given the major powers. He interpreted the proposals as a wise compromise embodying the desires of both realists and idealists. The General Assembly provided the nucleus for a genuine world parliament favored by utopians, while the Security Council incorporated the essence of his great-power alliance scheme. He thought it useless to worry about aggression by one of the permanent members of the Security Council, pointing out that a "realistic appraisal of the facts" led to the inescapable conclusion that "peace cannot be enforced against a great power." His old antagonist Sumner Welles had more reservations, but he urged his fellow Wilsonians to accept the proposals and work for their realization. "If the nations of the world seek today to achieve perfection in their plan for world organization before participating in it," Welles declared, "no world organization can be set up." [17]

Liberal journals agreed with Welles and Lippmann. The editors of the *Nation* and the *New Republic* frankly described the proposed United Nations organization as a "concert of power" and a "great-power alliance." They criticized the lack of an international police force, the flouting of the Moscow declaration's call for the "sovereign equality" of member nations, and the neglect of crucial economic reforms. But they dismissed these flaws as minor compared to the unity symbolized by this agreement among the Big Four. "As long as they stick together there is little chance for a new world war; if they drift apart a new war is almost inevitable," observed the *New Republic*. Above all else, liberal editors called on their readers to avoid the sin of perfectionism. Remembering 1919, when liberals opposed the Covenant because of injustices in the Treaty of Versailles, Freda Kirchwey exhorted, "The alternative to an unsatisfactory international order is not generally a satisfactory international order; it is uncontrolled power politics, international anarchy, and everything thrown into the lap of the nation with the fiercest appetite and most brutal arrogance." Max Lerner echoed her appeal, warning that the isolationists would seek to cripple the world organization not by frontal assaults but by reservations and amendments. "The wreckers are still in the Senate; never forget that," he wrote in *PM*. "The ghost of Henry Cabot Lodge still walks the Senate chamber."

A few liberals refused to be persuaded. In the *New Yorker*, E. B. White ridiculed the proposed world organization as the "Fifty Sovereign Nations of the World Solemnly Sworn to Prevent Each Other from Committing Aggression." He said the nations were united like marbles in a dish—"put your toe on the dish and the marbles will scatter, each to its own corner." An ardent advocate of world government, White found Roosevelt's ninety-percent statement incredible. Pointing out that the missing ten percent included the veto, he remarked, "But that, of course, isn't ten per cent; it is about 99.44 per cent." Louis Fischer, writing in the *Nation*, was also indignant. "What we are coming to is peace through dictatorship," he charged. "Some countries will be independent in name and colonies in fact." The bitterest complaint came from lifelong isolationist Oswald Garrison Villard: [18]

9. The Bi-Partisan Victory

A new crime has been added to the list of grave offenses, and no doubt the suitable punishment for it will soon be provided. The crime is nothing less than "perfectionism." It used to be considered praiseworthy to hitch your wagon to a star and determine to have only the best and to do the best within your power. Now, however, in the case of Dumbarton Oaks, perfectionism has become a penal transgression second in shame only to what is called "isolationism." All who refuse to agree that Dumbarton Oaks was a wonderful step forward and the very best that could have been accomplished under the circumstances, are now accused.

Religious groups were more cautious in their response. The National Catholic Welfare Conference issued a six-page statement in mid-November which avoided any direct censure but implied disapproval of the Dumbarton Oaks proposals. The Catholic Bishops urged the administration to put the ideals of the Atlantic Charter into effect and voiced their fear of Communist encroachment in Eastern Europe. Warning that the Security Council "must not be an instrument of imperialistic domination by a few powerful nations," they advocated a "universal institution" in which "every nation stands on its rights and not on its power." The editors of *Christian Century* praised this as a "lucid and courageous pronouncement" and urged all Protestants to join in a campaign to amend the administration's plan. Decrying the emphasis on the use of force to preserve peace, they demanded that the security provisions be removed from the proposals and be replaced by a covenant of peace, modeled after the Kellogg-Briand Pact. "The faith on which to build," declared the editors, "is the common and inclusive covenant never to resort to war."

The main Protestant voice in international affairs, the Commission on a Just and Durable Peace, mulled over the controversial issues for a long period of time. In September the Commission refused to accept Dulles' resignation as chairman, offered because of his political activities, and expressed the hope that the Dumbarton Oaks conference would not place too much emphasis on force. After the proposals were made public, the Commission remained conspicuously silent. Dulles revealed his own reservations in a speech to a Presbyterian conference in Brooklyn on November 24. Though he urged his audience to support the proposals as "a beginning" in the search for a new world order, he criticized the excessive reliance on power, saying, "The arrangement partakes too much of military alliance."

Four days later Dulles addressed the biennial meeting of the Federal Council of Churches in Pittsburgh. Surprisingly, he backed the Dumbarton Oaks proposals strongly, commenting that there had been an overemphasis on the provisions regarding the use of force in the public debate. "Almost all of us can accept the premise of Dumbarton Oaks that, in a world of imperfect individuals, some force-in-being of the nature of a police force is important for security," he affirmed. Stating that the only obstacle to world order was "the lack of any universal moral judgments about national conduct," he recommended that the Federal Council accept the Dumbarton Oaks proposals as "realistic" and work for their adoption. The Council then adopted a report of the Commission on a Just and Durable Peace which criticized some features of the plan but concluded, "We believe that the proposed organization can be developed into one that will commend itself to the Christian conscience." The press accepted this action as a firm Protestant endorsement of the Dumbarton Oaks proposals.[19]

Internationalist organizations differed in their responses to the administration's plan. Even before the conference was over, Edgar Ansel Mowrer was expressing his doubts to members of the Non-Partisan Council. "Those who are opposed to making World War III inevitable," he wrote on September 18, "will oppose the ineffectual and confusing Dumbarton formula." Three days after the proposals were made public, Mowrer drafted a statement urging drastic changes, including the elimination of the veto and the grant of more power to the General Assembly. The members divided on this statement, and for the next two months they debated the stand the Council should take. Malcolm Davis, representing the Carnegie Endowment, recommended a sweeping endorsement of Dumbarton Oaks while another member argued for its rejection, saying, "The spirit of Woodrow Wilson is not yet dead and must guide those who would have a decent world through an International Organization." In December, after an interview with Stettinius, Mowrer reported him as saying, "Needle us like Hell. Ask for the maximum." Finally, on December 27 the members voted to release a statement approving the Dumbarton Oaks proposals as a basis for discussion but stressing the many changes they wished to see adopted.

Americans United for World Organization was also lukewarm in its response. After a six weeks' lapse President Ernest Hopkins hailed the Dumbarton Oaks plan as "a first long step" on "the long road to making wars impossible." He stated that Americans United would promote public discussion of the proposals, but they would insist that the administration "stand for the principle that no veto should be made effective on the sole vote of one individual member." He also reserved the right of his organization to press for changes in the plan when all the nations met to draft the final charter.[20]

The League of Nations Association and the Commission to Study the Organization of Peace revealed no qualms about the Dumbarton Oaks proposals. The day after they were made public, Eichelberger announced that the League's executive committee had met and pledged to give "their full support" to the proposed world organization. "The statesmen in planning the United Nations," the executive committee declared, "have embodied the traditions of the Wilsonian ideal of a democratic world organization, but have provided, as the result of twenty years of trial, error, and tragedy, something stronger and better." At a meeting of the full board three days later, the directors heard Shotwell give a favorable analysis of the plan, and then voted unanimously to endorse it and work for its adoption. In *Changing World*, Eichelberger printed articles by Shotwell and Raymond Fosdick praising the plan. Fosdick thought it was a "decided improvement on the Covenant of the League of Nations." "Now we have the opportunity," he declared, "to take up where the League left off—with greater assurance and with more real confidence than was possible in 1919."

In early November the Commission to Study the Organization of Peace issued a slightly more restrained endorsement. "The statesmen have outlined a fundamentally democratic organization," read their statement, "while concentrating power for the suppression of aggression in the hands of those most capable of using that power." The Commission regretted the failure to include its plan for an international air force, and it advocated a voting formula in the Security Council based on "the equality of all states before the law." Nevertheless, the directors affirmed their belief that the United Nations organization would be the "spiritual and material heir of the League of Nations" and eventually become a "living and efficient world organization."

The Commission also published a pamphlet, *Proposals for the United Nations Charter*, written by Clark Eichelberger, which sold for ten cents and was widely distributed. He compared the proposed organization to the League of Nations and concluded that the United Nations would have the power its predecessor lacked to prevent aggression. He described its structure as "amazingly democratic" and expressed the belief that the "great powers will not place themselves above the law by exercising a veto in their own case." But most of all Eichelberger stressed the need for prompt action to implement these proposals. "Now," he concluded, "when the armies of the United Nations are marching together and the common people are working together in a great effort to defeat the common enemy and to save civilization, is the time to create the United Nations." [21]

V

The internationalists had no doubts about the importance of the 1944 elections. They had worked to secure favorable platform planks at the conventions, and they now concentrated on the Congressional races. Aware that the next Senate would pass on international organization, the Women's Action Committee, Americans United, the Non-Partisan Council, and the League of Nations Association asked their members to question the candidates closely and work against any who expressed isolationist views. The early developments were encouraging. Robert Reynolds of North Carolina, one of the noisiest isolationists in the Senate, announced at the beginning of the year that he would not run for reelection. In the spring Lister Hill and Claude Pepper, both strong internationalists, beat off challenges in the primaries and thus ensured their return to the Senate. In other southern primaries "Cotton Ed" Smith, an anti-administration Democrat, lost in South Carolina and William Fulbright defeated Hattie Carraway, the nation's first woman senator, to win the Democratic nomination in Arkansas. Other pre-war isolationist senators lost in Missouri and Montana; the only setback for the internationalists came in North Dakota, where Gerald Nye won a close race for renomination on the Republican ticket.[22]

Though the House of Representatives would not vote on the charter of the proposed international organization, intense interest developed in efforts to unseat Hamilton Fish of New York and Stephen Day of Illinois. Playwright Maxwell Anderson, actress Helen Hayes and many intellectuals backed Augustus Bennet in the Republican primary in New York, and even Thomas Dewey joined in the assault on Fish. When Fish eked out a narrow victory, Bennet announced that he would oppose him in the November election by running on a Good Government Party ticket. In Illinois, Emily Taft Douglas, wife of the future senator, announced she would oppose Day for the Congressman-at-Large seat in November. The Chicago *Tribune* backed Day, and a bitter campaign followed.

By the fall, internationalists were still deeply concerned about the composition of the next Senate. In a *New Republic* analysis, James Loeb pointed out that of 61 senators retaining their seats, 35 favored world organization, 14 were isolationists, and 12 were on the borderline. He believed that nearly half of the twenty-five incumbents running for reelection were either opposed to international organization or had not made clear their position. "If the 12 who are isolationists and doubtfuls are reelected," Loeb warned, "the next Senate will include 38 members in these two categories—more than enough to block the peace." Senator Joseph Ball had reached a similar conclusion, asking the voters to defeat eleven isolationists running for reelection to the Senate. Ball refrained from mentioning their names, but the press identified eight Republicans and three Democrats, including Robert Taft, Gerald Nye and Guy Gillette. Though these exhortations were designed primarily to prevent complacency in the internationalist ranks, the election of a Senate where isolationists could muster the one-third control required to defeat treaties remained a real possibility.[23]

In the presidential campaign, many observers who thought that Roosevelt's reelection was assured began to change their minds during the summer. The state of the President's health generated much of this doubt. Just before he left for a Pacific tour in July, a newsman had snapped a picture of him in San Diego that caught him in an unfortunate pose, with his head bowed and his mouth hanging open. The angle distorted his features and showed him as an emaciated, exhausted, utterly spent man. Stephen Early, who usually censored Roosevelt's pictures, was not along on this trip, and a few days later newspapers published the photograph. As the President toured Hawaii and Alaska, rumors developed that he was seriously ill. At the end of the trip he decided to speak to the nation from the deck of a destroyer at Bremerton, Washington. During the war years he had delivered his addresses sitting down, but he now insisted on wearing his heavy iron braces so that he could stand. Unaccustomed to the braces, which no longer fitted him properly, and bothered by the destroyer's curved deck, he delivered his speech in a halting, fumbling manner. It was the poorest public performance of his long career, and it fed the growing speculation that he could not stand the rigors of four more years in office.

Meanwhile, his opponent was planning a coolly professional campaign. Dewey believed that Willkie's mistake in 1940 had been to appeal to independent voters while neglecting the fundamentals of political organization. He decided to work with the party regulars, and instead of trying to convert Democrats and independents by emotional appeals, he planned to portray himself as a competent, tough-minded administrator who could restore order and efficiency to the government. Only forty-two, he played up his youthful appearance and hinted at the state of Roosevelt's health by attacking an administration of "tired old men." He hit hard at the intrusion of labor in the campaign, in the form of Sidney Hillman's CIO Political Action Committee, charging that the Communists were infiltrating the Democratic party and repeating over and over a statement Roosevelt supposedly made to Hannegan before the Democratic convention: "Clear it with Sidney." [24]

Dewey was handicapped by his vulnerability to the charge that he was not a genuine internationalist. Liberals cited his isolationism prior to Pearl Harbor and warned that even if he were sincere in avowing world organization, he would have a difficult time as President in handling the isolationists within his party. The *New Republic* continually referred to him as another Harding, and the New York *Times*, politically independent, kept asking him to clarify the vague Republican platform. In early September, Gerald W. Johnson published an open letter to Dewey in the *Atlantic Monthly*, asking, "What do you, as a Presidential candidate, offer me, as a voter, that Harding did not offer in 1920?"

Dewey replied in a major campaign address at Louisville on September 18. His speech, written by Dulles, contained a very forthright endorsement of the kind of world organization being discussed at Dumbarton Oaks. He specifically called for "effective cooperative means to prevent or repel military aggression," including the use of force. To distinguish his position from the President's, he stressed the role of small nations in the projected world body. "Some 60 nations, great and small, must help shape it, believe in it, join it, and make it work," he declared. He also took a swipe at Henry Wallace, attacking "Washington wasters" who "talk glibly of an American WPA for all the rest of the world." Though many internationalists winced at these words, Senator Connally expressed the prevailing view when he declared that he was "gratified" that Dewey had accepted the administration's plan for international organization.[25]

Dewey's adroit tactics alarmed Roosevelt. After his renomination he had said that he would not campaign with the war in progress, but in mid-September he announced a series of speeches to correct the misrepresentations of his opponents. The first was at a Teamsters Union dinner in Washington on September 23. Speaking from his chair, the President began, "Well, here we are together again—after four years—

and what years they have been! You know, I am actually four years older, which is a fact that seems to annoy some people." The friendly audience relaxed as Roosevelt gave a magnificent performance, taunting the Republicans with jibes, dismissing their attacks with sarcastic thrusts, ridiculing their charges. He reminded his listeners that his opponents were isolationists "who first woke up to the facts of international life a few short months ago—when they began to study the polls of public opinion." He welcomed them as converts to the cause of international collaboration, but he warned the voters not to risk having another Republican administration botch the peace. Then, with a straight face and a tone of righteous indignation, he dealt with the Republican charge that he had sent a destroyer back to the Aleutian Islands to retrieve his dog Fala, who had been left behind. "I don't resent attacks, and my family doesn't resent attacks, but *Fala* does resent them." While the audience howled with delight, Roosevelt berated the Republicans for libeling his dog. When he was finished, the audience gave him an ovation that astonished even his warmest supporters. "Never had there been a demonstration equal to this in sincerity, admiration and affection," commented Sam Rosenman. "In the mind of every friend and supporter who stood and cheered and applauded in that large dining hall was the same thought: 'The old maestro is back again—the champ is now out on the road.' " [26]

The race was going to be close, and both sides now realized that the support of Wendell Willkie could be crucial. He had several million followers, mainly independents whose loyalty he had won in 1940, who were waiting to see which candidate he would back. Willkie continued his deliberate silence in hopes of making the two candidates take a more specific stand on international organization, and in the summer of 1944 he skillfully dodged invitations by both Dewey and Roosevelt to confer in Albany and Washington. When Arthur Krock wrote a column in the New York *Times* on August 25 explaining Willkie's tactics, he thanked him and commented that Roosevelt and Dewey were "pragmatic politicians." "I am greatly interested in creating a body of public opinion which will force either or both of them to go in the direction in which I believe they should."

Willkie then wrote an article criticizing the party platform on foreign policy entitled "Cowardice at Chicago" which appeared in *Collier's* on September 16. Claiming that the failure of the politicians to face the issue of international organization squarely "prepared soil for the sowing of World War III," he attacked both parties for their insistence on preserving American sovereignty. "We are presented with an extraordinary proposition," he wrote. "We are jealously to guard our sovereignty; other nations are likewise to guard their sovereignty; but somehow all nations are to be welded together into an international organization with the *power* to prevent aggression and preserve peace." He urged the two candidates to go beyond their platforms and advocate the surrender of some degree of sovereignty to create an effective world organization. Declaring that he was a Republican, he hoped that Dewey would clarify the party's stand, but he urged all independents to vote for the man who took the most advanced position on international organization.[27]

The day before this article appeared Willkie entered a New York hospital for what reporters were told was a "check-up and rest." Actually, Willkie had already suffered a series of heart attacks, and he had several more in the hospital. He seemed to be getting better toward the end of the month, but he suffered a relapse and died on October 8, without disclosing his choice in the presidential race. Partisan journalists printed stories saying that he had endorsed Dewey or Roosevelt, until his widow finally put an end to this unseemly speculation by saying that no man could speak for her husband. Roscoe Drummond reported later that he had sneaked into the hospital on September 30 at Willkie's insistence. He told Drummond then that he did not trust either Dewey or Roosevelt and was having a difficult time making up his mind. Two days later he wrote Drummond, "Frankly, I cannot answer your ultimate question yet because I have not finally decided." [28]

When Willkie became ill, Senator Joseph H. Ball decided to take up his fight. On September 29 Ball, who had seconded Dewey's nomination at Chicago, startled his fellow Republicans by announcing, "I would violate my own deepest convictions if I were at this time . . . to campaign for Governor Dewey." He said that he had studied Dewey's statements and was not convinced Dewey "would fight vigorously for a foreign policy which will offer real hope of preventing World War III." Years later Ball said he made the statement because he feared Dewey had become the captive of isolationists within the party and he hoped to force him to disavow their support.

Democratic Chairman Robert Hannegan immediately issued a statement hailing Ball for exposing "Dewey's ersatz internationalism." Dismayed Republicans quickly disassociated themselves from Ball. Senator Harold Burton, co-sponsor of the B_2H_2 resolution, announced his support for Dewey, saying that the Governor could work with the Senate more effectively than Roosevelt in making the peace. Though Minnesota

Republicans denounced Ball and threatened to expel him from the party, the damage had already been done. Commentators believed that Ball's action might be decisive in several midwestern states where Dewey and Roosevelt were running evenly.[29]

After Willkie's death, Ball decided to go further. On October 12 he issued a public challenge to the two candidates, asking them three questions regarding international organization. The first two dealt with entering a world body before the end of the war and opposing crippling reservations, points that both candidates could easily answer affirmatively. But the third question raised a critical issue. "Should the vote of the United States' representative on the United Nations security council," Ball asked, "commit an agreed upon quota of our military forces to action ordered by the council to maintain peace without requiring further congressional approval?" Ball was raising the problem of a Congressional veto which Hull had tried to bury, and he requested the candidates to respond in their campaign speeches. "Safe, easy generalities on this issue are not enough," he told them, "when 11,000,000 American boys are facing death because of the failure of Governments, our own included, to solve this problem after World War I."

Dewey answered Ball in a major foreign-policy address at the New York *Herald Tribune* Forum on October 18. He said he favored creating the world organization before the peace settlement was made and he opposed amendments by the Senate. "The world organization must be enabled, through the use of force, when necessary, to prevent or repel military aggression," Dewey declared, but he refused to spell out who would decide how and when to use this force. Dewey went on to attack Roosevelt, accusing him of conducting secret diplomacy with Churchill and Stalin, and promising to restore the conduct of American diplomacy to the State Department. There was no further reference to international organization, nor did Dewey try to express his views to Ball privately. "Dewey never got in touch with me," Ball commented later. "That always puzzled me." [30]

It amazed Franklin Roosevelt, who had been following Ball's movements very closely. At Willkie's funeral on October 10, Ball told Ben Cohen of his plans to challenge the candidates. Cohen informed Roosevelt, who invited Ball to the White House for an hour-long conversation on October 15. Roosevelt had agreed to speak on world affairs at a Foreign Policy Association dinner on October 21, and the State Department was busy preparing drafts for Rosenman to rework at the White House. When Dewey failed to answer Ball's third question on October

238

18, the President ordered Rosenman to include a section opposing a Congressional veto on collective-security action. On October 20 Rosenman completed the statement, which was then worked into the final text.[31]

Roosevelt arrived in New York on the morning of October 21 so that he could take a campaign swing through the city to impress the voters with his vitality. Dressed in his traditional campaign outfit, a Navy cape and broad-brimmed fedora, he traveled by open car through a chilling rain. The caravan followed a fifty-one-mile route from Bronx to Brooklyn, winding up at a mass rally in Ebbets Field. The President went back to his wife's apartment for a bath and nap, and then appeared fresh and rested at the grand ballroom of the Waldorf-Astoria, the same room in which three days earlier Dewey had made his foreign-policy speech. For nearly an hour Roosevelt spoke in a low voice to the two thousand members and guests of the Foreign Policy Association. Once again he roasted the Republicans for their pre-war isolationism, drawing a huge response when he repeated his 1940 line about "Martin and Barton and Fish," reminding his listeners that Joseph Martin and Hamilton Fish were still in Congress and were still opposing a policy of international cooperation.

Midway through the speech the President turned to the plans for international organization. "The Council of the United Nations must have the power to act quickly and decisively to keep the peace by force, if necessary." Using one of his folksy similes, Roosevelt pointed out how foolish it would be if a policeman, when he saw someone breaking into a house, had to call a town meeting before he could arrest the intruder. "So to my simple mind," he continued, "it is clear that, if the world organization is to have any reality at all, our American representative must be endowed in advance by the people themselves, by constitutional means through their representatives in the Congress, with authority to act." He concluded by completing the analogy, saying that if we let the criminal escape because the town meeting has not passed an ordinance for his arrest, "then we are *not* doing our share to prevent another world war." [32]

Two days later, in a speech at Baltimore, Joseph Ball announced that Roosevelt had answered his third question satisfactorily and that he would support him for reelection. Regretting Dewey's refusal to speak out, Ball stressed the importance of the issue he had raised; if Congress reserved the right to decide whether American troops can be used every time there is a crisis, the world organization "will be simply a debating

239

society, without power to act, and future aggressors will sneer at it just as Hitler sneered at the League of Nations."

Internationalists praised Ball for his stand. The New York *Times* gave him credit "for his courage," and the *Nation* honored him for continuing Willkie's "gallant fight against the old-line isolationists who control his party." Harry Truman said, "He's a good man. I think he always was a Democrat and didn't know it." Republicans claimed Ball had made a "grievous mistake" and had done "a great disservice to the nation." They tried to dismiss him as "an insignificant voice," but Dewey belatedly paid tribute to him by announcing in a speech at Minneapolis on October 24 that he did not insist that the American delegate return to Congress for authority to use force in a crisis. Going almost as far as Roosevelt, Dewey asked only that Congress be allowed to decide how much authority it would surrender to the President in regard to the use of force for collective security.[33]

This concession came too late. Not only had Ball committed himself irrevocably, but a number of other prominent internationalists had also rejected Dewey. The New York *Times*, which had opposed Roosevelt's bid for a third term in 1940, came out for him in mid-October "with deep reluctance and strong misgivings." The sole reason the editors gave was Roosevelt's clear commitment to the cause of international organization. Walter Lippmann, who also had opposed Roosevelt in 1940, agreed. "I cannot feel that Governor Dewey can be trusted now with responsibility in foreign affairs," he wrote in his column on October 21. "He has so much to learn." Russell Davenport, Willkie's 1940 campaign manager, wrote an article entitled "Why I Cannot Vote for Dewey," and Hamilton Holt, after Dewey ignored a letter asking him to speak out boldly on foreign policy, announced for Roosevelt. ". . . much as I hate the third and fourth terms," he wrote to a friend, "I much prefer to do the utmost I can to prevent another world war."

In early November the GOP paid for a full-page statement by Robert Moses in the New York *Times* replying to that paper's endorsement of Roosevelt. Moses claimed that Roosevelt had won the support of internationalists by betraying the promise Hull had made to Dulles to keep the issue of world organization out of the campaign. Calling the President's idea of giving the American delegate the authority to commit troops for collective security "a fantastic scheme," Moses accused Roosevelt of wanting "a blank cheque to control our world relations without Congress." In the same issue the editors pointed out that Dewey had advocated a similar arrangement at Minneapolis and then asked Moses who his candidate was. Two days later Ball and Davenport asserted that

Moses' statement proved that the Republican party still stood where it did in 1919—for reservations. They did not admit that Moses was right in asserting that Roosevelt violated the promise to keep international organization out of the campaign. Dewey had provided the opportunity when he failed to answer Ball's third question promptly, and Roosevelt adroitly exploited this lapse to capture the internationalist vote.[34]

VI

The American people went to the polls on November 7 and sent Franklin Roosevelt to the White House for the fourth time. Though he won an overwhelming victory in the electoral college, Roosevelt defeated Dewey by only three million votes, making the election the closest since Wilson's narrow victory in 1916. The Democratic party, aided by the Political Action Committee's vigorous effort to get out a large vote, did better, picking up thirty seats in the House of Representatives and retaining a healthy margin in the Senate. A steady upward Republican trend in Congress was halted, to give Roosevelt the largest Democratic majorities since the heyday of the New Deal.

The election was a clear-cut mandate for international organization. Almost without exception, isolationists of both parties lost their seats in Congress. Fish in New York, Day in Illinois, Nye in South Dakota and many others went down to defeat while such internationalists as Wayne Morse, William Fulbright and Leverett Saltonstall won election to the Senate for the first time. The only newly elected senator who refused to commit himself on international organization was Republican Homer Capehart of Indiana.

"The election returns have announced to the world that 1944 is not 1920!" declared the editors of the *Nation,* and virtually all political commentators made the same contrast. *Time* remarked that Roosevelt had reversed a "historic decision of 25 years ago" and had achieved what Wilson had not, "an endorsement by the people of his general international program." Foreign newspapers, which had kept silent during the campaign, revealed their relief that the President had won and that the close working partnership between Roosevelt, Stalin and Churchill would continue, thereby ensuring that the United States would not retreat from the world again. The New York *Times* made this point again and again, calling the election "the great and solemn referendum that President Wilson asked for and failed to get." [35]

The internationalists rejoiced. Sumner Welles praised the American

241

people for their wisdom, commenting, "They have learned by the experience of a great tragedy. Today they see the truth." In the State Department, Breckinridge Long finally relaxed. In his diary he wrote, "Now we can go ahead with the war and exercise our authority, which assumes the form of a mandate, to arrange a peace organization. . . ." The editors of the *New Republic* were so elated by the outcome that they suggested that Wallace be named Secretary of State in place of the ailing Hull. "We do so, not merely because this is the only job the President can offer him that is an adequate reward for the service he has rendered, but because we think he is preeminently the best qualified man in the country for the place."

Even the Republican leaders took solace in the swing to internationalism. During the campaign Vandenberg wrote to Hull in appreciation of his "anxiety to proceed as far as possible on a bi-partisan basis in dealing with these post-war problems." Three days after the election Dulles wrote to the President, telling him that the American people had given a solid vote of confidence for his plans to create a new world body. "I wish you strength and wisdom in this great task," Dulles added, "and assure you of my continuing support, without regard to party, of constructive efforts along this line." In a letter to his brother Allen a month later Dulles admitted that, though he regretted Dewey's defeat, "I am glad that we succeeded in keeping the world organization out of politics. I think that was, at least, one important precedent established." Thus Dulles was very much aware that he had participated in a revolutionary experiment in American politics that had led to a truly bi-partisan victory.[36]

10

Winter of Discontent

THREE WEEKS after the election of 1944, President Roosevelt announced that Cordell Hull had resigned as Secretary of State because of ill health. After twelve years in office, twice as long as any other Secretary in the twentieth century, Hull was exhausted. He had developed a severe throat ailment at the end of the summer, and on September 30 he went to the White House to offer his resignation. The President asked him to wait until after the election, suggesting that a long rest might restore his health. Three days later, on his seventy-third birthday, Hull's doctor ordered him to bed in his apartment, and when he did not improve, the Secretary entered Bethesda Naval Hospital, where he remained for the next seven months. On November 21 he submitted a letter of resignation to the President, who again refused to accept it. Instead, Roosevelt proposed that Hull continue to serve until January 20 in order to round out a third full term in office. When Hull insisted that his resignation take effect immediately, Roosevelt visited him at the hospital, and then, unable to change Hull's mind, he revealed the Secretary's resignation on November 27.

In his letter to the President, Hull graciously acknowledged the warm personal relations he had enjoyed with Roosevelt and confessed his sorrow at not being able to complete the process of leading the United States into a new world organization. Privately, Hull expressed his growing sense of frustration and bitterness at the way in which Roosevelt had neglected to consult him on the conduct of wartime foreign policy. The Secretary had not taken part in either the Casablanca or the Teheran conference, and at the recent Quebec meeting between Roosevelt and Churchill, the President had overridden Hull's objections to a harsh plan for the future of Germany proposed by Secretary of the Treasury Henry Morgenthau. His health was failing, but he might well have stayed on if he had thought he still had the President's confidence. He poured out his grievances to Breckinridge Long on September 30, who recorded in his diary that Hull "was tired of intrigue. He was tired of being by-passed. He was tired of being relied upon in public and ignored in private. He was tired of fighting battles which were not appreciated."

There was no hint of this strained relationship in the President's letter of acceptance. Saying that Hull's resignation "has hit me between wind and water," Roosevelt praised his many services to the nation and expressed hope for his speedy recovery. To Hull's genuine delight, Roosevelt asked him to continue giving advice on the formation of an international organization and to preside over its first session as "the Father of the United Nations." [1]

On November 27, immediately following the disclosure of Hull's retirement, Roosevelt announced the appointment of Edward R. Stettinius as the new Secretary of State. This prompt action ended various rumors that Henry Wallace, Sumner Welles and James Byrnes were likely successors. Though most commentators praised the appointment, noting that Stettinius had proved a loyal aide as Under Secretary, they pointed out that it signified Roosevelt's intention of retaining full control over the conduct of American foreign policy. Stettinius was known to be a weak man whose pleasing personality and skills as an administrator masked a mediocre intellect and an almost complete lack of aggressiveness. Stettinius was at his best presiding over meetings. His ready grin, his conciliatory manner and his blithe disregard of subtle complexities enabled him to get people with conflicting ideas to reach at least superficial agreement. During his year as Under Secretary he had not gained any deep insight into the workings of diplomacy or the intricacies of international affairs. He spent most of his time on the reorganization of the Department, displaying a fondness for charts and lines of authority that helped streamline the day-to-day conduct of affairs but failed to remedy the Department's more serious administrative deficiencies, especially the lack of long-range planning. Snobbish foreign-service officers viewed him as a naive outsider; the press treated him as a good-natured Boy Scout, dubbing him "the White-Haired Boy" and commenting more on his handsome profile and genial manner than on his contributions to diplomacy.

Despite his obvious failings, Stettinius possessed qualities that made him an ideal choice for Secretary of State in the fall of 1944. He was well liked and respected in Congress, and thus he could continue to fulfill Hull's role as lightning rod against Senate criticism of administration policy. His big-business background reassured Republicans and ensured the continuation of bi-partisan policy that Hull had pioneered so effectively. Most significant, he realized the importance of influencing public opinion. Stettinius was a born salesman, and his major assignment as Secretary of State was to persuade the American people that their future well-being depended on their wholehearted willingness to enter a new world organization for peace. Letting others deal with the more complex problems of foreign policy, he wisely and single-mindedly concentrated on the great goal Hull had bequeathed to him.[2]

Stettinius began his crusade in mid-October, when he was Acting Secretary during Hull's illness. Responding to an overture from Ernest Hopkins, the head of Americans United for World Organization, he invited representatives of more than a hundred pressure groups to attend an informal, off-the-record briefing by State Department officers on the Dumbarton Oaks proposals. Private organizations ranging from patriotic and veterans' societies to women's clubs and labor unions sent delegates to the October 16 meeting, held in the Department's auditorium on the fourth floor of the old War-State-Navy building next to the White House. Stettinius told the representatives that the Dumbarton Oaks proposals were still tentative and subject to change, and he urged them to help bring about a "wide, intelligent, and maturing consideration of the proposals on the part of the American people." Then he introduced Leo Pasvolsky, who discussed the details of the plans and answered questions from the floor. After nearly three hours the meeting broke up with the delegates vowing to bring the proposals to the attention of the millions of members of their organizations.

A month later Stettinius, still Acting Secretary, had the Department begin distributing a brief pamphlet entitled *Questions and Answers on the Dumbarton Oaks Proposals*. Designed as a study guide, this brochure gave a recapitulation of the plan for international organization by comparing it with the League Covenant. The answers stressed the collective-security features, asserting, "The Security Council would have greater powers in the use of military and non-military enforcement measures than did the League Council." Many newspapers printed the text of this pamphlet, and in the next six months the Department distributed nearly two million copies of this and similar materials on the Dumbarton Oaks proposals.[3]

After his appointment as Secretary, Stettinius asked Archibald MacLeish, poet, former Librarian of Congress, and ardent internationalist, to direct the campaign as Assistant Secretary of State in charge of public and cultural relations. Under MacLeish's supervision, the State Department, traditionally insulated from public life in the United States, engaged in a heroic effort to reach the American people. In December five teams of State Department experts on international organization went out on the road, speaking to audiences of community leaders in sixteen cities. They varied the format from city to city, giving set speeches, running panel discussions and holding question-and-answer sessions. MacLeish sought out church, labor, business and professional groups to sponsor these meetings. He also arranged for a series of radio broadcasts over the NBC network on Saturday evenings and asked a Hollywood group to produce a short documentary film on international organization. Cooperating with the Office of War Information, Mac-Leish and Stettinius appeared before a group of prominent magazine editors and writers to engage in "an informal exchange of views on the Dumbarton Oaks proposals." On December 27 Stettinius spoke to one hundred members of the American Platform Guild, which included virtually all the country's well-known lecturers on international affairs, and gave them a thorough, off-the-record briefing on American plans for world organization.[4]

In the nearly three hundred public speeches they gave in the six months after Dumbarton Oaks, State Department officers reiterated a few basic themes. Uppermost in nearly all their addresses was the quest for security in a shrinking world. They pointed out how a reliance on isolation had failed to protect the United States in the 1930's, and they warned that the development of new weapons, notably the German V-2 rocket, had proven that the oceans could never again insure the United States against foreign attack. Above all, they asserted the importance of using force to prevent aggression. "Policing is as necessary as piety," declared Assistant Secretary Adolf A. Berle, Jr. In a radio speech on December 13, 1944, Under Secretary Joseph C. Grew, who had recently returned from internment in Japan, used an analogy that Stettinius and other speakers repeated in their addresses throughout the winter. Describing the League of Nations and the Kellogg-Briand Pact, Grew declared, "They failed because these peace plans were superficial. They were like poultices prescribed for cancer." Yet Grew, Stettinius and every other State Department official was careful to speak out against any idea of surrendering American sovereignty. "The thought of fashioning any kind of superstate is to us wholly repugnant," declared Stettinius in a New Year's message to the American people, "and no such thought has entered or can enter into our counsels." The United States planned to join its forces with those of other nations "not only for the common good *but for the future security of our own Nation*." MacLeish was equally insistent on the moderate nature of the State Department plan, stating, "The idea of a superstate has never entered our thoughts in connection with Dumbarton Oaks."

The State Department spokesmen prided themselves on their realism. They argued that two world wars had proven that only an international organization could prevent "a third world war within our lifetime." Archibald MacLeish affirmed, "The practical choice at this time is clearly between an organization of the type proposed at Dumbarton Oaks and international anarchy"; Stettinius was even blunter, saying that such a world body had to be created "for the sake of everything we hold dear and for our as yet unborn generations." All these speakers, however, were careful to avoid describing international organizations as a universal panacea. They referred to their plans as only the beginning of the search for peace, and they repeatedly warned that it would take decades to rid the world of war. "There is one mistake we must avoid at all costs," commented Grew, "and that is the mistake of thinking that the machinery itself will solve our problems." Dean Acheson agreed, calling the policy of international cooperation "a torturingly difficult process." "We must seek what is desirable within the realm of the attainable," declared both Grew and Stettinius in an effort to placate those who criticized the imperfections in the Dumbarton Oaks arrangements. Most of all, the State Department officers liked to portray their efforts toward international organization as a pioneering venture. Grew expressed it best when he said: [5]

> The way of international cooperation is hard; the process painful and grueling; initially the results may be far from perfect. But a generation which has learned the meaning of one world can take no other way, and the rewards for future generations of mankind may well be glorious.

I

Internationalists responded eagerly to the State Department campaign. For several months Clark Eichelberger had been planning a full-scale effort to reach the American people and arouse them to support the administration's final plan. At his request, the John Price Jones Corporation, a public-relations firm that had publicized the activities of the White Committee before the war, prepared a fifty-page prospectus outlining such an effort. "Now, for the second time in our lifetime, alone of all generations of Americans," this brochure began, "we have it within our power to do what we failed to do in 1919—to atone, in a measure, for the error of judgment which permitted us to witness the anguish, share the suffering and bear the stupendous costs of a second world war." The Jones Corporation went on to describe plans to flood the nation with pamphlets and leaflets, to organize public forums throughout the country, and to use radio, magazines, newspapers and every conceivable means of influencing the people. "The favorable public opinion that now exists for a world organization," concluded the prospectus, "must become a Rock of Gibraltar of public conviction."

When he discovered that this professional campaign would cost at least $200,000, Eichelberger turned to other alternatives. He hoped Americans United would take the lead in influencing public opinion, but the coolness of Ulric Bell to the Dumbarton Oaks proposals worried him. In early October he finally decided to offer his services as coordinator for all the many organizations interested in winning public support for the administration's proposals. On October 6 representatives of the various groups, including the Women's Action Committee, the League of Nations Association, the Carnegie Endowment, the Church Peace Union and the American Free World Association, met in the Woodrow Wilson Memorial Library to form the United Nations Educational Campaign Committee. Eichelberger received President Roosevelt's blessing for this effort on October 11, and by the end of the month the new drive was well under way.[6]

Eichelberger worked closely with the State Department, arranging many of the meetings addressed by the roving teams of officers. On November 3 Benjamin Gerig, a State Department specialist on international organization, met with the Campaign Committee to coordinate their activities, and the next week the committee sponsored an all-day conference at the Hotel Biltmore at which Gerig and his colleagues addressed some eight hundred people. Eichelberger set up a bureau to supply speakers to any group in the country who would listen to a ten-minute address on international organization. Proclaiming that "peace will be made on Main Street this time," Eichelberger supervised the preparation of leaflets designed to appeal to small businessmen and to farmers. " 'To be or not to be' is the burning issue of our day," proclaimed one of these brochures aimed at rural readers. "All hinges on the decision we shall make in accepting or rejecting a world organization for the prevention of wars." [7]

At a banquet of the League of Nations Association at the Biltmore on February 1, 1945, the board of directors disclosed their long-awaited change in name to the American Association for the United Nations. Promising to carry on the traditions of the past, Eichelberger announced that the AAUN would take charge of the educational campaign. He then introduced Raymond Fosdick, who gave the change his blessing. The featured speaker of the evening was Sumner Welles, who paid tribute to the "gallant campaign" waged by the League of Nations Association "during the 22 years of its valiant life." "In its new form," he added, "we must expect from it an even greater service." [8]

Other internationalist groups cooperated fully with the AAUN in the campaign to publicize the Dumbarton Oaks proposals. The Woodrow Wilson Foundation provided a meeting place for the coordinating committee in its library, and the directors voted to dip into their capital funds to finance the publication and distribution of educational materials, including 600,000 copies of the text of the Dumbarton Oaks plan. The Commission to Study the Organization of Peace opened a Washington office and began publishing a weekly newsletter focused on the prospects for Senate ratification of the final United Nations charter. In January the Women's Action Committee began a drive to engage 350,000 women, one percent of the nation's feminine population. Even the American Bar Association, which had stayed aloof from the internationalist movement, now cooperated by sponsoring forums on the Dumbarton Oaks plan in eighteen cities. The president, David Andrew Simmons, spoke on behalf of the administration's proposals at ten of these meetings, reporting "tremendous interest" everywhere he went.[9]

Americans United, founded to unify the internationalist movement, mounted its own independent campaign in November after Ulric Bell and Ernest Hopkins belatedly decided to endorse the Dumbarton Oaks proposals. They concentrated on winning mass support for international organization rather than working through established groups. They ran several full-page color advertisements in national magazines which played dramatically on the fear of losing the peace again. "Once in a great while mankind gets a second chance," ran their copy. "This is such a time." They adopted as their slogan Santayana's phrase "Those who do not remember the past are condemned to repeat it." Many prominent internationalists served on their board, including Robert E. Sherwood, Russell Davenport, Senator Joseph Ball and Thomas K. Finletter, but the leaders neglected the hard task of organizing local chapters and working through existing community groups. A membership drive, headed by industrialist Henry J. Kaiser, failed in its ambitious goal of signing up ten million recruits. Bell and Hopkins preferred to work on the national level, trying to influence public opinion by the media of mass communication.[10]

As they waged their campaign, internationalists continued to be handicapped by their own doubts about the Dumbarton Oaks plan. The Commission to Study the Organization of Peace, which had approved the proposals when they first appeared, came out in early 1945 with two major amendments. First, the members proposed the addition of a Commission on Human Rights as a permanent agency of the new world body, in the belief that "the violation of human rights anywhere may be a threat to world peace everywhere." Their other recommendation was for a Permanent Trusteeship Council to protect the rights of colonial peoples and prepare them for ultimate independence. Many members wanted to suggest more drastic changes in the proposed structure, but they held back, fearful that too many amendments would play into the hands of the isolationists. Joseph Ball warned against the dangers of perfectionism in two articles in the New York *Times Magazine*. Admitting that there were many flaws in the Dumbarton Oaks plan he said he would support it as the "best organization that can be agreed upon." "The only alternative to joining," he continued, "is to try to retire to our ivory tower of isolation that V-1 and V-2 have turned into rubble." [11]

In their pamphlets, speeches and radio talks, internationalists echoed the restrained, cautious approach of the State Department spokesmen. They warned against placing too much reliance on machinery, pointing out that the Covenant of the League of Nations was an admirable document, but one which failed because mankind did not support it. "Many people will have too much faith in just a document," cautioned Senator-elect William Fulbright, while Raymond Fosdick, speaking of the "failure of the human spirit" which had destroyed the League, pleaded, "It must not happen again." A pamphlet stressed the long and difficult task that lay ahead, noting realistically, "No utopian plans can solve the problem of bridging the chasm of mutual distrust between nations." The internationalists continually returned to the theme that there was no alternative. In a handbook of do's and don'ts, the Democratic National Committee Women's Division told workers, "Remember that the choice is not between the proposed world organization and some other one. The choice is between the proposed one and none. If

Dumbarton Oaks is discarded, we must begin to prepare for World War III." [12]

Among religious groups, the uneasiness over the Dumbarton Oaks proposals continued. In February the Catholic Association for International Peace labeled the plan a "death sentence" for small nations, and two months later the Catholic Bishops of America issued a statement denouncing the big-power dominance of the Security Council. Objecting to the central role given the Soviet Union, the bishops warned that democracy and Marxism could not exist side by side within a world organization. Religious pacifists joined in the attacks, decrying the emphasis on force and asking for universal disarmament as the only safe road to lasting peace. "The proposed five-power alliance," commented the director of the War Resisters League, "is unlikely to obtain security for small nations or even hold together long enough to set up a peace guaranteed by international force." The *Christian Century* concurred, predicting that the return of power politics would split apart the wartime coalition and lead to an immoral peace unless a truly democratic world organization was established. [13]

The religious controversy reached its climax in Cleveland when the Federal Council of Churches' Commission on a Just and Durable Peace held a National Study Conference on the Dumbarton Oak proposals in mid-January 1945. Dulles and Bishop J. Bromley Oxnam led an effort to secure unconditional approval for the Dumbarton Oaks proposals from the 481 lay and clerical delegates representing thirty-four Protestant denominations. They admitted that the proposed world organization was based on power politics, but they urged the churchmen to be realistic. "All politics deal with power," Oxnam told the delegates. "The primary issue is to bring power under control. . . . Dumbarton Oaks brings that power under the control of solemn agreement." Charles Clayton Morrison, the editor of *Christian Century*, challenged this view, asking the conference to approve a series of amendments qualifying the administration's plan. After two days of bitter argument, the conference adopted a message to the churches urging them to work for nine changes, including commissions on human rights and trusteeships for colonial peoples, the denial of the veto to a country involved in a dispute, and a broader role for small nations.

The press hailed the outcome of the Cleveland conference as a clear-cut endorsement of the Dumbarton Oaks plan by the Protestant churches. The New York *Times* spoke of "unconditional approval" and barely mentioned the nine specific amendments the delegates requested.

251

Time was more accurate in calling the result "a compromise compatible both with the highest Christian ethics and the ugly facts of human life in a sinful world." Morrison felt he had won substantial concessions from Dulles and Oxnam, and in the *Christian Century* he stressed the conditional nature of the conference's approval. Despite this confusion, it was clear that the Protestant churches had taken a positive stand on behalf of world organization. The final recommendation of the conference urged local churches to "use all their facilities, denominational and interdenominational, to secure American participation in international cooperation. New methods of education and all legitimate means by which public opinion is formed must be utilized in this effort." [14]

Bolstered by the support of the Protestant churches, the educational campaign conducted by the State Department and the internationalists seemed to be achieving results by the early months of 1945. Public-opinion polls showed a marked rise in support for international organization from the two thirds that had prevailed since 1943 to as high as 80 and 90 percent in March and April. The most widely cited figures were those disclosed by George Gallup in early April, indicating that 81 percent of the American people favored American entry into a "world organization with police power to maintain world peace." Gallup also asked those who responded affirmatively how important they thought such action was, and he reported that 83 percent answered "very important." A confidential poll taken for the State Department by the Office of Public Opinion Research at Princeton in the early fall confirmed these findings. Over 90 percent of those questioned favored American entry into a world body, and eight out of ten approved the use of force to keep the peace. [15]

At the same time, the American people were still skeptical of the effectiveness of the proposed world organization. Thirty-eight percent believed that the United States would find itself involved in another world war within twenty-five years, and more than half were certain this would happen within fifty years. There was no clear consensus on the crucial question of who should decide to commit American troops to a collective-security action in case of aggression; the secret State Department poll showed an even division on this point, while the National Opinion Research Center, in a special survey taken for *Free World* in March 1945, reported that among those favoring American entry into a world organization, two out of three wanted Congress to have the final authority. Internationalists were even more disturbed over polls which showed that the majority of the American people were unaware of the

Dumbarton Oaks proposals. In March the League of Women Voters surveyed ninety-eight people on the streets of Chattanooga, Tennessee. Forty-four approved of the Dumbarton Oaks plan, two opposed it, two had no opinion, and fifty said that they had never heard of it. The State Department reported to Roosevelt on March 17 that their private polls indicated that the percentage of Americans who had "heard or read about" the Dumbarton Oaks proposals had increased from 43 to 52 percent since December, but further questioning revealed that only 30 percent actually knew that they dealt with world organization.

The internationalists were still having difficulty bringing their message home to the man in the street. It was not a regional problem; Midwesterners were as committed as Easterners, with Southerners slightly more favorable than the rest of the nation. The level of education and the economic status of individuals were the major determinants. The wealthy and well-educated were almost unanimous in their support for international organization; the poor and those with only a grammar-school education were most resistant. Nearly all the promotional efforts of the internationalists were aimed at the first group, and thus failed to dissolve the hard core of apathy and ignorance which continued to flourish among the millions of Americans who rarely read a national magazine, did not go to internationalist rallies, and attended Catholic or fundamentalist Protestant churches which ignored international issues. These culturally deprived people remained impervious to the internationalist crusade and gave die-hard isolationists hope that they could still mount a successful counterattack.[16]

II

As soon as he became Secretary of State, Stettinius surprised everyone by accepting the resignations of Assistant Secretaries Breckinridge Long, Adolf Berle and Howland Shaw. Retaining only Dean Acheson, who was given Long's assignment of liaison with Congress, Stettinius asked Roosevelt to make Joseph Grew his Under Secretary, and to appoint five new assistant secretaries: Archibald MacLeish, William Clayton, James C. Dunn, Nelson Rockefeller and Julius Holmes. Grew, Dunn and Acheson were men with long experience in diplomacy whose appointments were not unusual, though all came from aristocratic backgrounds and were viewed with suspicion by New Dealers within the administration. Holmes was a former foreign-service officer and executive of

General Mills who had served as a brigadier general under Eisenhower, handling civil affairs in liberated areas of Italy and France; Clayton was a Houston cotton broker who had worked on international trade problems in the Department of Commerce during the war; Rockefeller had valuable experience as the Department's Coordinator of Inter-American Affairs for the previous four and a half years. With the exception of MacLeish, Stettinius' new "team," as he called them, reflected a conservative, business-oriented background which alarmed liberals. "These are men who cannot and could not possibly work with Soviet Russia, or a labor government in Great Britain," commented the *New Republic*. The *Nation* objected to having the State Department turned into "a millionaires' club" and noted that if Stettinius had only included Dulles, "Wall Street would have no cause to regret the failure to elect Dewey."

Many Democratic senators felt the same way. When Tom Connally presented the names of the new appointees to the Senate for confirmation, Joseph F. Guffey of Pennsylvania and Joseph O'Mahoney of Wyoming insisted that the Foreign Relations Committee hold public hearings on the nominations. Despite Connally's heated objections, the Senate voted 37 to 27 to return the names to his committee for further consideration. On December 12 a beaming Stettinius led his new team, characterized by one cynical observer as "a bevy of tycoons surrounding a poet," into the Senate caucus room. Stettinius played the role of master of ceremonies, introducing each nominee to the Foreign Relations Committee personally and trying to smooth over any hint of disagreement with his buoyant personality. The senators questioned Grew, Holmes and Rockefeller perfunctorily, but they went after Dunn for his pro-Franco views, and Bennett Clark, now a lame-duck senator, amused everyone by asking MacLeish to explain some of his more obscure poems. Will Clayton received a thorough going-over from southern liberals, who probed into his past as a cotton broker.[17]

When the hearings were over, the committee went into executive session and quickly voted to recommend the nominations of all but MacLeish. Two liberal senators who opposed the entire slate changed their vote to support the poet, enabling Connally to send all the names back to the Senate. Some senators were still unhappy, but when the President sent word that he wanted no further delay, they gave up their opposition and on December 19 the Senate confirmed all the nominations by a large margin. Liberal journalists were not satisfied, however, and they continued to criticize the appointments on the grounds that a pliable man like Stettinius should be surrounded by more progressive advisers. "To think of them as participating even remotely in a peace conference," commented the editors of the *New Republic*, "is to become acutely nauseated."

Undaunted by this criticism, Stettinius continued his program of invigorating the State Department after twelve years of genteel decay under Hull. Workmen swarmed through the old State Department building, putting in new plumbing, replacing the antique furniture with modernistic desks and chairs, and painting the gloomy halls a bright pistachio green. Even Cordell Hull's treasured rubber plant perished in the overhaul. On December 21 Stettinius assembled all 2,500 State Department employees for the first time in the DAR's Constitutional Hall, paying the $478 rental out of his own pocket. A Marine Corps band played "El Capitan" and the "Colonel Bogey March," and Stettinius presented his new assistants to the audience, asking each man to give a thirty-second speech. "It was encouraging to see the clubhouse so full of such team spirit," commented *Time* with tongue in cheek. "But the big game was waiting. The first half was over, the score looked bad, and the spectators were anxious." [18]

Stettinius did not neglect the issue of international organization. In November he resumed consultation with the Committee of Eight, meeting with Connally's group to explain the impasse with the Soviets over the voting formula on the Security Council. He described a compromise plan which enabled a major power to veto the use of economic or military sanctions, but which permitted the Council to discuss and make recommendations for the peaceful settlement of a dispute despite the objections of one of the permanent members. Vandenberg thought this was still an "unconscionable" surrender to the Soviet Union, but he agreed to go along with the other senators in backing this formula. On December 4 Stettinius invited a bi-partisan group from the House, including Speaker Sam Rayburn, Minority Leader Joseph Martin, Sol Bloom, chairman of the House Foreign Affairs Committee, and Charles Eaton, the ranking Republican member, for a briefing on the plans for international organization. Two days later he met with the four B_2H_2 senators for what he termed "a constructive discussion." "They made several good suggestions about the handling of public relations on the proposals," he told the President. Stettinius completed this round of bi-partisan talks on December 8 by conferring with John Foster Dulles and informing him of the voting formula. After the meeting, both Dewey and Dulles released statements promising to support the administration's policy and keep the issue of international organization out of partisan politics. [19]

Meanwhile, President Roosevelt sought to break the deadlock with the Soviet Union on Security Council voting. On December 5 he sent Stalin a message outlining the new State Department formula and urged his acceptance, saying that the great nations should exhibit "those enduring qualifications of moral leadership which can raise the whole level of international relations the world over." W. Averell Harriman, the American ambassador in Moscow, handed this message to Stalin on December 4, and though he asked for a prompt reply, the Soviet leader procrastinated. Finally, on December 27, Molotov handed Harriman a note from Stalin rejecting the American proposal. Insisting on the veto for all votes on the Security Council, Molotov said, "The principle of unity of action must be preserved from the inception of any dispute, it must never be diminished, and there must be no exceptions to it; otherwise, the entire organization would be emasculated." [20]

Although the British were willing to accept the American compromise, Roosevelt wavered on the veto issue. On January 8 he asked Stettinius if it would not be possible to find another formula that would satisfy the Russians. When the Secretary replied that both Congress and public opinion, as well as other members of the United Nations, opposed an ironclad veto, Roosevelt said he would take this issue up with Stalin personally in their next meeting, scheduled for Yalta in early 1945. Three days later Roosevelt met with the Committee of Eight for the first time to inform them of the topics he planned to discuss with Churchill and Stalin. He described the impasse on the voting formula, and surprised the State Department representatives by telling the senators that he "was unsure whether the Soviet position on unanimity was a bad position and that we might have to yield to them on this point." Then he mentioned the earlier Russian request for membership of all sixteen Soviet Republics in the General Assembly, hinting that he might have to concede the veto to force the Soviets to give up this demand. Calling it "ridiculous," Roosevelt said that if Stalin persisted he would counter by asking for General Assembly membership for each of the forty-eight states! The senators filed out convinced that Roosevelt was planning to compromise on the veto but stand firmly against the Soviet demand for extra seats in the General Assembly. [21]

III

By the end of 1944 the war was approaching its climax. In Europe the Allied armies had sped across France after breaking out of the Normandy beachhead in July. Paris was liberated in late August, and by September the German troops were retreating from French soil, taking refuge in the Siegfried Line, the fortifications Hitler had built along the German frontier in the 1930's. Supply problems hampered the American and British forces, but by November Eisenhower was preparing a broad advance on a three-hundred-mile front from the North Sea to the Swiss border. In the East the Soviet armies had swept the Germans out of Russia and had thrust deep into the Balkans. The Russian summer offensive had stopped at the Vistula, but Stalin was planning a mammoth winter assault across the plains of Poland and into Germany. In the war against Japan, American amphibious forces had captured the Marianas during the summer, and in November 1944 squadrons of B-29's, long-range bombers developed for the Pacific war, began their devastating raids on Japanese cities from airfields on Saipan and Tinian. When Japanese resistance proved lighter than expected, the Joint Chiefs of Staff gave General MacArthur permission to launch an invasion of the Philippines in mid-October. The landings on Leyte went smoothly, with the General splashing ashore two days later to announce, "I have returned," but the Japanese Navy gathered nearly all its remaining ships for a three-pronged attack on the American naval forces guarding MacArthur's landing. Though American task forces easily destroyed two of the Japanese units, only a brave stand by a frail American force of destroyers and escort carriers halted the third Japanese thrust and saved the defenseless supply and troop ships in Leyte Gulf. This great naval engagement wiped out the Japanese fleet, but it was a near thing, with the American commander attributing success to "bomb, torpedo and strafing air attacks, timely maneuvers, and the definite partiality of Almighty God." [22]

The stream of victories on all fronts brought political problems among the Big Three to the fore. Despite Japanese weakness, American military leaders believed that Russian assistance was essential to prevent enormous American casualties in the final invasion of the Japanese home islands. At Teheran, Roosevelt had raised this issue with Stalin, who had indicated a willingness to bring Russia into the war against Japan after the defeat of Germany, but he also expressed a desire for Chinese harbors and railroads as a reward. In December, Harriman reported from Moscow that Stalin's appetite had not diminished. The Russian invasion of the Balkans had raised even more immediate problems for the British, who had a traditional interest in this region. Fearful of a Communist take-over, Churchill had flown to Moscow in October and had suggested a division of the Balkans into spheres of influence pending a final peace settlement. "So far as Britain and Russia are concerned," Churchill proposed to Stalin, "how would it do for you to have ninety per cent predominance in Rumania, for us to have ninety per cent of the say in Greece, and go fifty-fifty about Yugoslavia?" Churchill wrote down the percentages on a piece of paper, Stalin studied it for a minute, then made a large check with his blue pencil and passed it back. "It was all settled in no more time than it takes to set down," Churchill commented. The United States did not take part in this arrangement, but when Churchill informed him, Roosevelt did not object, indicating that he considered the Balkans beyond the range of American interest. Two months later Churchill sent British troops to Athens to help install a conservative government over the armed opposition of Communist-dominated partisans. Heavy fighting ensued, but Stalin lived up to the bargain, refusing to aid the guerrillas.

The problem of Poland could not be settled so easily. Britain had gone to war against Germany in 1939 in defense of Poland, and after the Nazi conquest, accompanied by a Russian invasion from the East, the Polish government had operated from exile in London. In 1943, when the London Poles charged that the Russians had perpetrated the massacre of Polish officers at Katyn forest, Stalin severed diplomatic relations. At Teheran he told Churchill and Roosevelt that he intended to retain the portions of eastern Poland he had seized in 1939, and in the summer of 1944, as the Russian armies swept into this area, he created a Committee of National Liberation at Lublin composed of subservient Polish Communists. Churchill and Roosevelt tried to persuade the London government to give in on the territorial issue, but these men, staunchly opposed to Communism and bitterly anti-Russian, stubbornly refused. Finally, despite protests from the British and American governments, on the last day of 1944 the Soviet Union recognized the Lublin committee as the provisional government of Poland.[23]

"This war is being lost," commented the *Christian Century*. "It is being lost in the reversion to power politics, in the cynical evasion of solemn engagements with the peoples who have poured out their blood and treasure." Liberals and conservatives alike echoed this sentiment of frustration and disillusionment. "The news of Poland and Greece was that Britain and Russia each had specific, immediate well-planned aims in Europe," noted the editors of *Time*, urging the United States to halt this return to unilateral diplomacy. "In the absence of the United Nations Council," declared the *New Republic*, "the shape of the postwar world is being set along the lines of old-fashioned imperialism, power politics and economic rivalry." A few cynics charged that the peace was already lost. The editors of the New York *Times,* deeply concerned by the mood of unrest, published a long editorial reminding the American people that they were on the verge of triumphing over "the greatest threat that has ever arisen to the spiritual and moral vlaues of western civilization," and asking them to be patient and persevering in the minds of temporary political setbacks.

President Roosevelt returned to Washington after a three-week vacation in Warm Springs on December 19 and immediately made an off-the-cuff remark that heightened the turmoil. Responding to a reporter's question about whether Churchill had actually signed the Atlantic Charter, Roosevelt said, "Nobody ever signed the Atlantic Charter. Now that's an amazing statement." He went on to explain that the Charter was a press release, not a state paper like the United Nations Declaration, and thus did not require signatures. The next day newspapers headlined this disclosure, hinting that principles affirmed by Roosevelt and Churchill in 1941 were in the process of being discarded. In a press conference on December 22, Roosevelt tried to remedy his mistake, announcing that the ideals of the Charter were as valid as ever and that he stood squarely behind them. Isolationists refused to be convinced. The *Christian Century* commented that "no slippery words can disguise the fact that another great betrayal is under way," and the Chicago *Tribune* ran the following poem beneath a cartoon of Roosevelt on its front page: [24]

> For three long years you let us think
> The famed Atlantic Charter, Inc.,
> Was signed and sealed and guaranteed,
> By which all nations would be freed. . . .
> But now we're told the document
> Was just a memo of intent,
> An idyll written on a boat
> When you were fishing for our vote.

Roosevelt replied to his critics in his annual State of the Union message to Congress on January 6, 1945. Departing from tradition, he sent the full text over to the Capitol, where it was read by a clerk to a joint session. That evening the President delivered a briefer version to the American people by radio. Roosevelt grimly catalogued the political difficulties with the nation's allies, refusing to minimize their significance. But then he pleaded for understanding, declaring, "We must not let those differences divide us and blind us to our more important common and continuing interests in winning the war and building the peace." He denounced imperialism and power politics, but he also warned against "perfectionism," reminding his listeners that the return to isolationism after World War I had begun with attacks against "the alleged imperfections of the peace." "But we must not this time lose the hope of establishing an international order which will be capable of maintaining peace and realizing through the years more perfect justice between nations," he implored. "To do this we must be on our guard not to exploit and exaggerate the differences between us and our allies." [25]

As the new Congress began to organize, political observers took particular note of the composition of the Senate Foreign Relations Committee. Five isolationist members had been defeated in the 1944 elections, and their successors on the committee could determine the fate of international organization. A number of Democratic internationalists, including Carl Hatch, Lister Hill and freshman Senator William Fulbright, asked to be placed on the committee, but they lacked the seniority of such isolationist claimants as Burton Wheeler of Montana and Patrick McCarran of Nevada. The Democratic Steering Committee, however, ignored seniority and appointed Hill, Hatch and Scott Lucas of Illinois, an administration stalwart, to the three Democratic vacancies. The Republicans took a more careful step, choosing Styles Bridges of New Hampshire, a moderate internationalist, and Alexander Wiley of Wisconsin, a former isolationist, who announced cryptically, "I enter upon this task with no desire other than to safeguard the interests of my country first, last, and always, and, through so doing, to advance the interests of all other like-minded nations." Though some internationalists regretted the Republicans' failure to select such forthright applicants as Harold Burton and Chan Gurney of South Dakota, the men chosen ensured a heavy majority on the committee pledged to support international organization. Of the twenty-two members, there were only three staunch isolationists—Robert La Follette, Jr., Henrik Shipstead of Minnesota, and Hiram Johnson.

Though Fulbright failed to win a place on the Foreign Relations Committee, he gave the administration a great boost by arranging for the sixteen new senators—ten Democrats and six Republicans—to write a letter to Roosevelt supporting his foreign policy. Stating that they had not had a chance to vote for the Connally resolution, the sixteen senators affirmed, "We favor the formation at the earliest possible moment of a United Nations organization, to establish and preserve the peace of the world, along the general lines tentatively drafted at Dumbarton Oaks." The letter, written in early January, arrived at the White House after Roosevelt had left for Yalta, and it was finally made public on January 24 when Fulbright warned that several of the Republican signers were wavering and might retract their signatures at any moment.[26]

These developments encouraged Roosevelt, but he still feared a violent attack by Senate isolationists on the eve of his meeting with Churchill and Stalin. When the B_2H_2 senators announced plans to ask Congress to vote on a new resolution calling for the immediate formation of a United Nations Council, the President asked them to confer with him at the White House on December 23. For more than an hour he talked with Joseph Ball and Carl Hatch about the difficulties in Poland and Greece, trying to persuade them not to open up a debate in the Senate that could prove embarrassing to Britain and Russia. Ball and Hatch agreed not to introduce their resolution until after the Big Three had met, but when Congress convened on January 5, Senator Burton Wheeler threatened to launch a full-scale attack on the administration's foreign policy. On January 6 he inserted into the *Congressional Record* the text of a radio speech he had made the evening before, charging that "Dumbarton Oaks is a grim hoax." Citing recent events in Poland and Greece, he claimed that America's allies wanted an international organization "designed to put the United States in the position of holding the draw strings of an international grab bag while Britain and Russia connive or fight for the spoils."

Tom Connally pleaded with his fellow Democrats to refrain from such attacks until the President had had a chance to discuss the current problems face-to-face with Churchill and Stalin. After the Democratic caucus on January 5, he told reporters that he asked the senators "not to run off across the field after a rabbit while the fox is going down the road." A few days later, however, he told Roosevelt that there was strong pressure for "country-by-country debates on the floor," adding that he shared his colleagues' concern over Russian policy in Poland. At Connally's suggestion, Stettinius finally agreed to brief him every Thursday on the latest foreign-policy developments and to appear before the Foreign Relations Committee from time to time to answer the senators' questions. "While there are certain risks in the latter procedure," Stettinius told Roosevelt, "I feel it is worth trying and will plan to do it unless you feel it is unwise." The President had no objections, so Stettinius met with the committee on January 17, and after he left for Yalta, Assistant Secretary Dean Acheson continued to keep the members informed.[27]

Democratic senators reluctantly fell in line, but there was no way Roosevelt could prevent Republicans from speaking out. To their dismay, administration leaders discovered that Arthur Vandenberg planned to make a major foreign-policy speech to the Senate. Vandenberg came from a state with a heavy Polish population, and most observers expected him to deliver a tirade against Soviet expansion. Insiders knew that he was skeptical of the administration's ability to secure a fair peace and that he insisted on the right of Congress to retain a veto over the use of force for collective security. His reputation as a leading pre-war isolationist was untarnished, and few realized that he had been moving slowly toward acceptance of international organization. On January 4 he wrote Dulles that he shared a "sound middle ground" with him on foreign policy and asked Dulles to tell the people of Michigan in a forthcoming Detroit address of the identity of their views. Then for the next few days he drafted and redrafted his own speech, intent on challenging the President to end his silence and inform the nation of the policies he planned to pursue at Yalta.

"Mr. President, there are critical moments in the life of every nation which call for the straightest, the plainest, and the most courageous thinking of which we are capable," Vandenberg told the Senate on January 10. "We confront such a moment now." Citing the danger of disunity between the victorious United Nations, he called for "honest candor." Then, to the surprise of many of his colleagues, he affirmed "maximum American cooperation, consistent with legitimate American self-interest . . . to make the basic idea of Dumbarton Oaks succeed." He went on to describe the aggressive Soviet policy in Poland and eastern Europe, but he did not condemn the Russians. Instead, he attributed their policy to a fear of Germany, and argued that the United States would have to persuade Stalin that collective security provided a safe alternative to unilateral domination. He outlined a specific proposal—a treaty between the major allies to keep the defeated Axis powers permanently demilitarized and thus ensure lasting peace. With such a guarantee, Russia would abandon its aggressive behavior and the wartime unity could be preserved "at this moment when enlightened civilization is our common stake." Then, pleading for "honest candor" for the tenth time in thirty minutes, Vandenberg sat down amid the applause of his fellow senators.[28]

Time said "it might well prove to be the most important speech made by an American in World War II," while the *Christian Century* stated that Vandenberg had "pierced straight through the fog of mutual misunderstanding and recrimination which had begun to settle over the relations of Great Britain, Russia and the United States." The *New Republic* called the address "a turning point in world affairs," noting that the majority of Republican senators would follow Vandenberg down the trail to international organization. Most observers praised Vandenberg's proposal for a separate treaty to disarm Germany and Japan, and expressed the hope that Roosevelt would implement it at Yalta. An Associated Press poll in early February revealed that this plan had won the backing of sixty-eight senators, more than enough for treaty ratification.[29]

The administration, however, remained cool toward Vandenberg's proposal. Connally opposed it on the Senate floor, claiming that it would detract attention from the more important issue of international organization, and Roosevelt refused to commit himself when a reporter asked him about such a treaty. The President would only say that he had talked with Vandenberg at the White House recently; he did not reveal that he had asked for fifty reprints of the speech.

Republican leaders backed Vandenberg enthusiastically. Dulles issued a public statement endorsing the speech as "a notable contribution to the development of U.S. foreign policy" and in a letter to Dulles, Hugh Wilson said Vandenberg's remarks "will go far toward giving the party the reputation of forward thinking and constructive participation in the war effort." In a Lincoln's Birthday address in Washington a month later Dewey lauded the proposed demilitarization of Germany and Japan as "the clearest call for constructive action" since the election. Members of the Republican National Committee accepted the proposed treaty as party policy; a few party leaders even began talking of Vandenberg as a possible presidential candidate in 1948.[30]

Vandenberg's speech may not have been as epoch-making as contemporaries believed, but it did relieve the administration of the fear of an isolationist resurgence. When Burton Wheeler finally rose in the Senate a week later to charge that the Dumbarton Oaks proposals called for "a grim military alliance to underwrite tyranny," he attracted little attention, and Roosevelt was able to depart for the Yalta conference without a full-dress Senate debate on his policies. More significantly, he knew that Vandenberg had correctly interpreted the election results and would refuse to play the role of Henry Cabot Lodge in 1945. Indeed,

Vandenberg had changed from the potential saboteur of the peace to the leading Republican partner in the bi-partisan policy. As a former isolationist, he spoke for a group whose cooperation was essential to a sound peace, and he was shrewd enough to make the most of his conversion, supplanting such lifelong internationalists as Warren Austin and Wallace White as the Republican spokesman for foreign policy. "The moral of the Vandenberg story," commented Richard Rovere, "can be formulated in some such fashion as this: It is very often better to be wrong first and right afterward than to be right all along." [31]

IV

The President slipped quietly out of Washington on the morning of January 22. At Norfolk, Virginia, he boarded the U.S.S. *Quincy* for the first leg of the long journey to Yalta. Tired from the campaign, he had not snapped back as he usually did during his three weeks at Warm Springs, and his close associates hoped that the sea voyage would reinvigorate him. Those who did not see him daily were shocked by the change in his appearance—deep lines in his face and an ashen color revealed the heavy toll the war had taken in his health. His eyes still glowed with wit and humor, and as he crossed the Atlantic he seemed to gain energy. On February 2 the *Quincy* arrived at Malta, where the President conferred briefly with Churchill and then changed to a C-54 airplane for the long flight to the Crimea. The plane iced dangerously as it flew over the mountains of Greece, but the President slept peacefully and awoke refreshed just before the pilot landed on Russian soil at noon on February 3.

At Yalta, an old Czarist resort on the shores of the Black Sea, Roosevelt stayed in the Livadia Palace, built by Nicholas II in 1911. The Germans had stripped the building bare, and the Soviets had hastily filled it with furnishings from the Hotel Metropole in Moscow. The President had a spacious suite on the ground floor, complete with the only private bathroom in the fifty-room mansion. A corridor led to the huge ballroom where the plenary sessions of the conference would take place.[32]

A multitude of questions faced Roosevelt, Churchill and Stalin as they began their discussions on Sunday, February 4. Fifteen months had passed since they had last met at Teheran, and the war was speeding to a conclusion with vital political issues unresolved. The President, on the unanimous advice of his military counselors, wanted to ensure Soviet entry into the war against Japan. He was also concerned about the fate of Poland and the Balkans, though it was Churchill who took the lead on these European problems. And Stettinius, attending his first major diplomatic conference, pressed Roosevelt for the settlement of the issues left over from Dumbarton Oaks; aboard the *Quincy*, James Byrnes had suggested that the President alter the voting formula on the Security Council to prevent a major power from casting a veto in disputes in which it was involved. Aware that the Soviets would never agree to this modification, Stettinius finally convinced the President that he must stick to the State Department formula, which prevented a major power from vetoing the discussion of disputes but required unanimity of the permanent members for any decision involving economic or military sanctions. Stettinius then discovered that Churchill agreed with Stalin that the veto should be absolute, and he spent the first evening of the conference helping Anthony Eden change the Prime Minister's mind. Churchill finally gave in when Eden bluntly told him that if the big powers insisted on an unconditional veto, they might as well forget about a world organization—the small nations would refuse to participate.

On February 6, the third day of the conference, Stettinius presented the American voting plan to the plenary session. "We believe that unless this freedom of discussion in the Council is permitted, the establishment of the World Organization which we all so earnestly desire in order to save the world from the tragedy of another war would be seriously jeopardized," he declared. Churchill backed the American proposal forcibly, and when Stalin objected, saying that unanimity among the Big Three on all issues was essential, Roosevelt broke in to say that by permitting free discussion they would "demonstrate the confidence which the Great Powers had in each other and in the justice of their own policies." The Russians remained adamant, and finally Molotov moved that the issue be deferred.[33]

The next day Molotov began the plenary session by announcing that the Soviet Union accepted the American formula for voting on the Security Council. Then, as Stettinius broke out into a broad grin, he added that Russia had also modified its position on the other major issue left over from Dumbarton Oaks, the request for sixteen seats in the General Assembly. The Soviet Union, Molotov explained, would be content with the admission of only three, "or at least two," of the Soviet Republics: White Russia, the Ukraine and Lithuania. Roosevelt, who

265

had told Stettinius the day before that he was "unalterably opposed" to the Soviet request for sixteen votes in the General Assembly, was immediately on guard. He passed Stettinius a note reading, "This is not so good," and suggested to Stalin that the question of membership be left to the international organization to decide after it was operating. The Russians turned down this attempt at evasion, and the heads of state finally agreed to ask Stettinius, Eden and Molotov to take it up at the foreign ministers' level.

After dinner that evening Roosevelt told Stettinius that he was sympathetic to the scaled-down Soviet request for additional votes in the General Assembly. He said Stalin had told him that White Russia and the Ukraine had borne the brunt of the war against Germany and that giving them special consideration would guarantee wholehearted Soviet participation in the new world body. The President thought that the British, with five dominions possessing separate membership, would accept this compromise. Noting that the real power lay in the Security Council, Roosevelt told Stettinius he thought the United States could be accommodating. "As the President analyzed the question in my presence," Stettinius commented, "he said that the most important thing was to maintain the unity of the three Great Powers, to defeat Germany, and then to get them all around a table to work out a world organization."

At the foreign ministers' session the next day Eden announced British willingness to accept the Russian request. Stettinius reported that Roosevelt was sympathetic, but the Secretary could not commit the United States until he had checked again with the President. Stettinius was unable to see Roosevelt before the afternoon plenary session, and when it began he was startled to learn that Roosevelt had seen Eden and agreed to the Soviet request for two additional seats in the General Assembly. To avoid the appearance of big-power dictation, the agreement stated that when the United Nations met to form the new world organization, the United States and Great Britain would join the Soviet Union in asking for membership for the Ukraine and White Russia.

Other members of the American delegation were very upset when they learned of Roosevelt's concession. James Byrnes reminded the President that he had told the Senate Committee of Eight in January that he would never give in to the Soviet demand for sixteen votes. Byrnes and Edward J. Flynn, a professional politician, warned Roosevelt that isolationists in Congress would have a field day with charges that Britain had six votes, the Soviet Union three and the United States only one in the new world organization. On February 10, just before the conference ended, the President heeded their advice and wrote letters to Churchill and Stalin asking them to support a future American request for three votes in the General Assembly. Churchill immediately agreed, and a few hours later Stalin wrote that he was "prepared officially" to back two additional votes for the United States. In this correspondence, all pretense at granting membership to specific areas was dropped—it was simply a matter of achieving balance among the super-powers.[34]

With the important issues of voting and membership resolved, the Big Three had no difficulty in deciding that the United States should host the conference to launch the new world organization in late April. The State Department had been surveying various sites for several months, but Stettinius could not make up his mind. At three in the morning on February 9 he suddenly awoke with a vision of San Francisco. "I saw the golden sunshine, and as I lay there on the shores of the Black Sea in the Crimea, I could almost feel the fresh and invigorating air from the Pacific." The next day he told Roosevelt of his dream, and though the President was noncommital at first, he soon warmed to the idea as he realized it would help dramatize the war in the Pacific. On Saturday evening, February 10, just before the final dinner, Roosevelt announced that the United Nations conference would be held in San Francisco. Stettinius raised his glass of vodka and Eden and Molotov joined him in a toast to the success of the venture, while the three heads of state nodded their approval.

Roosevelt, Churchill and Stalin held their last meeting on Sunday afternoon, ironing out the text of the communiqué which they made public on February 12. The three leaders announced that they had decided to occupy Germany after the war and stamp out all traces of Nazism; that the Lublin committee would serve as the basis of a broader, more democratic Polish government; that the liberated peoples of Europe, including those in the Balkans, would be permitted to choose their own governments in free elections; and that all nations that had signed the United Nations Declaration would be invited to a conference at San Francisco on April 25, 1945, to create a new world organization. Significantly, the communiqué made no mention of a secret deal Roosevelt had made with Stalin whereby Russia promised to enter the war against Japan within three months after the defeat of Germany in return for control over Outer Mongolia, transfer of the Kurile Islands from Japan, return of the southern half of Sakhalin and rights to railroads and harbors in Manchuria. Nor did the three leaders reveal their continuing disagreement over the future of Germany, and over the make-up of the Polish government, which would clearly be Communist-dominated. The communiqué stated that they had agreed on a voting formula for the Security Council which would be made public once the other permanent members, France and China, expressed their approval. There was no hint of the deal on General Assembly membership, though Stettinius wanted to include it in the public statement. Roosevelt insisted on secrecy, saying that he preferred to explain the concession to Congressional leaders before it became public knowledge. "The President," Harry Hopkins cabled back to Washington, "is extremely anxious no aspect of this question be discussed even privately." [35]

"The results of the Crimea Conference," commented Clark Eichelberger after reading the communiqué, "have surpassed the hopes of the idealists and to a great extent confounded the cynics." Almost all the contemporary reactions were equally favorable. "BIG 3 DOOM NAZISM AND REICH MILITARISM," headlined the New York *Times*, while *Time* ran a picture of Roosevelt and Stalin at Yalta with the caption "Eight great days on the Russian Riviera." "On the basis of the Big Three's communiqué, no citizen of the U.S., the U.S.S.R., or Great Britain could complain that his country had been sold down the river," began the story. *Newsweek* believed that if any of the three leaders had dominated the conference, "that man was the President." Jonathan Daniels wired Stephen Early, who attended Yalta with Roosevelt, that the press reaction was "magnificent," adding that many Republicans made favorable comments, "including even Herbert Hoover." The only dissenting voices were those of Burton Wheeler and Arthur Vandenberg, who issued skeptical statements about the ambiguous Polish settlement, and the editors of the *New Republic*, who termed the conference a victory for Stalin.[36]

On February 10 Roosevelt had asked James Byrnes to fly back to Washington ahead of the presidential party in order to inform Congress of the achievements at Yalta. Byrnes, arriving a day after the communiqué was made public, held an hour-long public press conference and then met privately with the Committee of Eight at Connally's apartment, telling the senators that they could be proud of the way Roosevelt handled himself at Yalta. In this meeting, and at a larger gathering of senators the next day which included Fulbright and Wheeler, Byrnes carefully sidestepped questions about the Security Council voting formula and made no mention of the General Assembly deal. When James Reston published a slightly inaccurate version of the veto formula in the New York *Times* on February 14, Byrnes told Acting Secretary of State Grew to inform the Committee of Eight of the actual terms agreed on at Yalta. Then he cabled Roosevelt to assure him that he was keeping the membership arrangement confidential. "Up to this time," he wired, "no reference to the Assembly votes has appeared in the press." [37]

Meanwhile, Roosevelt was enjoying a leisurely sea voyage home aboard the *Quincy* after conferring with King Farouk, Haile Selassie and Ibn Saud in Egypt. The conference had exhausted his slender reserves of strength. On February 20 the death of his appointments secretary and close friend, "Pa" Watson, sent him into a mood of despondency that lasted for the remainder of the trip. Judge Rosenman had joined him at Algiers to work on the text of a report to the nation on Yalta, but Roosevelt could not concentrate, preferring to stay in his cabin mornings, and spending the afternoon on deck "quietly reading or just smoking or staring at the horizon." At dinnertime he became gay and animated, charming his companions with his keen wit. He held two press conferences with the three White House correspondents aboard the *Quincy* in which he carefully skirted the issues discussed at Yalta, casually describing the Crimean resort as "Hollywood and our South all rolled into one." He jocularly told them that he wanted the new world organization located in the Azores, where the press could be kept away. In a more serious vein, he said he was amazed at the degree of unanimity displayed at Yalta. When one reporter asked him if they had laid the foundations for a peace that would last more than one generation, Roosevelt replied, "We can look as far ahead as humanity believes in this sort of thing. The United Nations will evolve into the best method ever devised for stopping war. . . ." [38]

As they approached the United States, the President finally permitted Rosenman to show him the draft he had been preparing. On the advice of Byrnes and Vice President Harry Truman, Roosevelt decided to give his report to a joint session of Congress. When the *Quincy* arrived in Norfolk, the President went immediately to Arlington for the funeral services for "Pa" Watson and then returned to the White House, where Rosenman was preparing a fifth draft of the address. Roosevelt made a number of changes, and he specifically instructed Rosenman to make no mention of the agreement with Stalin to give the United States and Russia three votes in the General Assembly.

On March 1 Roosevelt went to the Capitol for his first appearance there in more than two years. Instead of standing on his braces at the rostrum, he spoke sitting down in a red plush chair in the well of the House chamber. Reporters commented on his "tanned and glowing" appearance from the weeks at sea, but they also noted that he looked "grayer, thinner and considerably aged." Departing from his usual style, he delivered his address in an informal, chatty manner, stopping frequently to insert impromptu comments that gave the speech a halting, uncertain quality. For nearly an hour he ranged broadly over the accomplishments at Yalta, stressing the unity which had characterized the conference but giving little information beyond that in the communiqué.

Conscious of the historical parallel with Wilson returning from Versailles in 1919, he spoke out boldly on international organization. He looked forward to the San Francisco conference, where he "confidently" expected the drafting of a charter "under which the peace of the world will be preserved and the forces of aggression permanently outlawed." Calling for a continuation of bi-partisanship, he warned against perfectionism, asking the members of Congress to join with him in a cooperative spirit in the hard tasks that lay ahead. Appealing directly to the senators and representatives who sat before him, he declared: [39]

> The Conference in the Crimea was a turning point—I hope in our history and therefore in the history of the world. There will soon be presented to the Senate of the United States and to the American people a great decision that will determine the fate of the United States—and of the world—for generations to come.
>
> There can be no middle ground here. We shall have to take the responsibility for world collaboration, or we shall have to bear the responsibility for another world conflict.

V

Roosevelt and Stettinius gave careful thought to the make-up of the American delegation to the San Francisco conference. When they arrived at Yalta, Roosevelt told the Secretary that he wanted a seven-member delegation to include a Democrat and a Republican from both the Senate and the House of Representatives. Stettinius conferred with the other Americans at Yalta, and on February 7 he suggested to Roosevelt the names of Senators Tom Connally and Arthur Vandenberg and Representatives Sol Bloom and Charles Eaton. The President, who disliked Vandenberg, said he preferred Warren Austin—who had always supported the administration's foreign policy—as the Republican member from the Senate, but Stettinius finally convinced him that Vandenberg possessed the seniority and influence that could ensure Senate ratification of the United Nations charter. Roosevelt accepted the Secretary's other nominees, Dean Virginia Gildersleeve of Barnard College and Lieutenant Commander Harold Stassen, and the two men agreed that Stettinius would head the delegation, with Cordell Hull, still recuperating at Bethesda Hospital, to serve as "senior advisor."

The White House announced the roster on February 13, although the formal letters of invitation did not go out until the end of the month. The press hailed the bi-partisan line-up, but Arthur Krock pointed out that in choosing Stassen the President had passed over the three distinguished Republicans who had run against him—Herbert Hoover, Alfred Landon and Thomas Dewey. Stassen's selection was actually a very shrewd one. As a naval officer, he represented the millions of young men serving overseas in the armed forces. Coming from the Midwest, he added regional balance to the American delegation, yet his firm internationalist views ensured that he would cooperate with the administration. Miss Gildersleeve was also a wise choice. She satisfied a growing clamor that American women take part in the making of peace. An intelligent and resourceful lady, she was one of the charter members of the Commission to Study the Organization of Peace, and her presence on the delegation was pleasing to internationalist leaders. The House members added less distinction. Bloom, as chairman of the House Foreign Affairs Committee, was a logical selection, but his brash manner and superficial knowledge of foreign affairs made him an ineffective delegate; Eaton was too old and infirm to make any significant contribution. Connally and Vandenberg tended to dominate the group. They possessed the political power and influence the others lacked, and Stettinius, never one to take charge, deferred to them in an effort to achieve harmony.[40]

As soon as he heard of his appointment, Vandenberg sent a letter to Roosevelt expressing his "deepest gratitude" but raising one vital reservation. Reminding the President that he had obligations to his own party, he asked if he could "present my own points of view to our Delegation" and "reserve the right of final judgment upon the ultimate results of the Conference." After reading this letter on board the *Qunicy*, Roosevelt commented to reporters, "He wants to be free to saw his head off." On February 26 the President replied evasively, thanking Vandenberg for his willingness to serve and ignoring completely his request for freedom of action. Vandenberg, who thought Roosevelt was using him "as a stooge," refused to be put off. On March 1 he wrote again, asking the President for a written pledge that he could voice his own views as a delegate and not be bound to support the administration's policy. When Roosevelt gave him this unqualified assurance, Vandenberg released a statement to the press saying that he accepted the appointment, adding that he planned to offer a series of amendments to the Dumbarton Oaks proposals.[41]

On the same day, March 5, Stettinius finally disclosed the Security Council voting formula agreed on at Yalta. Speaking from Mexico City, where he was attending an inter-American conference, the Secretary stressed the point that a great power could not block discussion of a dispute in which it was involved, only the use of force. The reaction to this news was quite favorable, though a number of commentators described it as a concession to Stalin. When a few isolationists condemned the veto in any form as undemocratic, Arthur Krock, one of Roosevelt's most persistent critics, reminded his readers that those same people insisted on the retention of sovereignty, which was precisely the purpose of the veto. In a letter to the *Times*, John Foster Dulles praised the Yalta formula as a "statesmanlike solution to a knotty problem," while the *New Republic* noted that the veto was simply a recognition of the fact that "the use of sanctions against any of the major powers undoubtedly means war." The New York *Times* pointed out that the peace rested on the continuing good faith between the great powers. "If they cannot get along together, then no machinery of voting in the Council, however elaborate or however ingenious on paper, will suffice to keep the peace." When a reporter asked Roosevelt if the voting formula was a victory for any nation, he replied, "I should say it was a common agreement. . . . If anybody has a better idea," he added, "we would be glad to consider it." [42]

The American delegation to San Francisco, meeting for the first time as a group on March 13, had no objections to the veto compromise. They spent the morning being briefed by State Department experts, and then at 11:30 Stettinius took them over to the White House to see Roosevelt. The President told them that he was besieged with requests to enlarge the delegation, but he was standing firm. Miss Gildersleeve thought he seemed tired. He talked for some time, even making a few indiscreet remarks about Churchill and Stalin, but he did not mention the General Assembly arrangement.

The delegates then returned to the State Department to continue their discussion of the forthcoming conference. When Stettinius said that each delegate could have a staff of two, Vandenberg asked for permission to name John Foster Dulles as his chief aide. Stettinius, who knew the President distrusted anyone closely associated with Dewey, evaded the request, saying that he was considering asking Dulles to serve as a consultant to the delegation in his capacity as a churchman. Dulles, aware of Roosevelt's hostility, decided to avoid any embarrassment by writing an open letter to Vandenberg in which he said he preferred to attend the conference as a private citizen. Intent on maintaining the bi-partisan policy, Stettinius finally prevailed on Roosevelt to invite Dulles to serve as an adviser to the entire American delegation. After conferring with Dewey, Vandenberg and Herbert Brownell, Dulles accepted the appointment, saying that he wanted to "consolidate the practice of bi-partisan action to establish world organization" which he and Hull had initiated during the presidential campaign. To accentuate the political nature of his role, he then resigned as chairman of the Commission on a Just and Durable Peace, saying that he was not representing the churches at San Francisco.[43]

The mood of harmony that had prevailed since Yalta suddenly dissolved in late March. On the twenty-third, Roosevelt met again with the American delegation, and this time he told them of the promise he had made to Stalin at Yalta to support the Soviet request for three votes in the General Assembly and of Stalin's willingness to back a similar American bid. "The delegates were rather stunned," commented Arthur Vandenberg, and they listened in silence as Roosevelt explained that they were not bound by his action, since he had only told Stalin that if he were a delegate he would vote for the admission of the Ukraine and White Russia into the General Assembly. It was up to them, and eventually the San Francisco conference, to make the final decision, the President finished lamely.

"This will *raise hell,*" Vandenberg wrote in his diary after the meeting with Roosevelt. He realized that when the arrangement was made public, people would demand to know why it had been kept secret so long. He tried to talk with Stettinius about it, but the Secretary was resting in Florida and Under Secretary Grew was home ill. He finally asked Assistant Secretary James Dunn to inform Cordell Hull and ask him to persuade the President to urge Stalin to drop the matter. The only other person he confided in was Dulles. "He agrees with me," Vandenberg noted, "that this effort to 'stack' the Assembly could easily dynamite San Francisco—or subsequent Senate approval of the entire treaty."

Someone else on the delegation was less discreet. On Thursday morning, March 29, the New York *Herald Tribune* ran a front-page story giving the full details of the General Assembly deal with the Soviet Union. Reporters bombarded harassed press secretaries at the State Department and the White House with questions they could not answer until finally Roosevelt, passing through Washington on his way from Hyde Park to Warm Springs, authorized confirmation of the story. The White House statement stressed that the "ultimate decision" on membership would be made at San Francisco, adding that "if the United Nations Organization agreed to let the Soviet Republics have three votes, the United States would ask for three votes also." Vandenberg, unhappy that Roosevelt had not indicated that the American delegates were free to ignore his promise to Stalin, issued his own statement denouncing the proposal, saying it "would destroy the promised 'sovereign equality of nations.'" [44]

On Friday morning Stettinius, just back from Florida, faced a crowded press conference at the State Department. Reporters wanted to know if there were any more secret agreements not yet made public, if the American delegation would honor Roosevelt's commitment, if the United States still upheld the sovereign equality of all nations in the proposed world organization. Stettinius took refuge in vague generalities, announcing that he still had "complete confidence" that all these problems would be dealt with successfully at San Francisco. Finally, he asked the reporters to put their questions in writing, promising to give them firm answers the following Tuesday.

While State Department experts spent the weekend trying to frame suitable replies to the twenty-seven questions the press submitted, the furor continued. On Sunday, Arthur Krock wrote a blistering column in which he charged that Roosevelt had now lost the confidence of the Senate, and he asked, "What will be the date-line on the leak of the next Yalta secret?" Periodical editors were equally critical in the copy they were preparing for the next week's editions. "The Big Three had practiced to deceive their Allies and the world," commented *Time*, calling the General Assembly arrangements "a sorry deal." The *Nation*, speaking for liberal internationalists, pointed out that under the Dumbarton Oaks plan the General Assembly had been designed "to reconcile the lesser nations to a plan of organization which gives special prerogatives and immunities to five great powers." And now even that concession to equality was compromised. The editors then reprinted a cartoon by David Low showing Churchill, Stalin and Roosevelt entering a

"Security Theatre" to see a movie entitled *Votes and Vetoes*. A group of children, labeled the small nations, were calling out, "Take me in, Mister?" as they pointed to a sign which read, "Little ones must be accompanied by grown-ups." [45]

On Monday morning, April 2, Stettinius telephoned the President in Warm Springs to secure his approval for a statement announcing that the United States did not intend to ask for three votes at San Francisco, but that the administration would support the Soviet request for membership for the Ukraine and White Russia. Roosevelt gave his consent, but the American delegation was still unhappy. Vandenberg conferred with Stettinius at Connally's office and insisted that the delegation be free to oppose the Soviet request. Connally and Vandenberg both wanted to issue a separate statement renouncing any desire for three votes for the United States, but they finally agreed to wait until the next day, when Stettinius would confer with all the delegates before facing the press.

"The Delegation went to the mat this morning over the Yalta episode," Vandenberg wrote disgustedly in his diary the next day after they agreed to honor Roosevelt's commitment to Stalin. Vandenberg took some solace in the willingness of the administration to give up its plan to ask for three votes for the United States, believing that it would place Russia in a bad light before the world. Later in the morning Stettinius gave the statement to the press, justifying the three votes on the ground that the two Soviet Republics had "borne great suffering in the prosecution of the war." He assured the reporters that there were no other secret agreements made at Yalta regarding international organization, and explained the forty-seven-day delay in informing the press by citing the need to permit the American delegation to make up its mind on the General Assembly issue free from public pressure. Then he concluded by reminding the press that none of the arrangements made at Yalta was binding on the San Francisco conference.

Reporters realized that, while Stettinius was technically correct, the small nations that would predominate at San Francisco had no choice but to go along with the plans already agreed upon by the Big Three. Nevertheless, most commentators accepted the administration's explanation of the General Assembly arrangements and applauded Roosevelt's decision to give up the idea of asking for three votes for the United States. But Stettinius and Roosevelt failed to comprehend the damage that had been done to the cause of international organization. Writing several years later, Stettinius, claiming that the Senate ignored the extra

275

votes for Russia, dismissed the episode as "a good example of 'Maginot Line' thinking—of preparing for the fight to ratify American participation in the United Nations as if it were the year 1919, not 1945." Roosevelt was even more insensitive. When reporters asked him in Warm Springs on April 5 about the General Assembly, he said, "It is not really of any great importance. It is an investigatory body only. . . . This business about the number of votes in the Assembly does not make a great deal of difference." But for millions of Americans it did make a difference, blighting their hopes for a truly democratic world body in which all nations, large and small, would join together in the quest for enduring peace. Roosevelt, usually so attuned to the nuances of public sentiment, had underrated the intelligence of the American people, a mistake, Robert E. Sherwood noted, that he usually left to his opponents.[46]

The General Assembly voting issue was only one of several disillusioning events during the first week of April. The Russians, growing ever more intransigent as the war moved toward a victorious end in Europe, refused to honor the Yalta agreements on Poland and insisted that the Lublin government be invited to the San Francisco conference. Then Moscow announced that Gromyko rather than Molotov would head the Soviet delegation, a sure sign that Stalin did not attach much importance to the creation of a new world organization. The press began printing stories that the administration was planning to postpone the San Francisco conference, and internationalists became alarmed. On April 2 Clark Eichelberger sent a letter to all chapters of the American Association for the United Nations to counter the growing disillusionment. "The whole future of humanity is at stake," he wrote. Denying that the government planned to delay the conference, he exhorted, "We are going to take a deep breath, clear our eyes and start meeting the greater obstacles to the success of the task of building a world organization—a task in which we dare not fail." To Eichelberger's intense relief, Stettinius announced the next day that, contrary to rumor, no nation had asked for a postponement and that the San Francisco conference would open as scheduled on April 25.[47]

VI

In Warm Springs a tired President was trying desperately to get back his strength. On March 30, William Hassett, who had succeeded "Pa"

Watson as appointments secretary, told Roosevelt's doctor that he was desperately concerned about the President's health. "He is slipping away from us and no earthly power can keep him here," he confessed. Dr. Bruenn disagreed, though he admitted that Roosevelt's health was "in a precarious condition." Hassett commented on the President's increasing apathy. "He was always willing to go through the day's routine, but there was less and less talk about all manner of things—fewer local Hyde Park stories, politics, books, pictures. The old zest was going."

Roosevelt still displayed a genuine interest in international organization. Anne O'Hare McCormick had an interview with him in late March and came away impressed by his determination to transform the United Nations into an effective agency for peace "while the force of war was still hot enough to fuse the nations together." When Harry H. Woodring wrote to him offering to speak in support of world organization in the Middle West, Roosevelt replied, "The tragic sequence of events through the last twenty-five years should be enough to convince all peace-loving Americans that the only alternative to another war is wholehearted membership in a plan to maintain the peace agreed to by our friends and allies." He decided to attend the opening session of the San Francisco conference, refusing to heed his doctor's request that he avoid the strenuous journey across the country. On April 6 he asked Archibald MacLeish to prepare a draft of the speech he would give in San Francisco. He wrote to Claude Pepper three days later, pointing out that give-and-take was the essence of diplomacy. "We cannot jump to what we consider perfection if the other fellow does not go the whole way," he counseled. "He might think that his point of view was just as good or better than ours." He closed by saying he hoped to see Pepper when he returned "from the opening day of the San Francisco parley."

On April 12, shortly after one in the afternoon, the President slumped in his chair in the living room of his cottage at Warm Springs, complaining of a "terrific headache." When the doctor reached him, he was unconscious, suffering from a massive cerebral hemorrhage, and two hours later he died.[48]

The nation went into mourning, but, despite their grief, the internationalists took heart. Since Yalta they had grown despondent, fearing that their dream would evaporate in the disillusionment engendered by big-power domination. Now they had something to fight for, a symbol that held greater meaning than the long-departed Wilson. "Franklin Roosevelt at rest in Hyde Park is a more powerful force for America's participation in a world organization than was President

Roosevelt in the White House," the *New Republic* proclaimed. "The only tribute we can pay worthy of him," wrote Clark Eichelberger, "is to see to it that the world organization is created with American membership just as quickly as possible." Thus to the very end Roosevelt proved to be the master of timing, providing in his death a final boost to a movement he had so often ignored.[49]

I I

San Francisco

HARRY TRUMAN was presiding over the Senate when President Roosevelt died. After the session was over, he went to Speaker Sam Rayburn's office to relax with a highball. Rayburn said Steve Early had just called from the White House, and when Truman returned the call, Early asked him to come over right away. At the White House, Eleanor Roosevelt broke the sad news to him. Early in the evening Chief Justice Harlan Fiske Stone administered the oath of office, and the new President then held his first Cabinet meeting. As he was about to speak, Early entered saying that the press wanted to know if the San Francisco conference would be postponed because of Roosevelt's death. Without a second's hesitation Truman replied that the conference would be held "as President Roosevelt had directed." The next morning the Secretary of State told the nation that "there will be no change of purpose or break of continuity in the foreign policy of the United States government." Under the new President, the United States would carry the war to a successful conclusion, Stettinius declared, and press toward "the establishment of a world organization endowed with the strength to keep the peace for generations and to give security and wider opportunity to all men." [1]

Truman's decision, made with his characteristic directness, was immensely reassuring to the millions of Americans who did not know their new President. In the many profiles and character sketches written to satisfy public curiosity, journalists stressed Truman's genuine commitment to the cause of international organization. They pointed out that he had been one of the small group of senators who developed the B_2H_2 resolution, and some even gave him credit for originating this proposal. Many recalled that Truman had spoken out boldly for international cooperation during the campaign, and that after becoming Vice-President he had been asked by Roosevelt to serve as the "go-between" on world organization between the Senate and the White House. He had reiterated his beliefs in a radio broadcast on February 23, saying, "America can no longer sit smugly behind a mental Maginot line." Some observers thought his rapport with the Senate would make ratification easier than it would have been under Roosevelt. His reputation for intense partisanship seemed to be an obstacle to the bi-partisan policy Hull and Roosevelt had developed, but those who knew him best pointed out that on the Senate investigating committee where he had gained prominence he had won the confidence and respect of the Republican members by handling politically sensitive issues of war contracts with scrupulous fairness.

One of Truman's first acts as President was to ask James Byrnes to come to the White House. Byrnes, who had just retired as War Mobilizer and "Assistant President," as the press dubbed him, accompanied Truman to Roosevelt's funeral. Byrnes had been a leading candidate for the vice-presidency in 1944, and many considered him far better equipped by experience and training than Truman for the presidency. In a long conference on April 16, Truman told Byrnes that he intended to appoint him Secretary of State at the end of the San Francisco conference, but in order not to undercut Stettinius, he would withhold any public announcement. The President did not inform Stettinius of his intentions, though Truman's obvious reliance on Byrnes for advice led to increasing public speculation about the impending change.[2]

The forthcoming conference occupied much of Truman's attention during his first week as President. On April 13 he spent the day going over foreign-policy problems with Stettinius, expressing concern at the impasse with the Soviets over Poland and their refusal to send Molotov to San Francisco. In mid-afternoon Ambassador Harriman sent in a cable reporting an interview he had just had with Stalin. The Russian leader had expressed a desire to work with Truman as he had with Roosevelt, and Harriman had immediately suggested that Stalin prove this by sending Molotov to Washington to confer with the President and then go on to the United Nations conference. Stalin, always cagey, said he would do so if he received a formal request from Truman. Without hesitation, the President told Stettinius to prepare such a cable, which was sent that evening. The next day Stalin, who was eager to get a first-hand report on the new American leader, announced that, at the personal request of Truman, Molotov would come to the United

States to confer with the President and then head the Soviet delegation to the San Francisco conference.

On April 16 Truman went to the Capitol to deliver his first major address as President to a joint session of Congress. When he entered the House chamber, the members gave him a standing ovation, and he looked proudly up to the galleries where his wife, Bess, and daughter, Margaret, were sitting. Sam Rayburn made the introduction, and then Truman, speaking in a flat, nasal voice that contrasted strikingly with Roosevelt's deep, rich tones, told how an hour after he became President he had decided that the San Francisco conference would proceed as scheduled. "We will face the problems of peace with the same courage that we have faced and mastered the problems of war," he declared. He went on to caution against distrust of the Soviet Union, saying that the continued unity of the Big Three was essential for the future peace of the world, but he did not overlook the other United Nations, saying, "The responsibility of the great states is to serve and not to dominate the world." He invoked the memory of Roosevelt, linking him with the thousands of soldiers and sailors who had given their lives in the war, and he closed by appealing "to every American, regardless of party, race, creed, or color, to support our efforts to build a strong and lasting United Nations organization." [3]

The next day Truman held his first conference with the American delegation. Earlier he had told Stettinius to consult with Vandenberg and Connally on all issues in order to assure eventual Senate approval. Now he told the delegates of his intense desire to avoid a repetition of the mistakes of 1919. "I emphasized," he recalled later, "that I wanted them to write a document that would pass the U.S. Senate and that would not arouse such opposition as confronted Woodrow Wilson."

Arthur Vandenberg remained the crucial figure. In March he had handed Stettinius eight amendments to the Dumbarton Oaks plan. Most were minor in nature, revealing Vandenberg's preoccupation with such abstract concepts as justice and peaceful change of the status quo, and did not touch on the vital issues of the veto, General Assembly membership and the use of force. His most significant suggestion was to broaden the authority of the Security Council so that whenever it found that "any situation which it shall investigate involved injustice to peoples concerned it shall recommend appropriate measures of adjustment which may include revision of treaties and of prior international decisions." Vandenberg showed this amendment to Warren Austin, who thought it proposed an "unwise" expansion of the authority of the

Security Council, writing that "the Republican party declared against a superstate." When Vandenberg persisted, the American delegation finally agreed to incorporate his idea in the section on the General Assembly, adopting a paragraph enlarging the power of investigation of that body, whose decisions were not binding.

The American delegation, which had been meeting continually in Washington since April 9, finally reached agreement on the position it would take on all disputed points at San Francisco. Stettinius passed on the recommendations to the President, and on April 21 Truman approved them in the form of written instructions to the delegation. The President concurred in the many minor changes in the Dumbarton Oaks plan that the delegates had suggested, and he agreed with their proposal, championed by Vandenberg, that the Charter include a declaration of human rights. On the controversial issue of General Assembly membership, Truman was blunt, stating, "I direct you to cast the vote of the United States in favor of the Ukrainian and White Russian Republics as initial members of the International Organization." [4]

As the delegates prepared to depart for San Francisco, Cordell Hull wrote Stettinius saying that he was too ill to go with them, though he hoped to join them at the end of the conference. Recalling the "grim memories" of hopes betrayed in 1919, of aggression and appeasement in the 1930's and of a second bloody world war, he said the conference would be "an acid test of whether mankind has suffered enough and has learned enough to have acquired the vision and the resolution to build a structure of organized international relations. . . ." He was hopeful, expressing his belief that it would be "one of the great turning points in history."

In the Senate chamber Connally and Vandenberg took leave of their colleagues. Brushing tears from his eyes, Connally announced that he was going to San Francisco neither as a Democrat nor as a Texan, but as a representative of all the American people. Vandenberg then said that they hoped to open "the golden gate upon a better, a happier, and a safer world." Vandenberg's son described the scene that followed: [5]

On both sides of the aisle men were getting to their feet, clapping their hands in violation of the Senate rules, and, after a moment, surging across the Chamber to shake hands, to put their arms around the shoulders of the two delegates and wish them well. America was going to San Francisco—to the second great international effort to establish lasting peace in the world—in a manner far removed from the lonely pilgrimage of Woodrow Wilson to Paris hardly a generation before.

I

The public-relations campaign on behalf of the Dumbarton Oaks proposals reached its climax in April. In the State Department, Archibald MacLeish, now assisted by Adlai Stevenson, used every conceivable means of influencing the American people. He distributed a film entitled *Watchtower over Tomorrow*, a very uncritical summary of the Dumbarton Oaks plan, to groups throughout the country; he continued the radio series "Building the Peace," announcing in early April that the broadcasts would be aired throughout the San Francisco conference; and he arranged for the publication of four pamphlets which were made available to churches, women's clubs and other civic groups without charge. In March, MacLeish ensured the active participation of every major government agency by having Jonathan Daniels telephone their chiefs to inform them that the President "is anxious to promote as much public understanding and disseminate as much information as possible about the proposed international organization in the weeks that remain before the San Francisco Conference." The message got through so well that by May, Senator Robert Taft was charging the administration with "superpropaganda . . . aimed directly at Congress." Letters to the State Department on international organization showed an amazing increase, jumping from a daily average of four hundred early in April to over five thousand by the end of the month. Radio stations cooperated so effectively that John T. Flynn claimed, "You cannot turn on the radio at any hour of the day—morning, noon, or night—whether you listen to the Metropolitan Opera or to a horse opera, a hill-billy band, a commentator or a newscaster, that you do not hear a plug for this great instrument of peace." [6]

In the course of this campaign the State Department developed a very close relationship with the many private organizations supporting international organization. When the American delegation was announced, these groups besieged the Department with requests to take part in the San Francisco conference. Typical of the pressure brought to bear were the letters sent out by David Andrew Simmons of Houston, president of the American Bar Association. On March 5 he wrote to Stettinius, asking to be made a member of the American delegation so that the

283

nation's lawyers would be represented. Leaving nothing to chance, Simmons also sent letters to Judge John T. Barker of Kansas City, whom he asked to plead his case with Truman, to Senator Tom Connally and to Assistant Secretary of State Will Clayton. The State Department, realizing that it could not honor all these requests, finally suggested that the American delegation choose a cross-section of organizations and ask them to send representatives to San Francisco to serve as "consultants."

The American delegates, particularly the Congressional members, shied away from this delicate task; instead, they recommended that all interested groups be encouraged to send "observers" to the conference. The State Department drafted an awkward press release to that effect and sent it to the White House for approval on March 25. The next day Jonathan Daniels returned it, saying the President preferred the original policy of inviting selected groups to send consultants, who would have a semi-official status. The American delegation reluctantly gave in, making it clear that they would take no part in the process of selection.

In early April, Stettinius and his aides worked on the list of more than a hundred organizations that wanted to be represented at San Francisco. They consulted with Clark Eichelberger and Malcolm Davis of the Carnegie Endowment, and finally on April 8 they agreed on the forty-two groups to be invited to send a representative and an alternate to serve as consultants to the American delegation. The list was a sweeping cross-section of American life, ranging from business and labor organizations through service and women's clubs to church, educational and peace societies. On April 9 Stettinius sent out telegrams to the favored groups, telling them that their representatives would be "consulted regularly" by the American delegates, and the next day he made the list of consultants public.[7]

In a final effort to publicize the San Francisco conference, the American Association for the United Nations and Americans United buried their differences and joined in sponsoring a Dumbarton Oaks Week from April 16 through April 22. Shortly before his death President Roosevelt issued a statement drafted by Eichelberger urging the American people to "observe this week by studying the Dumbarton Oaks proposals," and sixteen governors issued special proclamations in honor of the celebration. In March many New Hampshire town meetings voted on the question, "Do you favor United States participation in a world organization with automatic power to keep the peace?" The results were so overwhelmingly favorable, running nearly 20 to 1 in the affirmative, that Americans United decided to ask communities all across the land to hold "town meetings" during Dumbarton Oaks Week and vote on the same question as a way of expressing public confidence in the "town meeting of the world" that would open the following week in San Francisco. Such gatherings took place in cities throughout the country; the largest "town meeting" was held in Carnegie Hall in New York with stage, screen and radio personalities leading the discussion.

All kinds of civic groups cooperated in celebrating Dumbarton Oaks Week. The League of Women Voters and the YMCA distributed pamphlets and sent out sound trucks in New York City to stir up public interest. Merchants from Brooklyn to the Bronx covered their windows with posters and charts furnished by internationalist groups. In Detroit, Los Angeles and Milwaukee there were similar city-wide observances. The Federal Council of Churches asked all Protestant congregations to observe "United Nations Sunday" on April 22 by holding special services as a fitting climax to Dumbarton Oaks Week. On that Sunday, millions of men and women gathered in their churches to pray for the success of the San Francisco conference.[8]

Some churchmen still had doubts about the proposed international organization. On April 15 the National Catholic Welfare Conference called the Dumbarton Oaks plan "the draft of an alliance between great, victorious powers for the maintenance of peace and the promotion of international cooperation." Singling out the veto as the most objectionable feature, the Catholic bishops claimed that big powers could commit acts of aggression without fear of reprisal. *Christian Century* voiced similar criticisms and demanded that the San Francisco conference radically alter the Dumbarton Oaks proposals in framing the charter of the new world organization. On April 23 a group of distinguished Protestant clergymen, including such prominent theologians as Robert Calhoun of Yale Divinity School, Henry J. Cadbury of Harvard, and Bishop William Appleton Lawrence, released a declaration protesting the inequities in the Dumbarton Oaks plan. The existing proposals, they charged, "were a mere camouflage for the continuation of imperialistic policies and the exercise of arbitrary power by the Big Three for the domination of other nations."

Though few internationalists were as outspoken, many shared a feeling of uneasiness. The editors of *Time* feared that the charter written at San Francisco would not embody genuine collective security unless the delegates adopted amendments to define aggression, expand the role of the General Assembly and spell out fundamental human rights. Writing in the *Nation,* the political scientist Percy E. Corbett expressed a widespread desire that, instead of serving as a "gigantic rubber stamp," the San Francisco conference become a genuine congress that would produce "something infinitely better than . . . naked alliance of the great." The editors agreed, declaring, "The central tasks of San Francisco relate to the modification of the original Dumbarton Oaks charter to meet the larger requirement of justice and flexibility." [9]

A realistic outlook still predominated among the internationalists, however. Some, like Frederick Schuman, gloried in the implicit alliance between the Big Three, saying, "Peace for the next generation depends exclusively on Anglo-American-Soviet solidarity." Reinhold Niebuhr was more candid in admitting the risks in relying so heavily on the great powers, but he could see no alternative. "Nations cannot create a new universal sovereignty above themselves by a pure fiat of will," he warned, "and then turn around and subject themselves to this sovereignty." The editors of the *New Republic,* who ran a special supplement on "World Security" in late April, viewed San Francisco in a hopeful vein. The conference could not guarantee peace, they cautioned, but it offered "the possibility that out of this beginning a true, just and complete concert of the nations may ultimately grow." Any other course they prophesied, would lead to "a return to the international anarchy that existed prior to 1914."

Clark Eichelberger spoke for the handful of men and women who had labored so long for this moment. "Years of effort, of trial, of failure, and possibly of revolution, will be necessary before the several billion people inhabiting the earth can be united in a world government," he wrote. "But without the beginning at San Francisco, these years of successful effort will not be possible." Raymond Fosdick told the Women's Action Committee that internationalists faced "the most difficult, complex undertaking that mankind ever started," but he rejoiced at the opportunity. The most eloquent appeal came from Arthur Sweetser, a former League of Nations official and president of the Woodrow Wilson Foundation. In services dedicating the Foundation's new headquarters on April 17, 1945, he affirmed: [10]

God has given us a second chance, even those of us who were crushed last time. We owe it to the joint memory of Woodrow Wilson and Franklin Delano Roosevelt to take the solemn obligation never to relax till we fulfill the chance. Day in and day out, almost every hour of the day, we can each of us add our bit to

complete the work to which these two greatest of our countrymen
gave their lives.

II

At 4:30 on the afternoon of April 25 the United Nations Conference on
International Organization opened in San Francisco. A few hours earlier
an American patrol led by Lieutenant Albert Kotzebue had established
the first contact with Russian forces in Germany near the village of
Strehla on the banks of the Elbe. Kotzebue and his men accompanied
the Russians to their headquarters in a big farmhouse and soon they
were exchanging toasts to Roosevelt, Truman, Churchill and Stalin.
Though Hitler was still holding out in Berlin, refusing to sanction the
surrender proposals his subordinates urged on him, Germany was cut in
two and her final defeat imminent.

As the 282 delegates filed into the San Francisco Opera House for the
opening ceremony, they were unaware of this dramatic meeting, but
they did realize that the war in Europe was almost over. Their mood,
however, was grim; they still faced a stubborn enemy in the Pacific and,
beyond that task, the difficult and perplexing job of making a decent
peace. There were no bands, no gala ceremonies, and even the people
who crowded the street outside the Opera House were solemn and
quiet. The hall itself was tastefully and attractively decorated by Jo
Mielziner. On the stage there were four gold columns, symbolizing the
four freedoms, and the flags of the forty-six United Nations arranged in
a semicircle against a blue backdrop, all brilliantly lit by floodlights. The
opening speeches were brief and to the point. President Truman decided not to attend the opening session, but that evening he addressed
the delegates by radio from the White House. He welcomed them to the
United States and encouraged them in their momentous task. "We
must build a new world," he told them, "a far better world—one in
which the eternal dignity of man is respected." [11]

The first problem to arise at San Francisco came from the press. A
horde of reporters, nearly two thousand in all, descended on the city to
cover the conference for their papers, radio networks and magazines.
Some, like Eric Severeid, William Shirer, Walter Lippmann, James
Reston and Arthur Krock, were experienced journalists who had followed international affairs for many years. Others were gifted amateurs
like Sumner Welles, who was hired by a radio network to give a

fifteen-minute interpretive report on the conference each evening. But the glamour of the meeting also attracted hundreds of reporters from small-town papers who had no experience in dealing with diplomatic events and who were bewildered by the size and scope of their assignment. They flocked to the continual stream of press conferences in the hotel ballrooms, asked irrelevant and usually inane questions, and then filed stories which embodied the slanted releases handed out by the various national delegations. Even more irritating were the gossip columnists Hedda Hopper, Earl Wilson, Walter Winchell and Louella Parsons, who treated the conference like a Hollywood premiere, filling their stories with comments on the dress of the delegates, their more exotic manners and the intrigue that the columnists suspected was taking place behind closed doors. As a result, the American people received a distorted view of the conference; the reporters, confronted with little hard news and many rumors, blew up every minor difficulty into a major crisis and ignored the many constructive developments that characterized the day-by-day progress of the meeting. This over-reporting was accentuated by correspondents from such isolationist newspapers as the New York *Daily News* and the Chicago *Tribune*, who viewed every quarrel between the United States and Russia as proof of the inevitable failure of international cooperation.[12]

The United States, as host nation, supplied the clerks, translators and other staff members of the Secretariat that managed the conference. Alger Hiss, who had been serving as Deputy Director of the Office of Special Political Affairs, became the Secretary-General of the conference, in charge of the administrative and housekeeping chores. Of these, one of the most pressing was the allocation of hotel rooms. The American delegation took over the Fairmont Hotel, with Stettinius ensconced in a magnificent penthouse suite with a spectacular view of the city. The British were in the Mark Hopkins, across the street on Nob Hill, and the smaller nations spread out in less fashionable hotels across the city. The Russians, reluctant as usual to associate with foreigners, stayed on board a ship in San Francisco Bay.

The plenary sessions in the Opera House were purely ceremonial; the actual work of the conference went on in four commissions, each devoted to a section of the Dumbarton Oaks plan, and in twelve committees, which dealt with such specific subjects as the Security Council, peaceful settlement of disputes, and regional arrangements. Even these bodies were clumsy, since each nation had a representative on every committee, and many of the major decisions were reached in smaller, informal gatherings. A Steering Committee, composed of the chairmen of each delegation, and a more compact Executive Committee, consisting of fourteen members, directed the day-by-day course of the conference and served as a court of appeals for disputes that could not be ironed out in the commissions. The most powerful group, however, was an unofficial one. From the outset, the Big Four delegation leaders met every evening in Stettinius' penthouse to decide what changes they would permit in the Dumbarton Oaks structure, referring highly technical issues to a similar group of expert advisers in which Pasvolsky represented the United States. No decision was reached without their prior approval.

The American delegation quickly developed a rapport which lasted throughout the conference, though at times Vandenberg broke with his colleagues and opposed their otherwise unanimous decisions. The group met each morning at the Fairmont to discuss the day's agenda, and then the members scattered to attend their commission and committee meetings. Each day one or two of them met with the forty-two consultants from the private organizations in the Garden Room of the Fairmont, briefing them on the latest developments and occasionally asking their advice on particular problems. In the evening they would gather again at Stettinius' penthouse to compare notes and sit in on the Big Four deliberations. The House members, Bloom and Eaton, played very minor roles, and Virginia Gildersleeve spent most of her time dealing with social and economic issues which received little emphasis at San Francisco. Connally, Vandenberg and Stassen were America's most effective and influential delegates, taking a prominent part in commission meetings and advising Stettinius on all major decisions. Vandenberg displayed a very distrustful attitude toward the Soviets, and, with the backing of John Foster Dulles, he made sure that the United States made no unnecessary concessions to the many Russian demands. Stettinius proved to be a suprisingly able diplomat, negotiating smoothly and at times very stubbornly with Molotov and Anthony Eden, and using his charm and winning manner to preserve the fragile unity of the wartime allies.[13]

In the first week the United States and Russia clashed on three issues. The first was a minor point of great symbolic significance. Traditionally the head of the host nation's delegation serves as chairman of an international conference, but Molotov insisted that the leaders of the Big Four rotate as presiding officer. Backed by the entire American delegation, and with the support of nearly all the small nations, Stettinius fought against the Russian proposal in the Steering Committee. Eden suggested a compromise, with the chairmanship to rotate at the plenary meetings, but Stettinius to preside permanently over the all-important Steering and Executive committees. Molotov rejected it immediately, and Vandenberg was outraged by what he considered a British double-cross. On April 27, seeing that he was beaten, the Russian accepted Eden's formula, and though Vandenberg continued to grumble about "a victory for Molotov," the outcome was a fair compromise which saved Russia's face and yet retained American control over the course of the conference.

Molotov then challenged the United States again by demanding that the Lublin Polish government be invited to take part in the conference. Stettinius objected, pointing out that the Russians had not yet fulfilled their agreement at Yalta to reorganize the Lublin government by admitting democratic elements. Vandenberg, furious at Molotov's demand, warned Stettinius that concession on Poland would wreck "*any* chance of American approval of the work of the Conference," and he was greatly relieved when the British backed up Stettinius "magnificently." Realizing again that he lacked the votes, Molotov accepted a Belgian motion to defer the issue until the Polish government could be reorganized.

The strained relations between the two nations reached a peak on April 30. Following Truman's instructions, the American delegation planned to vote for the seating of White Russia and the Ukraine at the conference. But to ensure a majority for this proposal, the United States needed the cooperation of the twenty republics of Latin America, which were in a rebellious mood. At the inter-American conference in Mexico City in early March, Stettinius had promised to support the bid of Argentina, which belatedly joined the United Nations in March, for admission to the conference. Many of the countries at San Francisco opposed this, and the Latin American delegations informed the United States that they could not vote for the Soviet Republics without a guarantee that Argentina would receive favorable consideration. Accordingly, Stettinius asked the Executive Committee to approve the admission of Argentina as well as White Russia and the Ukraine on April 30. Molotov protested, pointing out that the Soviet Republics had fought "heroically" against Germany and that it was "incomprehensible" to admit Argentina and leave out Poland. The Executive Committee then voted unanimously to seat the Soviet Republics and split, 9 to 3, with 2 abstentions, in favor of Argentina. Later that day the Steering Committee concurred, and in the evening the matter came before the plenary session. When the recommendation to seat Argentina came up, Molotov rose to challenge it, making public for the first time the serious rift that had developed. With considerable logic, he asked that the question be deferred, pointing out that Argentina had refused to cooperate in the war against Germany until the last minute and condemning her government as "fascist." Though several of the smaller nations supported the Soviet move, Stettinius insisted on immediate action, and in the roll call that followed, Latin America led the way in securing Argentina's admission by a vote of 32 to 4, with 10 abstentions.[14]

"He has done more in four days," Vandenberg wrote of Molotov, "to solidify Pan America against Russia than anything that ever happened." But in defeat Molotov had also gained the sympathy of many small nations and even of some American journalists who shared his view of the Argentine government. "I saw Stettinius and Nelson Rockefeller marshal the twenty Latin American republics in one solid block," commented Walter Lippmann later, "and steamroller that through the United Nations." Many American internationalists felt that the United States had suffered a serious moral defeat, but actually this vote impressed the Russians with America's determination to use her voting majority if necessary to gain her objectives. From this time on, Molotov avoided public confrontations, and even in private he proved more gracious and willing to debate issues without rancor. Stettinius realized that he risked Russian withdrawal from the conference if he forced other issues to a vote, and so he was willing to seek agreement with the Soviets in behind-the-scenes negotiations. The showdown on Argentina thus cleared the air, leading the two dominant powers to disguise their differences and permit the conference to move on.[15]

III

The forty-two consultants grew restless as the delegates settled down to work; though they were briefed each morning, they had little opportunity to express their views. James Shotwell, representing the Carnegie Endowment, and Eichelberger, attending for the American Association for the United Nations, decided to organize the consultants. Since eighteen were members of the Commission to Study the Organization of Peace, Shotwell and Eichelberger had little difficulty in getting the group to form a core committee designed to place their views before the

American delegation. On May 2 Shotwell circulated a petition calling for the insertion of a declaration of human rights in the Charter and for the broadening of the Economic and Social Council to include a commission on human rights. That evening the consultants presented the document to Stettinius, who rather perfunctorily said he would pass it on to the other American delegates. But when Judge Joseph M. Proskauer of the American Jewish Committee reminded Stettinius that the consultants represented four million voters, the Secretary developed a sudden enthusiasm for the proposal.[16]

Later that same evening Molotov, Eden and T. V. Soong, the Chinese Foreign Minister, came to Stettinius' penthouse to begin considering amendments to the Dumbarton Oaks proposals that the Big Four would submit to the conference. For the next two days the four men conferred almost continually. Molotov was in a good mood, happy to show off his mastery of American slang by saying "O.K." frequently, though on occasion he reverted to form with a curt "No O.K." The foreign ministers approved the twenty-seven amendments, including the consultants' proposal on human rights, most of the suggestions Vandenberg had made to the American delegation, and several put forth by the smaller nations. None of these changes altered the fundamental nature of the proposed world organization, but all tended to make it more democratic and attractive. Stettinius released the text of the approved amendments to the press the evening of May 4, and the next morning he explained the changes in detail to the American consultants. Flashing his broad grin, he told them that they "could justly claim credit for getting a consideration of human rights into the Charter."

This Big Four agreement ended the first phase of the San Francisco conference. Much hard work remained, but the major decisions had been reached. Molotov departed from San Francisco on May 8, leaving Gromyko in charge of the Soviet delegation, which meant that all controversial matters had to be referred to Moscow for settlement. Eden left a few days later, putting Lord Halifax in command of the British group. Before he left, however, Germany surrendered unconditionally on May 8, and Eden was able to celebrate the long-awaited victory at a dinner with the Dominion Prime Ministers. Stettinius issued a public statement on V-E day saying that the German surrender created a new sense of urgency to those in San Francisco and encouraging the delegates to complete a Charter that would "make possible the development of an enduring peace in which wider freedom, justice, and opportunity for all men can be made secure." In a meeting of the consultants the next day, he predicted optimistically that the conference could finish up "in perhaps three weeks." [17]

Many Americans viewed the proceedings with pessimism. The liberal press regretted the hard line the American delegation was taking toward the Soviet Union. I. F. Stone claimed that the United States had organized an anti-Russian bloc at San Francisco, while Freda Kirchwey pleaded for a more understanding policy to preserve the unity of the Big Three. "Without it there is nothing," she wrote on May 5. "With it there is a hope and a machine." Two weeks later she admitted that the Russians were pursuing a unilateral policy as a hedge against the failure of world organization, but she thought the United States was equally guilty. "We, like Russia and Britain," she wrote, "will hold on to everything we think may augment our national security and will yield to the new League only such powers as will not interfere with basic measures of defense."

On May 3 Anthony Eden learned that sixteen Polish underground leaders loyal to the London regime who had gone to Moscow to negotiate had been arrested by the Russians and would be put on trial for aiding Germany. When Molotov confirmed this report, Eden and Stettinius bluntly denounced the Soviet government for betraying a promise to treat the sixteen Poles decently. "I have never seen Mr. Molotov look so uncomfortable," Eden reported afterward. For Vandenberg, this was "bad business" which confirmed his increasingly suspicious attitude toward the Soviets.[18]

Fear of postwar Communist expansion now led many to reconsider the wisdom of the great-power veto. Mitchell B. Carroll, an alternate consultant at San Francisco for the American Bar Association, left the conference in mid-May convinced that the Russians would use the veto to prevent any interference with their designs on eastern and central Europe. In a letter to David A. Simmons on May 16, he urged the American Bar Association to take a firm stand. "The new organization will never succeed," he wrote, "any more than did the League of Nations, if any of the big powers, and particularly Russia, has the power to veto action against itself. . . ." Senator Robert Taft had reached the same conclusion. Addressing a Polish-American rally in New York on May 20, he warned that the veto "makes almost impossible the establishment of international law." And in Washington, Acting Secretary of State Grew prepared a private memorandum on May 19; the veto, he wrote, will render the world organization being planned at San Francisco "powerless to act against the one certain future enemy,

Soviet Russia. In practice the main purpose of the organization will be annulled. . . . Its power to prevent a future world war will be but a pipe dream."

In San Francisco, Secretary Stettinius tried to combat this growing disillusionment. Speaking at the University of California in Berkeley on May 4, he stressed the "fundamental unity" of the Big Four. "It stands like a rock upon a shore resisting the waves which break upon it," he declared. "It is upon this strong and steady rock of unity that our work at San Francisco is firmly based." Two weeks later, in a radio report to the American people, Archibald MacLeish admitted that the deterioration of Soviet-American relations in Europe tended to overshadow "the new and shining structure in process of successful completion in San Francisco." He went on to deny that there was any fundamental conflict between the two nations and, paraphrasing Roosevelt's famous 1933 phrase, declared, "The basis of the fear is only fear itself."

Amid the doubts and the reassurances, a few observers perceived what was actually taking place. *Time* reported in mid-May that the conference was succeeding in its true objective—the creation of a system in which Russia and the West could live in peace. Only those who naively believed in genuine collective security would be disappointed, the editors continued. The split between the United States and Russia was real and deep, and the best that could be hoped for from San Francisco was "a charter for a world divided into power spheres" that would set peaceful limits to the rivalry. The *Nation* agreed, cautioning idealists not to "turn their backs on San Francisco and wander off into cynicism." Accepting big-power domination as foreordained, the editorial concluded, "The battle for effective world organization has not been lost; it is only beginning." [19]

IV

The conference made rapid progress through most of May, but toward the end of the month the commission dealing with the Security Council ran into trouble on the veto issue. The small nations, led by Australian Foreign Minister Herbert V. Evatt, resented the enormous power the permanent members of the Council would wield, and they realized that the Yalta voting formula was ambiguous. By its terms, the permanent members could clearly veto enforcement decisions but not procedural matters. But no one was sure what constituted procedural matters, and some delegates feared that this vague phrase would permit a great power to cast a veto to block discussion of disputes. To clear up the confusion and possibly gain some concessions from the permanent members, the small nations prepared a list of twenty-three questions about the voting formula which they asked the permanent members to answer.

On May 22, the day the questions were submitted, President Truman decided to call Stettinius to Washington for a conference. The Secretary flew back and reported the state of the negotiations to the President, pointing out that the Russians had indicated that they interpreted the Yalta formula as giving them a veto on whether the Council would take up a dispute or not. Truman instructed Stettinius to stand firmly for what the Americans believed they had secured at Yalta: Russian willingness to permit freedom of discussion on the Security Council, with only decisions to act being subject to the veto. Before returning to California, Stettinius held a press conference announcing that Truman would fly out to San Francisco to address the closing session, which Stettinius thought would be in early June. The Secretary was careful not to mention the veto issue to the press.[20]

Stettinius returned to find that the Russians refused to give in on their new interpretation of the veto. While the small nations waited for the answers to their questions, the big powers wrangled with one another in private. Gromyko finally referred the question to Moscow, and for five days the conference marked time while waiting for a decision from Stalin halfway around the world. On June 2 the answer came back: Russia demanded an absolute veto, even on the question of placing a dispute on the Security Council agenda. "When Gromyko made his report to us in the Pent-House," Vandenberg confided in his diary, "we all knew that we had reached the 'zero hour' of this great adventure."

Stettinius immediately telephoned President Truman, informed him of the impasse, and suggested that the Secretary ask Harry Hopkins, who was in Moscow in an effort to reach an agreement on Poland, to take up the veto directly with Stalin. Truman approved, and Stettinius drafted the cable, which was sent by way of Ambassador Harriman in Moscow. "We have reached a very serious crisis in the Conference in San Francisco," the Secretary began. He sketched out the dilemma, saying that he thought the Soviet position made a "farce" of the proposed world organization. He then asked Harriman and Hopkins to see Stalin and ask him to honor the Yalta agreement by abandoning the new Soviet interpretation of the voting formula. "Please tell him, in no uncertain words," Stettinius wrote, "that this country could not possibly join an organization based on so unreasonable an interpretation of the provision of the great powers in the Security Council."

On June 6 Hopkins brought up the veto issue during his last meeting with Stalin in the Kremlin. When he stated the American position, the Marshal seemed puzzled, and he turned to confer with Molotov, who explained the details to him. Stalin commented casually that he thought it was an insignificant matter and told Molotov that they should accept the American position. Stalin then turned back to Hopkins and Harriman and, after noting that "it was a mistake to believe that just because a nation was small it was necessarily innocent," said he agreed with the American position on the veto.[21]

Gromyko received his instructions on the morning of June 7, and he immediately informed the American delegation. "*America Wins!*" exclaimed Vandenberg. "The 'Veto' crisis broke today—and it broke *our* way." That afternoon the Big Five completed their answers to the small nations, stating that the veto applied only to the settlement of disputes and assuring them of a right to a hearing before the Security Council. But the Big Five refused to relinquish the power to veto recommendations for peaceful settlement of controversies, and the small nations were still unhappy. In Committee III/1, Australia put forward an amendment to the veto section, but Tom Connally opposed it. Refusing to mince his words, Connally told the other delegates that if they changed the veto provision, they would be tearing up the Charter, and as he spoke he "ripped the Charter draft in my hands to shreds and flung the scraps from the table." The Committee then rejected the Australian amendment by a vote of 20 to 10 with 15 abstentions, and at their next session the members approved the veto formula, though again 15 nations abstained to indicate their continued displeasure.[22]

Everyone now looked forward to the swift conclusion of the conference. President Truman, impatient at the delay, announced on June 15 that he would attend the closing ceremony now scheduled for the twenty-third. Reporters speculated that he wanted the Senate to ratify the Charter before the summer adjournment and thus before he left for a summit conference with Churchill and Stalin. "By sending President Truman to the coming Big Three meeting with ratification an accomplished fact," commented the *New Republic*, "we can do much to convince the people of the world that there is no doubt about our participating in a world organization."

But once again the Russians refused to cooperate. They suddenly objected to a sentence in the General Assembly section giving that body power to "discuss any matter within the sphere of International relations," and insisted on adding limiting language. After three days of hectic debate Gromyko finally accepted a phrase confining the Assembly to matters "within the scope of the present Charter." "Whoever holds out the *last* 15 minutes wins the battle," commented a triumphant Vandenberg, who had fought this battle for the American delegation. Truman had already left the capital for a visit to the state of Washington, and he was forced to spend several extra days in the Pacific Northwest waiting for the conference to wind up. On June 25 he flew into San Francisco, and the next day he closed the conference with his speech at the Opera House.[23]

The Charter drafted at San Francisco followed the basic outline agreed upon at Dumbarton Oaks, with the five big powers clearly dominant. The General Assembly was restricted to the discussion of problems; only the Security Council could take action. The members agreed to supply forces to the Security Council through separate agreements, and these troops would then be used, subject to big-power veto, in case of aggression. The most significant changes came in the Economic and Social Council, which was given greater authority and a wider role. The Charter included a draft statute for a new International Court of Justice which would succeed the existing World Court. A preamble, drafted by Jan Christian Smuts, "struck a muted millennial note," in the words of William H. McNeill, "which had been absent from the Dumbarton Oaks proposals." These and other "pious gestures" pleased the internationalists, but hardly altered the great-power alliance which remained the core of the new world organization. The delegates also included a highly ambiguous trusteeship section which looked forward to the eventual freedom and self-government of all colonial peoples but which did nothing to dismember the British or French empires, and which permitted the United States to retain the captured Japanese islands in the Pacific.

Most Americans accepted the document for what *Time* candidly said it was, "a charter written for a world of power, tempered by a little reason." Liberal journalists received it with "restrained optimism," likening it to a pontoon bridge thrown across a river "so that the armed forces can make some headway and set about building a more enduring structure." But for those who had labored so long and hard, it was much more. Cordell Hull called the Charter "one of the great milestones in man's upward climb toward a truly civilized existence," and Hamilton

11. *San Francisco*

Holt told friends that he had seen "my life's dream come true" at San Francisco. "It opens the door to the promised land," wrote Clark Eichelberger. "Whether or not man wishes to enter the door and turn his back on a third world war depends not upon the Charter but upon the people." [24]

12

Vindication

T HE DAY AFTER the San Francisco conference ended, Secretary-
General Alger Hiss placed the American copies of the Charter
inside a seventy-five-pound safe and boarded an army transport
plane for the flight back to the capital. Hiss took no chances on losing
his precious cargo. A separate parachute was attached to the safe, which
bore the legend: "Finder! Do Not Open. Send to the Department of
State, Washington."

In Congress, equally elaborate preparations were under way to ensure
favorable action on the Charter. Tom Connally had kept members of
the Foreign Relations Committee informed of the developments at San
Francisco, sending them copies of speeches and reports and welcoming
their advice on all problems. An Associated Press poll taken near the
end of the conference indicated that of seventy-five senators contacted,
fifty-seven favored the Charter, and none flatly opposed it. Many former
isolationists, including Burton Wheeler, Pappy O'Daniel of Texas, Pat
McCarran of Nevada and Wayland Brooks of Illinois, indicated their
intention of voting for ratification. On June 23 Charles Ross, the
President's press secretary, told reporters that Truman had spoken to
"virtually every Senator" about the Charter, and that the White House
expected no more than twelve men to vote against it.

On his way back from California the President announced that James
Byrnes would replace Stettinius as Secretary of State. Lauding Stettinius
for his performance at San Francisco, Truman announced that the former Secretary would be in charge of the administration's effort to win
ratification of the Charter and that he would serve as the American
delegate to the new world body. Stopping off in Kansas City to receive
an honorary LL.D., Truman asked Congress to act swiftly so that the
United States could be the first nation to approve the Charter. "I am

anxious to bring home to you that the world is one world, just as Wendell Willkie said," Truman declared. "It is a responsibility that this great republic ought to lead the way in—to carry out those ideas of Woodrow Wilson and Franklin D. Roosevelt." [1]

Tom Connally and Arthur Vandenberg flew back in Stettinius' plane, and when they arrived at National Airport in Washington on June 28, a large crowd, complete with a brass band was on hand to greet them. That afternoon the two entered the Senate chamber arm-in-arm to a standing ovation by their colleagues. In a press conference a few minutes before, Connally had told reporters that he would press for prompt action. Denying that he planned "to railroad the thing or jam it down anybody's throat," Connally explained, "I don't want the Senate dilly-dallying and honey-swoggling all through July and August just for the sake of making speeches to the people back home." When he reached the Senate rostrum to report on the San Francisco conference, he spoke with more restraint. He praised Vandenberg and the other Republican members of the American delegation for their contributions. He described the Charter as a carefully drawn document that provided a system of collective security without creating a "superstate." He admitted that it was far from a perfect instrument, but he pleaded with his colleagues to accept it as "a significant beginning." "The eyes of the entire world are centered on what we do here," he told them. "The world charter of peace is knocking at the doors of the Senate. We shall not turn it away." The people in the crowded galleries then rose to their feet as wave after wave of applause swept through the chamber.

The next day an even larger audience filled the galleries to hear Arthur Vandenberg give his views on the Charter. To the delight of Lord Halifax, who sat conspicuously in the front row of the diplomatic section, Vandenberg described the Charter as "a great, forward step" toward international understanding. Like Connally, he called it only a beginning—"an acorn, not an oak,"—but he prophesied that the "roots of peace" planted at San Francisco would eventually lead to a new age of tranquillity. He defended the veto, denying that it was a concession to Russia and pointing out how it preserved national sovereignty and prevented alien dictation of America's destiny. He concluded by affirming again the "promise" and the "hope" embodied in the Charter, saying, "It deserves a faithful trial." The senators responded with an ovation that matched the one they had given Connally.[2]

The next day Alben Barkley, the majority leader, announced that President Truman would deliver the Charter to the Senate and make a brief speech on Monday, July 2. Barkley then squelched rumors that ratification would be postponed until after the summer recess; the Senate, he declared, would stay in session until it acted on the Charter, even if that meant meeting all summer. He then said the Foreign Relations Committee would hold hearings on this issue beginning on July 9, and when they were over, he would move immediately for ratification of the Charter.

Over the weekend the President worked on his speech. Recalling Wilson's elaborate presentation to the Senate in 1919, he decided to be brief and informal. Aiming his remarks directly at the Senate, he insisted that there be no fanfare, no photographers, not even any radio microphones to carry his words to the nation. Shortly after one o'clock he entered the Senate chamber with a bulky manilla envelope under his arm. It was the first time he had been back since Roosevelt's death, and it was only the sixth time a President had appeared in person before the Senate. He handed the Charter, bound in blue with a great gold seal, to the presiding officer. "The choice before the Senate is now clear," he said. "The choice is not between this Charter and something else. It is between this Charter and no charter at all." Then in simple, direct language he asked the senators to approve the document and take the only road to peace. "Let us not hesitate to join hands with the peace-loving peoples of the earth and start down that road—with firm resolve that we can and will reach our goal." [3]

I

Internationalist organizations went all-out in an effort to secure prompt ratification. The consultants at San Francisco began planning the final public campaign in May, and by the first of June most of them had returned to their homes to concentrate on publicizing the Charter. On June 13 Clark Eichelberger spoke to the coordinating committee in charge of the educational drive, which had been meeting bi-weekly since October at the Woodrow Wilson Library. Representatives of more than a hundred organizations attended, and at the close they voted unanimously to continue cooperating until the Charter was approved. After the meeting Ulric Bell and Eichelberger sent letters to every member of the Senate urging them to act swiftly. The United States should be the first nation to join the world organization, wrote Bell; Eichelberger warned that a delay until fall "could not help but be discouraging to the world as well as to the American people."

On June 23 the American Association for the United Nations sponsored an all-day conference at the Hotel Commodore in New York at which State Department officers explained the Charter in great detail. In an attempt to reach all Americans, the AAUN joined with *True Comics* in preparing a special eight-page cartoon strip depicting examples of international cooperation from the Stone Age down to San Francisco. The final panels showed how the new world organization would function, and they featured captions taken from speeches by Presidents Roosevelt and Truman. The AAUN linked patriotism with the search for peace by asking its members to dedicate the Fourth of July to discussions of the Charter in their communities. This year, declared Eichelberger, the American people should observe Independence Day by celebrating "the birth of an orderly and peaceful world system." [4]

In *Changing World* and in specially prepared pamphlets, the AAUN leaders gave thorough and highly laudatory analyses of the Charter. They pointed up the many changes made in the Dumbarton Oaks proposals, and they contrasted the Charter with the League Covenant, affirming their belief that the United Nations would possess the power to stop aggression that the League lacked. They were careful not to oversell the Charter. "The organization will not automatically confer . . . benefits upon mankind," wrote Clark Eichelberger. "Rather it is an instrument to be used by courageous statesmen and an alert public opinion." Most of all, they stressed the importance of quick Senate ratification. Rejection of the United Nations, warned Livingston Hartley in a pamphlet entitled *It's Up to the Senate*, would imperil American security by creating "exactly the type of world system most dangerous to our future, an eventual world balance of power between two great regional blocs." Such a return to power politics, he concluded, could only mean a third world war. "Those of us who have served overseas feel that we have the right to ask that those at home do not fail again—that instead, they follow through and ensure the future of our country for which we fought this war."

Though Americans United joined with the AAUN in the drive for ratification, Ulric Bell was much less enthusiastic about the Charter. He agreed that it would be "disastrous" to reject it, but he warned that it would also be disastrous to be complacent about its many defects. The Charter marked a great step forward from Dumbarton Oaks, he commented, but it was still "a pact between sovereign states" designed "to obtain security from war by concentrating power in the hands of a few great powers." He urged members of Americans United to support it solely as a transitional body while they continued the quest for "a true world government before which all men are equal." [5]

The churches rallied strongly behind the Charter. John Foster Dulles left San Francisco before the signing to report favorably on the document to the Federal Council of Churches. He told his fellow churchmen that the conference had transformed the big-power alliance framed at Dumbarton Oaks into a world organization "which would promote justice and human welfare." Calling it "a Magna Carta for the world," he declared, "I can see no reasonable ground for Christian people now to hesitate in their support of the San Francisco charter." In a statement to the Commission on a Just and Durable Peace he praised it as "a great document of human rights" and said it was "the first duty of our Christian people . . . to assure that the organization will come into being." In a letter to Philip Marshall Brown he was more realistic, admitting the imperfections of the Charter, but still upholding it as "an inspiring document that starts off with a good spirit behind it" and one that "will afford mankind an opportunity if it really wants one." Dulles' enthusiasm was infectious. The Church Peace Union asked all denominations to observe "World Charter Day" on Sunday, July 1, and the Federal Council announced in late June that if the Senate procrastinated, it planned to have the Charter read from the pulpit of every Protestant church in the country.[6]

Republicans followed Vandenberg's lead in declaring for the Charter. In a radio address made just before he returned to active duty in the Pacific, Harold Stassen told a nationwide audience that, despite a few flaws, the United Nations promised to usher in a new reign of peace. Herbert Hoover had more doubts, lamenting the veto and the failure to fulfill all the ideals of the Atlantic Charter, but he did declare for ratification in a nationwide radio speech in mid-July. The party's leader, Thomas Dewey, was much less equivocal, calling for swift Senate action without any reservations. "There is a clear mandate from the American people for ratification of the Charter," he announced.

The policy of inviting private organizations to send consultants to San Francisco now paid rich dividends as group after group passed resolutions supporting the Charter. No major American association opposed it, and those that approved represented virtually every segment of American society. The AFL and the CIO joined with the United States Chamber of Commerce and the NAM in backing the Charter, as did the American Legion and the General Federation of Women's Clubs, the American Bar Association and the National Maritime Union, the National Congress of Parents and Teachers and Hadassah. Only the patriotic societies were missing from the ranks of the supporters.[7]

Public-opinion polls revealed that the American people were not quite as convinced as their leaders. Surveys taken in July showed that though three out of four Americans wanted the United States to enter the United Nations, nearly 20 percent had no opinion on this issue, and in one poll 12 percent said they had not even heard about the Charter. Those who were informed displayed a strong skepticism. Asked what chance they thought the new organization had of preventing future wars, 39 percent replied good, 44 percent said fair, and 17 percent expressed no opinion. A Gallup survey taken in late July indicated that only two out of five thought that the United Nations could preserve the peace. An equal number thought that war would occur again, while 22 percent expressed no opinion.

The growing tension with the Soviet Union over Poland, the many crises that had developed at San Francisco and the obvious big-power domination of the new organization had led to a more realistic evaluation of the United Nations than had prevailed in the earlier years of the war. Freda Kirchwey perceived the trend of public sentiment. Calling the new world organization "an instrument for holding together a coalition absolutely essential to the maintenance of peace," she urged the American people to accept it as "a plan to give frontier justice to a world just emerging from lawlessness." The New York *Times* took a more optimistic view. "We have the right to hope, as we must fervently pray," wrote the editors on the eve of the debate over ratification, "that the noble project launched in the Presidency of Woodrow Wilson, carried forward by Franklin D. Roosevelt, will win toward success under President Truman." [8]

II

On Monday morning, July 9, Chairman Tom Connally opened the Foreign Relations Committee's hearing on the Charter in the caucus room of the Senate office building. Connally had invited the entire Senate membership to attend so that they could be fully informed before the debate began on the floor, and many accepted his invitation and even participated by asking questions of the witnesses. Those who did not come found transcripts of the previous day's proceedings on their desks each morning. Newsmen and interested spectators filled the room, but the hearings proved very sedate. Reporters noted that Hiram Johnson, the last of the irreconcilables of 1919, sat at the table smoking a long black cigar in an even longer holder, but he did not produce the probing questions and tart comments they expected. Instead, he sat silently, making only an infrequent remark. Senator Eugene D. Millikin, a Colorado Republican, proved to be the most effective interrogator, and though he was not a member of the committee, he provided the few moments of tension when he challenged administration witnesses on specific points in the Charter.

For the first two days State Department officers appeared before the committee to explain the many detailed provisions of the Charter. Stettinius led off, spending much of his time defending the veto. "The Charter does not confer any power upon the great nations which they do not already possess in fact," he declared, and said that no one need fear the domination of the five permanent members of the Security Council since "their common interest in preventing another war is fully as urgent as that of any other nation." He also pointed out that the veto was essential to protect American sovereignty. Then, as did so many of the witnesses, he admitted that the Charter was not a perfect document, but he hastened to add that it offered the world "a truly effective instrument for lasting peace."

Leo Pasvolsky followed Stettinius to the witness chair, and for the next day and a half he went through the Charter article by article, explaining how the new world organization would function and clarifying many of its details. On Tuesday morning, when he came to the section on the Security Council, Senator Millikin interrupted to ask if the United States would violate the Charter if it reserved the right to decide in each case of aggression whether to furnish troops for collective security. Pasvolsky replied that the troops would be supplied under separate agreements between the member nations and the Security Council, and that the United States could always prevent collective military action by casting a veto. When Millikin pressed the point, raising the issue of Congressional approval on each occasion before American troops could be used, Connally and Vandenberg intervened to state that such a Congressional veto would violate the spirit of the Charter. Millikin countered by charging that then the Charter would violate the Constitution by depriving Congress of the right to declare war. Vandenberg replied, "But very clearly for 150 years the President has had the right to use our armed forces in a preliminary way for the national defense and in the interest of preventing war. That is a complete analogy to the intended use of preliminary force by the Security Council."

Millikin did not challenge this position, but later in the hearings he asked John Foster Dulles, who testified for the administration, if the Senate would have a chance to spell out the terms under which American troops would be supplied to the Security Council. Dulles, pointing out that the Charter stated that the special agreements providing the Security Council with troops must be approved by the "constitutional processes" of the member nations, replied that the President could not use the technique of an executive agreement. "It is clearly my view," Dulles added, "and it was the view of the entire United States delegation, that the agreement which will provide for the United States military contingent will have to be negotiated and then submitted to the Senate for ratification in the same way as a treaty." Dulles turned to Connally, who confirmed this statement. Millikin, satisfied that the Senate could pass on the question of a Congressional veto at a later date, then indicated that he would vote for approval of the Charter.[9]

The hearings came to life on the third day, when Connally announced that he would give anyone who wished to speak ten minutes to air his views. A parade of middle-aged women came forth to condemn the Charter as atheistic, Communist-inspired and un-American. One of these self-appointed patriots, Mrs. Agnes Waters of the National Blue Star Mothers of America, accused Eichelberger and Shotwell of being members of the Communist party, charged that the authors of the Charter planned to "make of this Nation a feeding trough for the 'have nots' of the world," and called the Second World War a "red plot" to take over the world. When she refused to stop after ten minutes, Connally finally had to have two policemen forcibly remove her. As she was dragged out, she screamed, "The real war criminals are right here in this room!"

Other nationalistic witnesses were almost as abusive. Most echoed Mrs. Waters' claims of a Communist conspiracy, but some directed their venom against the British and the Jews, seeing in the United Nations a "British-Israel World Federation movement." One midwestern woman attacked the committee for expressing too much concern for "the oppressed minority of Europe" and promised that the returning servicemen would "restore to its pristine freshness the temple of our American Republic." One of the few male isolationists to appear was Carl H. Mote, president of the Northern Indiana Telephone Company and a leader of Gerald L. K. Smith's American First party. He attacked Britain and Russia impartially, citing their wartime occupation of Iran and labeling them "the two most warlike nations in the world." The audience in the caucus room frequently broke into laughter at the wilder charges of these witnesses, and nothing infuriated them more. ". . . this country is in very bad case indeed," declared Mrs. L. Benge of Cincinnati, "when there is frivolity and laughter at the efforts of a group of middle-aged women who are trying to save what is left of their own country."

At the other extreme, a smaller group of witnesses came forward to attack the Charter as too timid and cautious a step toward world federation. David Darrin, who said he represented the United Nations of Earth Association, claimed that the proposed international organization would serve as an impediment to genuine world government and then went on to attack the Charter as "utterly Godless" because there had been no prayer at the opening of the San Francisco conference. When a senator interrupted him to ask how many people were in his association, he replied that he was the only member. Senator Barkley broke the silence that followed by commenting that, as far as he knew, there was no law against a man associating with himself.

Other advocates of world government argued more lucidly that the Charter established a "phoney internationalism" characterized by "world control of the Big Five." "The supreme danger in this Charter lies in the fact that once it is accepted," declared Mrs. Ruth Ann Baesler of Illinois, "no real plan for world federation, for instance a United States of the World, will be seriously introduced in our lifetime or perhaps ever." The head of the WCTU, who told the committee that her group opposed war as an evil comparable to alcohol, declared, "We must respectfully persist in believing that the future is for those who dare place what is right before what is expedient." Ely Culbertson told the committee that the United Nations perpetuated the fundamental flaw of the League, excessive reliance on national security, and he pleaded for consideration of his quota-force proposal as a way to prevent aggression by the large nations. "The Charter," he warned, "is a system of collective security which is neither collective nor secure." [10]

The views of the isolationists and the world federationists tended to cancel each other out. Charges that the United Nations was a dangerous superstate lost their impact when contrasted with accusations that the veto rendered the organization impotent. The advocates of the Charter, anxious to speed up the proceedings, limited themselves to very brief appearances. Spokesmen for churches, labor unions, farmers, educators and internationalist organizations stressed the theme that, while the Charter contained flaws it was "a step in the right direction." Representatives of Americans United called it a realistic document which would permit the American people to substitute "imperfect collaboration" for "perfect chaos." Only one witness, a Philadelphia judge, went all out, describing the Charter as "a marvelous document, notable for its directness, simplicity, and completeness." Many paused to pay homage to Woodrow Wilson, and none more passionately than former Senator Robert L. Owen of Oklahoma, who affirmed:

> That great man—a saint on earth, a martyr—who urged this country to establish the League of Nations did not succeed in having the United States enter the League. The world was not then ready for it. The world is ready for it now. The world has had another blood bath.

The most impressive testimony came from three pre-war isolationists. The first, Frederick H. Libby, Executive Secretary of the National Council for Prevention of War and a lifelong pacifist, criticized the Charter for relying on the use of force to preserve the peace. Libby praised many features of the United Nations, however, especially the Economic and Social Council and the General Assembly, and he indicated his willingness to support the Charter as an experiment for peace. Norman Thomas expressed many doubts, condemning the reliance on "the false and dangerous myth of absolute national sovereignty" and warning that the Charter failed to deal with the only real threat to world peace, the possibility of war between the United States and Russia. He suggested a number of reservations the Senate should enact, including a Congressional veto on the use of force, but he reluctantly advocated ratification, saying, "I agree with Senator Vandenberg that the world is even more at the mercy of the Big Three 'without the San Francisco Charter than with it.'" John T. Flynn, journalist, economist and professional Roosevelt-hater, gave the most savage indictment of the Charter. With considerable logic, he pointed out that the United Nations rested on the assumption that Germany and Japan were evil nations, and that peace could be maintained by keeping them in check. Nonsense, Flynn asserted, arguing that "you do not deal with the cause of war when you eliminate two aggressors and establish others of these aggressors in control of the world." Of the Big Four, only the United States had not committed acts of aggression, he maintained. "You have brought into existence a military alliance between four great powers, three of them great aggressors," he told the committee, "and around that central core of the military alliance you have placed a halo of small nations without any power to do anything, selling it to the world as a great organization for peace." Flynn concluded by urging the Senate to reject this structure of hypocrisy.

Flynn's comments hit home, and in an effort to counter them, the committee asked John Foster Dulles to give the concluding testimony. Dulles argued that the Charter protected American freedom of action through the veto, yet provided a way to halt aggression. He urged the senators not to insist on Congressional control over the use of force, pointing out that Stettinius, a man everyone could trust, would cast the American vote on the Security Council. Above all, he denied Flynn's charge that the Charter created a league of aggressors. Even the United States, Dulles confessed, had committed acts of aggression in the past. "Who, then, is to collaborate, and with whom are we to collaborate, and who is to collaborate with us, if no one is to collaborate with an aggressor?" he asked. "A collaboration which is limited to no collaboration between nations that have been aggressors is another way of saying that we must forever stand in isolation ourselves." [11]

It was shortly after four on Friday afternoon when Dulles completed his testimony. Connally quickly cleared the caucus room, and the committee went into executive session. Less than half an hour later Connally emerged to announce that all twenty senators present had voted to report the Charter favorably. Hiram Johnson did not attend this final meeting, but the next morning, while he was being shaved in the Senate barber shop, he called for Robert Shirley, the clerk of the committee. When Shirley entered, Johnson asked the barber to remove the towel from his face, sat up and told the clerk to record him as voting against the United Nations Charter. Then Johnson sat back in the chair and told the barber to continue shaving him. Later in the day Senator James E. Murray of Montana sent in his affirmative vote to make the final tally 21 to 1 in favor of ratification.

The Foreign Relations Committee's formal report, made public the next week, consisted of a strong plea for approval of the Charter without any amendments or reservations. The committee took special note of the demand for a Congressional veto raised by Senator Millikin, warning that such a proposal endangered the whole process of collective security, which rested on the swift and nearly automatic invoking of force to halt aggression. Any reservation adopted by the Senate to this effect, the committee declared, "would clearly violate the spirit of one of the most important provisions of the Charter." The report went on to note the many safeguards for American sovereignty—the veto in the Security Council; Article 51 permitting individual and collective acts of self-defense, thus preserving the Monroe Doctrine; and the clause exempting such domestic matters as the tariff and immigration restriction from international control. The committee concluded with the familiar refrain that, while the Charter was not a "perfect instrument," it was a "good beginning" in the search for world peace.

Internationalists breathed a great sigh of relief. In 1919 a hostile Foreign Relations Committee had laden down the Covenant of the League of Nations with reservations that led directly to its defeat on the Senate floor. The expeditious way Connally conducted the hearings, the far-out character of the opposition and the warm endorsement by the committee were all immensely encouraging to the men and women who could never forget the previous disaster. Now they could look forward with greater confidence to the final Senate debate. "It has taken twenty-five years and a second world war," commented the *Nation*, "but out of time and trial the nation has learned some world geography and a little political wisdom in the bargain." [12]

III

On Monday, July 23, Tom Connally rose in the Senate to begin the debate on ratification of the Charter. In a long, rambling speech he reminded his colleagues of the bi-partisan policy the administration had pursued on international organization and pointed up the overwhelming national support by citing public-opinion polls and reading a list of the organizations endorsing the United Nations. He made the usual reservations about the perfection of the Charter, but as he warmed to his subject, he described it "as the greatest document of its kind that has ever been formulated." Then he appealed to the senators to reassure a skeptical world by ratifying the Charter by such an overwhelming majority that it would erase the lingering memory of 1919. Other nations, he declared, "know how the League of Nations was slaughtered here on the floor. Can you not still see the blood on the floor? Can you not see upon the walls the marks of the conflict that raged right here in the Chamber where the League of Nations was done to death?" With a quiver in his voice, he closed by paraphrasing Emerson's "Concord Bridge," asking his colleagues to fire a shot for peace "that will be heard round the world."

Arthur Vandenberg followed him to the rostrum in a deliberate effort to underscore the bi-partisan backing for the Charter. The Republican leader carefully delineated the limits of the proposed world body, denying emphatically that it would become a superstate. "The United States retains every basic attribute of its sovereignty," Vandenberg affirmed, pointing out that the Charter "gives us a veto on war and on any steps leading to war." More significantly, Vandenberg argued that the United Nations would give America a security which two world wars proved it could not achieve on its own. The progress of science and technology, he warned, made a third world war too horrible to contemplate. "It clearly threatens the end of civilization," he prophesied. "Here is our chance to stop this disaster before it starts." [13]

For the next six days, fifty-six senators elaborated on the themes set forth by Connally and Vandenberg. The Democrats were drawn irresistibly back to the past, reliving again and again the moment of tragedy when the Senate killed the League. Brian McMahon of Connecticut remarked on how rare it was for a man "to be given a second chance in his lifetime to correct a great mistake. It is even more seldom that that chance comes to a nation." Others invoked the memory of Woodrow Wilson. Senator Andrews of Florida told the Senate of the inspiration he had received from a recent visit to Wilson's grave, and then read a passage from the former President's speech at Pueblo, Colorado, in 1919, when he had warned that rejection of the League would lead "with absolute certainty" to another world war within a generation. "After the First World War we failed to keep the pledge and the faith," Andrews declared. "God help us to keep it now." Claude Pepper was even more dramatic:

> I am sure that there is not one of us who does not have in his heart the feeling that in a gallery beyond this, through a veil which their immortal eyes can always penetrate, there are two other spectators of this scene. . . . Senators know who they are. One of them is Woodrow Wilson, and the other is Franklin D. Roosevelt.

Republican senators preferred to look to the future, repeating Vandenberg's warning that another world war would be disastrous. "In the normal developments of science," predicted Robert Taft, "a third world war might well bring about the complete destruction of modern civilization." Senators Ball and Burton both voiced similar fears about the fate of mankind, and several thoughtful Democrats concurred. "The V-bomb, the rocket plane, all the engines of destruction now being developed by science," declared Lister Hill of Alabama, "are too deadly to be used in organized warfare if civilization is to survive." [14]

As the flow of oratory continued day after day, the crowds in the galleries began to thin out and the presiding officer had to make frequent quorum calls to round up an audience on the Senate floor. The obvious majority in favor of ratification robbed the debate of any suspense, but the senators, aware of the historic nature of the event, insisted on putting their views on the record. Glenn Taylor, the singing cowboy from Idaho who would later be Henry Wallace's runningmate on the Progressive ticket, was more honest than most. Admitting that originally he had not planned to speak, he confessed, "In view of the fact that I am now talking to my future grandchildren and to the historians of the future, I feel more or less as though I were a voice from the grave."

Many of the speeches were filled with clichés as senators found it difficult to add anything significant to the discussion. Alexander Wiley of Wisconsin referred to the United Nations as "a great new adventure" and "a highway to peace," called the approaching vote "the hour of decision" and "a time for greatness," and warned his fellow countrymen to keep their powder dry! Denis Chavez could not resist commenting that "an ounce of prevention is still worth the proverbial pound of cure," and no less than eight senators praised the Charter as "a noble beginning." Senator Fulbright became suspicious of the endless string of platitudes that his colleagues were pouring forth in praise of the United Nations, noting that such "docility" was hardly characteristic of the Senate. He lamented the stress on the veto and national sovereignty, and reminded them that they were engaged in assuming awesome obligations and responsibilities for the future. Unless the senators were prepared to join "in the progressive building of the United Nations Organization into an effective system of law and order," their speeches and trite phrases were meaningless.

Burton Wheeler brought the Senate to life with a blistering three-hour speech in which he charged that the United Nations was likely to "legalize tyranny." Attacking both Britain and Russia, he declared that Roosevelt had been duped at Teheran and Yalta by smooth practitioners of power politics just as Wilson had been betrayed at Versailles. The Atlantic Charter had gone the way of the Fourteen Points, and instead of peace, the world was faced with "the ever-intensifying and expanding conflict between British and Russian interests." Then, to the amazement of his listeners, he announced that he would cast his vote for the Charter because "I do not see any alternative."

Only two men, William Langer of North Dakota and Henrik Shipstead of Minnesota, indicated that they would vote against ratification. Both were lifelong isolationists, and both expressed their sincere belief that international organization could never keep the peace. "I feel from the bottom of my heart that the adoption of the Charter . . . will mean perpetuating war," affirmed Langer. Shipstead decried the reliance on the use of force to keep the peace, saying, "Perpetual intervention means perpetual war." "We in the New World," he continued, "cannot and will not every 20 years redress the balance of the Old by sending our sons to war." [15]

The most heated controversy developed when supporters of the Charter differed on the method for approving the special agreement that the United States would negotiate with the Security Council to provide troops for collective action against aggression. Democratic senators, led by Scott Lucas of Illinois, preferred a joint resolution that required passage by both Houses, since the use of armed force related so closely to the Congressional power to declare war. Robert Taft and many other Republicans cited Dulles' testimony at the hearings and contended that such an agreement was a treaty which had to be ratified by a two-thirds majority of the Senate. The ensuing debate was highly technical and essentially sterile, since both sides were agreed on the major point: that the President should secure Congressional approval and not employ an executive agreement for such a major commitment. Vandenberg helped clarify the issue, informing the Senate of a telephone conversation in which Dulles said he preferred the treaty method but agreed that a joint resolution was perfectly acceptable. President Truman cleared up any lingering doubts when he sent a message from Potsdam, where he was conferring with Stalin and Churchill, saying that he intended "to ask Congress by appropriate legislation" to approve the special agreement with the Security Council. Senators interpreted this to mean a joint resolution, and the Republicans dropped their objection.[16]

On Saturday, July 28, Majority Leader Alben Barkley called the Senate into session at ten in the morning in an effort to wind up the debate. Twenty senators went to the rostrum before the roll was finally called. All but Langer and Shipstead answered "aye," and thus the Charter passed by a vote of 89 to 2. Of the five absent senators, only Hiram Johnson, who now lay fatally ill in Bethesda Naval Hospital, opposed ratification. Though the gallery was full, there were no cheers or applause; instead, the spectators filed quietly out of the chamber. Among them was Breckinridge Long, who went home to write in his diary, "The faith of Woodrow Wilson has been vindicated. The record of the United States of 1920 has been expunged. Civilization has a better chance to survive. . . ."

In Potsdam, President Truman had asked to be informed as soon as the Senate acted so that he could tell Stalin and Clement Attlee, who had replaced Churchill as Prime Minister. Just before the President went to bed, the flash came through, and he immediately released a statement to the press, declaring, "The action of the Senate substantially advances the cause of world peace."

Irving Fisher, the Yale economist and fighter for the League of Nations, anticipated the final victory. In a letter to Hamilton Holt early in July he wrote that he "almost shouted and cried with joy" at the prospect of Senate ratification. "If Lodge doesn't turn over in his grave," he continued, "I would be willing with you and other competent grave diggers to help him or even hang him up [by] his heels like Mussolini." [17]

Two days after the vote President Truman cabled Clark Eichelberger, thanking him for his work in securing the Charter and asking for his continuing help in the tasks that lay ahead. "We must all hope that the people of this country and the peoples of the rest of the United Nations will inform themselves of the possibilities which the Charter opens to them." More than anyone else, those who had labored so long for the United Nations knew that it was not a panacea that would automatically lead to a better world. "We threw away our first chance, and the cost has been very great," wrote Livingston Hartley. "Now we have a second under much more difficult conditions. Because it will be a continuous task for decades rather than for years, it represents an even greater challenge than this war to the American people."

Hartley did not realize how prophetic his words were. Nine days after the Senate ratified the Charter, the United States dropped the first atomic bomb over Hiroshima. Throughout the war the American people had looked forward to the creation of an international organization as the dominant feature of the postwar world. Their vision of the future centered in the fulfillment of Wilson's dream. Suddenly they discovered that scientists working secretly in laboratories in Chicago, Oak Ridge, Hanford and Los Alamos were the real architects of the brave new world. E. B. White caught the feeling of futility and despair which now blighted the triumph of the internationalists: [18]

12. *Vindication*

The preparations made at San Francisco for a security league of sovereign nations to prevent aggression now seem like the preparations some little girls might make for a lawn party as a thunderhead gathers just beyond the garden gate. The lemonade will be spiked by lightning.

Bibliographical Essay

Manuscripts

The most important collection of material on the internationalist movement is the Carnegie Endowment Archives at Columbia University. These papers include not only the records of the Endowment itself, but many of the minutes, reports and memoranda of groups subsidized by the Endowment, including the League of Nations Association, the Commission to Study the Organization of Peace, the Non-Partisan Council to Win the Peace, and Americans United for World Organization. The Hoover Library at Stanford University contains a wealth of pamphlets, leaflets and flyers sent out during the war years by the internationalist organizations. Since the records of the various internationalist groups are not available, these two collections proved to be indispensable for this study.

The private papers of a number of leading internationalist spokesmen were very helpful. The Hamilton Holt Collection at Rollins College in Winter Park, Florida, contains many letters that passed between Holt and other internationalists during the war years. The Dulles Papers at Princeton University are uneven, with a few valuable letters but many gaps. The Florence Harriman Papers in the Library of Congress are rich on the formation of the United Nations Association and Americans United for World Organization; the Norman H. Davis Papers in the same repository are disappointing for the war years. The David Andrew Simmons Papers in the University of Texas Archives contain much useful material, including a diary, on the role of the consultants at the San Francisco conference.

The State Department files in the National Archives, open only through December 31, 1943, at the time the research for this book was done, have very little on the activities of the various departmental committees and subcommittees engaged in postwar planning. The most valuable material is in the Pasvolsky Office Files: five boxes containing letters and memoranda of the Division of Special Research, which Leo Pasvolsky headed. The Hull Papers in the Library of Congress contain some material on postwar planning not available in the State Department records, as well as the Secretary's personal correspondence. These papers are open only through 1943, and the Historical Office of the Department of State reviews and censors all notes taken on them.

The most significant material on the State Department during the war years is in the Breckinridge Long Papers in the Library of Congress.

316

Throughout this period Long kept a diary which gives an intimate and penetrating view of the day-by-day activities of the Department's top officers. As Assistant Secretary of State in charge of Congressional affairs, Long played a central role in the planning for the United Nations, and both his diary and his letters add much to the meager records of the Department on the formation of the United Nations. Fred L. Israel has edited selections from the diary under the title *The War Diary of Breckinridge Long*.

The Franklin D. Roosevelt Papers in the Roosevelt Library at Hyde Park, a beautifully arranged and intelligently cross-listed collection, contain a great deal of valuable material on the President's view on international organization. Roosevelt's correspondence with Clark Eichelberger and Cordell Hull is particularly enlightening. The Roosevelt Library also houses a collection of Henry A. Wallace Papers, which consists almost exclusively of letters from the general public. Another Wallace collection at the Library of Congress is equally disappointing. The main body of Wallace material is at Columbia University and is not yet open for research.

The Senate Foreign Relations Committee Papers in the National Archives have very little on the Ball and Connally resolutions and nothing on the United Nations Charter. There are scattered items of interest in the Theodore Green, Tom Connally and Wallace White Papers in the Library of Congress. The Senate files in the Harry S. Truman Papers at the Truman Library in Independence, Missouri, consist primarily of constituent mail. The Frank McNaughton Papers in the Truman Library are more useful; McNaughton was a correspondent for *Time* whose background reports to his editors contain confidential information that was not published at the time. The Elbert Thomas Papers at the Roosevelt Library contain a few useful items relating to the Senate Foreign Relations Committee. Senator Ball disposed of his papers, but he still retains in his home a file of a newsletter to constitutents.

Interviews and Oral Memoirs

Interviews with two key participants in the internationalist movement proved very helpful. Joseph H. Ball, senator from Minnesota and author of the Ball resolution, graciously shared his memories of the war years with me at his farm outside Front Royal, Virginia, in July 1965. Clark M. Eichelberger, director of the League of Nations Association, the Commission to Study the Organization of Peace, and the American Association for the United Nations, spent an hour recalling the highlights of his role in the internationalist movement in his New York office in August 1965.

In his memoir in the Columbia Oral History Project in Butler Library, Walter Lippmann recorded his views concerning the reception of his books on postwar planning and his reactions to the internationalist movement. Malcolm Davis, an officer of the Carnegie Endowment charged with coordinating the internationalist effort, has a useful memoir in the same collection.

James Reston, in a letter to the author on May 17, 1966, disclosed that the Chinese provided the information for his exclusive account of the Dumbarton Oaks conference.

Government Documents

Foreign Relations of the United States: Diplomatic Papers, the official State Department publication of selected documents from its files, contains very little material on the planning and creation of the United Nations. None of the records or reports of the committees that were engaged in postwar planning appear in the volumes for 1942 and 1943. There is ample documentation on the Atlantic conference in the first volume of the 1941 series, and material on Roosevelt's views on international organization in the first volume of the 1942 series and in the first and third volumes of the 1943 series. Two special conference volumes, one on the Cairo and Teheran meetings and another on the Malta and Yalta gatherings, record the views of the wartime leaders on international organization.

The most useful source for the unfolding of State Department thinking on postwar international organization is the *Bulletin,* published weekly throughout this period. The *Bulletin* contains a complete record of all public releases of the Department as well as the texts of speeches by high-ranking officers. The official report on the San Francisco conference by Secretary of State Stettinius is given in the Department's publication *Charter of the United Nations: Report to the President on the Results of the San Francisco Conference.* The full documentation on the founding conference is given in *Documents of the United Nations Conference on International Organization,* compiled by the U.N. Information Organizations and the U.S. Library of Congress.

The *Congressional Record* provides a record of discussion on the postwar resolutions in 1943 and on the final debate on the United Nations Charter, as well as occasional speeches by members of the House and Senate on international organization throughout the war years. The Senate Foreign Relations Committee did not hold public hearings on the Ball or Connally resolutions; the only pertinent hearings are "The Charter of the United Nations," *Hearings* before the Senate Committee on Foreign Relations, 79th Congress, 1st Session.

Many very significant documents on the development of the administration's postwar policy, including some not available to scholars in any other form, appear in the appendixes of Harley Notter, *Postwar Foreign Policy Preparation, 1939–1945.* Notter includes the texts of several tentative drafts of an international organization which circulated through the Department in 1943 and early 1944.

Published Letters and Speeches

The *Public Papers and Addresses of Franklin D. Roosevelt* includes the texts of all of the President's major addresses, his official statements and excerpts from some of his press conferences. The Franklin D. Roosevelt Library has published the complete transcript of the President's press conferences on microfilm. A sampling of the rich correspondence in the files of the Roosevelt Library can be found in Elliott Roosevelt, ed., *F.D.R.: His Personal Letters, 1928–1945.*

The best source for the speeches of prominent public figures both in and out of government on international organization is the bi-weekly publication *Vital Speeches.* Russell Lord has edited two collections of Henry A. Wallace's addresses, *Democracy Reborn* and *The Century of the Common Man,* which contains the text of Wallace's most influential speech, "The Price of Free World Victory." Sumner Welles, *The World of the Four Freedoms* consists of the Under Secretary's wartime speeches through the spring of 1943.

318

Newspapers and Periodicals

The New York *Times*, with its very full coverage of national and international affairs and its extremely useful index, was indispensable for this study. The daily news reports provided an accurate account of the public discussion of international organization during the war, and two Washington correspondents, Arthur Krock and James Reston, had sources of information in Washington that permitted them to print stories on the inner workings of the administration. Krock, a close friend and confidant of Hull's, tended to be critical of President Roosevelt and Under Secretary Welles, and he wrote in favor of a very limited and carefully restricted form of international organization. Reston was inclined toward a more powerful world body, and his dispatches—particularly his revelations on the American plan at the Dumbarton Oaks conference, which won him the Pulitzer Prize—served to promote the internationalist cause. In addition, the New York *Times Magazine* printed many articles dealing with postwar planning. In its editorial policy the *Times* was unabashedly Wilsonian in viewpoint, and its pleas for action throughout the war years provide a very useful insight into the emotional reaction of internationalists to administration policy.

The two comprehensive news weeklies, *Time* and *Newsweek*, gave very full coverage to the development of sentiment in favor of world organization. Both reflected the strong internationalist views of their editors, and *Time* in particular infused its accounts with exhortations and editorial judgments. *Life* was even more open in its championship of the internationalist cause, printing editorials and articles on the postwar world and giving extensive coverage to internationalist leaders, particularly John Foster Dulles. Henry R. Luce's editorial "The American Century" (*Life*, February 17, 1941), reprinted as a pamphlet, *The American Century*, gives the fullest expression of the *Time-Life* brand of internationalism, which had a strong missionary thrust and imperialistic overtones.

Mass-circulation magazines carried occasional stories on postwar international organization. The *Saturday Evening Post, Collier's* and the *Reader's Digest* took a neutral position on the administration's postwar plans. Two articles by Forrest Davis, "Roosevelt's World Blueprint" (*Saturday Evening Post*, April 10, 1943) and "What Really Happened at Teheran" (*ibid.*, May 13 and 20, 1944), stirred up widespread public discussion. Davis' articles were based on personal interviews with the President, and they were shown to the White House staff prior to publication. Other significant articles include Herbert Hoover and Hugh Gibson, "New Approaches to Lasting Peace" (*Collier's*, June 5, 12, 19 and 26, 1943); William Hard, "Are We on the Wrong Road to Peace? (*Reader's Digest*, September 1944); and Joseph H. Ball, "Your Move, Mister President" (*Saturday Evening Post*, February 19, 1944).

The monthly magazines aimed at a more sophisticated audience, *Harper's, Atlantic Monthly* and *American Mercury*, printed occasional pieces on postwar planning, but did not give it much emphasis. In the "Talk of the Town" section of the *New Yorker*, E. B. White commented frequently on the administration's plans, ridiculing the cautious stance of the government and pleading for some form of world federation. White later reprinted these essays in *The Wild Flag. Foreign Affairs* did not become involved in the discussion over postwar international organization.

319

The weekly journals of opinion proved extremely fruitful. The *Nation* and the *New Republic* adopted firmly internationalist editorial positions early in the war. Their editors tended to be critical of the more idealistic expressions of Wilsonianism, advocating instead a realistic policy of cooperation with the Soviet Union coupled with an affirmation of the Wallace "people's revolution" on economic issues. The *Christian Century* took sharp issue with the liberal journals. The editors of this Protestant weekly, which had been strongly isolationist before the war, criticized the willingness of internationalists to rely on force to keep the peace. As the plans for international organization developed, *Christian Century* condemned them for failing to carry out the democratic ideals of the Atlantic Charter.

The periodicals published by internationalist organizations proved invaluable. The League of Nations Association began publishing the *League of Nations Herald* as a bi-weekly newsletter in 1923. Two years later the Association changed the name to *League of Nations News*, and it appeared monthly under this title until 1932, when it was replaced by the *Chronicle of World Affairs*, a six-page periodical in newspaper format which Clark Eichelberger began in the Chicago office of the Association. In 1939, *New World*, a monthly journal, replaced the *Chronicle*, and finally in 1941 the periodical, still edited by Eichelberger, assumed the name *Changing World*, which it retained through the war years. *Changing World*, normally twelve pages in size, was designed to give members of the Association news of the internationalist movement, and its issues chronicled the varying activities of the many organizations working for a new world order as well as the shifting hopes and visions of the Wilsonian internationalists. The Hoover Library at Stanford University has a complete file of this periodical, which was the single most important source for this study.

Other journals put out by internationalist groups give an insight into the movement. *Free World*, published by the American Free World Association, reported on the underground activities in Nazi-occupied Europe, the exile movements and the dreams for a new world organization. *Post War World*, begun in 1943 by Dulles' Commission on a Just and Durable Peace; *Freedom Digest*, the journal of Americans United for World Organization; and the *Bulletin* of the American Association for the United Nations also proved helpful.

Memoirs and Autobiographies

Very few of the leaders of the internationalist movement have written accounts of their efforts. *The Autobiography of James T. Shotwell* concentrates on his role in the peace movement in the 1920's and has very little on World War II. In *Chronicle of a Generation* Raymond B. Fosdick gives a very graphic account of the feelings and activities of internationalists in the early 1920's. Stephen Duggan, *A Professor at Large* contains a good deal of information on groups founded in the 1920's to stimulate an interest in international affairs among the American people. For the war years, Virginia C. Gildersleeve gives a picture of the formation of the Commission to Study the Organization of Peace and a keen analysis of the American delegation to the San Francisco conference in *Many a Good Crusade*.

The *Memoirs of Cordell Hull* contain a full account of the Secretary's ideas and actions in regard to world organization. Though Hull tries to put his policies in the best possible light, his personal traits of caution, extreme sensitivity to criticism, and political cunning come through clearly.

Samuel Rosenman sheds a good deal of light on Franklin Roosevelt's views on international organization, especially in the last year of his life, in *Working with Roosevelt*. Other useful memoirs on Roosevelt are William D. Hassett, *Off the Record with F.D.R., 1942–1945* and Ross T. McIntire, *White House Physician*. Admiral William D. Leahy, *I Was There* is valuable for the Yalta conference, as are the two volumes by James F. Byrnes, *Speaking Frankly* and *All in One Lifetime*.

The best source on the first months of the Truman administration is the first volume of Harry S. Truman's *Memoirs*. His blunt comments, evidently untouched by the softening hand of a ghostwriter, convey his sincere dedication to the task of fulfilling Roosevelt's plans for the United Nations. Joseph C. Grew, Under Secretary of State under Stettinius, gives his more pessimistic views on the postwar world in *Turbulent Era: A Diplomatic Record of Forty Years*.

The Private Papers of Senator Vandenberg, edited by his son, Arthur H. Vandenberg, Jr., gives a lively and detailed account of the Congressional role in the founding of the United Nations. Most of the material consists of diary entries, though there are occasional excerpts from Vandenberg's correspondence. Some of the diary entries were written well after the events recorded took place, and much of the material places Vandenberg in an unusually favorable light. There is nothing rehearsed about the Senator's prose, however, and his rhetoric comes through with a vivid, if at times painful, impact. The early publication of these papers, in the absence of accounts by other Congressional participants in the foreign-policy process, has led historians to give Vandenberg greater prominence, and often greater praise, than his achievements warrant. Tom Connally probably was as influential as Vandenberg in ensuring a majority in the Senate for the United Nations Charter, but *My Name Is Tom Connally*, his reminiscences as told to Alfred Steinberg, is marred by a self-laudatory tone and an extremely sketchy treatment of the war years. The only other Congressional memoir that proved helpful was Joseph W. Martin, as told to Robert J. Donovan, *My First Fifty Years in Politics*, which sheds some light on the struggle against isolationism inside the Republican party.

Winston Churchill gives his views on postwar planning in his personal history of World War II, especially in *Closing the Ring*, *The Hinge of Fate* and *Triumph and Tragedy*. The second volume of Anthony Eden's memoirs, *The Reckoning*, contains material on the Foreign Secretary's visit to Washington in 1943 and on the San Francisco conference, but Eden reveals very little of himself or his views on international organization. Raoul de Roussy de Sales, a French journalist in Washington, comments on the naiveté of American thinking on the postwar world in *The Making of Yesterday*.

In *War or Peace* John Foster Dulles gives his views on international affairs and recounts his role in developing a bi-partisan policy in 1944 with Cordell Hull.

Biographies

There are several biographies which give good insight into the internationalist movement in the 1920's. The two most useful are Hoyt L. Warner, *The Life of Mr. Justice Clarke*, dealing with the activities of the first president of the League of Nations Non-Partisan Association, and Warren F. Kuehl, *Hamilton Holt: Journalist, Internationalist, Educator,* covering the career of the most dynamic of the internationalists. Other biographies helpful for the 1920's are Irving N. Fisher, *My Father, Irving Fisher;* C. H. Cramer, *Newton D. Baker;* and Frank Freidel, *Franklin D. Roosevelt: The Ordeal.* Freidel has not yet treated Roosevelt's period in office in his multi-volume biography, and the most perceptive of other writers on Roosevelt, James MacGregor Burns, does not deal with the wartime years in *Roosevelt: The Lion and the Fox.* For a thorough appraisal of the state of the President's health see Herman E. Bateman, "Observations on President Roosevelt's Health During World War II" in the *Mississippi Valley Historical Review* (June 1956). Bateman concludes that Roosevelt's health began to decline in late 1943, improved briefly during the presidential campaign and then deteriorated sharply in the early months of 1945.

The best biography of Willkie is Ellsworth Barnard, *Wendell Willkie: Fighter for Freedom,* which was published after this book was written. Joseph Barnes, *Willkie* discusses his trip around the world in 1942 and gives an intimate glimpse of Willkie's personality; Mary E. Dillon, *Wendell Willkie* is uncritical, but it does set forth the major episodes in Willkie's political career. The best study of Willkie is Donald B. Johnson, *The Republican Party and Wendell Willkie,* which deals perceptively with his role as a political leader. Roscoe Drummond tells of his last days in "Wendell Willkie: A Study in Courage," in Isabel Leighton, ed., *The Aspirin Age, 1919–1941.*

The conflicting emotions aroused by Henry A. Wallace are revealed in Russell Lord, *The Wallaces of Iowa,* a warmly sympathetic biography by a close associate, and in Dwight Macdonald, *Henry Wallace: The Man and the Myth,* an extremely effective hatchet job. There are no biographies of Sumner Welles, but contemporary sketches by James Reston in the New York *Times Magazine* (August 3, 1941), and by Robert Bendiner in the *Nation* (August 1, 1942), and a cover-story profile in *Time* (August 11, 1941) give the details of his career.

The American Secretaries of State and Their Diplomacy series, edited by Robert H. Ferrell, includes two volumes covering the war years. The second volume of Julius Pratt, *Cordell Hull* is disappointing on the Secretary's role in planning the United Nations, simply summarizing the more detailed account in Hull's *Memoirs.* Richard L. Walker has a good sketch of Stettinius' contributions and George Curry describes the relationship between James F. Byrnes and Truman after Roosevelt's death in volume 14 of this series, *E. R. Stettinius—James F. Byrnes.*

John R. Beal has nothing but praise for Dulles in his biography *John Foster Dulles, 1888–1959.* Nat S. Finney, "Joseph H. Ball: A Liberal Dose of Candor," in J. T. Salter, ed., *Public Men In and Out of Office,* is sympathetic to the Minnesota senator; Richard Rovere gives a shrewd and unflattering reappraisal of Arthur Vandenberg in "New Man in the Pantheon" (*New Yorker,* March 24, 1962).

Public Opinion

The most comprehensive compilation of public-opinion polls for the war years is Hadley Cantril and Mildred Strunk, eds., *Public Opinion, 1935–1946.* More detailed breakdowns, including analysis by region, educational level and political preference, are given in the issues of *Public Opinion Quarterly* and the publications of the National Opinion Research Center, especially "Nationwide Survey of Postwar and Current Problems," *Report No. 5* (August 1942); "The Public Looks at World Organization," *Report No. 19* (April 1944); and "Public Opinion on World Organization up to the San Francisco Conference," *Report No. 25* (April 1945).

Jerome S. Bruner analyzes American attitudes during the war in *Mandate from the People* and concludes that the shift toward internationalism was more superficial than the polls would indicate. Selden Menefee, *Assignment: U.S.A.* and William A. Lydgate, *What America Thinks* also discuss trends in popular thought during World War II.

The views of members of the regional committees established by the Council on Foreign Relations in twelve American cities are given in two booklets edited by Percy Bidwell, *Our Foreign Policy in Peace and War* and *The United States and the United Nations.*

Publications of the Internationalist Movement

The major private organizations interested in international relations have published brief histories of their activities. The most noteworthy are *The Council on Foreign Relations: A Record of Twenty-Five Years, 1921–1946;* Paul U. Kellogg, *Ten Years of the Foreign Policy Association;* and the Commission to Study the Organization of Peace, *A Ten Year Record: 1939–1949.* The *Year Book* of the Carnegie Endowment for International Peace and the *Annual Report* of the Woodrow Wilson Foundation give basic information on the activities of these two important societies. Ruth Savord, *American Agencies Interested in International Affairs,* published by the Council on Foreign Relations, is a very useful checklist.

The most important publications of the Commission to Study the Organization of Peace are its four reports, all of which appeared in *International Conciliation.* The *Preliminary Report, November, 1940* was reprinted in 1942 with accompanying monographs by members of the studies committee. The others are *Second Report: The Transitional Period; Third Report: The United Nations and the Organization of Peace;* and *Fourth Report: Fundamentals of the International Organization—General Statement.* Of the many pamphlets and study guides the Commission put forth, the most significant are *11 Fundamentals for the Organization of Peace; The Peace We Want; A Design for a Charter of the General International Organization;* and two booklets by Clark M. Eichelberger, *The Time Has Come for Action* and *Proposals for the United Nations Charter.*

The Commission on a Just and Durable Peace, the agency of the Federal Council of Churches on the postwar world, headed by John Foster Dulles, published two pamphlets transmitting the Commission's views to the local churches, each titled *A Message from the National Study Conference on the Churches and a Just and Durable Peace* (1942 and 1945). The Commission's best-known formulation of its views, the Six Pillars of Peace, is contained in *A Just and Durable Peace: Statement of Political Propositions.*

Here Comes Your Last Chance, distributed by Americans United for World Organization, and *From the Garden of Eden to Dumbarton Oaks* are representative of the pamphlets the internationalists printed in their effort to sell the Dumbarton Oaks proposals to the people.

Contemporary Books on International Organization

Wendell Willkie's *One World* outsold all other books of the wartime period dealing with the future peace. Largely a chronicle of Willkie's trip around the globe in 1942, *One World* reflected a dominant Wilsonian belief that a new League of Nations would provide the surest bulwark against another world war. Sumner Welles put forth a more tightly reasoned argument for the collective-security school in his influential *The Time for Decision.* Other books arguing for a world organization along the lines of the League include Denna F. Fleming, *Can We Win the Peace?*; Philip C. Nash, *An Adventure in World Order*; and James T. Shotwell, *The Great Decision.*

Until the discussion of postwar plans became heated in 1943, Clarence Streit, *Union Now* was the best-known book on world order. Streit's plans for a union of democracies seemed modest compared to the world federation proposed by Ely Culbertson in his two books, *Summary of the World Federation Plan* and *Total Peace.* In *How to Think About War and Peace*, Mortimer J. Adler argued for an eventual world federation, though he was pessimistic about the immediate future.

The most significant books arguing for a realistic postwar policy were Walter Lippmann's *U.S. Foreign Policy: Shield of the Republic,* which enjoyed a very wide sale, and *U.S. War Aims,* which reached a much more limited audience. In these books Lippmann developed the idea of a nuclear alliance of the United States, Britain and Russia as the primary basis for permanent peace.

Herbert Hoover and Hugh Gibson, *The Problems of Lasting Peace* was one of the first influential treatments of postwar issues. The authors took a pessimistic view of mankind's future, arguing for a very cautious and limited form of internationalism. Other books skeptical of postwar aspirations include Carl Becker, *How New Will the Better World Be?*; Reinhold Niebuhr, *The Children of Light and the Children of Darkness*; Charles A. Beard, *The Republic*; and Norman Thomas, *What Is Our Destiny?*

Nicholas J. Spykman gave the most forthright statement of the balance of power position in *America's Strategy in World Politics* and *The Geography of the Peace.* Other books written from this point of view are George Fielding Eliot, *Hour of Triumph*, in which the argument is put moderately, and William T. R. Fox, *The Super-Powers,* an enthusiastic recital of the *Realpolitik* school.

The play by Howard Koch, *In Time to Come* was a forerunner of the Wilson revival which reached its peak in 1944. Biographies written in praise of Wilson include J. Eugene Harley, *Woodrow Wilson Still Lives—His World Ideals Triumphant*; David Loth, *The Story of Woodrow Wilson*; and Gerald W. Johnson, *Woodrow Wilson.* Charlotte B. Mahon stressed the relevancy of Wilson's ideas for the coming peace in *Our Second Chance.* Roger Burlingame and Alden Stevens played up the tragedy of Wilson's defeat in 1919 in *Victory Without Peace*, while Karl Schriftgiesser pilloried Henry Cabot Lodge in *The Gentleman from Massachusetts.* The only scholarly and balanced account of the peace-making after World War I published during this period was Thomas A. Bailey, *Woodrow Wilson and the Lost Peace.*

Historians and political scientists drew on Wilson's experience to suggest

324

ways of avoiding a repetition of his failure. In *America and Two Wars*
Dexter Perkins argued that recent history proved that only a new world
organization with the power to use force effectively could ensure lasting
peace. Edward S. Corwin and Kenneth Colgrove pleaded for a constitutional
amendment to abolish the two-thirds rule for Senate approval of treaties in
their books *The Constitution and World Organization* and *The American
Senate and World Peace*.

Among the very large number of wartime books dealing with the future
peace, other important ones are R. M. MacIver, *Towards an Abiding Peace*,
Irving Brant, *The Road to Peace and Freedom* and Norman Angell, *Let the
People Know*, which argue for collective security along Wilsonian lines;
Emery Reves, *A Democratic Manifesto*, Lionel Gelber, *Peace by Power* and
P. E. Corbett, *Post-War Worlds*, which stress Anglo-American cooperation;
William B. Ziff, *The Gentlemen Talk of Peace*, Henry Bamford Parkes, *The
World After War*, Neil MacNeil, *An American Peace* and Robert Kazmayer,
Out of the Clouds, which plead for a realistic peace; and Ross Hoffman, *The
Great Republic*, Paul Hutchinson, *From Victory to Peace*, and Walter Van
Kirk, *Religion and the World of Tomorrow*, which discuss the problems of
peace from religious perspectives.

Two significant books do not fit into the prevailing currents of thought in
the war years. Henry J. Taylor's *Men in Motion* is a frankly isolationist
account which is highly critical of the contemporary belief in postwar
cooperation with the Soviet Union. Michael Straight, a *New Republic*
editor, criticized the push for collective security as irrelevant to the fundamental economic and social upheavals going on in the world in *Make This
the Last War*.

Secondary Accounts

The State Department publication written by Harley Notter, *Postwar
Foreign Policy Preparation, 1939–1945*, and the study published by the
Brookings Institution, *A History of the United Nations Charter: The Role of
the United States 1940–1945* by Ruth B. Russell, assisted by Jeannette E.
Muther, are both works of outstanding scholarship which proved indispensable in the writing of this book. Notter details the constantly changing
organization inside the State Department which dealt with postwar issues,
and though his primary interest is in personnel and institutional arrangements, he gives a revealing picture of ideas and policies on international
organization. Miss Russell focuses on the writing of the Charter, and her
account of the San Francisco conference, which takes up nearly half of her
thousand-page book, is a model of painstaking research and careful analysis.
Both authors had access to State Department records which have not yet
been made available for research by other scholars.

American historians, preoccupied with the phenomenon of isolationism in
the twentieth century, have paid little attention to the internationalist
movement. The fullest account is Roland N. Stromberg, *Collective Security
and American Foreign Policy*, a highly partisan survey by a disillusioned
internationalist who sees the concept of collective security as the major flaw
in American foreign policy from Wilson to Eisenhower. Willard N. Hogan
gives a more balanced interpretation in *International Conflict and Collective
Security*, and there are several interesting essays in Alexander DeConde, ed.,
Isolation and Security, particularly Richard N. Current, "The United States

and 'Collective Security,' " and Kenneth W. Thompson, "Isolationism and Collective Security."

The best study of the origins of the internationalist movement is Ruhl Bartlett, *The League to Enforce Peace*, which traces this organization from its founding in 1915 down through the early 1920's. Thomas A. Bailey, *Woodrow Wilson and the Great Betrayal* is a thorough history of the Senate debate over the League of Nations. In his excellent study *The Isolationist Impulse: Its Twentieth Century Reaction* Selig Adler has an important chapter on the internationalists in the 1920's. Denna F. Fleming traces the limited American contact with the League of Nations and the World Court in *The United States and World Organization, 1920–1933*.

The role of private organizations in stimulating an interest in international affairs among the American people between the wars is surveyed by Edith E. Ware in *The Study of International Relations in the United States*. In this book, first published in 1934 and updated in 1937, Miss Ware gives a thorough description of the wide variety of groups engaged in this effort. Elton Atwater, *Organized Efforts in the United States Toward Peace* is a useful checklist of pacifist activities. J. Eugene Harley, *International Understanding*, Farrell Symons, *Courses on International Affairs in American Colleges, 1930–31* and Ida T. Jacobs and John J. DeBoer, eds., *Educating for Peace* give information on the role of universities and the schools in promoting interest in foreign affairs. The very active efforts of internationalists to align the United States with Britain against the Axis from 1939 to 1941 are described by Walter Johnson in *The Battle Against Isolation*.

The two excellent and thorough histories of the diplomacy of World War II, Herbert Feis, *Churchill, Roosevelt, Stalin: The War They Waged and the Peace They Sought* and William H. McNeill, *America, Britain, and Russia: Their Co-operation and Conflict, 1941–1946* (the third volume of the Royal Institute's *Survey of International Affairs* for the war years) focus on the interplay of policy between the leaders of the Big Three. Feis gives a good account of Roosevelt's Four Policemen concept, but he does not stress the issue of world organization. McNeill devotes more attention to this theme, and his section on the San Francisco conference is very perceptive. In his briefer survey of wartime diplomacy, *American Diplomacy During the Second World War, 1941–1945*, Gaddis Smith is highly critical of Roosevelt's casual approach to vital postwar issues.

Robert E. Sherwood, *Roosevelt and Hopkins: An Intimate History* is still the most absorbing book on the diplomacy of the war. Sherwood's account of the major conferences, based on Harry Hopkins' notes, gives an insight into Roosevelt's views on the postwar world. Other histories by participants that proved helpful are Edward R. Stettinius, Jr., *Roosevelt and the Russians: The Yalta Conference* and two books by Sumner Welles written after the war, *Where Are We Heading?* and *Seven Decisions That Shaped History*.

On the military side, Russell Buchanan, *The United States and World War II* gives a competent summary of the major campaigns. There is a wealth of detailed information, mostly the result of interviews with participants, on the closing stages of the war in Europe in John Toland, *The Last 100 Days*.

Roland Young, *Congressional Politics in the Second World War* chronicles developments in Congress without offering any interpretation. Robert Dahl gives a thoughtful analysis of the Congressional role in international affairs in *Congress and Foreign Policy*. The best brief account of the Senate's role in preparing for the peace is Joseph H. Ball, "How We Planned for the Postwar World," in Jack Goodman, ed., *While You Were Gone.*

The changing organizational structure of the State Department can be traced in Graham H. Stuart, *The Department of State.* Walter H. C. Laves and Francis O. Wilcox, "The Reorganization of the Department of State" (*American Political Science Review*, April 1944), describes and analyzes the changes Stettinius put into effect. In "Overselling the UN Charter—Fact and Myth" (*International Organization*, Spring 1960), Robert E. Riggs absolves the State Department from the charge of presenting the Charter as a millennial document to the American people.

The best study of the formation of the bi-partisan approach to postwar problems is H. Bradford Westerfield, *Foreign Policy and Party Politics: Pearl Harbor to Korea.* Westerfield carefully documents the way in which the Republican party joined with the Democrats in developing a consensus for international organization. Cecil V. Crabb, Jr., *Bi-partisan Foreign Policy, Myth or Reality* is a critical analysis by a political scientist.

Other useful books include John Snell, ed., *The Meaning of Yalta*, especially the article by Forrest C. Pogue, "The Big Three and the United Nations"; George Woodridge, *UNRRA*; Gabriel Almond, *The American People and Foreign Policy*; and David Elliott Weingast, *Walter Lippmann; A Study in Personal Journalism.*

List of Sources Cited in Notes

Manuscript Collections

Americans United for World Organization File, Hoover Library, Stanford, California

Joseph H. Ball Papers, Shannon Farm, Front Royal, Virginia

Carnegie Endowment for International Peace Archives, Butler Library, Columbia University

Commission to Study the Organization of Peace File, Hoover Library, Stanford, California

Tom Connally Papers, Library of Congress

Norman H. Davis Papers, Library of Congress

John Foster Dulles Papers, Firestone Library, Princeton University, Princeton, New Jersey

Federal Union File, Hoover Library, Stanford, California

Freedom House File, Hoover Library, Stanford, California

Theodore F. Green Papers, Library of Congress

Florence J. Harriman Papers, Library of Congress

Hamilton Holt Papers, Mills Memorial Library, Rollins College, Winter Park, Florida

Cordell Hull Papers, Library of Congress

Breckinridge Long Papers, Library of Congress

Frank McNaughton Papers, Truman Library, Independence, Missouri

Leo Pasvolsky Office Files, State Department Records, National Archives, Record Group 59

Republican Postwar Policy Association File, Hoover Library, Stanford, California

Franklin D. Roosevelt Papers, Roosevelt Library, Hyde Park, New York

San Francisco International Center File, Hoover Library, Stanford, California

Senate Foreign Relations Committee Papers, National Archives, Record Group 46

David Andrew Simmons Papers, University of Texas Library, Austin, Texas

State Department Records, National Archives, Record Group 59. All note references to decimal file numbers, such as 841.50/982, 111 Advisory Committee/11½, 500.CC/22, are to these records.

Elbert Thomas Papers, Roosevelt Library, Hyde Park, New York

Harry S. Truman Papers, Truman Library, Independence, Missouri

United Nations Association File, Hoover Library, Stanford, California
Henry A. Wallace Papers, Library of Congress
Henry A. Wallace Papers, Roosevelt Library, Hyde Park, New York
Wallace White Papers, Library of Congress
Women's Action Committee for Victory and Lasting Peace File, Hoover
    Library, Stanford, California
Woodrow Wilson Foundation File, Hoover Library, Stanford, California

Interviews and Oral Memoirs

Joseph H. Ball, interview with author, Front Royal, Virginia, July 23, 1965
Malcolm Davis Memoir, Oral History Project, Butler Library, Columbia
    University
Clark M. Eichelberger, interview with author, New York City, August 13,
    1965
Walter Lippmann Memoir, Oral History Project, Butler Library, Columbia
    University

Government Documents

U.S. Congress, *Congressional Record*
——, "The Charter of the United Nations," *Hearings* before the Senate
    Committee on Foreign Relations, 79th Congress, 1st Session (Wash-
    ington, 1945)
——, "House Joint Resolution 192," *Hearings* before the House Committee
    on Foreign Affairs, 78th Congress, 2nd Session (Washington, 1944)
——, "Nominations—Department of State," *Hearings* before the Senate
    Committee on Foreign Relations, 78th Congress, 2nd Session (Wash-
    ington, 1944)
——, *Senate Report No. 478*, 78th Congress, 1st Session (Washington,
    1943)
U.S. Department of State, *Bulletin*
——, *Charter of the United Nations: Report to the President on the Results
    of the United Nations Conference on International Organization*
    (Washington, 1945)
——, *Foreign Relations of the United States: Diplomatic Papers*

Periodicals

Specific articles are cited in full in notes.
American Mercury
Atlantic Monthly
Bulletin of the American Association for the United Nations
Changing World
Christian Century
Chronicle of World Affairs
Collier's
Foreign Affairs
Free World
Freedom Digest
Freedom House
Harper's

Ladies' Home Journal
League of Nations Chronicle
League of Nations Herald
League of Nations News
Life
Nation
New Republic
New World
New York *Times*
New York *Times Book Review*
New York *Times Magazine*
New Yorker
Newsweek
Post War World
Public Opinion Quarterly
Reader's Digest
Saturday Evening Post
Time
Vital Speeches

Books and Pamphlets

Adler, Mortimer J., *How to Think About War and Peace* (New York, 1944)
Adler, Selig, *The Isolationist Impulse: Its Twentieth Century Reaction* (New York, 1957)
Almond, Gabriel A., *The American People and Foreign Policy* (2nd edition, New York, 1960)
American Association for the United Nations, "Washington Letter on the 'United Nations,'" No. 23 (July 7, 1945) and No. 26 (July 31, 1945)
Americans United for World Organization, *Here Comes Your Last Chance* (New York, 1945)
Atwater, Elton, *Organized Efforts in the United States Toward Peace* (Washington, 1936)
Bailey, Thomas A., *Woodrow Wilson and the Great Betrayal* (New York, 1945)
——, *Woodrow Wilson and the Lost Peace* (New York, 1944)
Barnes, Joseph, *Willkie* (New York, 1952)
Bartlett, Robert M., *They Work for Tomorrow* (New York, 1943)
Bartlett, Ruhl J., *The League to Enforce Peace* (Chapel Hill, 1944)
Baruch, Bernard, *Baruch: The Public Years* (New York, 1960)
Beal, John Robinson, *John Foster Dulles: 1888–1959* (2nd edition, New York, 1959)
Beard, Charles A., *The Republic* (New York, 1944)
Becker, Carl, *How New Will the Better World Be?* (New York, 1944)
Bidwell, Percy W., ed., *Our Foreign Policy in Peace and War* (New York, 1942)
——, ed., *The United States and the United Nations: Views on Postwar Relations* (New York, 1943)
Bruner, Jerome S., *Mandate from the People* (New York, 1944)
Buchanan, A. Russell, *The United States in World War II* (2 vols.; New York, 1964)
Burlingame, Roger, and Alden Stevens, *Victory Without Peace* (New York, 1944)

Byrnes, James F., *All in One Lifetime* (New York, 1958)
Cantril, Hadley, and Mildred Strunk, eds., *Public Opinion, 1935–1946* (Princeton, 1951)
Carnegie Endowment for International Peace, *Year Book—1920* (Washington, 1920)
——, *Year Book—1942* (Washington, 1942)
——, *Year Book—1943* (Washington, 1943)
——, *Year Book—1944* (Washington, 1944)
——, *Year Book—1945* (Washington, 1945)
Churchill, Winston S., *Triumph and Tragedy* (Boston, 1953)
Colegrove, Kenneth, *The American Senate and World Peace* (New York, 1944)
Commission on a Just and Durable Peace, *A Guidebook for Action* (New York, 1944)
——, *A Just and Durable Peace: Statement of Political Propositions* (New York, 1943)
——, *A Message from the National Study Conference on the Churches and a Just and Durable Peace* (New York, 1942)
——, *A Message from the National Study Conference on the Churches and a Just and Durable Peace* (New York, 1945)
Commission to Study the Organization of Peace, *Comment on the Eight-Point Declaration . . .* (New York, 1941)
——, *A Design for a Charter of the General International Organization* (New York, 1944)
——, *11 Fundamentals for the Organization of Peace* (New York, 1944)
——, *Fourth Report* (New York, 1943)
——, *In Time of War Prepare for Peace* (New York, 1940)
——, *The Peace We Want* (New York, 1944)
——, *Preliminary Report, November, 1940* (New York, 1940)
——, *Second Report—The Transitional Period* (New York, 1942)
——, *Study Course on Immediate Post-War Problems* (New York, 1942)
——, *A Study of the Organization of Peace* (New York, 1940)
——, *Ten Year Record, 1939–1949* (New York, 1949)
——, *Third Report* (New York, 1943)
——, *Toward Greater Freedom* (New York, 1942)
——, *The United States and Postwar International Organization* (New York, 1944)
Connally, Tom, and Alfred Steinberg, *My Name Is Tom Connally* (New York, 1954)
Corwin, Edward S., *The Constitution and World Organization* (Princeton, 1944)
Council on Foreign Relations: A Record of Twenty-Five Years, 1921–1946 (New York, 1947)
Crabb, Cecil V., Jr., *Bipartisan Foreign Policy, Myth or Reality?* (Evanston, Ill., 1957)
Cramer, C. H., *Newton D. Baker* (Cleveland, 1961)
Culbertson, Ely, *Summary of the World Federation Plan* (New York, 1943)
——, *Total Peace* (New York, 1943)
Curry, George, "James F. Byrnes," in Robert H. Ferrell and Samuel F. Bemis, eds., *American Secretaries of State and Their Diplomacy* (15 vols.; New York, 1927–1966), XIV
de Sales, Raoul de Roussy, *The Making of Yesterday* (New York, 1947)

Dillon, Mary Earhart, *Wendell Willkie* (Philadelphia, 1952)

Drummond, Roscoe, "Wendell Willkie: A Study in Courage," in Isabel Leighton, ed., *The Aspirin Age, 1919–1941* (New York, 1949)

Duggan, Stephen, *A Professor at Large* (New York, 1943)

Dulles, John Foster, *Long Range Peace Objectives* (New York, 1941)

——, *War or Peace* (New York, 1950)

Eagleton, Clyde, "Aggression and War," in Commission to Study the Organization of Peace, *Preliminary Report and Monographs* (New York, 1942)

Eden, Anthony, *The Reckoning* (Boston, 1965)

Eichelberger, Clark M., "The League of Nations Association," in Ida T. Jacobs and John J. DeBoer, eds., *Educating for Peace* (New York, 1940)

——, *Proposals for the United Nations Charter* (New York, 1944)

——, *The Time Has Come for Action* (New York, 1944)

——, *The United Nations Charter: What Was Done at San Francisco* (New York, 1945)

Eliot, George Fielding, *Hour of Triumph* (New York, 1944)

Feis, Herbert, *Churchill, Roosevelt, Stalin: The War They Waged and the Peace They Sought* (Princeton, 1957)

Finney, Nat S., "Joseph H. Ball: A Liberal Dose of Candor," in J. T. Salter, ed., *Public Men In and Out of Office* (Chapel Hill, 1946)

Fisher, Irving Norton, *My Father, Irving Fisher* (New York, 1956)

Fleming, Denna F., *Can We Win the Peace?* (Nashville, Tenn., 1943)

——, *The United States and World Organization* (New York, 1938)

Fosdick, Raymond B., *Chronicle of a Generation: An Autobiography* (New York, 1958)

——, *The Humanitarian Work of the League of Nations* (New York, 1923)

——, *The Meaning of Dumbarton Oaks* (New York, 1945)

——, *An Opening Chapter in World Cooperation* (New York, n.d.)

Fox, William T. R., *The Super-Powers* (New York, 1944)

Freidel, Frank, *Franklin D. Roosevelt: The Ordeal* (Boston, 1954)

Gelber, Lionel, *Peace by Power* (Toronto, 1942)

Gildersleeve, Virginia C., *Many a Good Crusade* (New York, 1954)

Grew, Joseph C., *Turbulent Era: A Diplomatic Record of Forty Years, 1904–1945* (2 vols.; Boston, 1952)

Harley, John Eugene, *International Understanding* (Stanford, Calif., 1931)

——, *Woodrow Wilson Still Lives—His World Ideals Triumphant* (Los Angeles, 1944)

Hartley, Livingston, *It's Up to the Senate* (New York, 1945)

Hassett, William D., *Off the Record with F.D.R., 1942–1945* (New Brunswick, N.J., 1958)

Hoover, Herbert, and Hugh Gibson, *The Problems of Lasting Peace* (New York, 1942)

Hull, Cordell, *The Memoirs of Cordell Hull* (2 vols.; New York, 1948)

Israel, Fred L., ed., *The War Diary of Breckinridge Long* (Lincoln, Neb., 1966)

Jessup, Philip C., *International Security* (New York, 1935)

Johnson, Donald Bruce, *The Republican Party and Wendell Willkie* (Urbana, Ill., 1960)

Johnson, Gerald W., *Woodrow Wilson: The Unforgettable Figure Who Has Returned to Haunt Us* (New York, 1944)

Johnson, Walter, *The Battle Against Isolation* (Chicago, 1944)
Kellogg, Paul U., *Ten Years of the Foreign Policy Association* (New York, 1929)
Koch, Howard, *In Time to Come* (New York, 1942)
Kuehl, Warren F., *Hamilton Holt: Journalist, Internationalist, Educator* (Gainesville, Fla., 1960)
League of Nations Association, *Essential Facts in Regard to the League of Nations, the World Court and the International Labor Organization* (10th edition, New York, 1937)
Leahy, William D., *I Was There* (New York, 1950)
Lerner, Max, *Public Journal* (New York, 1945)
Lippmann, Walter, *U.S. Foreign Policy: Shield of the Republic* (Boston, 1943)
——, *U.S. War Aims* (Boston, 1944)
Lord, Russell, *The Wallaces of Iowa* (Boston, 1947)
Loth, David, *The Story of Woodrow Wilson* (New York, 1944)
Lydgate, William, *What Our People Think* (New York, 1944)
Macdonald, Dwight, *Henry Wallace: The Man and the Myth* (New York, 1947)
McIntire, Ross T., *White House Physician* (New York, 1946)
McNeill, William Hardy, *America, Britain and Russia: Their Co-operation and Conflict, 1941–1946* (London, 1953)
Mahon, Charlotte Burnett, *Our Second Chance* (New York, 1944)
Martin, Joseph W., as told to Robert J. Donovan, *My First Fifty Years in Politics* (New York, 1960)
Menefee, Selden, *Assignment: U.S.A.* (New York, 1943)
Nash, Philip C., *An Adventure in World Order* (Boston, 1944)
National Opinion Research Center, *Report Number 5: Post-War and Current Problems* (Denver, 1942)
——, *Report No. 19: The Public Looks at World Organization* (Denver, 1944)
Niebuhr, Reinhold, *The Children of Light and the Children of Darkness* (New York, 1944)
Notter, Harley A., *Postwar Foreign Policy Preparation, 1939–1945* (Washington, 1950)
Padover, Saul K., ed., *Wilson's Ideals* (Washington, 1942)
Perkins, Dexter, *America and Two Wars* (Boston, 1944)
Pusey, Merlo J., *Charles Evans Hughes* (2 vols.; New York, 1951)
Reves, Emery, *A Democratic Manifesto* (New York, 1942)
Roosevelt, Elliott, ed., *F.D.R.: His Personal Letters, 1928–1945* (2 vols.; New York, 1950)
Rosenman, Samuel, ed., *The Public Papers and Addresses of Franklin D. Roosevelt* (13 vols.; New York, 1938–50)
——, *Working with Roosevelt* (New York, 1952)
Russell, Ruth B., assisted by Jeannette E. Muther, *A History of the United Nations Charter: The Role of the United States 1940–1945* (Washington, 1958)
Schriftgiesser, Karl, *The Gentleman from Massachusetts: Henry Cabot Lodge* (Boston, 1944)
Sherwood, Robert E., *Roosevelt and Hopkins: An Intimate History* (New York, 1948)
Shotwell, James T., *The Autobiography of James T. Shotwell* (Indianapolis, 1961)

333

Shotwell, James T., *The Great Decision* (New York, 1944)
——, "War as an Instrument of Politics," in Commission to Study the Organization of Peace, *Preliminary Report and Monographs* (New York, 1942)
Smith, Gaddis, *American Diplomacy During the Second World War, 1941–1945* (New York, 1965)
Spykman, Nicholas J., *America's Strategy in World Politics* (New York, 1942)
——, *The Geography of the Peace* (New York, 1944)
Stettinius, Edward R., Jr., *Roosevelt and the Russians: The Yalta Conference* (New York, 1949)
Streit, Clarence K., *Union Now* (New York, 1939)
Stuart, Graham H., *The Department of State* (New York, 1949)
Symons, Farrell, *Courses on International Affairs in American Colleges, 1930–31* (Boston, 1931)
Taylor, Henry J., *Men in Motion* (Garden City, N.Y., 1943)
Thomas, Norman, *What Is Our Destiny?* (New York, 1944)
Toland, John, *The Last 100 Days* (New York, 1966)
Truman, Harry S., *Memoirs* (2 vols.; Garden City, N.Y., 1955)
Union for Democratic Action, *From the Garden of Eden to Dumbarton Oaks* (New York, 1945)
Van Kirk, Walter, *Religion and the World of Tomorrow* (New York, 1941)
Vandenberg, Arthur H., Jr., ed., *The Private Papers of Senator Vandenberg* (Boston, 1952)
Walker, Richard L., "E. R. Stettinius, Jr.," in Robert H. Ferrell and Samuel F. Bemis, eds., *American Secretaries of State and Their Diplomacy* (15 vols.; New York, 1927–1966), XIV
Wallace, Henry A., *Democracy Reborn* (Russell Lord, ed.; New York, 1941)
Ware, Edith E., ed., *The Study of International Relations in the United States* (New York, 1945)
Warner, Hoyt Landon, *The Life of Mr. Justice Clarke* (Cleveland, 1959)
Weingast, David Elliott, *Walter Lippmann: A Study in Personal Journalism* (New Brunswick, N.J., 1949)
Welles, Sumner, *Seven Decisions That Shaped History* (New York, 1951)
——, *The Time for Decision* (New York, 1944)
——, *Where Are We Heading?* (New York, 1946)
——, *The World of the Four Freedoms* (New York, 1943)
Westerfield, H. Bradford, *Foreign Policy and Party Politics: Pearl Harbor to Korea* (New Haven, 1955)
White, E. B., *The Wild Flag* (Boston, 1946)
Willkie, Wendell, *One World* (New York, 1943)
Woodbridge, George, *UNRRA* (3 vols.; New York, 1950)
Woodrow Wilson Foundation, *Annual Report, 1943–1944* (New York, 1944)
——, *Annual Report, 1944–1945* (New York, 1945)

Notes

LIST OF ABBREVIATIONS USED

AAUN   *American Association for the United Nations*
CEA   *Carnegie Endowment Archives*
CJDP   *Commission on a Just and Durable Peace*
CSOP   *Commission to Study the Organization of Peace*
LNA   *League of Nations Association*
NPC   *Non-Partisan Council to Win the Peace*
UNA   *United Nations Association*
WAC   *Women's Action Committee For Victory and Lasting Peace*

PROLOGUE

1. Truman, *Memoirs*, I, 289; New York *Times*, June 26, 1945.
2. *Time*, XLVI (July 2, 1945), 21; *Newsweek*, XXVI (July 2, 1945), 48; New York *Times*, June 27, 1945.
3. Truman, *Memoirs*, I, 290–91.
4. Russell, *History of the United Nations Charter* and the official State Department history, Notter, *Postwar Foreign Policy Preparation*, provide very thorough coverage of United States governmental policy. I have relied extensively on the work of Miss Russell and Mr. Notter for an understanding of the government's role in the founding of the United Nations.

CHAPTER ONE

1. New York *Times*, January 11, 1923; Warner, *Clarke*, pp. 131–2.
2. Bartlett, *League*, pp. 37–43, 50–1, 88–93, 121; Kuehl, *Holt*, pp. 119–27.
3. Bartlett, *League*, pp. 143–54; Bailey, *Wilson and the Great Betrayal*, pp. 185–6.
4. Bartlett, *League*, pp. 187–8; Kuehl, *Holt*, pp. 151–3; Fisher, *Fisher*, p. 207.
5. Bartlett, *League*, pp. 191–6.
6. Fleming, *U.S. and World Organization*, p. 45; Pusey, *Hughes*, II, 432–4; Kuehl, *Holt*, p. 160; Bartlett, *League*, p. 202.
7. Kuehl, *Holt*, pp. 158–61; *Hull Memoirs*, I, 118, 124; Warner, *Clarke*, p. 123.
8. Fosdick, *Chronicle*, pp. 188, 211–13, 220–3; Pusey, *Hughes*, II, 436.
9. Warner, *Clarke*, pp. 115–28; Kuehl, *Holt*, pp. 166–7; Fosdick, *Chronicle*, p. 224.
10. Warner, *Clarke*, pp. 128–30; Kuehl, *Holt*, p. 167.
11. Warner, *Clarke*, pp. 140–1; Kuehl, *Holt*, pp. 168–9; *League of Nations Herald*, I (April 1, 1924), 7; Fosdick, *Humanitarian Work*, p. 2; Fosdick, *Opening Chapter*, p. 39.

12. Warner, *Clarke,* pp. 146–9, 153–4; *League of Nations Herald,* I (March 1, 1924), 4; *ibid.,* I (May 15, 1924), 11; *ibid.,* I (June 1, 1924), 1, 4; *ibid.,* I (March 15, 1924), 3.

13. Warner, *Clarke,* pp. 154–7; *League of Nations Herald,* I (June 15, 1924), 1–2; Fleming, *U.S. and World Organization,* p. 275; Fosdick, *Chronicle,* pp. 241–2; Cramer, *Baker,* pp. 219–20.

14. Warner, *Clarke,* pp. 163–4; *League of Nations News,* II (July 1925), 10.

15. *League of Nations News,* II (November 1925), 21; *ibid.,* III (September 1926), 9–12; League of Nations Association, *Essential Facts,* pp. 7, 39.

16. Eichelberger, "League of Nations Association," pp. 97–9; Ware, *Study of International Relations,* p. 330; *League of Nations News,* III (April 1926), 29; *ibid.,* IV (June 1927), 22; *ibid.,* VI (September 1929), 4–5.

17. *League of Nations News,* II (July 1925), 10; Kuehl, *Holt,* pp. 172–5; Fosdick, *Chronicle,* p. 225; Warner, *Clarke,* pp. 173–4; Adler, *Isolationist Impulse,* pp. 216–17.

18. *League of Nations News,* VI (January 1929), 3; *ibid.,* VI (March 1929), 3–4; *ibid.,* VI (April 1929), 3; *ibid.,* VII (April 1930), 19.

19. Harley, *International Understanding,* p. xiii; Freidel, *Roosevelt: Ordeal,* p. 124; Kuehl, *Holt,* pp. 163–5; Ware, *Study of International Relations,* p. 34; *Chronicle of World Affairs,* VIII (April 17, 1936), 6.

20. Kellogg, *Ten Years,* pp. 7–15; Duggan, *Professor at Large,* pp. 13, 29; Ware, *Study of International Relations,* p. 348.

21. *Ibid.,* p. 75; Council on Foreign Relations: *Record of Twenty-Five Years,* pp. 6–9, 11–12; Duggan, *Professor at Large,* pp. 25–6.

22. Ware, *Study of International Relations,* pp. 26–9; *Changing World,* XII (May 1940), 13; Carnegie Endowment, *Year Book—1920,* pp. 55–7; Symons, *Courses on International Affairs,* pp. vii, xi.

23. Freidel, *Roosevelt: Ordeal,* pp. 126–7; Duggan, *Professor at Large,* pp. 33–4; Ware, *Study of International Relations,* pp. 119, 127, 129; Harley, *International Understanding,* pp. 98, 221–38; Baruch, *Baruch: Public Years,* p. 88.

24. *League of Nations News,* VII (November 1930), 1; *League of Nations Chronicle,* V (February 1933), 1; *ibid.,* V (December 1933), 4; *ibid.,* VI (July 1934), 4; *ibid.,* VI (October 1934), 4; *ibid.,* VII (February 28, 1935), 6; *Chronicle of World Affairs,* VIII (March 18, 1936), 6; Directors of the League of Nations Association to Butler, April 28, 1933, Holt Papers, Box 73; Ware, *Study of International Relations,* p. 352; Atwater, *Organized Efforts,* p. 29.

25. Jessup, *International Security,* p. 19.

26. Freidel, *Roosevelt: Ordeal,* pp. 235–40; Adler, *Isolationist Impulse,* p. 251; Hull *Memoirs,* I, 153; Holt to Cummings, March 14, 1933, Holt Papers, Box 4.

27. Fosdick, *Chronicle,* pp. 251–2; *League of Nations Chronicle,* V (May 1933), 1; Shotwell *Autobiography,* pp. 38–48, 60–7, 77–9, 82, 134; *League of Nations Chronicle,* V (November 1933), 4.

28. *Chronicle of World Affairs,* VIII (May 15, 1936), 1; *ibid.,* VIII (July 8, 1936), 1; *ibid.,* VIII (June 19, 1936), 1; *ibid.,* X (January 1938), 8; *ibid.,* X (February 1938), 8; *ibid.,* X (November 1938), 5.

29. *Ibid.,* IX (October 1937), 1, 3; *ibid.,* X (January 1938), 1; *ibid.,* XI (March 1939), 5; *ibid.,* XI (April 1939), 1; *ibid.,* XI (May 1939), 7.

30. *Public Opinion Quarterly,* VIII (Fall 1944), 454; *Chronicle of World Affairs,* X (March 1938), 1; *ibid.,* X (October 1938), 4; *ibid.,* XI (March 1939), 4; *ibid.,* X (September 1938), 4.

CHAPTER TWO

1. *New World,* XI (October 1939), 6; Rawlings to Holt, June 6, 1940, Holt Papers, Box 5; *New World,* XI (September 1939), 2, 14; *ibid.,* XI (October 1939), 7.

2. *Ibid.,* XI (September 1939), 2; *ibid.,* XII (February 1940), 15; *ibid.,* XII (May

1940), 7; Johnson, *Battle Against Isolation, passim; Changing World*, XII
(October 1940), 7; *ibid.*, XII (November 1940), 7.
3. Commission to Study the Organization of Peace, *Ten Year Record*, pp. 7–8;
Shotwell Autobiography, p. 312; Gildersleeve, *Many a Good Crusade*, p. 254;
New World, XI (November 1939), 15.
4. *New York Times*, January 3, 1940; *New World*, XI (December 1939), 15; *ibid.*,
XII (March 1940), 12; CSOP, *In Time of War Prepare for Peace*; New York
Times, February 26, 1940.
5. Council on Foreign Relations, *Record of Twenty-Five Years*, pp. 15–18; Joseph
H. Willits to Edward R. Stettinius, November 15, 1943, Pasvolsky Office Files,
Box 5; *Hull Memoirs*, II, 1626–7; Notter, *Postwar Foreign Policy Preparation*,
pp. 19–21.
6. *New York Times*, November 19, 1940; text of radio broadcast, November 9,
1940, in CSOP file, Hoover Library.
7. CSOP, *Preliminary Report, November, 1940*, pp. 5, 8, 10–12, 14; Shotwell, "War
as an Instrument of Politics," p. 15; Eagleton, "Aggression and War," p. 32.
8. *Changing World*, XIII (March 1941), 2; *ibid.*, XIII (April 1941), 4; *ibid.*, XIII
(June 1941), 2, 7.
9. *Ibid.*, XIII (April 1941), 3, 15; *ibid.*, XIII (June 1941), 15; *ibid.*, XIII (July
1941), 7.
10. *Ibid.*, XII (May 1940), 10; *ibid.*, XII (December 1940), 15; *ibid.*, XIII (May
1941), 15; *ibid.*, XIII (July 1941), 8; undated memorandum, Harriman Papers,
Box 16; *Free World*, I (October 1941), 7–8.
11. "Work of the Commission to Study the Organization of Peace," memorandum,
December 6, 1941, CEA, 123379; *Study of the Organization of Peace*, p. 3;
Clyde Eagleton to members of the Commission, January 21, 1941, CEA,
123370; *New York Times*, June 7, 1941.
12. Beal, *Dulles*, pp. 89–91; Bartlett, *They Work for Tomorrow*, pp. 107–9; New
York *Times*, February 25, 1941; speech draft, May 13, 1941, Dulles Papers;
speech draft, May 28, 1941, Dulles Papers; Dulles to Lawrence, June 27, 1941,
Dulles Papers.
13. *Time*, XXXVII (March 17, 1941), 15–16; Streit, *Union Now*, pp. 3, 35,
passim.
14. *Time*, XXXVII (March 17, 1941), 15–16; *Headquarters Bulletin No. 1*, Federal
Union file, Hoover Library; *New York Times*, November 27, 1940; *ibid.*,
January 23, 1941; *New World*, XII (February 1940), 8; *Changing World*, XIII
(April 1941), 11.
15. Cantril and Strunk, *Public Opinion*, p. 373; *Public Opinion Quarterly*, VIII
(Fall 1944), 454; *Life*, X (February 17, 1941), 61–5.
16. Rosenman, *Public Papers of FDR*, IX, 672; Eichelberger to Roosevelt, April 6,
1941, and Roosevelt to Eichelberger, May 12, 1941, FDR Papers, OF 394,
Box 5.
17. Notter, *Postwar Foreign Policy Preparation*, pp. 41–2, 45; *Hull Memoirs*, II,
1630; *Newsweek*, XXIII (May 1, 1944), 37.
18. Wallace, *Democracy Reborn*, pp. 176–7; *New York Times*, April 9, 1941.
19. James B. Reston, "Acting Secretary," *New York Times Magazine*, August 3,
1941, pp. 9, 22; *Time*, XXXVIII (August 11, 1941), 10–13; *Nation*, CLV
(August 1, 1942), 87–90.
20. Welles, *World of the Four Freedoms*, pp. 11–13; *New York Times*, July 23,
1941; *ibid.*, July 24, 1941; *ibid.*, July 28, 1941; *Changing World*, XIII
(September 1941), 15.
21. *Foreign Relations of the United States, 1941*, I, 355, 363; Welles, *Seven
Decisions*, pp. 176–80; Welles, *Where Are We Heading?* pp. 5–15; Sherwood,
Roosevelt and Hopkins, p. 360.
22. *Changing World*, XIII (September 1941), 2, 9; CSOP, *Comment on the
Eight-Point Declaration*, pp. 10, 12–13; speech draft, November 24, 1944,
Dulles Papers; Dulles, *Long Range Peace Objectives*, pp. 8–9, 15–16, 19–21;
Van Kirk, *Religion and the World of Tomorrow*, pp. 52–3.

23. *Vital Speeches*, VIII (October 15, 1941), 18, 21; New York *Times*, October 2, 1941; Welles, *World of the Four Freedoms*, pp. 29–30, 32; New York *Times*, November 12, 1941.

CHAPTER THREE

1. Rosenman, *Public Papers of FDR*, X, 528–30; *Changing World*, XIII (December 1941), 3, 7, 13; *ibid.*, XIV (January 1942), 21.
2. Andrews to Holt, January 8, 1942, Holt Papers, Box 7; Ball, "Notes from Washington," December 24, 1941, Ball Papers; *Vital Speeches*, VIII (January 15, 1942), 202.
3. New York *Times*, January 3, 1942; *Hull Memoirs*, II, 1116–23; Sherwood, *Roosevelt and Hopkins*, pp. 446–53; Rosenman, *Working with Roosevelt*, pp. 316–17; Israel, *Long Diary*, pp. 239–40.
4. *Changing World*, XIV (January 1942), 3; *New Republic*, CVI (January 12, 1942), 35; Rosenman, *Public Papers of FDR*, XI, 35–46; New York *Times*, February 24, 1942; Eichelberger to McIntyre, April 11, 1942, and Roosevelt to Eichelberger, April 30, 1942, FDR Papers, PF 3833; Eichelberger to McIntyre, May 21, 1942, and Roosevelt to McIntyre, May 25, 1942, FDR Papers, PPF 3833.
5. Notter, *Postwar Foreign Policy Preparation*, pp. 58–9; Welles to Roosevelt, October 18, 1941, FDR Papers, OF 4351, Box 1; *Hull Memoirs*, II, 1632–3; *Foreign Relations, 1941*, I, 494–5.
6. Notter, *Postwar Foreign Policy Preparation*, pp. 72, 79–80, 82–3; Welles to Norman Davis, February 9, 1942, Norman H. Davis Papers, Library of Congress, Box 54; Welles, *Where Are We Heading?* pp. 20–1; Leo Pasvolsky to Walter Mallory, August 7, 1942, Pasvolsky Office Files, Box 3.
7. *Hull Memoirs*, II, 1635–8; minutes of Advisory Committee meeting, May 2, 1942, Cordell Hull Papers, Library of Congress, Box 82; Notter, *Postwar Foreign Policy Preparation*, pp. 74, 91–2; Israel, *Long Diary*, pp. 241, 243–4, 268; Hull to Austin, May 27, 1942, State Department files, National Archives Record Group 59, 111 Advisory Committee/11½; Connally and Steinberg, *Connally*, p. 262.
8. Notter, *Postwar Foreign Policy Preparation*, pp. 88–9, 108–9; Welles, *Where Are We Heading?* p. 22; Hull to Shotwell, June 25, 1942, 111 Advisory Committee/15D; Pasvolsky to Welles, July 31, 1942, Pasvolsky Office Files, Box 3; *Shotwell Autobiography*, p. 312; interview with Clark M. Eichelberger, New York City, August 13, 1965.
9. Yost to Pasvolsky, April 14, 1942, and Joseph M. Jones to Pasvolsky, April 11, 1942, Pasvolsky Office Files, Box 2; Notter, *Postwar Foreign Policy Preparation*, p. 149; memorandum of conversation by Harley Notter, June 17, 1942, Pasvolsky Office Files, Box 3; Hull to Austin, May 27, 1942, 111 Advisory Committee/7A; New York *Times*, July 12, 1942.
10. Eagleton memorandum, December 12, 1941, CEA, 123380; text of radio broadcast by Shotwell, December 13, 1941, CSOP file, Hoover Library; New York *Times*, February 15, 1942; CSOP, *Second Report*, pp. 3, 20, 22.
11. Eichelberger to Henry Haskell, March 10, 1942, CEA, 123404; Eichelberger to members of studies committee, February 13, 1942, CEA, 123416; *Changing World*, XIV (July 1942), 2; *ibid.*, XIV (April 1942), 10; CSOP flyer, "Victory in War—Victory in Peace"; CSOP, *Study Course on Immediate Post-War Problems*, pp. 3, 5–8; CSOP, *Toward Greater Freedom*, pp. 2, 5, 25.
12. Carnegie Endowment, *Year Book—1942*, p. 93; minutes of executive committee meeting, May 7, 1942, CEA, 4481; Shotwell to William P. Maddox, June 15, 1942, CEA, 120201; Shotwell to trustees, November 24, 1942, CEA, 120247; Eichelberger memorandum, July 8, 1942, CEA, 120210; "What Is the International Center?" San Francisco International Center files, Hoover Library; Eloise ReQua to Shotwell, May 2, 1942, CEA, 120183; Wright memorandum, undated, CEA, 120198.

13. *Changing World*, XIV (May 1942), 4; minutes of executive committee, CSOP, May 24, 1942, CEA, 123426; memorandum by Clark Eichelberger, July 24, 1942, CEA, 123466; Eichelberger to Shotwell, December 10, 1942, CEA, 120251; Shotwell to W. W. Waymack, July 9, 1942, CEA, 120211.

14. John R. Van de Water to Eichelberger, June 17, 1942, CEA, 120199; Eichelberger to McIntyre, May 21, 1942, FDR Papers, PPF 3833; *Changing World*, XIV (July 1942), 4; *ibid.*, XIV (May 1942), 2, 13; *ibid.*, XIV (April 1942), 15; *ibid.*, XIV (October 1942), 8; *ibid.*, XV (April 1943), 4; *ibid.*, XIV (January 1942), 6, 20.

15. New York *Times*, May 12, 1943; *Changing World*, XIV (May 1942), 12; press release, November 3, 1942, Woodrow Wilson Foundation files, Hoover Library.

16. Koch, *In Time to Come*, pp. 73–84, 93–4; New York *Times*, December 29, 1941; *ibid.*, January 4, 1942; *Time*, XXXIX (January 12, 1942), 42; *Changing World*, XIV (January 1942), 23; Padover, ed., *Wilson's Ideals*, p. 4; *Changing World*, XIV (November 1942), 1.

17. *Time*, XXXIX (March 16, 1942), 44–5; *Message from the National Study Conference on the Churches and a Just and Durable Peace* (1942), pp. 10–13, 19; Dulles to Sumner Welles, April 13, 1942, and Pasvolsky to Dulles, April 16, 1942, Pasvolsky Office Files, Box 2.

18. *Changing World*, XIII (July 1941), 15; *ibid.*, XIV (March 1942), 15; *ibid.*, XIV (June 1942), 15; New York *Times*, March 27, 1943.

19. New York *Times*, January 10, 1942; *ibid.*, January 20, 1943; *ibid.*, February 8, 1942; press release, May 4, 1942, Federal Union file, Hoover Library; New York *Times*, June 29, 1942; "Summary of Opinions and Ideas on International Post-War Problems," July 29, 1942, Hull Papers, Box 82; *Newsweek*, XX (November 16, 1942), 56.

20. Reves, *A Democratic Manifesto*, pp. 134–5; Gelber, *Peace by Power*, pp. 36–7, 127; Lord Davies to Hamilton Holt, January 2, 1942, Holt Papers, Box 7; New York *Times*, May 23, 1942; *ibid.*, May 24, 1942; Davies to Holt, July 9, 1942, Holt Papers, Box 7.

21. Spykman, *America's Strategy*, pp. 41, 446–7, 458, 461.

22. *Reader's Digest*, XLI (August 1942), 124–42; *Time*, XL (July 6, 1942), 14; Dulles to Hugh Gibson, June 22, 1942, Dulles Papers; Stanley Hornbeck to Hull, July 14, 1942, Hull Papers, Box 87; Hoover and Gibson, *Problems of Lasting Peace*, pp. 21, 105, 125, 143, 178, 201, 262–8.

23. *Foreign Relations*, 1942, III, 568–9, 573–4, 580–1.

24. Johnson, *Republican Party and Willkie*, pp. 50–2, 179; Dillon, *Willkie*, pp. 234, 243; Wendell Willkie, "Let's Look Ahead," New York *Times Magazine* (February 15, 1942), pp. 5, 33.

25. Johnson, *Republican Party and Willkie*, pp. 204–7; Westerfield, *Foreign Policy and Party Politics*, pp. 136–7; New York *Times*, April 21, 1942; *ibid.*, April 26, 1942; *Time*, XXXIX (April 27, 1942), 14; Israel, *Long Diary*, p. 259; *Private Papers of Vandenberg*, p. 30.

26. Hubert Herring, "Henry III of Iowa," *Harper's*, CLXXXVI (February 1943), 287–8; Lord, *Wallaces of Iowa*, pp. 483–4, 486, 489, 492; Louis Dolivet to Harriman, April 6, 1942, Harriman Papers, Box 15; Wallace to Roosevelt, May 4, 1942, FDR Papers, OF 12; Henry A. Wallace, "The Price of Free World Victory," *Free World*, III (June 1942), 9–13.

27. New York *Times*, May 9, 1942; Macdonald, *Wallace*, pp. 65, 98–9; *Newsweek*, XIX (June 1, 1942), 32; *New Republic*, CVI (May 25, 1942), 717, 725–6; Dulles to Wallace, July 27, 1942, Dulles Papers; *Atlantic Monthly*, CLXX (July 1942), 113; Carnegie Endowment, *Year Book—1943*, p. 63; Mary Huss to Michael Arond, June 29, 1942, Wallace Papers, Library of Congress, Box 9; *Vital Speeches*, VIII (July 15, 1942), 588; de Sales, *Making of Yesterday*, p. 254.

28. Welles, *World of the Four Freedoms*, pp. 70–2, 78; New York *Times*, May 31, 1942; *ibid.*, June 1, 1942; Shotwell to Norman Davis, June 2, 1942, Davis Papers, Box 8; New York *Times*, June 3, 1942; *ibid.*, June 6, 1942.

29. *Hull Memoirs*, II, 1227–8; Israel, *Long Diary*, pp. 271, 273, 277; Long diary, June 12, 15 and 22, 1942, Long Papers, Box 5; Rosenman, *Public Papers of FDR*, XI, 301.
30. Israel, *Long Diary*, p. 278; *Vital Speeches*, VIII (August 1, 1942), 611–13; New York *Times*, July 26, 1942; *Time*, XL (August 3, 1942), 16; *New Republic*, CVII (August 3, 1942), 131; Raoul de Roussy de Sales, "The Making of Yesterday, III," *Atlantic Monthly*, CLXXII (October 1943), 85, 88; New York *Times*, August 15, 1942.
31. New York *Times*, July 5, 1942; National Opinion Research Center, *Report Number 5*, p. 9; Bruner, *Mandate*, pp. 28, 30, 35–7; "Survey of Opinion and Ideas on International Post-War Problems," July 15, 1942, Hull Papers, Box 82; *Public Opinion Quarterly*, VI (Fall 1942), 491; Bidwell, *Our Foreign Policy*, pp. 53–69.
32. New York *Times*, July 5, 1942; *ibid.*, May 10, 1942; *ibid.*, June 23, 1942; Westerfield, *Foreign Policy and Party Politics*, p. 138; *Changing World*, XIV (May 1942), 3–4; *ibid.*, XIV (July 1942), 5.
33. Dillon, *Willkie*, p. 263; New York *Times*, August 4, 1942; *ibid.*, September 23, 1942; *ibid.*, September 24, 1942; *Time*, XL (October 5, 1942), 21; *ibid.*, XL (August 24, 1942), 15; *Newsweek*, XX (September 21, 1942), 40, 42; *ibid.*, XL (August 24, 1942), 76.
34. Rosenman, *Public Papers of FDR*, XI, 353, 425; Rosenman, *Working with Roosevelt*, pp. 362–3; Marvin McIntyre to Roosevelt, August 5, 1942, FDR Papers, OF 4040.
35. Johnson, *Republican Party and Willkie*, pp. 215, 220; Dillon, *Willkie*, p. 289; Barnes, *Willkie*, pp. 289–90; *Time*, XL (October 19, 1942), 16; Roosevelt to Willkie, October 13, 1942, FDR Papers, PPF 7023; *Vital Speeches*, IX (November 1, 1942), 34–9.
36. Barnes, *Willkie*, pp. 310–11; New York *Times*, October 27, 1942; *New Republic*, CVII (November 9, 1942), pp. 594–5, 608; Raoul de Roussy de Sales, "The Making of Yesterday, V," *Atlantic Monthly*, CLXII (December 1943), 71–2; Rosenman, *Public Papers of FDR*, XI, 436; Roosevelt to Arthur Proctor, November 2, 1942, FDR Papers, PPF 4242.
37. New York *Times*, November 4, 1942; *ibid.*, November 5, 1942; *Newsweek*, XX (November 16, 1942), 43, 46; *Time*, XL (November 16, 1942), 16–17, 20; *New Republic*, CVII (November 16, 1942), 623–8, 638.

CHAPTER FOUR

1. Buchanan, *United States in World War II*, I, 148–9, 235–42.
2. Welles, *World of the Four Freedoms*, pp. 97–8, 101, 108, 120–1.
3. New York *Times*, November 7, 1942; *Vital Speeches*, IX (December 15, 1942), 135; New York *Times*, January 3, 1943.
4. Johnson, *Republican Party and Willkie*, pp. 222–6; Martin and Donovan, *My First Fifty Years in Politics*, pp. 132–5; New York *Times*, December 8, 1942; *ibid.*, December 9, 1942; *Time*, XL (December 21, 1942), 30.
5. *Vital Speeches*, IX (January 1, 1942), 185–7; *ibid.*, IX (March 1, 1943), 318–20.
6. Wallace, *Democracy Reborn*, pp. 196–200; New York *Times*, December 3, 1942; *ibid.*, January 12, 1943; Wallace to Krock, December 8, 1942, and Krock to Cecil Grey, December 9, 1942, Hull Papers, Box 50; New York *Times*, December 24, 1942.
7. Wallace, *Democracy Reborn*, pp. 201–3, 205, 207; *Christian Century*, LX (January 13, 1943), 36; *Nation*, CLVI (January 2, 1943), 1; Freeman Matthews (London) to Hull, December 30, 1942, 840.50/982; Long diary, December 29, 1942, and January 10, 1943, Long Papers, Box 5.
8. Wallace, *Democracy Reborn*, pp. 199, 208; New York *Times*, December 13, 1942; *ibid.*, January 1, 1943; Wallace to Roosevelt, February 5, 1943, Wallace Papers, Roosevelt Library, Box 88; Welles to Wallace, March 3, 1943, Wallace Papers, Roosevelt Library, Box 109; *Newsweek*, XXI (January 25, 1943), 34.

9. Memorandum of conversation with Sir Ronald Campbell by Hull, August 14, 1942, 840.50/577; Jones to Pasvolsky, September 24, 1942, November 25, 1942, and February 3, 1943, Pasvolsky Office Files, Box 4; Daniels to McIntyre, December 5, 1942, FDR Papers, OF 394, Box 5.

10. *New Republic*, CVII (December 14, 1942), 779–80; *Life*, XIV (January 18, 1943), 28; Luce to Hull, January 25, 1943, and Hull to Luce, January 29, 1943, Hull Papers, Box 51; Kingsbury Smith, "The American Plan for a Reorganized World," *American Mercury*, LV (November 1942), 536–47.

11. Welles, *Where Are We Heading?* pp. 22–3; Welles, *Seven Decisions*, pp. 184–6; *Shotwell Autobiography*, pp. 312–13; Israel, *Long Diary*, pp. 284, 285, 297–8; Harley Notter to Welles, March 10, 1943, 500.CC/7; Notter, *Postwar Foreign Policy Preparation*, p. 74.

12. Daniels to Roosevelt, December 9, 1942, and Roosevelt to Daniels, December 14, 1942, FDR Papers, PPF 86, Box 2; *Christian Century*, LX (January 20, 1943), 79–80; Roseman, *Public Papers of FDR*, XII, 3, 5.

13. *Ibid.*, XII, 30, 32–3; *Newsweek*, XXI (January 18, 1943), 34; Feis, *Churchill, Roosevelt, Stalin*, pp. 108–11.

14. *Public Opinion Quarterly*, VII (Spring 1943), 173; Cantril and Strunk, *Public Opinion*, p. 907; *Free World*, IV (November 1942), 103; *ibid.*, V (January 1943), 4; *Changing World*, XIV (September 1942), 13; *ibid.*, XV (January 1943), 8; *New Republic*, CVIII (February 1, 1943), 136; *ibid.*, CVIII (February 8, 1943), 165.

15. Eichelberger to Roosevelt, October 19, 1942, and Eichelberger to Edwin Watson, November 9, 1942, FDR Papers, PPF 3833; memo by Grace Tully, November 13, 1942, *F.D.R.: Personal Letters*, II, 1366–7; interview with Clark M. Eichelberger, New York City, August 13, 1965; *Changing World*, XIV (November 1942), 2; minutes of CSOP executive committee, December 13, 1942, CEA, 123532; Frederick C. McKee to Florence Harriman, December 28, 1942, Harriman Papers, Box 15.

16. Eichelberger to Roosevelt, December 22, 1942, Eichelberger to McIntyre, December 22, 1942, Roosevelt to McIntyre, December 30, 1942, and Eichelberger to McIntyre, December 31, 1942, FDR Papers, PPF 3833.

17. Undated memo, Harriman Papers, Box 13; Eichelberger to McIntyre, January 8, 1943, and Herbert Houston to Roosevelt, January 4, 1943, FDR Papers, OF 4725A; Eichelberger to Harriman, February 15, 1943, Harriman Papers, Box 20; *Changing World*, XV (March 1943), 1, 4.

18. *New York Times*, February 28, 1943; *Changing World*, XV (March 1943), 2, 3, 8; CSOP, *Third Report* (New York, 1943), pp. 7, 11, 33.

19. Dulles to Welles, November 11, 1942, Pasvolsky to Welles, December 7, 1942, and Pasvolsky to Dulles, December 8, 1942, Pasvolsky Office Files, Box 4; draft of Dulles statement, December 10, 1942, Dulles Papers; Van Dusen to Dr. William Paton, February 9, 1943, Dulles Papers; *New York Times*, March 19, 1943; *Vital Speeches*, IX (April 15, 1943), 406.

20. CJDP, *A Just and Durable Peace*, pp. 7–8, 10–11; *New York Times*, March 19, 1943; Dulles to Roosevelt, March 26, 1943, Dulles to Stephen Early, March 29, 1943, and William Hassett to Rosenman, March 31, 1943, FDR Papers, OF 213.

21. *New York Times*, January 5, 1943; *ibid.*, January 8, 1943; *ibid.*, January 9, 1943; *Congressional Record* (January 6, 1943), p. 14; *ibid.*, (January 18, 1943), pp. 209–10; Hull to Wiley, October 21, 1942, 711.00/1614; Israel, *Long Diary*, p. 300.

22. Sol Bloom to Hull, February 3, 1943, 500.CC/1; Foster Stearns to Sumner Welles, March 4, 1943, 840.50/1570; *Congressional Record* (February 4, 1943), pp. 571–2; *New Republic*, CVIII (January 11, 1943), 38; *Time*, XLI (January 25, 1943), 21; *New York Times*, February 14, 1943; *ibid.*, February 17, 1943; *ibid.*, March 3, 1943; *ibid.*, March 4, 1943; *Nation*, CLVI (March 13, 1943), 365.

23. Hull to Bloom, February 16, 1943, 500.CC/1; *Foreign Relations, 1943*, III, 2, 5; Hackworth to Welles, March 6, 1943, 840.50/572; Felton Johnson to Long,

March 6, 1943, Long Papers, Box 198; Connally to Gillette, March 6, 1943; Papers of the Senate Foreign Relations Committee, National Archives, Record Group 46, File R–6 78–1.

24. Potomacus, "The Senator from Minnesota," *New Republic*, CVIII (May 31, 1943), 727–8; Roscoe Drummond, "Senator Ball of Minnesota," *American Mercury*, LX (May 1945), 530–3; Finney, "Ball," pp. 303–4; Ball, "Notes from Washington," June 18 and June 25, 1942, Ball Papers.

25. Interview with Joseph H. Ball, Front Royal, Virginia, July 25, 1965; Helena Huntington Smith, "The Man Who Stuck His Neck Out," *Collier's*, CXI (June 5, 1943), 29; *Congressional Record* (March 16, 1943), p. 2030.

26. Frank McNaughton to James McConaughy, March 13, 1943, McNaughton Papers; *Nation*, CLVII (October 16, 1943), 427; New York *Times*, March 14, 1943; *ibid.*, March 15, 1943.

27. *Congressional Record* (March 16, 1943), pp. 2030–1; typescript of press conference, March 16, 1943, FDR Papers, PPF 1–P, XXI, 206; New York *Times*, March 17, 1943; *Atlantic Monthly*, CLXXI (May 1943), 23; typescript of press conference, March 19, 1943, FDR Papers, PPF 1–P, XXI, 210.

28. *Hull Memoirs*, II, 1260–2; *Private Papers of Vandenburg*, pp. 40–1; *Foreign Relations, 1943*, III, 11, 30–1; New York *Times*, March 19, 1943.

29. New York *Times*, March 25, 1943; *ibid.*, March 26, 1943; McNaughton to McConaughy, March 26, 1943, McNaughton Papers; Ball interview, July 23, 1965; Connally and Steinberg, *Connally*, p. 263; Grace Tully to Roosevelt, March 24, 1943, and Roosevelt to Byrnes, March 25, 1943, FDR Papers, OF 394, Box 6.

30. *Hull Memoirs*, II, 1261; text of press release, March 22, 1943, Long Papers, Box 198; Vandenberg to Hull, March 24, 1943, and Hull to Vandenberg, March 26, 1943, Hull Papers, Box 51.

31. New York *Times*, March 16, 1943; *ibid.*, March 17, 1943; *ibid.*, March 22, 1943; Israel, *Long Diary*, p. 301; New York *Times*, March 28, 1943; *New Republic*, CVIII (March 19, 1943), 400; *Nation*, CLVI (March 27, 1943), 436.

CHAPTER FIVE

1. Eichelberger to United Nations committees, April 3, 1943, CEA, 63011; *Changing World*, XV (April 1943), 1–2; *Free World*, V (April 1943), 294; minutes of LNA board meeting, March 27, 1943, CEA, 63017; Victor Elting to Malcolm Davis, July 20, 1943, CEA, 63018; minutes of UNA executive committee meeting, August 27, 1943, CEA, 63021; New York *Times*, July 31, 1943.

2. *Changing World*, XV (July 1943), 6, 7; Samuel Myres to Malcolm Davis, June 15, 1943, CEA, 120370; *Changing World*, XV (October 1943), 3; *ibid.*, XV (September 1943), 5; "Unite for Lasting Victory," UNA file, Hoover Library; *Changing World*, XV (September 1943), 1.

3. Minutes of NPC organizing meeting, March 11, 1943, CEA, 63759; Mowrer to Malcolm Davis, March 19, 1943, CEA, 63765; New York *Times*, April 17, 1943; Carnegie Endowment, *Year Book—1944*, p. 45; Davis to Mowrer, July 9, 1943, CEA, 63791; Mowrer to Davis, May 14, 1943, CEA, 63783; minutes of NPC meeting, June 17, 1943, CEA, 63786; NPC, "Your Congress Can Win the War," Freedom House file, Hoover Library; New York *Times*, June 28, 1943.

4. Almond, *American People and Foreign Policy*, p. 177; undated leaflet, WAC file, Hoover Library; *Changing World*, XV (March 1943), 8; *ibid.*, XV (April 1943), 6; "Twenty Questions on an International Police Force," June 1943, WAC file, Hoover Library.

5. New York *Times*, June 6, 1943; "For This We Fight," undated brochure, CSOP file, Hoover Library; *Changing World*, XV (May 1943), 7; *ibid.*, XV (July 1943), 2, 8; *ibid.*, XV (September 1943), 8; "Winning the War on the

Spiritual Front," undated pamphlet, CSOP file, Hoover Library; Eichelberger to members of studies committee, April 15, 1943, CEA, 123581; Margaret Olson to members of CSOP, August 31, 1943, CEA, 123686.

6. Interview with Clark Eichelberger, New York City, August 13, 1965; Malcolm Davis Memoir, Oral History Project, pp. 343, 350; George Finch to Eichelberger, July 20, 1943, CEA, 123540; Davis to Mowrer, April 5, 1943, CEA, 63763.
7. New York *Times*, March 26, 1943; Barnes, *Willkie*, pp. 313–14.
8. Willkie, *One World*, pp. 2, 102, 158, 161, 177, 203.
9. *Nation*, CLVI (April 24, 1943), 605; *New Republic*, CVIII (April 19, 1943), 513; New York *Times*, April 11, 1943; *Foreign Affairs*, XXII (October 1943), 161; *Atlantic Monthly*, CLXXI (May 1943), 125; *Nation*, CLVII (November 6, 1943), 515; Barnes, *Willkie*, pp. 314–15; New York *Times*, May 16, 1943; *New Yorker*, XIX (May 15, 1943), 14; *Newsweek*, XXI (May 31, 1943), 78; *New Republic*, CIX (October 11, 1943), 483.
10. *Changing World*, XV (April 1943), 7; Johnson, *Republican Party and Willkie*, pp. 241–2; New York *Times*, May 4, 1943; undated brochure, Republican Postwar Policy Association file, Hoover Library; *Nation*, CLVI (June 12, 1943), 822; *Newsweek*, XXII (July 19, 1943), 42, 44; New York *Times*, July 20, 1943.
11. Johnson, *Republican Party and Willkie*, p. 243; Westerfield, *Foreign Policy and Party Politics*, pp. 150–1; Washington *Times-Herald* clipping, June 2, 1943, Hull Papers, Box 87; *Newsweek*, XXI (June 14, 1943), 32; *Time*, XLI (June 7, 1943), 26.
12. *Private Papers of Vandenberg*, pp. 42–51; Connally and Steinberg, *Connally*, p. 257; New York *Times*, April 1, 1943; *ibid.*, April 16, 1943.
13. Frank McNaughton to James McConaughy, March 26, 1943, McNaughton Papers; Migel to Green, May 4, 1943, Green Papers, Box 284; Fisher to Green, May 7, 1943, Green Papers, Box 284; R. F. Wood to Truman, March 23, 1943, Truman Papers, Senatorial Files, Box 149; Connally to Archie Bahm, May 13, 1943, Senate Foreign Relations Committee Papers, File R–9 78–1.
14. New York *Times*, April 3, 1943; *ibid.*, July 1, 1943; Frances L. Landry to Connally, May 12, 1943, and Brunauer to Connally, July 13, 1943, Senate Foreign Relations Committee Papers, R–9 78–1.
15. New York *Times*, April 1, 1943; *ibid.*, April 13, 1943; *Nation*, CLVI (April 24, 1943), 590; New York *Times*, April 15, 1943; *ibid.*, April 11, 1943; McNaughton to McConaughy, March 29, 1943, McNaughton Papers; New York *Times*, June 20, 1943; *ibid.*, May 26, 1943; *ibid.*, April 16, 1943.
16. *Ibid.*, April 19, 1943; *Private Papers of Vandenberg*, p. 47; *New Republic*, CVIII (April 26, 1943), 547; undated Mowrer memo, CEA, 63779.
17. New York *Times*, May 2, 1943; Bruner, *Mandate*, pp. 45–7; *Public Opinion Quarterly*, VII (Summer 1943), 299; *New Yorker*, XIX (May 15, 1943), 11; Cantril and Strunk, *Public Opinion*, p. 373.
18. *Newsweek*, XXI (June 28, 1943), 38; *Congressional Record* (February 16, 1943), p. 1012; Fulbright to Welles, April 9, 1943, and Welles to Fulbright, April 13, 1943, 500.CC/22; Westerfield, *Foreign Policy and Party Politics*, pp. 148–9; *Congressional Record* (June 15, 1943), p. 5934; *ibid.* (June 16, 1943), p. 5971; New York *Times*, June 16, 1943.
19. *Congressional Record* (June 16, 1943), pp. 5943–4; *Time*, XLI (June 28, 1943), 15; *Nation*, CLVI (June 26, 1943), 878; New York *Times*, June 16, 1943; *ibid.*, June 30, 1943.
20. Fulbright to Roosevelt, June 26, 1943, Roosevelt to Hull, June 28, 1943, Hull to Roosevelt, June 28, 1943, and Roosevelt to Fulbright, June 30, 1943, FDR Papers, OF 3575 and OF 394, Box 6.
21. *Congressional Record* (July 2, 1943), pp. 6998, 7019–21; *Private Papers of Vandenberg*, pp. 53–5.
22. New York *Times*, March 22, 1943; *Time*, XLI (March 29, 1943), 18–19; "Draft Constitution of the International Organization," March 26, 1943, Hull Papers, Box 87; *Foreign Relations*, 1943, III, 37–9; Eden, *The Reckoning*, pp. 436–7.

23. Memo by Stephen Early, December 2, 1942, and Roosevelt to Welles, February 16, 1943, FDR Papers, OF 4287; Forrest Davis, "Roosevelt's World Blueprint," *Saturday Evening Post*, CCXV (April 10, 1943), 20–1, 109–10.
24. Dunn to Hull, April 9, 1943, Hull Papers, Box 82; Long diary, April 21, 1943, Long Papers, Box 5; memo by Bowman, April 24, 1943, Hull Papers, Box 87; *Hull Memoirs*, II, 1639; Russell, *United Nations Charter*, p. 219; Hull to Luther Johnson, July 12, 1943, 111 Advisory Committee/93A; Notter, *Postwar Foreign Policy Preparation*, p. 167; Eichelberger interview, August 13, 1965.
25. Typescript of press conference, February 23, 1943, FDR Papers, PPF 1–P, XXI, 184; Welles to Hull, March 3, 1943, and Hull to Welles, March 7, 1943, Hull Papers, Box 51; *Newsweek*, XXI (March 8, 1943), 39; typescript of press conference, March 19, 1943, FDR Papers, PPF 1–P, XXI, 209–10; Rosenman, *Public Papers of FDR*, XII, 133.
26. New York *Times*, March 31, 1943; *Time*, XLI (April 19, 1943), 50–1; *Congressional Record* (April 2, 1943), p. 2895; *ibid.*, (April 14, 1943), p. 3342; *Newsweek*, XXI (May 31, 1943), 34, 36; *Time*, XLI (May 31, 1943), 22; State Department, *Bulletin*, VIII (June 19, 1943), 553; *ibid.*, VIII (June 12, 1943), 518, 520; New York *Times*, June 8, 1943.
27. Notter, *Postwar Foreign Policy Preparation*, p. 137; State Department, *Bulletin*, VIII (June 12, 1943), 523–8; Kenneth Colegrove, "The Role of Congress and Public Opinion in Formulating Foreign Policy," *American Political Science Review*, XXXVIII (October 1944), 959–60; Westerfield, *Foreign Policy and Party Politics*, p. 153; *Congressional Record* (July 6, 1943), p. 7237; *Private Papers of Vandenberg*, p. 67.
28. Connally and Steinberg, *Connally*, p. 262; Colegrove, *American Senate and World Peace*, pp. 29–30; *Congressional Record* (July 8, 1943), pp. 7434–6; *Private Papers of Vandenberg*, pp. 70–2; Hull to Roosevelt, August 10, 1943, Long Papers, Box 211; memo by Sayre, August 16, 1943, 840.50/2696; New York *Times*, August 18, 1943; Vandenberg to Acheson, August 19, 1943, 840.50/2697.
29. Rosenman, *Public Papers of FDR*, XII, 333.
30. Hull to Wallace, June 2, 1943, Hull Papers, Box 51; Wallace, *Democracy Reborn*, pp. 239, 244; Roosevelt to Wallace, July 28, 1945, Wallace Papers, Roosevelt Library, Box 88; New York *Times*, June 1, 1943.
31. Barnes, *Willkie*, pp. 314–16; *New Yorker*, XIX (May 15, 1943), 14; *Time*, XLII (August 2, 1943), 44; *Atlantic Monthly*, CLXXII (July 1943), 121; *Prefaces to Peace*, p. ii; New York *Times Book Review* (July 18, 1943), p. 1.
32. *Vital Speeches*, IX (May 15, 1943), 457–9; Roberts to Hull, August 11, 1943, Hull Papers, Box 52; Harold E. Stassen, "We Need a World Government," *Saturday Evening Post*, CCXV (May 22, 1943), 11, 41, 44, 48; Harold E. Stassen, "Blueprint for a World Government," New York *Times Magazine* (May 23, 1943), pp. 1, 34.
33. *Time*, XLI (April 12, 1943), 24; Ely Culbertson, "A System to Win This War and the Peace to Come," *Reader's Digest*, XLII (February 1943), 135–42; Culbertson, *Summary of the World Federation Plan*, pp. 2–3, 14, 23, 30, 36, 47–50; Culbertson, *Total Peace*, pp. 8–9, 14, 245–6.
34. *Time*, XLII (September 13, 1943), 106; *New Republic*, CVIII (June 28, 1943), 865; *Nation*, CLVI (April 24, 1943), 582–3, 585–6; Rowe to Pasvolsky, July 23, 1942, Pasvolsky Office Files, Box 3; Holt to Culbertson, December 14, 1942, Holt Papers, Box 7; *Nation*, CLVI (June 5, 1943), 818.
35. *Newsweek*, XXI (April 19, 1943), 96; *Vital Speeches*, IX (July 1, 1943), 568; *Life*, XIV (September 20, 1943), 106; Dulles to Luce, September 29, 1943, Dulles Papers; Luce to Holt, September 22, 1943, Holt Papers, Box 7; Taylor, *Men in Motion*, pp. 41, 277, 281.
36. Herbert Hoover and Hugh Gibson, "New Approaches to Lasting Peace," *Collier's*, CXI (June 5, 1943), 11–12; *ibid.*, CXI (June 12, 1943), 74–5; *ibid.*, CXI (June 26, 1943), 33.
37. *Vital Speeches*, IX (October 1, 1943), 761–5; *Time*, XLII (September 6,

1943), 22; *Nation,* CLVII (September 4, 1943), 255; New York *Times,* August 17, 1943; *Collier's,* CXII (August 7, 1943), 74.

38. Weingast, *Walter Lippmann,* pp. 15–17; Walter Lippmann Memoir, Oral History Project, pp. 203–4.

39. Lippmann, *U.S. Foreign Policy,* pp. 7, 25–6, 100–1, 107, 136, 146, 164–5, 168.

40. Lippmann Memoir, Oral History Project, p. 215; New York *Times Book Review* (July 4, 1943), p. 9; *Atlantic Monthly,* CLXXII (October 1943), 132; *Reader's Digest,* XLIII (July 1943), 119; *Ladies' Home Journal,* LX (August 1943), 31.

41. New York *Times Book Review* (June 13, 1943), p. 1; *Harper's,* CLXXXVII (July 1943); *Atlantic Monthly,* CLXXII (July 1943), 70–2; *New Republic,* CIX (July 5, 1943), 27; Mary Workman to Malcolm Davis, October 8, 1943, CEA, 63044; Long to Hull, August 28, 1943, and Warren to Long, July 11, 1943, Long Papers, Box 194; Roosevelt to Grace Tully, April 1, 1943, FDR Papers, PPF 2037.

42. "Notes from Washington," July 15, 1943, Ball Papers; Ball interview, July 23, 1965; New York *Times,* July 4, 1943; *Changing World,* XV (July 1943), 2; *ibid.,* XV (September 1943), 2; Malcolm Davis to Mrs. A. J. McGuire, August 30, 1943, CEA, 120454.

43. *Changing World,* XV (July 1943), 5; Talbott to Eichelberger, July 15, 1943, CEA, 120390; Harry E. Terrell to Davis, August 14, 1943, CEA, 120429; Truman to Leonard Williams, August 23, 1943, Truman Papers, Senatorial Files, Box 150.

44. Minutes of UNA meeting, August 27, 1943, CEA, 63022; Eichelberger to Butler, August 18, 1943, CEA, 63018; Butler to Eichelberger, August 20, 1943, CEA, 63019; Davis to Robert Gulich, August 16, 1943, CEA, 123680; Dickey to Hull, September 25, 1943, Long Papers, Box 204.

45. F. B. Sayre to Davis, July 23, 1943, CEA, 63804; minutes of NPC meetings, July 29 and August 24, 1943, CEA, 63806 and 63832; New York *Times,* September 13, 1943; Wallace to Roosevelt and Roosevelt to Hull, September 8, 1943, FDR Papers, OF 12; *Vital Speeches,* IX (October 1, 1943), 754–7; New York *Times,* September 12, 1943.

46. New York *Times,* July 22, 1943; *ibid.,* July 28, 1943; *Newsweek,* XXII (August 9, 1943), 40, 42; *ibid.,* XXII (September 13, 1943), 33; New York *Times,* August 27, 1943; *Private Papers of Vandenberg,* pp. 55–8; Johnson, *Republican Party and Willkie,* pp. 244–5; Westerfield, *Foreign Policy and Party Politics,* p. 151.

47. *Ibid.,* pp. 152–3; New York *Times,* September 3, 1943; *ibid.,* September 4, 1943; *ibid.,* September 6, 1943; *Newsweek,* XXII (September 13, 1943), 33; *ibid.,* XXII (September 20, 1943), 40; New York *Times,* September 7, 1943; *Time,* XLII (September 20, 1943), 19–20.

48. New York *Times,* September 9, 1943; *Newsweek,* XXII (October 25, 1943), 60; Crabb, *Bipartisan Foreign Policy,* pp. 49–50; *Private Papers of Vandenberg,* pp. 59–60.

49. New York *Times,* September 8, 1943; *Nation,* CLVII (September 18, 1943), 311; *Free World,* VI (October 1943), 298; minutes of NPC meeting, September 9, 1943, CEA, 63840; New York *Times,* September 11, 1943; typescript of press conference, September 7, 1943, FDR Papers, PPF 1–P, XXII, 93–4; *Hull Memoirs,* II, 1258–9; New York *Times,* September 8, 1943.

50. *Ibid.,* September 24, 1943; *New Republic,* CXI (September 18, 1944), 331; New York *Times,* September 30, 1943; *ibid.,* October 1, 1943.

51. *New Republic,* CVIII (February 15, 1943), 197; *Vital Speeches,* IX (August 1, 1943), 619–20; CSOP, *U.S. and Postwar International Organization,* pp. 10–11; New York *Times,* October 7, 1943; *Christian Century,* LX (October 13, 1943), 1158–9.

52. *Public Opinion Quarterly,* VII (Winter 1943), 760; Menefee, *Assignment: U.S.A.,* pp. 142–4; *Public Opinion Quarterly,* VII (Summer 1943), 304.

53. Bidwell, *U.S. and the United Nations, passim; Public Opinion Quarterly,* VII

(Winter 1943), 759; memorandum of conversation with Litvinov by Hull, May 8, 1943, Pasvolsky Office Files, Box 5; *Changing World*, XV (June 1943), 6–7.
54. *Public Opinion Quarterly*, VII (Summer 1943), 267–79; *Time*, XLII (October 11, 1943), 18; Bruner, *Mandate*, p. 230.

CHAPTER SIX

1. Taylor memo, July 8, 1943, Hull Papers, Box 52; Pasvolsky memo, August 9, 1943, Hull Papers, Box 82; Notter, *Postwar Foreign Policy Preparation*, pp. 172, 188, 553; Russell, *United Nations Charter*, pp. 119–24; *Hull Memoirs*, II, 1238–9; Rosenman, *Public Papers of FDR*, XII, 368.
2. Washington *Star*, August 24, 1943, clipping in Long Papers, Box 5; New York *Times*, August 25, 1943; *ibid.*, August 4, 1943; *ibid.*, August 5, 1943; *ibid.*, August 6, 1943; Israel, *Long Diary*, pp. 281, 322–5.
3. Israel, *Long Diary*, pp. 323, 327; *Hull Memoirs*, II, 1230; *Foreign Relations, 1943*, I, 519.
4. *New Republic*, CIX (September 6, 1943), 319; *Nation*, CLVII (September 4, 1943), 253; *Newsweek*, XXII (September 6, 1943), 48; *Atlantic Monthly*, CLXXII (October 1943), 21; *Time*, XLII (September 6, 1942), 21; *Nation*, CLVII (September 4, 1943), 259; typescript of press conference, August 31, 1943, FDR Papers, PPF 1–P, XXII, 82–5.
5. Israel, *Long Diary*, pp. 326–9; State Department, *Bulletin*, IX (September 18, 1943), 177, 179.
6. *Ibid.*, IX (September 25, 1943), 208; New York *Times*, September 26, 1943; *Nation*, CLVII (October 9, 1943), 402; *New Republic*, CIX (October 4, 1943), 441.
7. *Nation*, CLVII (September 18, 1943), 312; *Newsweek*, XXII (September 13, 1943), 18; *Time*, XLII (July 19, 1943), 23; New York *Times*, September 17, 1943; *Congressional Record* (September 17, 1943), pp. 7618, 7623.
8. Westerfield, *Foreign Policy and Party Politics*, pp. 155–6; New York *Times*, September 19, 1943; *ibid.*, September 21, 1943; *Congressional Record* (September 20, 1943), pp. 7646, 7655, 7657, 7659, 7666.
9. *Ibid.* (September 20, 1943), pp. 7659–60, 7670–1, 7680, 7706; *ibid.* (September 21, 1943), pp. 7724, 7726–8.
10. *Ibid.* (September 20, 1943), pp. 7651, 7665–6, 7677; *ibid.* (September 21, 1943), 7712–14.
11. *Ibid.* (September 20, 1943), pp. 7647, 7660–1, 7672, 7675–6; *ibid.* (September 21, 1943), p. 7709.
12. *Ibid.* (September 21, 1943), pp. 7723, 7728–9; *Nation*, CLVII (October 2, 1943), 370–1; New York *Times*, September 22, 1943; *Newsweek*, XXII (October 4, 1943), 42; State Department, *Bulletin*, IX (September 25, 1943), 207–8; *Congressional Record* (October 4, 1943), p. 8028.
13. McNaughton to Eleanor Welch, September 25, 1943, McNaughton Papers; New York *Times*, September 25, 1943; *New Republic*, CIX (September 27, 1943), 408; New York *Times*, October 4, 1943.
14. McNaughton to Eleanor Welch, September 30, 1943, McNaughton Papers; New York *Times*, September 30, 1943; *Nation*, CLVII (October 16, 1943), 428.
15. Connally and Steinberg, *Connally*, p. 264; *Private Papers of Vandenberg*, p. 62; New York *Times*, October 14, 1943; Stettinius to Hull, October 15 and 25, 1943, Hull Papers, Box 83; *Congressional Record* (October 14, 1943), pp. 8293–4; New York *Times*, October 16, 1943; Ball interview, July 23, 1965.
16. Theodore Green to Mrs. Thomas M. Claflin, October 20, 1943, Green Papers, Box 283; Elbert Thomas to R. W. Lovell, October 19, 1943, Thomas Papers, Box 55; New York *Times*, October 20, 1943; transcript of press conference by Senator Connally, October 21, 1943, Senate Foreign Relations Committee Papers, R–25 78–1; *Senate Report No. 478*, 78C., 1S., pp. 1–2; New York *Times*, October 22, 1943; *Newsweek*, XXII (October 25, 1943), 42; *Time*, XLII (October 25, 1943), 19; *New Republic*, CIX (October 25, 1943), 555.

17. *Changing World*, XV (December 1943), 1; minutes of NPC meeting, October 22, 1943, CEA, 63844; Ryan to Connally, October 22, 1943, and Dulles to Connally, October 22, 1943, Senate Foreign Relations Committee Papers, R–25 78–1; Flora M. Hesse to Truman, October 25, 1943, Truman Papers, Senatorial Files, Box 150; Murray to Green, October 28, 1943, Green Papers, Box 283; *Free World*, VI (December 1943), 513; Calvin B. Haver to Connally, October 26, 1943, Senate Foreign Relations Committee Papers, R–25 78–1.

18. New York *Times*, October 26, 1943; *ibid.*, October 27, 1943; *Nation*, CLVII (November 6, 1943), 518–19; *Newsweek*, XXII (November 8, 1943), 35–6; *Congressional Record* (October 25, 1943), pp. 8650, 8665–7, 8672, 8685; *ibid.* (October 26, 1943), p. 8732.

19. *Ibid.* (October 25, 1943), pp. 8678–88; *ibid.* (October 26, 1943), pp. 8627–40; *ibid.* (October 27, 1943), pp. 8785–8, 8791–804; *ibid.* (October 28, 1943), pp. 8843–53; *ibid.* (October 29, 1943), pp. 8887–95, 8898.

20. Stettinius to Hull, October 22, 26, and 30, 1943, Hull Papers, Box 52; Stettinius to Hull, October 27, 1943, Hull Papers, Box 83; Rosenman, *Public Papers of FDR*, XII, 460–1; *F.D.R.: Personal Letters*, II, 1460.

21. *Hull Memoirs*, II, 1274, 1279, 1281, 1307; *Foreign Relations, 1943*, I, 597–8; Feis, *Churchill, Roosevelt, Stalin*, pp. 208, 216–17; State Department, *Bulletin*, IX (November 6, 1943), 309.

22. *Congressional Record* (November 1, 1943), pp. 8920–2, 8937, 8944; New York *Times*, November 3, 1943; *Newsweek*, XXII (November 15, 1943), 52, 54; Long diary, November 3 and 7, 1943, Long Papers, Box 5; Stettinius to Hull, November 3, 1943, Hull Papers, Box 83.

23. "hd" to Green, November 3, 1943, Green Papers, Box 266; undated memo, Thomas Papers, Box 55; *Private Papers of Vandenberg*, p. 63; Byrnes to Roosevelt, November 3, 1943, FDR Papers, OF 419; *Congressional Record* (November 3, 1943), pp. 9066–8.

24. *Ibid.* (November 2, 1943), p. 9006; *ibid.* (November 3, 1943), pp. 9045, 9075; *ibid.* (November 4, 1943), pp. 9083, 9087, 9096–9, 9106; *ibid.* (November 5, 1943), pp. 9182, 9206, 9213.

25. *Ibid.* (November 5, 1943), pp. 9221–2; New York *Times*, November 6, 1943; *Time*, XLII (November 15, 1943), 18.

26. New York *Times*, November 6, 1943; *New Republic*, CIX (November 15, 1943), 668; New York *Times*, November 29, 1943; Stettinius to Hull, November 5, 1943, Hull Papers, Box 84; *F.D.R.: Personal Letters*, II, 1467; Ball interview, July 23, 1965; New York *Times*, November 7, 1943; Israel, *Long Diary*, p. 333.

27. Lippmann to Roosevelt, November 2, 1943, FDR Papers, PPF 2037; *Vital Speeches*, X (December 15, 1943), 139; *Newsweek*, XXII (November 15, 1943), 112; *Nation*, CLVII (November 13, 1943), 545, 546; *Newsweek*, XXII (December 13, 1943), 44; *ibid.*, XXII (November 29, 1943), 47; New York *Times*, November 14, 1943; *Christian Century*, LX (December 1, 1943), 1392–3.

28. *Free World*, VI (December 1943), 487; *Newsweek*, XXII (November 22, 1943), 34, 37; Carlton Savage to Stettinius, November 3, 1943, Long Papers, Box 204; Israel, *Long Diary*, pp. 333–4; *Newsweek*, XXII (November 29, 1943), 42; *Hull Memoirs*, II, 1314; *New Republic*, CIX (November 29, 1943), 743; State Department, *Bulletin*, IX (November 20, 1943), 341–5.

CHAPTER SEVEN

1. State Department, *Bulletin*, IX (November 13, 1943), 317–19; memo by Francis B. Sayre, September 22, 1943, 840.50/2659; New York *Times*, September 24, 1943; "House Joint Resolution 192," *Hearings* before the House Committee on Foreign Affairs, 78C., 2S., pp. 9–10, 48, 53; Woodbridge, *UNRRA*, I, 32; *Congressional Record* (November 15, 1943), p. 9485; *ibid.* (January 25, 1944), pp. 694–5; *ibid.* (February 17, 1944), p. 1829; *Nation*, CLVII (November 13, 1943), 548.

2. Smith, *American Diplomacy*, p. 75; Sherwood, *Roosevelt and Hopkins*, p. 799; Lippmann Memoir, Oral History Project, p. 217.
3. Sherwood, *Roosevelt and Hopkins*, pp. 785–6; *Foreign Relations: Cairo and Tehran*, pp. 530–1, 595–6; Feis, *Churchill, Roosevelt, Stalin*, pp. 270–1; McNeill, *America, Britain and Russia*, pp. 356–7.
4. State Department, *Bulletin*, IX (December 11, 1943), 409; *Nation*, CLVII (December 11, 1943), 683; *New Republic*, CIX (December 13, 1943), 835; State Department, *Bulletin*, X (January 1, 1944), 3–7.
5. *New York Times*, October 29, 1943; *Time*, XLII (November 8, 1943), 34; *Christian Century*, LX (November 10, 1943), 1292; text of Dulles speech, October 28, 1943, Dulles Papers; *Post War World*, I (December 15, 1943), 1; CJDP, *Guidebook for Action*, p. 11.
6. Oxnam to Hull, March 1, 1943, Hull Papers, Box 51; *Time*, XLII (November 22, 1943), 43; *New York Times*, January 13, 1944; *Christian Century*, LXI (January 26, 1944), 124.
7. *Congressional Record* (February 8, 1944), pp. 1408–9; various letters to Henry Wallace, February and March 1944, Wallace Papers, Library of Congress, Boxes 39 and 48; various letters to Senator Green, spring 1944, Green Papers, Box 343; various letters to Senator Truman, spring 1944, Truman Papers, Box 139; A. C. Ames to Truman, January 22, 1944, and Frances Robertson to Truman, February 22, 1944, Truman Papers, Senatorial Files, Box 150; *Christian Century*, LXI (March 22, 1944), 356; *ibid.*, LXI (April 19, 1944), 485–6; *Post War World*, I (April 15, 1944), 1; *Changing World*, XVI (May 1944), 5.
8. *Post War World*, I (December 15, 1943), 1; *New York Times*, January 22, 1944; *ibid.*, February 9, 1944; Tucker to Roosevelt, February 2, 1944, FDR Papers, OF 213; *New York Times*, February 16, 1944; *Post War World*, I (April 15, 1944), 1; *Christian Century*, LXI (May 3, 1944).
9. *Time*, XLII (November 22, 1943), 19–20; *New York Times*, November 14, 1943; minutes of NPC meeting, November 19, 1943, Harriman Papers, Box 16; minutes of NPC meetings, January 20 and February 3, 1944, CEA, 63881 and 63891; *Changing World*, XVI (May 1944), 5; *New York Times*, May 15, 1944; Louise Warren Johnson to Truman, May 22, 1944, Truman Papers, Box 139.
10. *New York Times*, November 21, 1943; CSOP, *Fourth Report*, pp. 10–12, 14, 25–7; Shotwell to Hull, November 26, 1943, Hull Papers, Box 52.
11. William Allan Neilson to Florence Harriman, December 10, 1943, Harriman Papers, Box 16; minutes of CSOP executive committee meeting, February 14, 1944, CEA, 123795; "Fundamentals for Permanent United Nations Organization," flyer in CSOP file, Hoover Library; CSOP, *11 Fundamentals*; CSOP, *Peace We Want*, pp. 3–6; *Changing World*, XVI (March 1944), 8; CSOP, *U.S. and Postwar International Organization*, pp. 1–2, 5, 7, 14.
12. Minutes of UNA executive committee meeting, September 10, 1943, CEA, 63027; minutes of LNA board of directors meeting, February 11, 1944, CEA, 63054; Eichelberger to members of LNA, March 21, 1944, and Holt to Eichelberger, March 28, 1944, Holt Papers, Box 7; *Changing World*, XVI (April 1944), 3, 5, 6; minutes of LNA board of directors meeting, June 15, 1944, CEA, 63082; Eichelberger to members of LNA board of directors, June 3, 1944, CEA, 63077.
13. *New York Times*, March 21, 1944; minutes of NPC meeting, April 7, 1944, CEA, 63908; minutes of Free World meeting, April 29, 1944, Harriman Papers, Box 15; Bell to Grace Tully, March 18, 1944, FDR Papers, PPF 2409; Eichelberger interview, August 13, 1965; Eichelberger memo, June 20, 1944, CEA, 68162; Bell to Malcolm Davis, July 15, 1943, CEA, 68163; Harriman to Roosevelt, June 10, 1944, and Roosevelt to Harriman, June 12, 1944, Harriman Papers, Box 18.
14. Mahon, *Our Second Chance*, p. 5; Woodrow Wilson Foundation, *Annual Report*, 1943–1944, pp. 2, 4, 5, 7–9; Loth, *Wilson*; Harley, *Wilson Still Lives*, pp. 44, 75; Johnson, *Wilson*, pp. 271, 291, 292–3.

15. Bailey, *Wilson and the Lost Peace*; Burlingame and Stevens, *Victory Without Peace*; *Nation*, CLVIII (May 13, 1944), 569; Schriftgiesser, *Gentleman from Massachusetts*, pp. 300, 304–5, 324, 343; *Newsweek*, XXIV (September 11, 1944), 100; *Nation*, CLIX (October 14, 1944), 439; Bartlett, *League*, p. 212; Holt to W. T. Couch, September 6, 1943, and Holt to Bartlett, June 14, 1944, Holt Papers, Box 7; *Changing World*, XVI (April 1944), 4.
16. Barnes, *Willkie*, p. 374; Woodrow Wilson Foundation, *Annual Report*, *1944–1945*, p. 10; *New Republic*, CXI (August 14, 1944), 187–8; *Newsweek*, XXIV (August 14, 1944), 72; *Nation*, CLIX (August 19, 1944), 221; *Time*, XLIV (August 7, 1944), 84, 87–8; New York *Times*, September 10, 1944.
17. *Changing World*, XVI (September 1944), 6; Holt to Ruhl Bartlett, September 27, 1944, Holt Papers, Box 7; Long diary, September 8, 1944, Long Papers, Box 5.
18. Colegrove, *American Senate and World Peace*, pp. 25–6, 60–1, 134–5; Corwin, *Constitution and World Organization*, pp. 20–30; *New Republic*, CIX (November 22, 1943), 704–5; Claude Pepper, "A Summons Against the 'Kiss of Death,'" *New York Times Magazine* (December 12, 1943), pp. 5, 40–1; Lerner, *Public Journal*, p. 339.
19. Perkins, *America and Two Wars*, pp. 100, 197; Fleming, *Can We Win the Peace?* pp. 17–18, 105–6, 110–11; Nash, *Adventure in World Order*, pp. 26–7, 51–2; Shotwell, *Great Decision*, pp. 95, 101, 115–22, 124, 131, 208.
20. Thomas, *What Is Our Destiny?* p. 89; *New York Times Book Review* (July 2, 1944), p. 3; *Christian Century*, LXI (October 4, 1944), 1139; *New Republic*, CXI (September 11, 1944), 294.
21. Beard, *Republic*, pp. 302–30.
22. Becker, *How New Will the Better World Be?* pp. 71, 84–5, 125–6, 203.
23. Niebuhr, *Children of Light*, pp. 162–5, 168–9, 174, 176, 187.
24. Adler, *How to Think About War and Peace*, pp. 21, 69–70, 157–8, 282, 301.
25. Eliot, *Hour of Triumph*, pp. 38–9, 162–5, 167, 176, 190.
26. Spykman, *Geography of the Peace*, pp. 3, 6, 60–1.
27. Fox, *Super-Powers*, pp. 3–4, 9, 85, 147, 162.
28. *Time*, XLIV (December 18, 1944), 99; *Atlantic Monthly*, CLXXIV (August 1944); *Reader's Digest*, XLV (September 1944), 108–28; New York *Times Book Review, passim*; Lippmann Memoir, Oral History Project, pp. 146, 204, 216; Lippmann, *U.S. War Aims*, pp. vii, 3; Welles, *Time for Decision*, p. 3.
29. *Ibid.*, pp. 328, 334–5, 370–7, 387, 414.
30. Lippmann, *U.S. War Aims*, pp. 6, 53, 64–5, 76, 91, 99, 131, 138, 143, 149–50, 165, 170–82, 194, 197.
31. *Freedom House*, I (August 1944), 4; New York *Times Book Review* (July 23, 1944), p. 1; *Newsweek*, XXIV (December 18, 1944), 91; Lerner, *Public Journal*, pp. 348–9; *Free World*, VIII (September 1944), 278; Russell, *United Nations Charter*, pp. 395–6; Long to Roosevelt, July 12, 1944, Long Papers, Box 189.
32. *Newsweek*, XXIV (August 21, 1944), 96–107.
33. *Public Opinion Quarterly*, VIII (Summer 1944), 301; *ibid.*, VIII (Fall 1944), 454; National Opinion Research Center, *Report No. 19, Public Looks at World Organization*, pp. 5, 16–17.
34. Lydgate, *What Our People Think*, pp. 40–5; Edward L. Bernays, "Preview of American Public Opinion," *American Mercury*, LVIII (March 1944), 340–5.

CHAPTER EIGHT

1. Leo Pasvolsky to Hull, November 30, 1943, Hull Papers, Box 82; Notter, *Postwar Foreign Policy Preparation*, pp. 248–51, 576–81; Russell, *United Nations Charter*, pp. 220–1; Hull Memoirs, II, 1649–50.
2. State Department, *Bulletin*, X (January 1, 1944), 8; Eichelberger to Roosevelt, January 7, 1944, and Roosevelt to Eichelberger, January 11, 1944, FDR Papers, OF 4725; State Department, *Bulletin*, X (January 15, 1944), 76–7.

3. New York *Times*, February 3, 1944; *Newsweek*, XXII (November 29, 1943), 47–8; Johnson, *Republican Party and Willkie*, p. 261; *Congressional Record* (March 3, 1944), p. 2206; New York *Times Magazine* (February 6, 1944), pp. 8, 34; New York *Times*, January 16, 1944; *ibid.*, April 5, 1944.

4. *Ibid.*, December 12, 1943; *ibid.*, February 11, 1944; *ibid.*, February 13, 1944; *Congressional Record* (February 15, 1944), pp. 1670–2; Bowers to Long, March 30, 1944, Long Papers, Box 149.

5. Johnson, *Republican Party and Willkie*, pp. 268–80; New York *Times*, March 22, 1944; *ibid.*, March 24, 1944; *ibid.*, April 6, 1944; *Newsweek*, XXIII (April 17, 1944), 22.

6. *Free World*, VII (May 1944), 413; New York *Times*, April 7, 1944; *Saturday Evening Post*, CCXVI (May 13, 1944), 112; *Time*, XLIII (April 17, 1944), 18; Dillon, *Willkie*, pp. 329, 332; Johnson, *Republican Party and Willkie*, p. 282.

7. *Vital Speeches*, X (May 15, 1944), 451; *Newsweek*, XXIII (May 8, 1944), 38; *New Republic*, CX (May 8, 1944), 661; *Nation*, CLVIII (May 6, 1944), 526–7; *Time*, XLIII (May 8, 1944), 15–16; New York *Times*, April 28, 1944; Westerfield, *Foreign Policy and Party Politics*, p. 163.

8. Memo of conversation by R. W. Morin, December 13, 1943, Pasvolsky Office Files, Box 5; State Department, *Bulletin*, X (January 8, 1944), 30–5.

9. *Ibid.*, X (January 15, 1944), 43; Notter, *Postwar Foreign Policy Preparation*, pp. 213–14; Walter H. C. Laves and Francis O. Wilcox, "The Reorganization of the Department of State," *American Political Science Review*, XII (April 1944), 295–6; Stuart, *Department of State*, pp. 389–92.

10. Long diary, March 3, 11, 15 and 19, and May 11, 1944, Long Papers, Box 5; *Hull Memoirs*, II, 1652–4.

11. *Christian Century*, LXI (April 5, 1944), 419; New York *Times*, March 7, 1943; *ibid.*, March 29, 1943; Joseph H. Ball, "Your Move, Mister President," *Saturday Evening Post*, CCXVI (February 19, 1944), 19, 86; Joseph H. Ball, "Are We Losing the Peace?" *Collier's*, CXIII (April 22, 1944), 24; *Nation*, CLVIII (March 11, 1944), 300, 302; *ibid.*, CLVIII (April 1, 1944), 383; New York *Times*, March 17, 1944; *Time*, XLIII (March 20, 1944), 17–18; New York *Times*, March 23, 1944.

12. State Department, *Bulletin*, X (March 25, 1944), 275–6; New York *Times*, March 22, 1944; *Christian Century*, LXI (April 5, 1944), 419; Kingsbury Smith, "Spotlight on the State Department," *Reader's Digest*, XLIV (May 1944), 1, 7; *Hull Memoirs*, II, 1657–8; Notter, *Postwar Foreign Policy Preparation*, pp. 259–60; *Newsweek*, XXIII (April 3, 1944), 62–3.

13. Long diary, March 28, 29, 30, and April 9, 1944, Long Papers, Box 5; State Department, *Bulletin*, X (April 15, 1944), 335–42; New York *Times*, April 10, 1943; *ibid.*, April 11, 1943; *Christian Century*, LXI (April 26, 1944), 516; *New Republic*, CX (April 17, 1944), 515.

14. New York *Times*, April 22, 1944; Connally and Steinberg, *Connally*, p. 265; *Time*, XLIII (May 22, 1944), 20; *ibid.*, XLV (April 30, 1945), 21–2; Richard Rovere, "New Man in the Pantheon," *New Yorker*, XXXVIII (March 24, 1962), 151–5.

15. *Hull Memoirs*, II, 1658–9; Connally and Steinberg, *Connally*, p. 266; *Private Papers of Vandenberg*, pp. 95–6.

16. Long diary, April 27, May 1, 3, 8 and 12, 1944, Long Papers, Box 5; Long to Davis, May 2, 1944, and Davis to Long, May 8, 1944, Long Papers, Box 150; *Private Papers of Vandenberg*, pp. 96–8; *Hull Memoirs*, II, 1660–7.

17. Forrest Davis, "What Really Happened at Teheran," *Saturday Evening Post*, CCXVI (May 13, 1944), 13, 37; *ibid.*, CCXVI (May 20, 1944), 22–3, 44, 46; Stephen Early to Edwin Watson, March 2, 1944, and Davis to Early, March 23, 1944, FDR Papers, OF 4287.

18. *Saturday Evening Post*, CCXVI (May 20, 1944), 112; Davis to Roosevelt, June 20, 1944, FDR Papers, OF 4287; Demaree Bess, "The Cost of Roosevelt's 'Great Design,' " *Saturday Evening Post*, CCXVI (May 27, 1944), 27, 90, 92;

Christian Century, LXI (May 31, 1944), 668–9; New York *Times*, May 19, 1944; *Nation*, CLVIII (May 27, 1944), 609; *New Republic*, CX (May 29, 1944), 729; *Saturday Evening Post*, CCXVI (June 24, 1944), 104.

19. *Private Papers of Vandenberg*, pp. 99–103; Connally and Steinberg, *Connally*, pp. 266–7; Israel, *Long Diary*, pp. 344–50.

20. *Private Papers of Vandenberg*, p. 106; *Hull Memoirs*, II, 1667–9; State Department, *Bulletin*, X (June 3, 1944), 510; New York *Times*, May 30, 1944; Israel, *Long Diary*, p. 346.

21. *Hull Memoirs*, II, 1657; Roosevelt to Mrs. Harriman, June 12, 1944, Harriman Papers, Box 18; Eichelberger to Daniels, April 8, 1944, Daniels to Roosevelt, May 9, 1944, and Roosevelt to Hull, May 18, 1944, FDR Papers, OF 4725.

22. Rosenman, *Public Papers of FDR*, XIII, 133–7, 140–2, 147; *Time*, XLIII (June 12, 1944), 11.

23. *Ibid.*, 11–12; New York *Times*, May 31, 1944; *New Republic*, CX (June 12, 1944), 787; *Nation*, CLVIII (June 10, 1944), 669.

24. State Department, *Bulletin*, X (June 3, 1944), 509; Israel, *Long Diary*, pp. 355–6; *Hull Memoirs*, II, 1687–8; *Time*, XLIII (June 26, 1944), 17; State Department, *Bulletin*, X (June 17, 1944), 552–3.

25. Ely Culbertson to Roosevelt, June 16, 1944, FDR Papers, OF 5557; Vera A. Harmer to Roosevelt, June 23, 1944, Truman Papers, Box 139; *Nation*, CLVIII (June 24, 1944), 722; New York *Times*, June 16, 1944; Eichelberger to Roosevelt, June 19, 1944, FDR Papers, OF 4725; *Changing World*, XVI (July 1944), 3.

26. William Hard, "Are We on the Wrong Road Toward Peace?" *Reader's Digest*, XLV (September 1944), 1–8; *Time*, XLIII (June 26, 1944), 18; New York *Times*, June 17, 1944; *New Republic*, CX (June 26, 1944), 835–6.

27. *Hull Memoirs*, II, 1669–70; Notter, *Postwar Foreign Policy Preparation*, p. 286; Reynolds to Long, June 6, 1944, and Long to Hull, June 7, 1944, Long Papers, Box 204; Israel, *Long Diary*, pp. 356–8.

28. Barnes, *Willkie*, pp. 264–5; Johnson, *Republican Party and Willkie*, p. 291; New York *Times*, June 18, 1944; *New Republic*, CX (June 26, 1944), 833; *Private Papers of Vandenberg*, p. 87.

29. Westerfield, *Foreign Policy and Party Politics*, p. 164; New York *Times*, June 21, 1944; *ibid.*, June 22, 1944; *ibid.*, June 23, 1944; *ibid.*, June 24, 1944; *ibid.*, June 25, 1944; Ball interview, July 23, 1965; *Changing World*, XVI (July 1944), 2, 8; *Newsweek*, XXIV (July 3, 1944), 27–8.

30. New York *Times*, June 27, 1944; Johnson, *Republican Party and Willkie*, pp. 292–3; *Nation*, CLIX (July 1, 1944), 1; New York *Times*, June 28, 1944; *Vital Speeches*, X (July 15, 1944), 579; Israel, *Long Diary*, p. 363; New York *Times*, June 28, 1944; *Nation*, CLIX (July 8, 1944), 36–8; New York *Times*, July 2, 1944.

31. Rosenman, *Public Papers of FDR*, XIII, 197–8, 199–200; Rosenman, *Working with Roosevelt*, p. 439; Lord, *Wallaces of Iowa*, p. 530; *Time*, XLIV (July 24, 1944), 15–16.

32. New York *Times*, July 10, 1944; Israel, *Long Diary*, pp. 365–7; Connally to Gilbert May, August 1, 1944, Connally Papers, Box 104; New York *Times*, June 25, 1944.

33. *Ibid.*, July 20, 1944; press release, July 27, 1944, Connally Papers, Box 104; Long diary, July 25, 1944, Long Papers, Box 5; New York *Times*, July 21, 1944.

34. *Vital Speeches*, X (August 1, 1944), 611–15; New York *Times*, July 21, 1944; Israel, *Long Diary*, pp. 369–70; *Time*, XLIV (July 31, 1944), 9; *Free World*, VIII (September 1944), 199; *Freedom Digest*, I (August 1944), 1.

CHAPTER NINE

1. Hudson to Long, May 17, 1944, Long Papers, Box 150; Hudson to Cohen, June 3, 1944, and Cohen to Grace Tully, June 5, 1944, FDR Papers, OF 5557;

Shotwell to Holt, June 7, 1944, Holt to Shotwell, June 22, 1944, and Shotwell to Holt, June 28, 1944, Holt Papers, Box 7; New York *Times*, August 1, 1944; CSOP, *Design for a Charter*; Eichelberger, *Time Has Come for Action*, pp. 8–9, 12, 31–2.

2. Edgar Mowrer to members of NPC, August 3, 1944, CEA, 64001; Mowrer to members of NPC, July 26, 1944, CEA 63991; New York *Times*, August 9, 1944; *ibid.*, September 3, 1944; *Changing World*, XVI (September 1944), 4; Hopkins to Nicholas Murray Butler, September 14, 1944, CEA, 68168; Bell to Roosevelt, September 18, 1944, FDR Papers, OF 54.

3. State Department, *Bulletin*, XI (July 23, 1944), 84; New York *Times*, July 18, 1944; *ibid.*, August 2, 1944; *Hull Memoirs*, II, 1676; New York *Times*, August 15, 1944; *ibid.*, August 16, 1944; Israel, *Long Diary*, pp. 370–3; Russell, *United Nations Charter*, pp. 396–7, 406–8; Notter, *Postwar Foreign Policy Preparation*, p. 290.

4. New York *Times*, August 17, 1944; Stuart Haydon to Malcolm Davis, August 21, 1944, CEA, 64016; *New Republic*, CXI (August 28, 1944), 237, 247; *Christian Century*, LXI (August 30, 1944), 987; *Time*, XLIV (August 28, 1944), 13; *Hull Memoirs*, II, 1689; New York *Times*, August 18, 1944; *ibid.*, August 19, 1944; Israel, *Long Diary*, p. 372.

5. John Chamberlain, "John Foster Dulles," *Life*, XVII (August 21, 1944), 85, 95, 96; Dulles to Dewey, June 27, 1941, Dulles Papers; *New Republic*, CXI (September 4, 1944), 265; *Time*, XLIV (August 28, 1944), 14; typescript of press conferences, August 19 and 20, 1944, Dulles Papers; Dulles, *War or Peace*, pp. 123–4; Dillon, *Willkie*, p. 352; New York *Times*, August 22, 1944; *Time*, XLIV (September 4, 1944), 22.

6. Gerald L. K. Smith to Hull, August 20, 1944, Long Papers, Box 153; Dulles, *War or Peace*, pp. 124–5; draft statement, August 24, 1944, Long Papers, Box 191; *Hull Memoirs*, II, 1690–3; New York *Times*, August 26, 1944; *Time*, XLIV (September 4, 1944), 22; State Department, *Bulletin*, XI (September 10, 1944), 255; Israel, *Long Diary*, pp. 375–6.

7. *Time*, XLIV (August 21, 1944), 19; *ibid.*, XLIV (August 28, 1944), 14; *Newsweek*, XXIV (August 21, 1944), 37; New York *Times*, August 22, 1944; State Department, *Bulletin*, XI (August 27, 1944), 199; Rosenman, *Public Papers of FDR*, XIII, 232–3; *Time*, XLIV (September 4, 1944), 21, 22–3.

8. New York *Times*, August 23, 1944; *ibid.*, May 8, 1945; letter from James Reston to author, May 17, 1966; *Atlantic Monthly*, CLXXIV (October 1944), 23; *Congressional Record* (August 28, 1944), pp. 7334–6; *Newsweek*, XXIV (September 4, 1944), 48; *ibid.*, XXIV (September 11, 1944), 42; State Department, *Bulletin*, XI (September 3, 1944), 233–4.

9. *Hull Memoirs*, II, 1695–6; *Private Papers of Vandenberg*, pp. 115–18; Notter, *Postwar Foreign Policy Preparation*, p. 316; Rosenman, *Public Papers of FDR*, XIII, 251–2; Israel, *Long Diary*, pp. 377–8.

10. *Congressional Record* (September 5, 1944), pp. 7522–8.

11. *Hull Memoirs*, II, 1694–5, 1697–9; Notter, *Postwar Foreign Policy Preparation*, p. 323; New York *Times*, September 13, 1944.

12. *Congressional Record* (September 19, 1944), pp. 7919–21.

13. McNeill, *America, Britain, and Russia*, p. 506; Feis, *Churchill, Roosevelt, Stalin*, pp. 430, 432–3; *Hull Memoirs*, II, 1678–80, 1700–1; Stettinius, *Roosevelt and the Russians*, pp. 18–19, 20–22.

14. Long diary, September 8, 14, and 19, 1944, Long Papers, Box 5; *Hull Memoirs*, II, 1702–5; New York *Times*, September 21, 1944; *ibid.*, September 23, 1944; typescript of press conference, September 22, 1944, FDR Papers, PPF 1–P, XXIV, 130; *Christian Century*, LXI (October 11, 1944), 1155; New York *Times*, September 28, 1944.

15. Notter, *Postwar Foreign Policy Preparation*, pp. 335–6; Hull to Truman, October 7, 1944, Truman Papers, Box 164; Hull to Theodore Green, October 9, 1944, Green Papers, Box 338; State Department, *Bulletin*, XI (October 8, 1944), 365–74.

16. New York *Times*, October 10, 1944; Dulles to Hull, October 13, 1944, Long Papers, Box 191; Orlando *Sentinel*, October 12, 1944, Holt Papers, Scrapbook #23; New York *Times*, October 15, 1944.

17. *Time*, XLIV (October 16, 1944), 19; *Newsweek*, XXIV (October 9, 1944), 40–1; Walter Lippmann, "Pacification for Peace," *Atlantic Monthly*, CLXXIV (December 1944), 46–52; New York *Times*, October 5, 1944; *ibid.*, October 25, 1944.

18. *New Republic*, CXI (September 18, 1944), 326; *ibid.*, CXI (October 23, 1944), 510–11; *Nation*, CLIX (September 16, 1944), 312–13; *ibid.*, CLIX (October 21, 1944), 451; Lerner, *Public Journal*, p. 336; White, *Wild Flag*, pp. 39, 40; *Nation*, CLIX (September 16, 1944), 316; *Christian Century*, LXI (December 13, 1944), 1444.

19. New York *Times*, November 19, 1944; *Time*, XLIV (November 27, 1944), 21; *Christian Century*, LXI (December 6, 1944), 1406–7; *ibid.*, LXI (November 29, 1944), 1375–6; New York *Times*, September 21, 1944; *ibid.*, September 23, 1944; *ibid.*, November 25, 1944; speech text, November 28, 1944, Dulles Papers; *Christian Century*, LXI (December 13, 1944), 1452; New York *Times*, November 29, 1944.

20. Mowrer to NPC members, September 18, 1944, CEA, 64031; minutes of NPC meeting, October 12, 1944, CEA, 64040; Davis to Mowrer, October 24, 1944, CEA, 64045; Courtenay Barber, Jr., to NPC members, November 18, 1944, CEA, 64054; Mowrer to NPC members, CEA, 64062; NPC press release, December 27, 1944, CEA, 64065; Americans United press release, November 21, 1944, CEA, 64055; Eichelberger interview, August 13, 1965.

21. New York *Times*, October 11, 1944; minutes of LNA directors meeting, October 13, 1944, CEA, 63112; *Changing World*, XVI (November 1944), 1, 4, 5; Eichelberger, *Proposals*, pp. 7, 14, 23.

22. *Changing World*, XVI (September 1944), 8; *Nation*, CLVII (November 20, 1943), 571; *ibid.*, CLVIII (April 29, 1944), 306–7; *Changing World*, XVI (May 1944), 2–3; *Newsweek*, XXIV (July 10, 1944), 44; *Time*, XLIII (June 19, 1944), 20; *ibid.*, XLIV (August 7, 1944).

23. *Ibid.*, XLIV (August 7, 1944), 17; *ibid.*, XLIV (August 14, 1944), 21; *New Republic*, CXI (October 9, 1944), 450; *ibid.*, CXI (October 16, 1944), 489.

24. Rosenman, *Working with Roosevelt*, pp. 453, 461–2, 471–2; *Time*, XLIV (October 30, 1944), 11.

25. New York *Times*, August 11, 1944; *New Republic*, CXI (September 25, 1944), 396, 407; Gerald W. Johnson, "A Letter to the Honorable Thomas E. Dewey," *Atlantic Monthly*, CLXXIV (September 1944), 39–41; *Newsweek*, XXIV (September 18, 1944), 39–40; New York *Times*, September 9, 1944; *New Republic*, CXI (September 18, 1944), 327.

26. Rosenman, *Working with Roosevelt*, pp. 473–8; Rosenman, *Public Papers of FDR*, XIII, 284–5, 290; Sherwood, *Roosevelt and Hopkins*, pp. 821–2.

27. Johnson, *Republican Party and Willkie*, p. 284; Roosevelt to Willkie, August 21, 1944, FDR Papers, PPF 7023; New York *Times*, August 26, 1944; Barnes, *Willkie*, pp. 381–3; Wendell Willkie, "Cowardice at Chicago," *Collier's*, CXIV (September 18, 1944), 11, 77–9.

28. Johnson, *Republican Party and Willkie*, pp. 305–6; *New Republic*, CXI (October 16, 1944), 479; *Time*, XLIV (October 30, 1944), 14; Drummond, "Willkie," p. 467.

29. Westerfield, *Foreign Policy and Party Politics*, pp. 173–4; New York *Times*, September 30, 1944; Ball interview, July 23, 1965; press release by Robert Hannegan, October 3, 1944, Green Papers, Box 331; New York *Times*, October 3, 1944; *Nation*, CLIX (October 14, 1944), 423.

30. New York *Times*, October 13, 1944; *Christian Century*, LXI (November 8, 1944), 1281; *Time*, XLIV (October 23, 1944), 18; New York *Times*, October 19, 1944; *Newsweek*, XXIV (October 30, 1944), 47; Ball interview, July 23, 1965.

31. Rosenman, *Working with Roosevelt*, pp. 480–2; *Time*, XLIV (October 30,

1944), 15; speech draft, October 6, 1944, Long Papers, Box 194; Long diary, October 12 and 20, 1944, Long Papers, Box 5.
32. Sherwood, *Roosevelt and Hopkins*, pp. 825–6; *Newsweek*, XXIV (October 30, 1944), 42, 44; *Time*, XLIV (October 30, 1944), 12–13; New York *Times*, October 22, 1944; Rosenman, *Public Papers of FDR*, XIII, 344–5, 348, 350.
33. *Time*, XLIV (October 30, 1944), 15; New York *Times*, October 23, 1944; *ibid.*, October 24, 1944; *ibid.*, October 25, 1944; *Nation*, CLIX (October 28, 1944), 503; *Newsweek*, XXIV (November 6, 1944), 48; Westerfield, *Foreign Policy and Party Politics*, pp. 174–5.
34. New York *Times*, October 16, 1944; *Newsweek*, XXIV (October 30, 1944), 52; Russell Davenport, "Why I Cannot Vote for Dewey," *American Mercury*, LIX (October 1944), 391–9; Orlando *Sentinel*, November 2, 1944, clipping, Holt Papers, Scrapbook #23; Holt to Dewey, September 26, 1944, and Holt to Mrs. Henry A. Strong, November 1, 1944, Holt Papers, Box 7; New York *Times*, November 3, 1944; *ibid.*, November 5, 1944.
35. New York *Times*, November 9, 1944; *Newsweek*, XXIV (November 13, 1944), 4, 8; *Nation*, CLIX (November 11, 1944), 573–4; *ibid.*, CLIX (November 18, 1944), 604–6; *Time*, XLIV (November 13, 1944), 19, 20–1; New York *Times*, November 10, 1944; *ibid.*, November 12, 1944.
36. New York *Times*, November 16, 1944; Israel, *Long Diary*, p. 389; *New Republic*, CXI (November 20, 1944), 645; Vandenberg to Hull, October 18, 1944, Long Papers, Box 154; Dulles to Roosevelt, November 10, 1944, FDR Papers, PPF 8988; John Foster Dulles to Allen Dulles, December 20, 1944, Dulles Papers.

CHAPTER TEN

1. *Hull Memoirs*, II, 1715–18; State Department, *Bulletin*, XI (December 3, 1944), 649; Israel, *Long Diary*, pp. 386–8; New York *Times*, November 28, 1944.
2. Walker, "Stettinius," pp. 10–11; *Newsweek*, XXIV (December 4, 1944), 47; *Time*, XLIV (December 11, 1944), 20–1.
3. *Free World*, VIII (December 1944), 562; State Department, *Bulletin*, XI (October 22, 1944), 450–2; *ibid.*, XI (November 26, 1944), 631–5; New York *Times*, November 21, 1944; State Department, *Charter of the United Nations*, p. 27.
4. *Ibid.*, p. 27; Notter, *Postwar Foreign Policy Preparation*, pp. 378–9; *Free World*, IX (January 1945), 86; State Department, *Bulletin*, XI (December 10, 1944), 713; *ibid.*, XI (December 31, 1944), 848; *ibid.*, XII (January 21, 1945), 82.
5. State Department, *Bulletin*, XI (October 22, 1944), 459, 479; *ibid.*, XI (December 10, 1944), 709–10; *ibid.*, XI (December 17, 1944), 742; *ibid.*, XII (January 7, 1945), 31; *ibid.*, XII (January 28, 1945), 116–17; *ibid.*, XII (February 11, 1945), 179–80; *ibid.*, XII (February 25, 1945), 285; *ibid.*, XII (March 4, 1945), 360; *ibid.*, XII (March 18, 1945), 434; Robert E. Riggs, "Overselling the UN Charter—Fact and Myth," *International Organization*, XIV (Spring 1960), 277–90.
6. Eichelberger interview, August 13, 1965; "Our Second Chance," September 1944, CEA, 63096; CSOP, *Ten Year Record*, pp. 26–7; New York *Times*, November 24, 1944; Edwin Watson to Eichelberger, October 2, 1944, FDR Papers, OF 3833; Eichelberger to Roosevelt, October 17, 1944, FDR Papers, PPF 1820.
7. Clark Eichelberger to organization representatives, October 25, 1944, CEA, 64047; New York *Times*, November 11, 1944; Carnegie Endowment, *Year Book—1945*, p. 114; *Changing World*, XVI (November 1944), 8; *ibid.*, XVI (December 1944), 2, 4, 6, 7; *ibid.*, XVII (February 1945), 7; George Fulk, "What Is Your Answer Now?" undated pamphlet, CSOP file, Hoover Library.
8. Minutes of LNA board of directors, November 3, 1944, CEA, 63114; New York *Times*, February 2, 1945; *Changing World*, XVII (March 1945), 5.
9. Woodrow Wilson Foundation, *Annual Report*, 1944–45, pp. 7–9; form letter, December 28, 1944, Woodrow Wilson Foundation file, Hoover Library; Wil-

liam Allan Neilson to members of executive committee, March 19, 1945, CSOP file, Hoover Library; New York *Times*, January 16, 1945; Simmons to Tom Connally, March 5, 1945, Simmons Papers, Box 26.

10. Eichelberger interview, August 13, 1965; New York *Times Magazine* (February 25, 1945), p. 13; sample ads, Americans United file, Hoover Library; Hopkins to Nicholas Murray Butler, November 20, 1944, CEA, 68173; Americans United, *Here Comes Your Last Chance.*

11. *Changing World*, XVII (January 1945), 5, 6; *ibid.*, XVII (March 1945), 1, 8; Joseph H. Ball, "Isolationism Is Far from Dead," New York *Times Magazine* (October 29, 1944), pp. 5, 53; Joseph H. Ball, "There Is No Ivory Tower for Us," *ibid.* (January 14, 1945), pp. 5, 37.

12. New York *Times*, December 12, 1944; Raymond B. Fosdick, "The Hour Is Late—We Must Not Fail," New York *Times Magazine* (February 11, 1945), 5, 43, 45; Union for Democratic Action, *From the Garden of Eden to Dumbarton Oaks*; undated leaflet, Green Papers, Box 367.

13. New York *Times*, February 2, 1945; *New Republic*, CXII (April 23, 1945), 543; *Christian Century*, LXII (January 10, 1945), 39–40, 60.

14. CJDP, *Message to the Churches* (1945), pp. 3, 9, 15; *Changing World*, XVII (February 1945), 7; New York *Times*, January 20, 1945; *Time*, XLV (January 29, 1945), 22–3; *Christian Century*, LXII (February 7, 1945), 166–7.

15. Cantril and Strunk, *Public Opinion*, pp. 908, 910; Stettinius to Roosevelt, October 19, 1944, FDR Papers, OF 5557.

16. *Public Opinion Quarterly*, IX (Spring 1945), 101; *Free World*, IX (March 1945), 35; *Time*, XLV (March 26, 1945), 23; Dean Acheson to Roosevelt, March 17, 1945, FDR Papers, OF 857, Box 3; Harry H. Field and Louise M. Van Patten, "If the American People Made the Peace," *Public Opinion Quarterly*, VIII (Winter 1944–45), 501–4; Frederick W. Williams, "Regional Attitudes on International Cooperation," *ibid.*, IX (Spring 1945), 38–40, 50.

17. Walker, "Stettinius," pp. 20–1; Stuart, *Department of State*, pp. 397–9; State Department, *Bulletin*, XI (December 10, 1944), 685–6; *Nation*, CLIX (December 9, 1944), 703–4; *New Republic*, CXI (December 25, 1944), 857; New York *Times*, December 7, 1944; "Nominations—Department of State," *Hearings* before the Senate Foreign Relations Committee, 78th Congress, 2nd Session (Washington, 1944), *passim.*

18. *Newsweek*, XXIV (December 25, 1944), 30; *Congressional Record* (December 19, 1944), pp. 9716–17, 9737, 9742–3; *New Republic*, CXI (December 25, 1944), 857; *ibid.*, CXII (January 1, 1945), 18; *Time*, LV (January 1, 1945), 12–13.

19. Stettinius to Connally, November 11, 1944, Long Papers, Box 149; Notter, *Postwar Foreign Policy Preparation*, pp. 380–1; Russell, *United Nations Charter*, pp. 498–9; *Private Papers of Vandenberg*, p. 121; Stettinius, *Roosevelt and the Russians*, p. 45; Stettinius to Roosevelt, December 7, 1944, FDR Papers, OF 5557; New York *Times*, December 9, 1944.

20. Feis, *Churchill, Roosevelt, Stalin*, pp. 551–2.

21. Russell, *United Nations Charter*, pp. 500–7; Notter, *Postwar Foreign Policy Preparation*, p. 384.

22. Buchanan, *U.S. and World War II*, II, 415–18, 523–5, 537–40.

23. Smith, *American Diplomacy*, pp. 137–44; Feis, *Churchill, Roosevelt, Stalin*, pp. 447–9, 510–11; Churchill, *Triumph and Tragedy*, pp. 227–8.

24. *Christian Century*, LXII (January 3, 1945), 6; *Time*, XLV (January 8, 1945), 13; *New Republic*, CXII (January 8, 1945), 36; New York *Times*, January 5, 1945; typescript of press conferences, December 19 and 22, 1944, FDR Papers, PPF 1–P, XXIV, 266, 276; New York *Times*, December 20, 1944; *Christian Century*, LXII (January 3, 1945), 4; *Time*, XLV (January 1, 1945), 12.

25. State Department, *Bulletin*, XII (January 7, 1945), 26–8; New York *Times*, January 7, 1945.

26. New York *Times*, December 21, 1944; Fulbright to Elbert Thomas, September 7, 1944, Thomas Papers, Box 80; *New Republic*, CXII (January 22, 1945),

102; *Changing World*, XVII (January 1945), 3; New York *Times*, January 11, 1945; Joseph H. Baird, "Will the Senate Hamper the Peace?" *American Mercury*, LX (June 1945), 649–51; State Department, *Bulletin*, XII (January 28, 1945), 121; Jonathan Daniels to Roosevelt, January 24, 1945, FDR Papers, OF 4675, Box 61.

27. New York *Times*, December 24, 1944; *ibid.*, December 26, 1944; *Congressional Record* (January 6, 1945), p. 85; New York *Times*, January 6, 1945; Connally and Steinberg, *Connally*, p. 271; Stettinius to Roosevelt, January 9, 1945, FDR Papers, OF 20; Notter, *Postwar Foreign Policy Preparation*, p. 384.

28. Vandenberg to Dulles, January 4, 1945, Dulles Papers; *Private Papers of Vandenberg*, pp. 128, 130–1; *Congressional Record* (January 10, 1945), pp. 164–7.

29. *Time*, XLV (January 22, 1945), 15; *Christian Century*, LXII (January 24, 1945), 100–1; *New Republic*, CXII (January 22, 1945), 103; *Nation*, CLX (January 20, 1945), 59–60; New York *Times*, January 12, 1945; *ibid.*, February 4, 1945.

30. *Congressional Record* (January 10, 1945), p. 168; typescript of press conference, January 16, 1945, FDR Papers, PPF 1–P, XXV, 33; *Private Papers of Vandenberg*, p. 139; press release, January 11, 1945, Dulles Papers; Wilson to Dulles, January 11, 1945, Dulles Papers; New York *Times*, February 9, 1945; *ibid.*, January 21, 1945; *ibid.*, January 22, 1945.

31. *Congressional Record* (January 15, 1945), pp. 236–45; Richard Rovere, "New Man in the Pantheon," *New Yorker*, XXXVIII (March 24, 1962), 166.

32. Hassett, *Off the Record with F.D.R.*, p. 313; McIntire, *White House Physician*, pp. 210–11; Leahy, *I Was There*, pp. 294–7.

33. Byrnes, *All in One Lifetime*, p. 256; Stettinius, *Roosevelt and the Russians*, pp. 115–16, 138–45; *Foreign Relations: Malta and Yalta*, pp. 661–2, 667.

34. *Foreign Relations: Malta and Yalta*, pp. 712–14, 736–7, 966–8; Stettinius, *Roosevelt and the Russians*, pp. 171–3, 187–8, 196–7; Feis, *Churchill, Roosevelt, Stalin*, p. 555; Byrnes, *All in One Lifetime*, pp. 261–2.

35. Stettinius, *Roosevelt and the Russians*, pp. 190–1, 203–6, 280–2; Byrnes, *All in One Lifetime*, pp. 262–3; *Foreign Relations: Malta and Yalta*, pp. 969–73.

36. *Changing World*, XVII (March 1945), 2; New York *Times*, February 13, 1945; *Time*, XLV (February 19, 1945), 15, 22; *Newsweek*, XXV (February 19, 1945), 37; Daniels to Early, February 13, 1945, FDR Papers, OF 4675, Box 61; New York *Times*, February 14, 1945; *New Republic*, CXII (February 19, 1945), 243.

37. Byrnes, *All in One Lifetime*, pp. 266–7; *New Republic*, CXII (February 26, 1945), 294; *Newsweek*, XXV (March 19, 1945), 52; New York *Times*, February 14, 1945; Byrnes to Roosevelt, February 17, 1945, FDR Papers, OF 4675, Box 61; Notter, *Postwar Foreign Policy Preparation*, p. 408.

38. Sherwood, *Roosevelt and Hopkins*, pp. 873–4; Rosenman, *Working with Roosevelt*, pp. 522–3; Leahy, *I Was There*, pp. 325–8; McIntire, *White House Physician*, pp. 232–4; typescript of press conferences, February 19 and 23, 1945, FDR Papers, PPF 1–P, XXV, 47, 58.

39. Rosenman, *Working with Roosevelt*, pp. 527–8, 537; Byrnes to Roosevelt, February 20, 1945, FDR Papers, OF 4675, Box 61; *Time*, XLV (March 12, 1945), 17; New York *Times*, March 1, 1945; Rosenman, *Public Papers of FDR*, XIII, 578, 585.

40. Stettinius, *Roosevelt and the Russians*, pp. 118, 186; Byrnes, *All in One Lifetime*, p. 265; State Department, *Bulletin*, XII (February 18, 1945), 217; Rosenman, *Public Papers of FDR*, XIII, 565–6; New York *Times*, February 23, 1945; Gildersleeve, *Many a Good Crusade*, pp. 320–2.

41. Vandenberg to Roosevelt, February 15, 1945, Roosevelt to Vandenberg, February 26, 1945, Vandenberg to Roosevelt, March 1, 1945, and Roosevelt to Vandenberg, March 3, 1945, FDR Papers, OF 4725G; typescript of press conference, February 19, 1945, FDR Papers, PPF 1–P, XXV, 55; *Private Papers of Vandenberg*, pp. 149, 151, 153–4.

42. State Department, *Bulletin*, XII (March 11, 1945), 394–5; New York *Times*,

March 6, 1945; *ibid.*, March 7, 1945; *New Republic*, CXII (March 12, 1945), 350; Rosenman, *Public Papers of FDR*, XIII, 591.

43. *Private Papers of Vandenberg*, pp. 156–7, 159; Gildersleeve, *Many a Good Crusade*, p. 318; New York *Times*, March 22, 1945; *ibid.*, April 6, 1945; memorandum by Dulles, April 5, 1945, Dulles Papers.

44. *Private Papers of Vandenberg*, pp. 159–60; Gildersleeve, *Many a Good Crusade*, p. 319; State Department, *Bulletin*, XII (April 1, 1945), 530; Hassett, *Off the Record with F.D.R.*, p. 327.

45. State Department, *Bulletin*, XII (April 8, 1945), 636; Daniels to Hassett, March 31, 1945, FDR Papers, OF 4675, Box 61; New York *Times*, March 31, 1945; *ibid.*, April 1, 1945; *Time*, XLV (April 9, 1945), 23; *Nation*, CLX (April 7, 1945), 376.

46. *Private Papers of Vandenberg*, pp. 161–2; Hassett, *Off the Record with F.D.R.*, p. 329; State Department, *Bulletin*, XII (April 8, 1945), 600–1; *Time*, LXV (April 16, 1945), 19–20; *New Republic*, CXII (April 16, 1945), 493; Stettinius, *Roosevelt and the Russians*, p. 282; Rosenman, *Public Papers of FDR*, XIII, 611; Sherwood, *Roosevelt and Hopkins*, pp. 876–7.

47. *Time*, XLV (April 9, 1945), 17, 23; *Nation*, CLX (April 14, 1945), 403; New York *Times*, April 2, 1945; *ibid.*, April 3, 1945; Eichelberger to AAUN chapters, April 2, 1945 , CEA, 63135; State Department, *Bulletin*, XII (April 8, 1945), 608.

48. Hassett, *Off the Record with F.D.R.*, pp. 327–8, 331, 333–7; Anne O'Hare McCormick, "His 'Unfinished Business'—and Ours," New York *Times Magazine* (April 22, 1945), p. 5; Woodring to Roosevelt, March 19, 1945, and Roosevelt to Woodring, March 24, 1945, FDR Papers, PPF 663; Stettinius to Roosevelt, April 7, 1945, FDR Papers, OF 4725; Roosevelt to Pepper, April 9, 1945, FDR Papers, OF 3575; McIntire, *White House Physician*, pp. 241–3.

49. *New Republic*, CXII (April 23, 1945), 539; Eichelberger to members of AAUN, April 13, 1945, CEA, 63137.

CHAPTER ELEVEN

1. Truman, *Memoirs*, I, 4, 9; State Department, *Bulletin*, XII (April 15, 1945), 669.

2. *Nation*, CLX (April 21, 1945), 437; *New Republic*, CXII (April 23, 1945), 554; *ibid.*, CXII (April 30, 1945), 579; New York *Times*, February 23, 1945; *ibid.*, March 6, 1945; *Time*, XLV (April 23, 1945), 28; Truman, *Memoirs*, I, 22–3; Curry, "Byrnes," pp. 102–4; Walker, "Stettinius," pp. 78–9.

3. Truman, *Memoirs*, I, 26, 41–2; New York *Times*, April 15, 1945; State Department, *Bulletin*, XII (April 22, 1945), 722.

4. Truman, *Memoirs*, I, 46, 73, 272, 277–80; *Private Papers of Vandenberg*, pp. 157, 162–4; Austin to Vandenberg, March 19, 1945, White Papers, Box 60; Russell, *United Nations Charter*, pp. 608–9; New York *Times*, April 11, 1945; *ibid.*, April 19, 1945.

5. State Department, *Bulletin*, XII (April 22, 1945), 726; *Congressional Record* (April 20, 1945), pp. 3611–13; Connally and Steinberg, *Connally*, p. 276; *Private Papers of Vandenberg*, p. 171.

6. State Department, *Bulletin*, XII (February 25, 1945), 316; *ibid.*, XII (April 1, 1945), 555–73; *ibid.*, XII (April 8, 1945), 629; *ibid.*, XII (April 29, 1945), 806; MacLeish to Daniels, March 2, 1945, FDR Papers, OF 5557; *Congressional Record* (May 3, 1945), pp. 4125, 4128; "The Charter of the United Nations," *Hearings* before the Senate Committee on Foreign Relations, 79C., 1S., p. 613.

7. Russell, *United Nations Charter*, pp. 594–5; CSOP, *Ten Year Record*, p. 27; Simmons to Stettinius, Connally, Clayton, and Barker, March 5, 1945, Simmons Papers, Box 26; Daniels to Hassett, March 26, 1945, and Hassett to Daniels, March 27, 1945, FDR Papers, OF 4725G; Eichelberger to Davis, March 27, 1945, CEA, 63132; State Department, *Bulletin*, XII (April 15, 1945), 671;

Stettinius to Simmons, April 9, 1945, Simmons Papers, Box 26; New York *Times*, April 11, 1945.

8. Eichelberger to Daniels, March 21, 1945, and Roosevelt to Eichelberger, March 24, 1945, FDR Papers, OF 5557; AAUN bulletin to branches, March 30, 1945, CEA, 68180; AAUN, *Bulletin*, No. 4 (May 1, 1945), 4–5; *Changing World*, XVII (March 1945), 8; *ibid.*, XVII (April 1945), 5, 7; Anna Lord Strauss to Roosevelt, February 9, 1945, FDR Papers, PPF 1439; New York *Times*, April 16, 1945; *ibid.*, April 23, 1945.

9. New York *Times*, April 15, 1945; *Christian Century*, LXII (April 18, 1945), 485–7; New York *Times*, April 23, 1945; *Time*, XLV (April 30, 1945), 26–7; *Nation*, CLX (April 28, 1945), 473, 482–3.

10. *Ibid.*, CLX (April 28, 1945), 480; *ibid.*, CLX (April 7, 1945), 382–3; *New Republic*, CXII (April 30, 1945), 603–16; *Changing World*, XVII (April, 1945), 2, 4; Fosdick, *Meaning of Dumbarton Oaks*, p. 7; Raymond B. Fosdick, "Our Last Chance—at San Francisco," New York *Times Magazine* (April 22, 1945), pp. 8, 41; Woodrow Wilson Foundation, *Annual Report, 1944–45*, p. 18.

11. Toland, *Last 100 Days*, pp. 460–1; New York *Times*, April 26, 1945; *Time*, XLV (May 7, 1945), 25–6; Truman, *Memoirs*, I, 94–5.

12. *Time*, XLV (April 16, 1945), 70; *ibid.*, XLV (May 7, 1945), 66; *New Republic*, CXII (May 7, 1945), 633–4; *Newsweek*, XXVI (July 2, 1945), 79.

13. *Time*, XLV (April 16, 1945), 27; Connally and Steinberg, *Connally*, pp. 277–80; Russell, *United Nations Charter*, pp. 639–42; David A. Simmons diary, April 26 and 27, 1945, Simmons Papers, Box 26; Gildersleeve, *Many a Good Crusade*, p. 335; Eichelberger interview, August 13, 1965.

14. Russell, *United Nations Charter*, pp. 634–9; McNeill, *America, Britain and Russia*, pp. 594–5; *Private Papers of Vandenberg*, pp. 179–82; Eden, *Reckoning*, pp. 616–17; Truman, *Memoirs*, I, 280–2.

15. *Private Papers of Vandenberg*, p. 182; Lippmann Memoir, Oral History Project, p. 262; *Nation*, CLX (May 12, 1945), 534; McNeill, *America, Britain and Russia*, pp. 595–6.

16. Simmons diary, May 1 and 2, 1945, Simmons Papers, Box 26; undated list of CSOP members at San Francisco, Thomas Papers, Box 109; CSOP, *Ten Year Record*, p. 31; *Shotwell Autobiography*, p. 313–14; Eichelberger interview, August 13, 1965; State Department, *Charter of the United Nations*, pp. 28, 114, 118.

17. *Private Papers of Vandenberg*, pp. 183–5; Simmons diary, May 5 and 9, 1945, Simmons Papers, Box 26; State Department, *Bulletin*, XII (May 6, 1945), 851–7; *ibid.*, XII (May 13, 1945), 887; Eden, *Reckoning*, pp. 617–18.

18. *Nation*, CLX (May 12, 1945), 534; *ibid.*, CLX (May 5, 1945), 501–2; *ibid.*, CLX (May 19, 1945), 560–1; *New Republic*, CXII (May 14, 1945), 665–7; Eden, *Reckoning*, p. 620; *Private Papers of Vandenberg*, pp. 185–6.

19. Carroll to Simmons, May 16, 1945, Simmons Papers, Box 26; New York *Times*, May 21, 1945; Grew, *Turbulent Era*, II, 1446; State Department, *Bulletin*, XII (May 6, 1945), 859; *ibid.*, XII (May 27, 1945), 950–1; *Time*, XLV (May 21, 1945), 23; *Nation*, CLX (May 26, 1945), 588.

20. Russell, *United Nations Charter*, pp. 716–19; McNeill, *America, Britain and Russia*, pp. 600–1; Truman, *Memoirs*, II, 285–6; New York *Times*, May 24, 1945.

21. Stettinius, *Roosevelt and the Russians*, pp. 319–21; *Private Papers of Vandenberg*, pp. 201–6; Truman, *Memoirs*, I, 287; Sherwood, *Roosevelt and Hopkins*, pp. 910–12.

22. *Private Papers of Vandenberg*, p. 208; Russell, *United Nations Charter*, pp. 735–9; McNeill, *America, Britain and Russia*, pp. 602–3; Connally and Steinberg, *Connally*, p. 283.

23. New York *Times*, June 16, 1945; Russell, *United Nations Charter*, p. 897; New York *Times*, June 15, 1945; *New Republic*, CXII (June 25, 1945), 860;

McNeill, *America, Britain and Russia*, p. 603; *Private Papers of Vandenberg*, pp. 212–14; Truman, *Memoirs*, I, 287–8.

24. New York *Times*, June 7, 1945; McNeill, *America, Britain and Russia*, pp. 596–7, 599; *Time*, XLV (June 18, 1945), 24–5; *Nation*, CLX (June 30, 1945), 709; *New Republic*, CXII (June 25, 1945), 862–3; New York *Times*, June 27, 1945; Holt to Dr. and Mrs. Sidney Homer, July 7, 1945, Holt Papers, Box 8; *Changing World*, XVII (May 1945), 2.

CHAPTER TWELVE

1. *Time*, XLVI (July 9, 1945), 22; New York *Times*, June 29, 1945; Connally to Theodore Green, May 4, 1945, Green Papers, Box 379; New York *Times*, June 24, 1945; AAUN, "Washington Letter on the 'United Nations,'" No. 23 (July 7, 1945), p. 2; New York *Times*, June 28, 1945.

2. Connally and Steinberg, *Connally*, p. 285; *Private Papers of Vandenberg*, pp. 216–17; *Time*, XLVI (July 9, 1945), 13–14; *Newsweek*, XXVI (July 9, 1945), 27–8; *Congressional Record* (June 28, 1945), pp. 6874–8; *ibid.* (June 29, 1945), pp. 6981–5.

3. *Congressional Record* (June 30, 1945), pp. 7038–9; *ibid.* (July 2, 1945), pp. 7118–19; *Newsweek*, XXVI (July 9, 1945), 28.

4. Simmons diary, May 25, 1945, Simmons Papers, Box 26; *Changing World*, XVII (May 1945), 6; *ibid.*, XVII (July 1945), 7; Bell to members of the Senate, June 13, 1945, CEA, 68185; Eichelberger to Elbert Thomas, June 11, 1945, Thomas Papers, Box 109; *Changing World*, XVII (June 1945), 8; New York *Times*, June 24, 1945; *ibid.*, June 27, 1945.

5. *Changing World*, XVII (June 1945), 5, 8; *ibid.*, XVII (July 1945), 2, 7; Eichelberger, *United Nations Charter*, pp. 29–30; Hartley, *It's Up to the Senate*, pp. 23, 31; *Freedom Digest*, II (June 1945), 1; *ibid.*, II (July 1945), 2.

6. *Time*, XLVI (July 2, 1945), 21; Dulles statement, June 25, 1945, Dulles Papers; Dulles to Brown, July 18, 1945, Dulles Papers; New York *Times*, June 23, 1945; *ibid.*, June 27, 1945.

7. *Time*, XLVI (July 16, 1945), 17; New York *Times*, July 19, 1945; *ibid.*, July 2, 1945; "United Nations Charter," Senate *Hearings*, 79C., 1S., pp. 418, 473–81.

8. Cantril and Strunk, *Public Opinion*, pp. 908–9, 910, 914–15; *Public Opinion Quarterly*, IX (Fall 1945), 385; *Nation*, CLXI (July 7, 1945), 5; New York *Times*, July 1, 1945.

9. New York *Times*, July 10, 1945; *ibid.*, July 11, 1945; "United Nations Charter," Senate *Hearings*, 79C., 1S., pp. 1, 215–16, 221, 224, 298–300, 644–7; *Congressional Record* (July 16, 1945), p. 7553.

10. New York *Times*, July 12, 1945; "United Nations Charter," Senate *Hearings*, 79C., 1S., pp. 351–5, 375, 380, 401, 403, 405, 415–18, 562, 570, 571, 580–4.

11. *Ibid.*, pp. 394, 398, 418, 432–3, 444, 446, 450, 454–5, 533, 534–7, 565, 584–9, 591, 606–15, 641–3.

12. New York *Times*, July 14, 1945; *ibid.*, July 15, 1945; *Newsweek*, XXVI (July 23, 1945), 25–6; New York *Times*, July 17, 1945; *Nation*, CLXI (July 21, 1945), 50.

13. *Congressional Record* (July 23, 1945), pp. 7950–7.

14. *Ibid.* (July 24, 1945), 7971; *ibid.* (July 25, 1945), pp. 8017, 8019; *ibid.* (July 26, 1945), p. 8068; *ibid.* (July 27, 1945), pp. 8106, 8108; *ibid.* (July 28, 1945), pp. 8152, 8177.

15. *Ibid.* (July 23, 1945), pp. 7957, 7962–3, 7964–6; *ibid.* (July 24, 1945), pp. 7973–92; *ibid.* (July 27, 1945), pp. 8116–21; *ibid.* (July 28, 1945), pp. 8167, 8188.

16. *Ibid.* (July 24, 1945), pp. 7987–90, 8000; *ibid.* (July 25, 1945), pp. 8021–5, 8027–8, 8030; *ibid.* (July 28, 1945), pp. 8134–5, 8185, 8188; Truman, *Memoirs*, I, 399; New York *Times*, July 28, 1945.

17. *Congressional Record* (July 28, 1945), p. 8190; New York *Times*, July 29, 1945;

Time, XLVI (August 6, 1945), 21; Long diary, July 28, 1945, Long Papers, Box 5; Truman, *Memoirs,* I, 399–400; Fisher to Holt, July 5, 1945, Holt Papers, Box 8.

18. Truman to Eichelberger, July 30, 1945, CEA, 63139; AAUN, "Washington Letter on the 'The United Nations,'" No. 26 (July 30, 1945), 4; White, *Wild Flag,* p. 109.

Index

361

Index

Robert A. Divine

———

Robert A. Divine was born in Brooklyn, New York, in 1929 and educated at Phillips Exeter Academy and Yale University, where he received his Ph.D. in 1954. Since then Professor Divine, who has won a teaching-excellence award, has been at the University of Texas, and he is now Chairman of its History Department. A specialist in American diplomatic history, he began research for this book while a Fellow at the Center for Advanced Study in the Behavioral Sciences at Stanford, California. His other books are *American Immigration Policy, 1924–1952; American Foreign Policy: A Documentary History; The Illusion of Neutrality;* and *The Reluctant Belligerent*. He lives in Austin, Texas, with his wife and three children.